Applications in Basic Marketing

Clippings from the Popular Business Press

1990 Edition

E. Jerome McCarthy
Michigan State University

and

William D. Perreault, Jr.
University of North Carolina

IRWIN

Homewood, IL 60430
Boston, MA 02116

ISBN 0-256-08522-6

Printed in the United States of America

1 2 3 4 5 6 7 8 9 0 VK 7 6 5 4 3 2 1 0

Preface

We developed this set of marketing "clippings" from popular business publications to accompany our texts-- the new 10th edition of *Basic Marketing* and the 4th edition of *Essentials of Marketing*. All of these clippings report interesting case studies and current issues that relate to topics covered in our texts and in the first marketing course. We will publish a new edition of this book *every year*. That means that we can include the most current and interesting clippings. Each new copy of *Basic Marketing* will come shrink-wrapped with a free copy of the newest (annual) edition of this book. It can also be ordered from the publisher separately for use in other courses or with other texts.

Our objective is for this book to provide a flexible and helpful set of teaching and learning materials. We have included clippings (articles) on a wide variety of topics. The clippings deal with consumer products and industrial products, goods and services, new developments in marketing as well as traditional issues, and large well known companies as well as new, small ones. They cover important issues related to marketing strategy planning, including ideas related to selecting target markets and developing a marketing mix. The readings can be used for independent study, as a basis for class assignments, or as a focus of in-class discussions. Some instructors might want to assign all of the clippings, but we have provided an ample selection so that it is easy to focus on a subset which are especially relevant to specific learning/teaching objectives. We have put special emphasis on selecting highly readable, short articles--ones which can be read and understood in 10 or 15 minutes--so that they can be used in combination with other reading and assignments for the course. For example, they might be used in combination with assignments from *Basic Marketing*, exercises from the *Learning Aid to Accompany Basic Marketing*, the *Computer-Aided Problems to Accompany Basic Marketing*, or *The Marketing Game!* micro-computer strategy simulation.

All of the articles are reproduced here in the same style and format as they originally appeared. This gives the reader a better sense of the popular business publications from which they are drawn, and stimulates an interest in ongoing learning beyond the time frame for a specific course.

We have added this new component to our complete set of **P**rofessional **L**earning **U**nits **S**ystems (our P.L.U.S.) to provide even more alternatives for effective teaching and learning in the first marketing course. It has been an interesting job to research and select the readings for this new book, and we hope that readers find it of true value in developing a better understanding of the opportunities and challenges of marketing in our contemporary society.

E. Jerome McCarthy and William D. Perreault, Jr.

Acknowledgments

We would like to thank all of the publications that have granted us permission to reprint the articles in this book. Similarly, we value and appreciate the work and skill of the many writers who prepared the original materials.

Linda G. Davis played an important role in this project. She helped us research thousands of different publications to sort down to the final set, and she also contributed many fine ideas on how best to organize the selections that appear here.

The ideas for this new book evolve from and build on previous editions of *Readings and Cases in Basic Marketing*. John F. Grashof and Andrew A. Brogowicz were coauthors of that book. We gratefully recognize the expertise and creativity that they shared over the years on that project. Their fine ideas carry forward here and have had a profound effect on our thinking in selecting articles that will meet the needs of marketing instructors and students alike.

We would also like to thank the many marketing professors and students whose inputs have helped shape the concept of this book. Their ideas--shared in personal conversations, in focus group interviews, and in responses to marketing research surveys--helped us to clearly define the needs that this book should meet.

Finally, we would like to thank all of the people at Richard D. Irwin, Inc., our publisher, who have worked hard to turn this idea into a reality. We respect their commitment to excellence in all stages of the project, and are grateful for their vision in making these materials widely available.

Contents

Product

Place—Channel Systems and Physical Distribution

Promotion

Price

Marketing Strategies: Planning, Implementation, and Control

Marketing Strategy Planning for International Markets

Marketing in a Consumer-Oriented Society: Appraisal and Challenges

Marketing's Role in Society

Small Shopkeepers Losing Grip on Japanese Consumers

Mom-and-Pop Stores, Wholesalers Who Supply Them Fall Out of Favor

By Christopher J. Chipello
Staff Reporter of The Wall Street Journal

TOKYO—In the shopping arcade next to a train station in Tokyo's upper-middle-class Meguro ward, Yoshiyuki Abe and his wife operate the Japanese equivalent of a delicatessen. Wielding chopsticks, they insert pieces of marinated meat, fish and vegetables into takeout boxes.

The couple's teen-age sons help part time, as does their grandmother. But while the sons lend a hand, their friends scoff at the thought of working in such a place, says Mr. Abe, rubbing a hand over his shaved head.

The Abes are fortunate. Three other shops in the arcade have shut down this year because the owners' sons didn't want to help keep them going. "It's got everyone around here talking," Mr. Abe says.

What's happening in his neighborhood is no isolated event. Throughout Japan, small businesses like Mr. Abe's—the mom-and-pop stores that once dominated retailing—are losing their clout.

Emerging in their place are convenience stores and chains specializing in everything from shoes to audio equipment. At the same time, department stores and supermarkets are stepping up efforts to sell their own brands directly. Manufacturers, too, are moving to establish their own marketing channels.

Wholesale Scramble

As a result, wholesalers are being squeezed, and some are scrambling to find new roles in a changing system.

"A vast restructuring of the Japanese retail industry is under way," says a recent report by Salomon Brothers Inc. Adds Yoshihiro Tajima, president of the Distribution Economics Institute of Japan, "The basic picture is changing."

A shifting distribution structure ultimately could help restrain Japan's notoriously high prices. It will certainly offer consumers more choices. And the move by some big Japanese companies to set up wholesale importing operations may even help foreigners crack the world's second-largest consumer market.

But the changes are bad news for the hundreds of thousands of people who run Japan's candy stores, vegetable stands, fresh-fish outlets and other small shops.

After decades of uninterrupted growth, the number of stores run by individuals stagnated between 1976 and 1982, and declined by 8% from 1982 to 1985, the latest year for which figures are available. Corporate-run stores in the most recent four-year period increased by 35%.

Chain Reactions

"The small-scale traditional type of stores are disappearing," says Mr. Tajima, of the economics institute, making it likely that "the wholesalers who supply them will also disappear."

The forces behind these changes range from a new breed of fashion-conscious Japanese consumers to the strong yen. Computerized check-out systems and data networks linking retailers with suppliers are pushing the process along. The government's proposed 5% value-added tax—if it survives the storm of criticism it has generated—could accelerate these trends.

Japan's sprint from deprivation to affluence has altered personal values and tastes. Young Japanese are less interested in taking over the family business and squirreling away money than they are in working for prestigious companies and skiing on weekends. Buying habits have shifted, forcing retailers to adjust or be left behind.

The three defunct shops near the train station fell victims to what Mr. Tajima calls the "bubble effect." As Japan rebuilt itself helter-skelter on the rubble of World War II, people returning from China and Korea made a living peddling goods on the streets, moving to indoor premises when they had saved enough. With the economy rising fast through the early 1970s, there was enough new business to accommodate big and little retailers alike. But since the mid-1970s, the surge in oil prices and other factors have made Japan's double-digit growth a thing of the past.

"The bubble became bigger and bigger," says Mr. Tajima. "But now it's finished."

Of Japan's 1.3 million small shops, industry analysts say, the ones that specialize stand the best chance of surviving.

Take Kojima Denki, a small electronics shop across the street from the Abes' establishment. Two years ago the store was a typical neighborhood *denkiya*, a house-

hold-appliances shop crammed with everything from televisions to washing machines. Today, disco music spills out of the store, and the shelves are filled with videotapes, pocket radios, floppy disks and a few compact blow-dryers.

A gray-haired employee who has spent much of the past 25 years making house calls on regular customers sits these days behind a partition keeping the books. Targeting the *shinjinrui*—literally, the "new humankind," as Tokyo's upwardly mobile trendies are known—has paid off, he says. For small retailers, "It's hard to get by anymore being a we've-got-it-all shop."

Seven-Eleven Japan Co. has it all—or so it might seem. Thirteen years after the first Japanese Seven-Eleven opened for business, under an agreement with Southland Corp. of the U.S., some 3,000 of the convenience stores, with their orange, green and red trim, dot the country's urban neighborhoods and rural highways.

A First for Japan

In 1983, Seven-Eleven became the first Japanese retail chain to introduce computerized check-out systems in all its outlets. It also pioneered a system in which suppliers pool their deliveries to outlets. Before this so-called vendor system was introduced, "it was unthinkable to put one maker's goods on another's trucks," says Yoshinobu Naito, spokesman for Ito Yokado Co., which owns 51% of publicly traded Seven-Eleven Japan.

The strong yen is also encouraging retailers to go bargain hunting overseas. Last September, for instance, Korean-assembled rolls of Fuji Photo Film Co. film began showing up on the shelves of a major superstore chain. The retailer's representative in Seoul had discovered that exchange-rate shifts made it possible to repatriate the film and still undercut the standard Japanese price.

The 5% value-added tax before Japan's parliament could speed consolidation of the distribution industry. Despite exemptions for 51 product categories and measures to insulate small businesses from the proposed levy, many small operations will be hit hard, analysts believe. "We expect the small middleman to virtually disappear," says the Salomon report.

UNDERGROUND ECONOMY

THE PARADOX OF *PERESTROIKA* : A RAGING BLACK MARKET

Reforms are making the sale of illicit goods more lucrative than ever

Eyes peeled for plainclothes cops, two lookouts dressed in sporty windbreakers scan hordes of Saturday shoppers. In a narrow alley lined with aluminum kiosks, goods of all kinds are going fast at markups of 50%, 100%, even 200% over state stores. The lookouts swing into action as I push my way in to photograph a man hawking a vial of perfume. One shoves a newspaper in front of my camera lens, while the other shouts a warning: "Be careful. You don't know who he is. Could be KGB."

Welcome to Ryzhki Rinok, one of at least 25 illegal outlets in Moscow for black market goods. Can't find blue jeans in the state stores? Buy them here for 150 rubles—about three weeks' pay for the average worker. Want some Beluga caviar? Just ask the guy leaning on his car. Need an AK-47? It can be obtained, perhaps from an Afghan vet. Here, and at other markets in town, you can also shell out 85 rubles for Polish sneakers—or 6,000, two years' pay, for a Japanese videocassette recorder.

When Mikhail S. Gorbachev's *perestroika* can't deliver the goods, the Soviet Union's *fartsovshiki*—black marketers—can. Four years after Gorbachev began his economic reform campaign and crackdown on corruption, the black market is stronger than ever. Fully 84% of the Soviet population gets the goods they need on the black market, estimates the Soviet economic journal *Eco*. Illegal trade is worth some 150 billion rubles a year—but it may exceed 350 billion, some $560 billion at official exchange rates. "The black market passes through everyone," says Yuri Shchekoshikin, an investigative reporter for the newspaper *Literaturnaya Gazeta*.

Goods sold at markets such as Ryzhki Rinok are believed to be produced in hundreds of underground factories across the country. Perhaps up to 20 million people earn their living from it.

In an economy straitjacketed by central planning, *fartsovshiki* can easily make a killing. One example is a black marketer from the republic of Uzbekistan. When he traveled to Moscow, he lived in the style of a Soviet Al Capone, with a limousine and eight rooms at a pricey foreigners' hotel.

BRIBES. He supplied wood and sheet metal to individuals and enterprises at prices far above those fixed by the state. To get supplies, he bribed top officials in the state planning and supply agencies and persuaded them to send telexes authorizing deliveries. "He had everything just like the Italian mafia—bodyguards, weapons, his own special communications network," Shchekoshikin says. The black marketer, who ran his illegal business in the late 1970s and early 1980s, was tried and convicted a few years ago.

In the years of Soviet leader Leonid I. Brezhnev, the authorities turned a blind eye to many such cases. The black market seemed to be officially sanctioned as a way to keep the rigid Soviet economic system moving. But that changed when former KGB chief Yuri Andropov became leader and won support from both reformers and the KGB to root out corruption. Gorbachev, Andropov's protégé, stepped up the campaign. Last year, Yuri Churbanov, Brezhnev's son-in-law, was sentenced to 15 years in prison for taking bribes.

Yet it's plain that Gorbachev's cleanup campaign has backfired. To stop corruption and provide consumer goods, he tried to bring the black market into the open by legalizing small private businesses. In two years, more than 100,000 of the businesses, called cooperatives, have sprouted. They now employ some 2.7 million, or 2.1% of the labor force.

But the co-ops haven't become substitutes for the black market. In fact, they are regularly accused of spawning crime. Some are believed to launder black market funds. Others, if they are successful, provide gangsters with cash-laden targets for extortion or robbery.

Indeed, violent crime is on the rise. In 1987 and 1988, armed robbery went up nationwide by 42.8%. For the first four months of this year alone, violent crime rose 40%. Many blame Gorbachev's reform efforts. They maintain that by freeing debate through *glasnost* and encouraging political activity, Gorbachev is breaking down the social order that gave Soviets few choices but did keep violent crime in check.

Moreover, there's a paradox in the attitude of many Soviets toward cooperatives. People often express anger at cooperatives that charge high prices or envy at owners who make high salaries. Yet, Soviets hardly think twice about paying higher prices on the black market. It's a mindset that says: "If you're doing it illegally, it must be O. K."

A RUSE. Even more subversive is the outright sabotage black marketers may be wreaking on Gorbachev's reforms. Soviets believe that *fartsovshiki* and state officials who fear the destruction of their businesses are the cause of shortages in the state stores. What's really happening, they think, is that state officials and black marketers collude to prevent goods from reaching the shelves.

Citizens of the Caucasian city of Grozny were mystified recently when soap miraculously appeared in large quantities in state stores the moment rationing was introduced. Up to then, it couldn't be found. Apparently, soap had been available all along but had been secretly stockpiled in local warehouses.

The 1964 downfall of another reformer, Nikita Khrushchev, was at least partly brought about by similar sabotage. Such a fate seems unlikely for Gorbachev, but it's scant consolation to know that *perestroika's* biggest unintended result so far is the booming underground. Now, if only the legal economy could do so well.

By Peter Galuszka in Moscow

Going It Alone

East Germany Opens A Front in Cold War: The Kitchen Freezer

Stalinist Central Planning, Passe in the Soviet Union, Is Making Its Last Stand

Ilona Enthofer Breaks Out

By BARRY NEWMAN
Staff Reporter of THE WALL STREET JOURNAL

KARL MARX STADT—In 1981, the all-powerful Politburo of the Central Committee of the ruling Communist Party secretly decided to open a new front in the Cold War: East Germany would build home freezers—and they would open at the front.

The deep-freeze directive, embedded in the five-year plan, won unanimous assent at the Party Congress. And Parliament gave it the force of law. The Council of Ministers then ordered the State Planning Commission to order the Ministry of General Machines to order the giant state household-appliance combine in Karl Marx Stadt to make front-loading freezers.

The combine passed the deep-freeze directive to its refrigerator enterprise in the town of Scharfenstein. The central plan clanked into gear. And so it is that in the hamlet of Niederschmiedeberg, home freezers by the hundred thousand march along a computerized assembly line, opening and closing at the front.

The Cold War these freezers are then shipped off to fight may be the only real Cold War left: the one that pits East German freezers against the freezers (and washing machines and food processors) advertised, for all East Germans to see, on West German television.

New and Improved

"If you live far from the competition, the situation never confronts you," says Reinhart Greuner, an economics journalist. "Here, everybody can compare." So far, the East's freezers have held the fort. They fit kitchens a lot better than those bulky top-loaders the combine used to turn out. But Dieter Buttner, technology chief at the household-appliance combine, can never relax. "We are feeling a certain pressure," he says, "on microwave ovens."

At nearly every other point on the Communist compass, the thrill of competing with capitalism by responding to central command is gone. Even Czechoslovakia, which persists in clobbering dissidents, mimics the reformist fashions of the Soviets and Chinese. Only a few zealots resist: Cuba, North Korea, Albania, Romania—economic invalids all. And East Germany.

But East Germany is no invalid. Someday, forces closing in from both West and East may undo it. For now, however, it remains the richest country under communism—the one place where unreconstructed planners can utter the words "commence production" and actually see it commence. This is where Stalin's cherished system of central planning is making its last stand.

Best There Is

"The German Democratic Republic," says a Western diplomat in Berlin, "is as well-organized as a planned economy can be and does as well as a planned economy can do." The system is "efficient, dynamic and flexible," party chief Erich Honecker once crowed. "While it has not yet reached a state of perfection," he admitted on another occasion, "we have made good headway."

This country has no debt problem. The 17 million East Germans earn 30% more than their next-richest partners, the Czechoslovaks, and not much less than the English. East Germans build 32-bit minicomputers and a socialist "Walkman," and the only queue in East Berlin forms at the opera.

From this vantage, today's thinking in the Soviet Union has turned stagnation in the U.S.S.R. into catastrophe, while reform has produced chaos in Yugoslavia, class conflict in Hungary and political defeat in Poland. Who needs it? Certainly not a functioning planned economy.

"We are different from our fraternal countries," says Karl-Heinz Stiemerling, an economist presented by the authorities to outline the skeptical official view. "If they can produce more success, we will use their ideas."

German Thinking

East German Communists never did like the Bolsheviks. The Berlin party declared back in 1945 that "it would be wrong to force the Soviet system on Germany." It soon was made to eat those words and find a new slogan: "Learn from the Soviet Union! Learn the way to victory!" Today, the party has reprised its old line. "We have never yet regarded copying as a replace-

ment for our own theoretical thinking," Mr. Honecker said recently, "nor shall we ever do so."

For all its bravado, however, East Germany has gotten itself caught between capitalism and Gorbachevism, and that makes the planned life less and less predictable.

West German consumer goods touted on TV may well keep the East on its toes. But West Germany also hands East Germany's repressive regime some $2 billion a year in handouts—tax rebates on imports, currency conversion at the silly official rate, and such. That prop helps keep potentially destabilizing cracks from widening in the East's poor housing and worse cars. The country's rulers can thank Mikhail Gorbachev, too, for their greater "independence" to suppress free speech and fresh ideas—but only so long as the economy holds.

The planners are running scared. They have to spend more on high-tech heavy industry without shortchanging consumers, who see the West pulling ahead ever faster. And the Soviets won't stay satisfied too long with the less-advanced imports it gets from its biggest trading partner; if the Gorbachev economic reform succeeds, the Soviets will raise standards and insist on more goods—not just freezers, but microchips—and a leap in quality.

Toward Perfection

Yet to escape these pressures from both sides of the ideological wall, the East Germans ask no favors. They seek neither loans from the West nor ideas from the East. They just want to perfect the plan.

Enter the combine, an invention Mr. Honecker considers "the most important step toward perfect management and planning."

"Here's the concept," says technology chief Buttner of VEB Haushaltsgeraete, the household-appliance combine. "Bring it all together—a totally closed production cycle. We don't just produce the product, but the parts, and the machines to make the parts."

In a camel jacket with a Communist Party pin on the lapel, he sits on a velour sofa in the headquarters reception room, flanked by three colleagues, also party members. Pots and pans nest in glass cases. Illuminated graphs show the progress of freezer production. Downstairs, on the main square of Karl Marx Stadt, broods a massive stone head of Marx himself.

Here at combine headquarters, a staff of 1,000 directs 28 factories, where 28,000 workers make 10,000 things—meat grinders, spoons, kitchen sinks—all sold under one name: "Foron."

(cont.)

All-Purpose Logo

"It doesn't mean anything," Mr. Buttner says. "It's easy to remember. If you have one combine, you need one logo."

East Germany, over a decade, has conglomerated all its sizable factories into 133 of these vertical monopolies. No other socialist country has concentrated control this way. It means planners at the top can, and do, call the entire industrial elite into one room to tell them what's what. The process doesn't appear to strain the managerial imagination. How, for example, does the appliance combine know that East Germans are hot for front-loading freezers?

"There is a certain demand," says planning chief Eckhard Bohmke, who sits beside Mr. Buttner, taking notes. "This becomes known to the Planning Commission. They have years of experience. They give us quotas for individual products."

Mr. Buttner adds: "There is a certain body under the Ministry of Trade and Supply. It has contact with the wholesale trade organization, which is in contact with distribution bodies. They know what deliveries are necessary."

More With Less

Market research made simple. Demand established, the planners then ordain what the economy can afford to supply—steel, plastic, paint, wages—to get the freezers made. In a country with a shrinking work force and scant resources, it is never enough. The combine asks for more, rarely gets it, and then struggles to hit the target with less. The East Germans call this "intensification."

"We try to prove our case," Mr. Bohmke says. "But the Commission has the final say. It knows what's in the interest of the economy." Says Mr. Buttner: "We are forced—really forced—to think about what we have to do to meet the demand."

The planners have devised an ingenious instrument of compulsion. They call it "profit." But it is simply a percentage dreamed up at the State Planning Commission: the difference between fixed revenue and fixed taxes. Here, profit resembles the engine of capitalism less than a beaver resembles a platypus.

The profit target assigned to the appliance combine is 7.5%. Achieving higher

profit means more pay and lower taxes, so naturally the combine craves that. But to increase profit, it can't raise prices; they're fixed. It can try to cut costs. Better yet, it can make new products, like freezers.

Why bother? Because the planners will arbitrarily assign a higher profit to a new product. If a product isn't improved for five years, according to the rules, the permissible profit drops. This is innovation the way East Germans like it—on command.

"The rules set by the state make profit our central figure," says Mr. Buttner. Yet that isn't enough to make him promote sales; they cruise along at $2 billion a year. If a freezer proved wildly popular, the combine wouldn't be able to expand production, even if it wanted to. "In a market, you'd go out and buy more steel. Here, we have a long-term national material supply policy, based on the central plan, elaborated on a long-term basis."

Mr. Bohmke gets up to shake hands. "One must see oneself," he says, "as a component part of the whole society."

Once a combine meets its planned profit, state inspectorates armed with all manner of guidelines and indicators, order how the profit gets spent, from bonuses for workers to summer camps for their children. The system may not create wealth on a Western scale, but it does parcel out the wealth evenly. And, more efficiently than in any fraternal country, it works by the book.

Where it doesn't work is on the world market. The appliance combine, as hard up for hard currency as all the other combines are, has to sell its freezers in competitive West Germany for less than it charges consumers at home. The state's own economists admit the technological revolution is steadily being lost. Innovation can't keep up. Growth has slowed.

Ever Better Planning

Outsiders blame planning. They say that its phony prices produce phony profits, and that the total absence of a market leads to higher costs and a colossal waste of materials. The planners know all about it. Their answer is to keep on perfecting. They would rather cut the budgets of education and health care than give East Germany a dose of capitalism. Instead, combines will soon load on new car-

goes of incentives and indexes, governing every part of production but the one no central plan has ever seemed to reach: human motivation.

Scharfenstein, home of the refrigerator factory, is a hill town of rushing brooks and stone bridges on the road to Prague. Siegfried Haase joined it as an apprentice in 1944 when it already was making refrigerators. Now he is in charge of contacts with the planners and the combine's central management—"those superior to us." He wears a blue suit. His style is practical and calm. What motivates him?

"It's not just a matter of taking orders," he says. "If you don't know people, if you don't have contacts, you don't get anything done. I grew up with this factory. My father worked here. My whole career has taken place here. I know what I'm talking about. We export hundreds of thousands of compressors, and it has nothing to do with the central plan. It's tradition."

A few miles away, in tiny Niederschmiedeberg, freezer bodies pass through a West German epoxy bath and onto an assembly line run by a Philips computer. A blackboard displays the month's target. A chart records waste. A poster proclaims: "Initiative For All!"

What Makes Ilona Enthofer Run

As the production chief glares at them from across a table in the canteen, two workers are asked what makes them run.

"Pressure is put on you to work fast," Peter Wittig says.

"If you don't fulfill the quota," says Ilona Enthofer, "you get wage deductions." The production chief leans toward her. Miss Enthofer squirms nervously. A wine-red rash appears above the neck of her T-shirt.

"Germans generally show commitment to work," she says, trying to scratch unobtrusively. "It raises the living standard. It's a whole cycle. I have a freezer. Almost everybody has a freezer."

And what is it, after all, that makes everybody want a freezer? The answer becomes clear at the appliance combine's Berlin showroom. East Germans need freezers, buyers there explain, because they have to snap up all the meat and vegetables they can, when they are available. People never know when to expect more. Centrally planned agriculture is too unpredictable.

Glutted Markets

A Global Overcapacity Hurts Many Industries; No Easy Cure Is Seen

Among Those Hit Are Autos, Steel, Computers, Chips; Some Chemicals Recover

One Winner: The Consumer

A WALL STREET JOURNAL *News Roundup*

Raise the subject of America's industrial problems, and you hear a lot of complaints. You are told that much of U.S. industry is performing sluggishly because Americans don't want to work anymore or have forgotten how; that foreign rivals are competing unfairly through government machinations, ridiculously low wages or both; that the U.S. just hasn't surmounted the legacy of an overvalued dollar.

But all this emphasis on what is going wrong in the U.S. and in its relations with trading partners—especially Japan, with its mercantilist drive to export—tends to obscure a world-wide problem: Many major industries, all around the globe, are burdened with far too much capacity.

"Overcapacity is a world-wide problem, and it's getting worse," says Lester Thurow, an economist at the Massachusetts Institute of Technology. "We're still investing as if the world economy were growing at 4% a year instead of the actual rate of about 2%."

Demand Sluggish

While a lot of automated capacity has been added, effective demand has been sluggish. Knocking many buyers out of the market have been the debt burdens in Latin America, the political and economic slide of much of Africa, and the torpor of most Communist economies.

Even then, the forces of supply and demand should, theoretically, produce prices that clear the markets. But they seem not to be doing so, or are working only slowly and painfully, partly because of protectionism, government subsidies and other forms of political interference with the process of economic adjustment. In many industries, moreover, declining prices have rendered some high-cost facilities uneconomic.

Not everyone is rattled by the overcapacity, however. Marvin Runyon, a former Ford executive who runs Nissan's plant in Smyrna, Tenn., says: "You read that we're putting too much capacity in place, but that's the way it has to be in a competitive industry. I say hooray for the American consumer, because somebody is going on political interference with the process of economic adjustment. In many industries, moreover, declining prices have rendered some high-cost facilities uneconomic.

Not everyone is rattled by the overcapacity, however. Marvin Runyon, a former Ford executive who runs Nissan's plant in Smyrna, Tenn., says: "You read that we're putting too much capacity in place, but that's the way it has to be on a competitive industry. I say hooray for the American consumer, because somebody is going to have to do things better than somebody else. The consumer will benefit."

Many Industries Afflicted

Whether good or bad, overcapacity is obvious in many industries. Among them:

Autos. Roger Vincent, an expert at Bankers Trust Co., estimates that world automotive demand stands in the "low 30 millions" of vehicles annually, while capacity "is in the low to mid-40s." By 1990, capacity should rise to the mid-40s, he says, and demand won't grow very much. Thus, world overcapacity could expand to about 15 million units from about 10 million currently, he believes.

Steel. Estimates vary, but most economists calculate the annual global overcapacity at 75 million to 200 million metric tons—compared with total capacity of 570 million tons in non-Communist countries and 455 million tons in industrialized nations. John Jacobson, an economist at Chase Econometrics, figures that only if the entire U.S. steel industry shut down would demand equal supply in the non-Communist world.

Computers. Although no figures on the industry's capacity use are published, most computer makers are clearly being plagued with overcapacity. The problem is reflected in declining orders and intense competition.

Semiconductors. In the U.S. and Japan, which together account for 87% of global chip making, the equipment-use rate—the best measure of overcapacity—skidded from nearly 100% in 1984 to about 60% in 1985. However, Dataquest Inc., a market-research firm, says it is now back up to roughly 70% and rising.

Heavy Equipment. Makers of farm and construction equipment are buried in overcapacity, but, surprisingly, some countries, especially South Korea, are nonetheless believed to be planning more plants.

Textiles. In the textile industry, cheap-labor foreign competition is causing the howls. Overcapacity lingers on as more and more mills are built in less developed nations, with more and more mills in the U.S. thus turned into surplus capacity.

Rebound in Chemicals

However, some once-glutted industries have got supply and demand back into balance. For example, much of the chemical and plastics group has cut capacity and expanded sales, and the glut of a few years ago has been largely cured.

Looking at many troubled industries, Joseph L. Bower, a Harvard Business School professor, attributes much of the excess capacity to "country after country building world-scale facilities." Newly industrializing countries have ample reason for fostering development, of course. They want to create industrial jobs at a time of rapidly expanding populations, of an influx into the cities and of rising educational levels, which create labor forces sufficiently skilled for factory work. The weakness in many commodity markets also encourages the idea that any hope for economic growth lies in industry.

Industrialization has been rapid, Mr. Bower adds, "because technology and capital are now highly mobile—it's staggering how fast they can move around the world nowadays." No longer, he says, is the game played by "just four or five good players." He urges that American companies "understand that we've moved from Ivy League football to the Big Ten."

Many economists trace the overcapacity back to the booming early 1970s, when many manufacturers saw tremendous growth in demand ahead and expanded accordingly. Other analysts go back much further. Jay W. Forrester, also of MIT, traces the problem—which he thinks will get worse—largely to "the big buildup of capacity during and after World War II." He recalls that "the idea took hold that more capital plant was invariably desirable," and building it was facilitated by "the enormous forced savings that had accumulated during the war years."

Also greasing the path to industrial overcapacity are plentiful supplies and low prices of many raw materials—an incentive for marginal manufacturers to keep producing and for newcomers to enter the game. The gluts affect a wide range of commodities. For example, producers of nickel and molybdenum, both used in pro-

(cont.)

ducing steel, are operating at roughly 70% to 75% of capacity world-wide, estimates Robin Adams, the president of Resource Strategies Inc., a consulting firm in Exton, Pa. The copper industry is operating at a little over 80% of capacity, he adds.

The stage for the commodity gluts was set in the inflationary 1970s, when price shocks stimulated investment in production capacity in many commodities. But in many cases, demand hasn't grown to meet the increased production.

Pressure to Produce

Moreover, many debt-laden countries increased the output of commodities to avoid spending precious foreign exchange on imports. Others invested in commodity-producing capacity to generate export cash regardless of price. Many countries "only had one option, and that was to produce more. So we didn't follow the normal corrective path," says Donald Ratajczak, the head forecaster at Georgia State University. Copper, for example, has responded slowly to reduced demand.

Oil is abundant, too. The Organization of Petroleum Exporting Countries is producing less than 15.8 million barrels of oil a day, compared with capacity of nearly 30 million. However, the surplus is mainly in crude oil—both in the ground, in production capacity, and above it, in inventories. In petroleum refining, much of the overcapacity has been trimmed back. U.S. refineries are operating at about 80% of capacity, a relatively high level, and as gasoline demand rises, processing facilities may be approaching their effective limits.

But the oil-service sector remains awash in red ink. After the collapse in petroleum prices last year, oil companies slashed exploration and production spending by 40% to 50%. This year, spending remains depressed. Thus, only 25% of the U.S. drilling-rig fleet is active, and manufacturers of oil-field equipment have several times the capacity currently needed.

Here is a detailed look at the overcapacity problems in major industries.

Autos

Automotive experts agree that the industry suffers from vast overcapacity world-wide and that Japan, like North America and Europe, will soon be hit as it builds more U.S. plants. But they disagree about the extent of the overcapacity; some measure cars, for example, and others measure all vehicles.

Ford, which gauges capacity quite differently from Bankers Trust, estimates 1985 world-wide overcapacity at 3.8 million cars and trucks, and it believes that by 1990, world-wide excess capacity will rise to six million units, 5.7 million of which will be aimed at North America.

The principal force behind the projected increase is the expansion of Japanese auto manufacturing. The Japanese, having pushed aggressively into the U.S. auto market, are reacting to the voluntary export restraints and the threat of more American protectionism. "The building of Japanese plants in the U.S. wasn't motivated by economics," Bankers Trust's Mr. Vincent says. "It was motivated by concern over future protectionism."

As a result, the auto glut bedeviling the U.S. industry is being worsened. Starting in 1989, Daihatsu Motor will be producing cars in Canada, thus becoming the last of Japan's nine auto makers to put an assembly plant in North America.

Meanwhile, other players keep getting into the game. In the wake of the success of South Korea's Hyundai Excel, Kia Motors of Korea is planning to export cars and vans world-wide by the end of this decade. Yugoslavia is exporting its Yugos to the U.S., and Malaysia plans to send its Proton Sagas here next year. Thailand and Taiwan also are trying to export.

Japanese Auto Makers

A comprehensive listing of Japanese companies that build cars in North America or are planning production:

COMPANY	YEAR: TOTAL CAPACITY
Honda of America Marysville, Ohio	1986: 220,000
Nissan Motor Mfg. U.S.A. Smyrna, Tenn.	1986: 65,690
Toyota Motor Mfg. U.S.A.[1] Fremont, Calif.	1987: 50,000
Georgetown, Ky.	1988: 75,000
	1989: 200,000
Mazda Motor Mfg.[2] Flat Rock, Mich.	1988: 135,000
	1989: 240,000
Diamond Star Motors[3] Bloomington-Normal, Ill.	1989: 182,400
Daihatsu Motor[4] Valcourt, Que.	1989: 37,200
Isuzu-Subaru Lafayette, Ind.	1990: 240,000
Suzuki/GM Ingersoll, Ont.	1990: 200,000

[1]Joint venture with General Motors
[2]Joint venture between Mazda and Ford
[3]Joint venture between Mitsubishi Motors and Chrysler
[4]Joint venture with Bombardier

Source: Chase Econometrics

"Newly industrialized countries all want auto companies so they can have steel industries and reasons to build roads and purchase technology from the outside world," says Susan Jacobs, the manager of automotive research at Merrill Lynch Economics Inc.

However, she also attributes the excess capacity to sluggish world-wide demand. In addition, she says, new plants were built to make the small cars that became popular during the energy crisis of the 1970s and to enter new market niches, such as that for light trucks.

Japan hasn't had more automobile start-up companies than Europe or the U.S., Mr. Vincent says. "It's just that they all managed to survive"—with government help. Other nations have done much the same, however. The U.S. government saved Chrysler. And Donald Petersen, Ford's chairman, notes the heavy French subsidies for Renault and American Motors and says he expects the two French producers, Renault and Peugeot, to survive "as long as there is a France."

Japan and South Korea also have stimulated their auto industries by closing their home markets to outsiders and encouraging exports. Moreover, the Japanese also have helped South Korea develop its auto industry. Mr. Vincent believes that the Japanese are saying, "It's inevitable, and why not be part of it?"

Mr. Vincent notes that in the past, American auto companies, looking forward to the next auto-buying boom, often created excess capacity. If the market grew, "you are bailed out by higher demand; otherwise, you get stuck with overcapacity—which is what has happened to some companies," he says.

But the patterns have shifted. Ford reacted to flatter demand by changing its philosophy—keeping capacity tight, forgoing some sales but betting that lower capacity would cut costs and keep it profitable when demand fell. But until recently, General Motors kept more capacity running than its sales warranted. Now, however, GM also is closing more plants.

James P. Womack, the research director of the international motor-vehicle program at MIT, believes that apparent world overcapacity might not be as large as it seems because "some plants are dedicated [to a certain type of vehicle] and can't be switched from product to product." While the Japanese have built flexible plants that can make more than one vehicle, he says, "the North American philosophy has been not to complicate matters by mixing products"—a policy that aggravates the overcapacity.

7

(cont.)

Steel

The global glut of steel reflects poor investment decisions in the 1970s, dwindling use of steel in industrialized economies, burgeoning production in industrializing countries, and high financial and political barriers to closing mills.

Anticipating shortages, steelmakers in Europe and Japan greatly expanded capacity in the 1970s, and U.S. producers modernized existing mills. Not only did scarcity never come, but consumption fell sharply in industrialized countries. Between 1970 and 1980, according to the World Bank and International Iron and Steel Institute, capacity in industrialized nations climbed 14% to 485 million metric tons, while consumption dropped 8% to 334 million metric tons.

Yet despite mounting evidence of a "phony boom," steel executives "just wouldn't give up the illusion that the market was headed up," says Hans Mueller, a steel-industry consultant.

Plunging consumption in industrialized nations, which is expected to continue into the 1990s, reflects the maturation of their economies. Construction of railroads and highways has largely been completed. And in other big steel markets—autos and containers, for example—alternative materials are increasingly supplanting steel. Donald F. Barnett, a World Bank consultant, calculates that had U.S. steel usage since 1960 matched the growth in gross national product, steel consumption in 1985 would have been some 70% higher.

Faced with excess capacity, European and Japanese steelmakers, in particular, have turned to export markets. But there they are increasingly finding limits. U.S. producers have won import curbs, and less developed countries, though consuming more and more steel, are producing much of it themselves.

Some, moreover, are becoming major exporters, penetrating traditional European and Japanese export markets. In 1976, Brazil, for instance, produced 7.3 million metric tons of steel products and exported a mere 264,000 tons. Today, it is the world's fifth-largest non-Communist steelmaker, and it exported 40% of the 17.3 million tons it produced in 1985.

Rapid growth in steelmaking capacity may have as much to do with nationalism and industrial prestige as economic growth. Today, Zimbabwe and Qatar have steel industries. "Every industrializing country wants an airline and a steel mill," Chase's Mr. Jacobson says. "It's something that planning ministers push for."

Capacity has fallen modestly among in-dustrialized nations since 1980, and the reductions are continuing. In the U.S., steel-making capacity (including recently announced cutbacks) is being slashed to 111.9 million short tons from its 1977 peak of 160 million tons. Even with the cutbacks that have been carried out, the U.S. industry is operating at only 55% of capacity, Georgia State's Mr. Ratajczak estimates.

In Japan, all five major steelmakers are cutting production capacity, although only one, Nippon Steel, has specified its plan in terms of crude steel-production capacity; it is cutting back to 24 million metric tons annually from 34 million tons.

Louis L. Schorsch, a consultant at

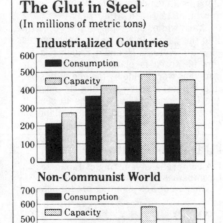

The Glut in Steel
(In millions of metric tons)

Industrialized Countries

■ Consumption
▨ Capacity

Non-Communist World

■ Consumption
▨ Capacity

1960   1970   1980   1985

NOTE: Consumption figures are on a crude-steel-equivalent basis (number of tons of raw steel needed to make finished products)

Sources: Economic Associates Inc; World Bank. International Iron and Steel Institute.

McKinsey & Co., expects future mill closings to be much more difficult. In the U.S., many steelmakers, saddled with huge unfunded pension liabilities, are reluctant to shut even unprofitable plants because they can't absorb the cost of paying off workers and other expenses. Chase Econometrics estimates the total cost of closing a mill at $75,000 per employee. "Given an average of 4,000 employees per plant," Mr. Jacobson says, "we estimate that a typical integrated-plant closure today would cost over $300 million."

Mr. Barnett adds: "So far, steelmakers have closed mostly old plants that hadn't been in operation anyway. Now, they've got to get rid of relatively modern capacity that can still make a satisfactory product. The hard part is just beginning."

Computers

Seduced by huge sales gains during the 1983-84 boom, computer companies expanded rapidly. Most "invested in growth rates that aren't materializing," says Ulric Weil, a Washington-based securities analyst. "Demand just didn't develop." According to Commerce Department figures, factory orders for the office-equipment and computer industry plunged 15% in the two-year period ended in 1986.

A good barometer is International Business Machines, which accounts for 40% of the world's computer sales. Last year, IBM's revenue rose only 2% to $51.25 billion, and profit slumped. This isn't the type of growth IBM anticipated. In the past five years, IBM spent more than $20 billion on plant and equipment, says Steven Milunovich, a First Boston analyst.

IBM responded to last year's disappointments by consolidating operations at several U.S. locations "to bring capacity in line with current and projected needs," IBM Chairman John Akers said in the company's 1986 annual report.

Nevertheless, many computer makers expanded in the fight for sales. "People who participated in niches in the past want to expand and provide complete systems for their customers," says David Penning, the director of manufacturing-automation service at Dataquest. For instance, he adds, some personal-computer companies now make work stations, while some computer makers best known for mainframes make personal computers.

Technological advances have aggravated the overcapacity. With more power being stored on silicon chips, computer companies can make smaller, more powerful machines. "Any given square footage of plant can produce a lot more stuff in terms of horsepower," Mr. Weil says. The minicomputer market is being squeezed from two sides: on the lower end, by more powerful personal computers, and on the upper end, by lower prices on computers with the power once associated with mainframes.

The emergence of manufacturers in the Far East, especially those in Japan and South Korea, has compounded the overcapacity problem for U.S. computer makers. Last year, the U.S. computer and parts trade deficit with Far Eastern countries

(cont.)

soared 77% to $5.3 billion, according to the Commerce Department. Japan's exports to the U.S., ranging from parts to portable personal computers to supercomputers, surged 43% to $4.75 billion last year.

Moreover, countries that had primarily produced peripherals are exporting full machines now, says Tim Miles, a program manager in the department's Office of Computers. "The South Koreans began penetrating the U.S. market in terminals and other areas," Mr. Miles says. "Now, they're producing complete PC systems."

Not all computer makers have been suffering, however. Some companies, such as Tandy Corp., which makes personal computers, and Digital Equipment Corp., a minicomputer maker, have grown rapidly, primarily because of revamped product lines. Moreover, the pressure on the industry would be reduced by any pickup in sales. Already, there are signs of rebounding volume in personal computers.

Semiconductors

The glut in the semiconductor industry eased last year, as orders picked up from a disastrous 1985, but most chip makers remain deeply troubled. The roots of the problems are twofold: Huge miscalculations of future demand and Japanese producers' targeting practices, under which they ignored market conditions while aggressively pursuing market share.

The introduction of the personal computer early this decade spawned a sudden surge in demand for chips. Global chip consumption jumped from about $15 billion in 1982 to $29 billion in 1984. Thus, chip makers rushed to add capacity to meet growing, apparently insatiable demand. Japanese chip makers' capital spending rose a total of 116% in 1983 and 1984, while U.S. chip-company spending doubled in 1984. World-wide capacity to produce chips increased about one-third in 1984 alone.

Then, when falling personal-computer sales sent global chip demand plummeting about 14%, to $25 billion, in 1985, chip companies started losing big money. Dataquest says the chip industries in Japan and the U.S. each lost about $1 billion last year.

Moreover, Japanese producers exacerbated the industry's overcapacity problems by continuing to add production and slash prices on certain products right through the slump. Taking advantage of their lower-cost capital, patient stockholders and government research assistance, the Japanese drove U.S. producers out of some major commodity markets by drastically underselling them.

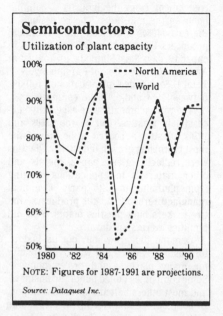

Semiconductors
Utilization of plant capacity

········ North America
—— World

NOTE: Figures for 1987-1991 are projections.

Source: Dataquest Inc.

Indeed, the U.S. government found that Japanese companies "dumped" certain chips in the U.S. and other markets, and the U.S. may soon penalize them if they don't raise their prices. Japan's Ministry of International Trade and Industry, trying to save a semiconductor trade pact signed last summer, has told Japanese chip makers to cut production 10%.

Heavy Equipment

Plunging demand has blighted the farm-equipment industry with huge worldwide overcapacity. The glut has persisted despite sharp cutbacks in the number of factories producing tractors, combines and other agricultural equipment.

Sales have consistently trailed even the most pessimistic forecasts. In retrospect, that isn't surprising. The world is awash in food. A few years ago, fears of shortages, embargoes and price gouging led many food-importing countries, such as Japan, to give agriculture a high priority. Many nations imported new agricultural technology that now has borne fruit.

The global surplus of food and feed grains is expected to surge to a 13-week supply this year; an eight-week supply would be ample. The U.S. has more than a one-year supply of wheat, enough for both exports and domestic consumption.

With farmers in dire financial trouble, the business of supplying them with new equipment is as dead as last year's corn-

field. World-wide tractor output fell to 120,000 units last year from 230,000 in 1979. For larger equipment, the declines have been even sharper. Manufacturers produced 20,000 over-100-horsepower tractors last year, down from 80,000 in 1979.

"The downturn has been so dramatic that no one has done anything but cut back," says John Ruth, Massey-Ferguson's president. He says he doesn't know of any additions to industry capacity anywhere in the past five years. Because of high costs, some U.S. facilities were among the first to close, with part of their production moving to existing foreign plants.

Mr. Ruth sees further cutbacks in capacity needed for anyone to make a profit. But for now, companies are playing an industrywide game of chicken. No one wants to get out of the business so that rivals can make money again.

In construction equipment, too, demand is down, but, surprisingly, capacity is still rising.

In the late 1970s, construction-equipment sales surged, and plants were operating at close to capacity even though Japan was working hard to build a construction-equipment industry. But from 1980 to 1983, demand plunged 70%, beaten down by reduced demand for coal as well as a decline in world-wide construction activity. Construction was hurt in part by declining oil profits and international-debt problems.

Now, demand has recovered a bit, but the industry is still running only at about 60% of capacity. Nevertheless, some countries are planning to expand even more. Industry analysts expect South Korea soon to begin an assault on the market. "Korea is a big emerging threat," says Frank Manfredi, the publisher of Machinery Outlook, an industry newsletter. "Everyone is expecting them to come into the market like gangbusters." Other countries that have added capacity in construction equipment are China and Italy.

"It's ironic that even though sales have been lousy, there's more capacity in the industry than there was five years ago," says Mitchell Quainn, a securities analyst at Wertheim Shroder & Co. "It's almost as if every country wants to have its own bulldozer manufacturer."

Textiles

Seeking crucial foreign exchange and jobs for surging populations, many developing nations are producing textiles and apparel at rates far above domestic de-

(cont.)

mand. Building a textile industry "is the first thing that a developing nation does" as it moves toward industrialization, says Ron Levine, a Commerce Department official. He notes the abundance of raw materials and such countries' cheap labor.

Cheap labor is at the heart of the overcapacity problem cited by the U.S. industry. For six years, foreign producers have flooded the American market with goods, principally apparel fabrics and finished garments, and forced the domestic industry to shrink dramatically to survive.

Arriving in the U.S. last year were some 12.7 billion square yards of imports, 17% more than in 1985 and more than double the 1980 level. "Imports have achieved a successively increasing share of the [U.S.] market," says Donald R. Hughes, the chief financial officer at Burlington Industries, the nation's largest publicly held textile concern. In six years, imports have taken 55% of the total market, up from about 25% in 1980, he says.

"Historically, the level of increase in [U.S.] demand has been about 1% annually. Yet imports have been growing at a rate of 15%," he adds.

Domestic textile leaders blame the Reagan administration's trade policies for the surge in imports. And the drop in the dollar hasn't slowed the imports because most of them come from Asian nations with currencies pegged to the dollar.

The glut of imports has forced the domestic industry to reassess its basic structure and make sweeping changes. Domestic companies have closed dozens of plants—at a cost of about 700,000 jobs—and installed high-tech equipment designed to make mills more efficient and versatile. They also are emphasizing marketing and customer services, and some analysts see domestic retailers and garment makers gradually shifting back to buying from U.S. sources because of improved quality and quicker deliveries.

Chemicals

Chemical companies have scrapped scores of plants in recent years, spurring a long-awaited growth in plant-capacity use. Last year, chemical-plant use rates rose to an estimated 80.5% from 66% five years ago, according to the Chemical Manufacturers Association. The trade group expects plant use to reach 82.3% this year, Myron Foveaux, a spokesman, says.

The wave of plant closures reflects retrenchment from the industry's building boom in the mid-1970s. The recessions of the early 1980s convinced many chemical producers that the industry was awash in capacity, says Sano Shimoda, an analyst at Anantha Raman & Co., of Parsippany, N.J. Total U.S. chemical-plant capacity fell 3% between 1984 and 1986, he estimates.

The retrenchments were especially successful in plastics. During the 1960s and 1970s, plastics appeared to be one of the most promising growth industries. Plastics were replacing glass, paper, metals and other materials in applications ranging from plumbing to auto parts. Chemical manufacturers, oil and gas producers, and tire makers built plastics plants. Few old facilities were shut down.

Demand did grow, but not as fast as forecast. By 1980, there was overcapacity for many plastics, and prices plunged. Some companies pulled out of the business, and most others halted plant construction. In both Europe and North America, some old plants were closed. Gradually, the cutbacks and rising consumption brought supply and demand for some common resins in better balance.

Polyvinyl chloride illustrates the trend. U.S. capacity more than doubled between 1965 and 1974, dipped briefly during the 1973-75 recession and then doubled again. By the end of 1983, U.S. capacity was about 8.5 billion pounds a year, up from two billion in 1965. But although PVC has grown rapidly in pipe, siding and other construction applications, no major plant has been built since 1983, and U.S. PVC plants are running at close to 90% of capacity. In Europe, there still is some overcapacity, but some plant closings are planned. Worldwide capacity is likely to be tight for five years or so, according to Richard Roman, the manager of marketing research for the Geon Vinyl division of B.F. Goodrich.

Among the large-volume resins, polystyrene, used for many inexpensive molded products, now is in the tightest supply. Dow Chemical, a major producer, is running its polystyrene plants at about 94% of capacity, "right at the ragged edge of what we can do," a spokesman says.

In contrast, the fertilizer industry, suffering along with the farmers, is still in trouble. Between 1984 and 1986, capacity reductions reached 7%, but plant-use rates are still only 74%, Mr. Shimoda says.

By spurring demand for chemicals, lower oil prices have helped U.S. chemical producers increase plant use, Mr. Foveaux says. Cheaper oil, along with chemical producers' sweeping cutbacks in personnel and productivity gains stemming from development of improved chemical catalysts, has enabled the companies to reduce plant break-even points to 70% from 75% five years ago, Mr. Foveaux says. "It's still not ringing bells, but, as a whole, the industry is much better off," he adds.

Although some small specialty chemical plants are likely to be built soon, both Messrs. Foveaux and Shimoda expect U.S. basic-chemical production to shrink further. "Profitability is improving, but people are still very hesitant to build," Mr. Shimoda says.

The Outlook

In view of the problems, what is the outlook for American companies struggling in industries with global overcapacity?

Noting that "manufacturers have sharply reduced operating costs and restructured their industries," Alan Greenspan, a New York consultant, says, "We still have problems because the real cost of capital is too high. That slows the replacement of obsolete capacity." He adds:

"Funds are diverted away from research, away from long-term projects. The emphasis is on high-tech investments that pay off fast—and become obsolete quickly. There's no incentive for the sort of investments that would bring back the Rust Belt. Economic policy really does matter."

Saying that "a variety of industries still have huge readjustment problems . . . associated with the excess capacity," Karl Brunner of the University of Rochester adds:

"If we want to be competitive in the world, we have to stand back and let the adjustments take place. We can't protect these industries from change, any more than we protected the Pony Express riders of a century ago. We have to improve our use of resources and our productivity.

"Sure, it would help if we could distribute more products overseas to people who need them. But we aren't going to solve the U.S. auto industry's problems by selling more cars to Africa in the next decade. We have to begin with adjustments here at home. We have to mitigate the hardships for the people caught in these adjustments, but we can't let that stand in the way of the adjustments being made."

Marketing's Role in the Firm

BALDOR'S SUCCESS: MADE IN THE U.S.A.

When the motor industry conked out, this Arkansas company looked foolish for not moving production abroad. Now it's booming—and exporting to Japan.　　■ *by Alan Farnham*

CHASTITY IS NICE. And temperance gets applause. But constancy, among the virtues, pays off in cash when properly employed—as Baldor Electric, an electric motor maker in Fort Smith, Arkansas, is finding. Along with much bigger brethren like General Electric, Reliance Electric, and Emerson Electric, Baldor slogged through a decade of lousy sales for the U.S. motor industry. But unlike some of those others, it emerged with bigger market share, record sales and profits, and a reputation for quality second to none. How Baldor accomplished this has something to do with a resource Fort Smith has plenty of: grit.

Peaceful enough today, this town of 76,000 on the Oklahoma-Arkansas line was known in the 1870s as Hell on the Border. The Dalton Boys, Cattle Annie, Belle Starr, and a horde of generic rowdies galloped up and down its streets, making commerce difficult. Rather than turn tail and run, its citizens stayed put, dug in, and fought back, in the person of Judge Isaac Charles Parker. Judge Parker's prescription for soothing social eruptions was sim-

REPORTER ASSOCIATE *Darienne L. Dennis*

ple. He hanged people. Lots of them.

In 21 years on the bench, he spoke these words into the faces of 160 accused: "I sentence you to hang from the neck until you are dead, dead, dead." So many irritants left life by way of his chambers that Fort Smith had to build a 12-man gallows just to keep up with the volume. Persistence paid off, and the town's law-abiding citizens buried their competition. Before Parker: rapine and mayhem on an epic scale. After: opera and the Rotary.

The threat Baldor Electric faced down was, admittedly, somewhat less dramatic. But the company's triumph was just as complete. Sales that dwindled in the early Eighties jumped almost 40% between 1985 and 1988, hitting an all-time high of $243 million last year. In this year's first quarter they climbed 22% from a year ago. Profits rose 53% last year, to $10.6 million, and another 40% in the first quarter of 1989. Today's profit margins of 4.5% compare with 3.3% two years ago. Return on equity has improved in the past year from 7.3% to 10.6%, and the stock, recently around $30, is 13% above its 1988 high.

The danger to Baldor came from overseas. In the late 1970s foreign manufacturers began pumping out low-cost commodity-type motors from automated factories in Japan, South Korea, and Taiwan. "And they weren't even breathing hard," says Jim Raba, spokesman for the National Electrical Manufacturers Association. The dollar's rise increased their advantage. Some American manufacturers, including Westinghouse, originator of the alternating-current motor, got out of the business altogether. Others—including GE and Emerson—moved some production offshore to capture lower costs. In effect, they got out of town.

BALDOR did not. It stayed the course—which sounds great if you're on the right course. Staying the *wrong* course has little merit, as the crew of the *Exxon Valdez* can attest. More than a few security analysts thought Baldor's compass had been magnetized. They kept asking when management would wise up. Remembers Roland Boreham Jr., 64, Baldor's chairman: "We caught hell because we looked like an oddball."

> ## *Baldor targets niche markets ... it adjusts so much of its production to suit special demands that on average it only produces 50 units of any given motor.*

If not actually odd, Baldor is at least a niche player. The company makes only industrial electric motors, not the kind found in consumer appliances, the business that Emerson dominates. Baldor's motors turn up in factories and work sites. There are explosion-proof motors (for mining, oil, and gas applications) and lint-proof motors (for the textile industry). Small Baldor motors run heart pumps in hospitals. Larger ones flip battleship windshield wipers back and forth. The largest, at 500 horsepower, roll steel. Being specialized, such motors command premium prices. While none is a big seller by McDonald's standards, collectively they give Baldor more than 10% of the $.1-billion-a-year U.S. industrial motor market.

Half the company's 1988 sales came from selling standard motors (over 2,500 different models). The rest came from custom work—building motors for a variety of manufacturers, most of which require short lead times. Baldor can design, produce, and deliver a motor in six weeks.

Boreham, the man most people credit with keeping Baldor home, worried about going offshore. Trained at UCLA as a meteorologist (and electrical engineer), he forecast that when updrafts buoying the dollar subsided, Baldor would lose any price advantage gained by moving. And as a quality maven, he feared production abroad might damage Baldor's reputation. Engineers consistently give the company's motors high marks for reliability and workmanship.

Tolerant of nothing less than total quality where copper wire and insulation are concerned, Boreham is somewhat less scrupulous about personal possessions. He speaks admiringly of a friend's Yamaha graphite golf clubs but plays with a set Andrew Carnegie would have recognized. His daughters, he says, needle him to buy better clothes. A contemplative man who likes to help write the company's annual report, he smokes Prince Albert tobacco ($8.50 the pound) in pipes he suspects "may not be very good." (They aren't.) So absorbed is he in motors that his wife—whose sense of humor is perhaps obscure—once hung a picture of one over their bed.

Since Baldor adjusts so much of its production to suit special demands—the company's average lot produced is only 50

> ## *Contemplating Baldor's past, Chief Executive Officer Boreham muses, "Pride takes you in one direction, short-term profit in another."*

motors—it was insulated, to a degree, from commodity competition. It felt the squeeze another way. "A flood of motors coming over wasn't our big worry," Boreham says. "Our fear was foreign machinery coming in." When the dollar rose, foreign-made industrial machinery began entering the U.S., all of it powered by foreign motors. By 1987, the National Electrical Manufacturers Association estimates, $1 billion a year in offshore motors was arriving via this channel. As these wore out, U.S. owners began ordering overseas replacements. Making matters worse, two markets Baldor relied on—energy and agriculture—coincidentally went into slumps. By 1982 the combined effects on sales were hard to ignore. Recalls Boreham: "After 21 straight years of sales increases, we learned humility." From 1981 to 1983 profits tumbled by a third.

Baldor now entered its Judge Parker phase, battling back on every front: equipment, manufacturing, training, and marketing. When the dust settled, Baldor had prevailed.

THE VICTORY cost plenty. Between 1977 and 1982—around the same time other motor companies were bowing out—Baldor tripled its rate of capital investment, upgrading milling equipment, cutters, lathes, and winders. President and chief operating officer Quentin Ponder designed a home-grown version of just-in-time manufacturing, which Baldor calls flexible flow. Under Baldor's batch system, making an order had taken up to four weeks. Ponder cut that time to five days.

Flex-flow eliminates progressive assembly. Each worker puts together a complete motor from a tray of parts in front of him. The tray is tagged with a computer printout telling him what kind of motor he's building, how to assemble the parts, and how to test the completed product. Successive trays may hold parts for different kinds of motors, and a worker may assemble as many as 20 different models in a shift. (Note to purchasing agents: Dan Quayle, campaigning for the vice presidency, dropped by

(cont.)

Baldor to assemble a motor. Don't worry. It wasn't shipped.)

To bolster its reputation for quality, Baldor in 1987 sent all 96 of its middle-level managers through quality expert Philip Crosby's training program in Orlando, Florida. It sent nearly 2,000 of its 2,500 employees through in-house classroom instruction. Baldor's investment in training confirms the company's commitment to—and high opinion of—its non-union work force. The company hasn't laid off a worker in Fort Smith since 1962. It offers profit sharing (a local rarity) and pays close to union wages. Its workers by and large return the compliment. Turnover is low, and workers tend to regard jobs at Baldor as careers. Workers voted 10 to 1 to reject an attempt to unionize a Baldor plant in Oklahoma. "It's hard to get a 10-to-1 vote on whether it's a nice day or not," says Boreham. Tom Netherton, business manager for the International Brotherhood of Electrical Workers, says he plans to make his own effort next year. Isn't he fighting an uphill battle? "Well," he allows, "you have to do something for entertainment in Fort Smith."

Randy Goldsmith, a 32-year-old lathe operator, says he has seen big changes since he arrived at Baldor in 1975. "Nobody had the pride then they do now," he says. "Not the workers, not the company. It used to be we had these clips to check the tolerances of the shafts we made. If the clip didn't fit—well, you could push on it harder and say it was OK. Now we check with these electronic snap gauges." The digital gauges are accurate to one ten-thousandth of an inch. Goldsmith, who signs off on every shaft he makes, says, "If anything's wrong with it, they know my address."

CHASTENED BY its onetime dependency on agriculture and oil, Baldor has been broadening its product line, adding 300 new models to its last catalogue alone, as it explores less cyclical markets such as food handling and fitness. The fitness motor turns joggers' treadmills, while the food industry product, called a Wash Down motor, is designed to take dousings with hot, soapy water. It sells at a 40% to 50% premium over competing alternatives, yet Dick James, engineering manager of Mushroom Cooperative Canning, a mushroom growers' association in Kennett Square, Pennsylvania, uses at least 140 of them to drive his canning and freezing lines. He says, "Downtime is costly. We had several motors prior to Baldor, but they didn't last. They're bombarded all day long with hot water, and at night, when they cool, ordinary motors suck in water, ruining the bearings." Since Baldor introduced its first Wash Down four years ago, the model's unit sales have grown nearly 50% annually.

Perhaps the most impressive evidence of Baldor's renewed staying power is its sales abroad, which began expanding even when the dollar was high. These now account for 11% of total sales, with exports growing at twice the rate of domestic sales. The company's strategy overseas is to sell to neglected niches. In Japan it found one: dental lathes. "It took us three years to get an order," says John McFarland, Baldor's director of international sales. "We had to make quite a few modifications to suit the buyers." This small bite into the Japanese mo-

tor business has led to orders from Toyota, among others. In selling to foreign markets, whose design standards often differ from those of U.S. customers, Baldor has an important edge in its ability to fine-tune small orders, even from across an ocean.

Contemplating Baldor's past, especially its decision not to move production abroad, Boreham puffs his pipe and muses, "Pride takes you one direction, short-term profit another. Pride usually wins out if you're a confident person." In Baldor's case, pride —a stubborn, costly, and almost atavistic commitment to home, work force, and product—has served the company well. Contemplating the future, what could go wrong? For the near term, at least, not much. Unless scientists at the University of Utah discover perpetual motion. **F**

INVESTOR'S SNAPSHOT

BALDOR ELECTRIC	
SALES (latest four quarters)	**$255.5 MILLION**
CHANGE FROM YEAR EARLIER	UP 22.8%
NET PROFIT	**$11.5 MILLION**
CHANGE	UP 58.5%
RETURN ON COMMON STOCKHOLDERS' EQUITY	**10.8%**
FIVE-YEAR AVERAGE	9.0%
STOCK PRICE RANGE (last 12 months)	**$22.625–$30.00**
RECENT SHARE PRICE	**$29.875**
PRICE/EARNINGS MULTIPLE	**17**
TOTAL RETURN TO INVESTORS (12 months to 6/12)	**16.9%**

Stung by Rivals, AT&T Is Fighting Back

It Trims Prices, Offers a Variety Of New Services

By JANET GUYON
Staff Reporter of THE WALL STREET JOURNAL

BEDMINSTER, N.J.—Nowhere is the new AT&T more apparent than in the men's room of the Bedminster Inn.

This popular watering hole for employees of **American Telephone & Telegraph** Co.'s network operations center features graffiti alleging deviant acts by employees of rival **MCI** Communications Corp. and **US Sprint Communications** Co. Other wall-art attributes scatological appetites to various members of AT&T's slow-moving bureaucracy.

Until recently, AT&T hardly seemed to realize it had any competitors. Old-fashioned methods and ponderous decision-making were esteemed features of the corporate culture. But that was before customers like United Airlines Inc., Sears, Roebuck & Co. and Merrill Lynch & Co. took some of their business elsewhere.

Fighting Back

Stung by seeing its rivals steal market share with cheaper rates, AT&T is fighting back in long distance. Thousands of sit-around staffers have been sent out to the field to sell, and new services are rolling out. Meanwhile, the company that used to take pride in selling gold-plated service at higher prices is running promotional discounts that sometimes make it cheaper than competitors. Big customers say for the first time AT&T is asking them what they want and selling it to them. And yesterday the company said that, effective tomorrow, it will lower prices on basic long-distance service, selected international calls and Reach Out America, its optional long-distance plan for consumers.

It's too soon for AT&T to tell whether its new sales efforts are regaining any market share, but first-quarter earnings surged 21%, mainly on the strength of better long-distance results. And the stock market is pleased; AT&T's shares closed at $35.50 yesterday, compared with $26.50 a year ago.

The idea of a former monopolist aggressively cutting prices delights federal regulators who were hoping for such competition at the Bell breakup five years ago. But even as the Federal Communications Commission is pondering whether to further lift restrictions on AT&T's ability to sell, competitors are raising the specter of an AT&T so successful that it regains its monopoly power. "If you deregulated AT&T, they would blow MCI and Sprint out of the water by cutting price," says one big US Sprint customer.

AT&T continues to dominate the residential side of the long-distance market, with a 75% share by some estimates. But the residential market isn't all that profitable, and there really isn't that much difference in prices for consumers choosing

> **THE IDEA** of a former monopolist aggressively cutting prices delights federal regulators who were hoping for such competition at the Bell break-up five years ago. But competitors are raising the specter of an AT&T so successful that it regains its monopoly power.

among AT&T, US Sprint and MCI. It is in the lucrative corporate market, in which competition based on price and service is at an all-time high, that AT&T has begun to hurt. In one major business service, Wide Area Telecommunications Service, AT&T's market share has fallen to 60% from 77% just a couple of years ago.

Long distance remains vitally important to AT&T. Despite its new competitive vigor, the company has failed to make handsome profits in its other major businesses—computers and office equipment. Last year, for example, long distance accounted for 53% of AT&T's revenue but a huge 90% of its profit, according to analysts' estimates.

In an internal speech last year, AT&T senior executive John Smart warned that the company's "basic financials are at stake" if the slide in long distance that began soon after the Bell breakup isn't turned around. Stanley Welland, General Electric Co.'s manager of telecommunications, says that AT&T is "losing more corporate customers to MCI and Sprint than most people realize."

Of late, even top AT&T executives, including Chairman Robert E. Allen, have

put on their salesmen's hats. To solidify AT&T's relationship with First Interstate Bancorp in Los Angeles, Mr. Allen recently had breakfast with that bank's president, Edward Carson. Says Mr. Carson, who had never met Mr. Allen: "Our company's relationship with AT&T now is closer than it was. That's just a human factor." Corporate telecommunications managers say close relationships between AT&T's top brass and theirs often give AT&T the edge on really big orders.

That Mr. Allen wants change was clearly signaled last September when he blessed the choice of Joseph Nacchio as head of the $14 billion corporate long-distance operation. The 40-year-old Brooklyn native, colleagues say, was talking back to upper managers long before it became fashionable; as a salesman, he made a name for himself by brazenly warning customers switching to AT&T's rivals that they were making a grave mistake.

In an interview, Mr. Nacchio says with typical bravado that "I don't see any reason to be any smaller [in long distance] than we are now." Indeed, he even talks about growing market share.

To back up his boasts, Mr. Nacchio has transferred 5,500 staffers into sales jobs, allowing the company to recapture several hundred million in revenue, he says.

Clients say the sales force as a whole has become much more responsive. Wayne Davidson, manager of telecommunications at United Technologies, says AT&T salesmen now call him almost every day to tell him about price cuts or specific proposals on how he can improve his communications system. "In the past I would have learned about the price reductions in the newspaper," he says.

To lure customers with technology, AT&T salesmen sweep them down to Jacksonville, Fla., where the company runs a high-tech telemarketing center that can display an incoming caller's phone number

(cont.)

and other such information. After some early-morning golf last fall, officials from Champion International Corp. of Hamilton, Ohio, spent six hours touring the facility. The Champion men were impressed, but the paper firm hasn't decided whether the AT&T system is worth the cost.

PaineWebber Group recently asked MCI, US Sprint and AT&T for proposals about installing a cheaper, faster system linking its stockbrokers with computers that store customer-account data. In less than 24 hours, AT&T had seven salesmen and a half-dozen pricing analysts poring over PaineWebber's phone and computer records.

Forty-four days later, the brokerage firm says, AT&T came back with a plan designed to save PaineWebber an estimated $1 million a month. "MCI hasn't gotten back to us yet," says Robert Benmosche, executive vice president of operations. "US Sprint says they can beat AT&T's price. But anybody can quote a cheaper rate. We need a solution to our phone problems." MCI and US Sprint both decline to comment on the PaineWebber matter.

While AT&T's hustle won the PaineWebber account, price is gaining in importance since many corporate customers say AT&T no longer enjoys a significant advantage over US Sprint and MCI in terms of billing systems and transmission quality. "We have reached a point where quality is no longer a major issue," says United Technologies' Mr. Davidson. "Now, a lot of decisions are based on price."

The lingering FCC restrictions still pose a big pricing problem for AT&T. And FCC rules permit competitors to intervene every time AT&T asks permission to sell a new service.

Some customers say this regulatory morass leads them to shift at least some of their business to an AT&T rival. "AT&T competitors are free to market without any sort of regulatory handicap," notes GE's Mr. Welland, who does business with all three major long-distance concerns.

The FCC recently lifted restrictions on the amount of money AT&T can earn from long distance and relaxed its restrictions on prices it allows the company to charge customers. FCC staffers say the commission may propose further changes this year that will give AT&T more freedom to introduce new services by lifting a regulation that classifies AT&T as a "dominant" carrier. A recent paper by two FCC staffers proposes that only prices for such "core" services as residential long distance continue to be regulated.

AT&T has also won FCC permission to hold promotional sales on some of its products. It has won back more than 20,000 small-business customers with a promotion that waived a one-time service order charge for PRO WATS, a discount plan for businesses using over $120 a month in long-distance services. AT&T promised new PRO WATS customers that if they weren't satisfied, it would pay to reconnect them to their old carrier. The promotion, begun on Super Bowl Sunday in January, has been extended through August.

'Customers Weren't Happy'

AT&T is appealing an FCC decision that denied it permission to give away phone equipment to customers that order a high-speed digital phone line, which allows faster, more-accurate data transmission. Meanwhile, AT&T is pressing for permission to waive $7,500 in monthly charges for customers buying the same high-speed lines. "Customers weren't happy with the FCC decision" denying the equipment giveaways, says the network design manager at one major company who is part of an AT&T user group. "A lot of people had orders in."

Mr. Nacchio says AT&T also plans to make more use of a pricing scheme called Tariff 12, which gives discounts for specialized packages of AT&T services. The FCC has ruled tariffs illegal but lets them go into effect anyway with minor changes to encourage competition for big accounts.

This has competitors once again complaining about an unfair monopoly and calling for a reassessment of the wisdom of deregulation. MCI and US Sprint have taken the FCC to court over its Tariff 12 decision. "AT&T is a very healthy competitor with enormous market power," says David Dorman, head of US Sprint's national sales force. "They can intimidate customers almost to the point of coercing them."

ACCOUNTANTS STRUGGLE AS MARKETERS

By LEE BERTON

Staff Reporter of THE WALL STREET JOURNAL

A recent **Touche Ross** & Co. brochure for prospective clients plays up the accounting firm's "competitive edge." **Peat Marwick** titles its recruitment brochure "The Peat Marwick Edge." And a **Deloitte, Haskins & Sells** brochure is titled: "The Competitive Edge in Health Care."

Marketing originality clearly isn't accountants' strong suit. In fact, *marketing* isn't accountants' strong suit. Many of them have an instinctive aversion to it. They refuse to spend much of their money or time on it. Even worse, what they do spend often results in promotions that are, well, dull.

"To accountants, marketing is like Greek," says Ken Davis, who recently left as a director at **BDO Seidman**, a big New York accounting firm. "They just refuse to learn the language."

Growing Competition

But they may have to. The '80s merger boom has shrunk the number of public companies, making the market for audit and tax clients more competitive. Moreover, accounting firms are seeking to increase their relatively small share of the lucrative—but highly competitive—computer-consulting market.

"There's no question it's become more of a dog-eat-dog world out there for getting new business, and firms that don't learn how to market will be out in the cold," says Charles Kaiser, chairman of **Pannell Kerr Forster** and chairman-elect of the American Institute of Certified Public Accountants, which has 280,000 members.

At the same time, a wave of accounting-firm mergers—such as that planned for Oct. 1 between **Ernst & Whinney** and **Arthur Young** & Co., and one agreed to by Deloitte and Touche Ross—offers a chance for the combined firms to establish strong new identities.

"If ever there was an opportunity for all accounting firms, including the newly merged ones, to put their best foot forward, this is it," says Bruce Marcus, a marketing consultant for professional firms. "But they'll flub it, as they have in the past, because marketing gives them the whim-whams."

Part of the problem is financial: Partners at accounting firms are reluctant to spend money on marketing because it comes directly out of their pockets. But there's also a huge psychological obstacle. To put it simply, many accountants feel marketing—no matter how low-key—is beneath their dignity.

In 1987, Mr. Davis, a former investment banker, convinced Seidman to run a "tombstone" ad in a financial publication, citing a merger in which the firm had played a part. Seidman partners were never really comfortable with the ad, says Mr. Davis. "It was our last, even though we helped in eight more mergers."

John Abernathy, Seidman's chairman, admits that many of the firm's 315 partners consider marketing "undignified" for a professional. "It's the way accountants have been brought up," he adds.

The upshot is that since 1977, when an ad ban was lifted under pressure from federal regulators, the Big Eight firms combined have put just $2 million to $4 million a year into advertising. Even with **Arthur Andersen** & Co. spending more than $10 million this year in an ad blitz for its consulting business, the industry's ad spending will be dwarfed by outside competitors.

That's a particular problem when it comes to competing with computer companies for the computer-systems consulting business. It's a business that accounting firms desperately want to crack. After all, revenue from computer consulting totals more than $90 billion a year, dwarfing the $4 billion combined annual consulting revenue of the Big Eight firms.

"Accounting firms aren't likely to take a much bigger bite out of this growing business because their marketing is so poor," says David Lord, managing editor of Consultants News, a monthly based in Fitzwilliam, N.H.

Competitors long have used marketing incentives that accounting firms are only just discovering. **International Business Machines** Corp., for example, gives commissions to thousands of sales representatives and systems engineers who bring in computer-consulting business. "We're not selling Fuller brushes," says David Harrah, an IBM program administrator. "We sometimes have to keep personnel at the customer's office for up to five years."

Accounting firms, on the other hand, are only now becoming able to pay commissions to their personnel as the CPA institute phases out a longtime ethics ban against them. And the firms rarely have enough personnel to keep an office at a client company for long.

Many companies wooing computer-consulting clients spend freely. **General Motors** Corp.'s Electronic Data Systems Corp. subsidiary, which sells computer systems, did "hundreds of dog-and-pony demonstrations to Florida's state officials before winning a $100 million contract to install a computer system to keep tabs on people receiving state aid," says Stewart Reeves, a senior vice president.

That kind of spending—and hard selling—doesn't come naturally to accounting firms looking to win computer-consulting business. In 1983, Peat Marwick began marketing a computer-systems service that helps companies rewrite computer language to make different systems and software compatible. "We found that we weren't comfortably equipped to do the telemarketing and direct-sales work needed to sell the product," says Richard Worrall, Peat's partner in charge of information-technology consulting. So Peat last month sold the service to **XA Systems** Corp., a Los Gatos, Calif., computer concern that specializes in such software and has a much bigger sales force.

Lacy Edwards, president and chief executive officer of XA, says: "The software business is intensively competitive right now, and the culture of a big accounting firm is too conservative" to build an aggressive sales organization. "We're willing to make unsolicited phone calls to executives, which would make accounting firms uncomfortable," he adds. "Also, accounting firms are protective of their audit and tax clients and are hesitant to hard-sell them, as we can."

Sometimes, problems arise from a lack of coordination between marketers and accountants. For example, many firms undertake marketing efforts without ensuring that partners will have time to follow up on any leads generated. Mr. Marcus, the consultant, recalls that when he worked for **Coopers & Lybrand** eight years ago, the firm ran ads with coupons in Dallas newspapers asking potential small-business clients to write in. "We got over 500 coupons back in 13 weeks, but partners in Dallas just didn't follow up with the leads," says Mr. Marcus. "It was a disaster."

James Lafond, a Coopers & Lybrand vice chairman and former marketing director, says marketing by accounting firms was "in its infancy back then." Partners "couldn't afford to do that today because business has become so competitive," he adds.

In other cases, partners become too closely involved in marketing projects. A former marketing executive for Peat Marwick says: "Because accountants are business advisers, they think they walk on the water and can do everything. The partners

(cont.)

find it hard to turn over responsibility for marketing to the marketing group."

Familiar Ring

Some marketing copy certainly sounds as though it is written by accountants. A Deloitte brochure has this to say about a service called strategic profit planning: "SPP utilizes a customized methodology that involves a detailed analysis of your organization and banking environment, the development of a strategic framework, and a plan for tactical implementation."

John C. Burton, former chief account-

ant of the Securities and Exchange Commission, says, "A lot of accountants' marketing literature sounds like footnotes in an annual report."

Despite the criticism, few marketers—and many accountants—don't see much changing. Accountants will continue to be uncomfortable with marketing. They will spend a bit more, and talk about it a lot more, but there's a limit. "Advertising has a place in accounting, but a very modest place, from our point of view," says Ray Groves, chairman of Ernst & Whinney

and co-chief executive of the future Ernst & Young. "A big ad campaign could turn out to be a gimmick, and accountants aren't impressed by gimmicks."

Thomas Phillips, marketing director for Spicer & Oppenheim, New York, says the big mergers "should give all accounting firms a chance to reposition themselves to grab new clients." But "not many will," he adds. "Accountants are like Indian chiefs. They feel that marketing is like selling trinkets by the roadside. They can't and won't do it."

Global Reach

Citicorp Strives to Be McDonald's and Coke Of Consumer Banking

Despite Far-Flung Network, It Faces Large Hurdles; Needed: Big Acquisitions

A Spanish Coup, French Flop

By ROBERT GUENTHER
Staff Reporter of THE WALL STREET JOURNAL

In West Germany, its bankers are making house calls to time-pressed yuppies. In Spain, it quickly became the biggest auto lender. In Taiwan, it introduced the 20-year home mortgage.

Citicorp is trying, in short, to become the world's first global consumer bank, with the Citibank branch, credit card and mortgage eventually becoming as ubiquitous around the world as the McDonald's hamburger, Coca-Cola or Italian knitwear.

"We want to be like Benetton—location indifferent," says Pei-yuan Chia, the Shanghai-born chief of Citicorp's international consumer business. Already, eight million households in 40 foreign countries are Citicorp customers, and Mr. Chia is aiming for 16 million within five years.

"No one else has the network that Citicorp does," says Robin Monro-Davies, who heads IBCA Ltd., a London bank-ratings firm. "They've got as good a shot as anybody at building a global consumer business."

A Difficult Game

Whether the biggest U.S. banking company can achieve that won't be known for years. Selling as basic a product as soap world-wide isn't easy, and global marketing of banking services is far tougher. It runs into a welter of government regulations and cultural differences, and it requires huge commitments of managerial talent and capital.

"Personally, I don't know how to make a retail bank work outside my own country: Mr. Meunier isn't Mr. Mueller," says Marc Vienot, the chairman of Societe Generale, a major French bank that has been frustrated in its attempts to serve con-

sumers in other nations.

Other grand visions of global consumer franchises have already faltered. After big losses in mobile-home financing, Britain's Barclays Bank PLC is shifting its U.S. focus to corporations. Midland Bank PLC, similarly disenchanted, sold Crocker National Bank in California to Wells Fargo & Co. several years ago.

U.S. banks have fared little better. Chase Manhattan Corp. has retrenched, selling its Belgian bank earlier this year. BankAmerica Corp., Chemical Banking Corp. and Manufacturers Hanover Corp. have largely quit trying to serve consumers overseas. Japanese banks, despite their huge size, haven't tried hard to get into consumer banking abroad.

Reasons for Optimism

Nevertheless, Richard S. Braddock, who heads Citicorp's consumer business, contends that it can succeed where others have stumbled. He gives three reasons: "First, the fundamental needs of consumers world-wide differ only in degree. We also believe that we can lever our size quite effectively and export financial products from one market to another. Lastly, we're perceived as large and innovative. We're quite credible in other countries."

Even some Citicorp executives are dubious, however. They argue that the company is stretching itself too thin and should focus on a relatively few foreign countries. Thomas Theobald, former vice chairman for investment banking at Citicorp and now chairman of Continental Bank Corp., strongly opposed Citicorp's push for European consumers and instead favored expansion in the U.S.

But the critics have been wrong before. In the 1970s, Citicorp lost millions trying to build its U.S. consumer banking business. That business is now highly profitable, and John S. Reed, who led the effort, has become Citicorp's chairman. Citicorp, a leader in back-office automation, is convinced that its marketing and technological know-how can make global banking work. So, it is hunting for big overseas acquisitions.

"It's no secret that we're looking to buy in the U.K. and France," Mr. Reed says.

Profits Already Healthy

The bank's international consumer business already is churning out healthy profits. Last year, according to a source at the bank, it earned about $170 million and posted a return on equity exceeding 20%. Meanwhile, Citicorp's U.S. consumer business, which has 20 million households as customers, earned about $500 million. Internal plans call for Citicorp's consumer

banking, domestic and international, to earn more than $1 billion a year in the 1991-93 period. Last year, Citicorp's total net was $1.9 billion.

How has Citicorp been able to penetrate foreign consumer markets? It has made the right acquisitions on favorable terms, exploited underserved markets and used its back-office technology to provide superior service. It also has tried hard to look like a local bank by employing local people; Mr. Chia says only 2% of its branch managers or higher executives overseas are U.S. citizens. And it has attempted to introduce a "sales culture" in its foreign banks and to make customers comfortable during their bank visits, countering the old hat-in-hand atmosphere.

As one Citicorp executive says, "There's enough anxiety associated with financial services that people will pay a premium for comfort and peace of mind. This is a people business, not a money business."

This approach to foreign banking worked in Spain and West Germany.

In 1983, Citicorp bought Banco de Levante from the Spanish government. The bank was a mess; about 65% of its commercial loans had soured. Margins between what it paid for funds and what it charged on loans were anemic. Its 100 branches were spread too thinly across the country to give it strong market presence anywhere. Its biggest asset, an ornate marble and brass headquarters, was a white elephant. Moreover, Spain, with about one bank branch for every 1,300 residents, is so overbanked that a Spanish businessman says half-jokingly, "Banking and bullfighting are our national sports."

For Citicorp, Spain's entry into the Common Market in the early 1980s outweighed those problems; it galvanized the Spanish economy. Moreover, Citicorp sensed an opportunity because Spanish banks had disdained retail banking; many viewed consumers primarily as a source of deposits for commercial loans.

The bank, renamed Citibank Espana, quickly began pursuing consumer loans. It realigned its branches to concentrate on big urban centers; Madrid now has 20 branches, up from four. To mesh with the local culture, Citicorp brought in Hispanic executives from its operations in Chile and London.

And to differentiate itself from rivals, Citibank Espana tried to seem friendlier. Personnel seated at desks replaced tellers at long, elevated counters. Stylish furniture, ebony stone floors and artwork decorated the branches. And Citibank Espana promised mortgage commitments in 15 days to consumers used to waiting as long

(cont.)

as two months. Now, they wait only 48 hours.

Auto-Loan Coup

Citibank Espana also introduced point-of-sale auto financing. Tomas Martinez Perez, a Madrid Peugeot dealer, says, "Before Citibank, banks didn't make auto loans. Private finance companies were the primary source of financing. . . . Now, the finance companies aren't in the car business at all because the banks are cheaper." With Citibank's computer systems recently upgraded, car buyers can get loans approved in minutes.

The bank also exploited a regulatory loophole that in effect allowed it to pay interest on checking accounts and avoid having to lure deposits through high-rate savings accounts. The checking account has attracted $600 million in deposits, and other Spanish banks have copied it.

Since 1983, Citibank Espana's assets have grown to $1.2 billion from $43 million. It began turning a profit in 1986.

In contrast to its turnaround of a sick Spanish bank, Citicorp bought the thriving Kundenkreditbank, West Germany's biggest consumer bank, and developed it into the crown jewel of Citicorp's overseas empire. In 1974, Citicorp paid about $100 million for a stake in the well-regarded KKB when a KKB partner needed cash and apparently feared that KKB would fall into hands of Deutsche Bank AG, Germany's largest bank. German bankers say the remaining partners figured that eventually they could buy back Citicorp's stake. Instead, Citicorp bought them out.

"One of the keys to Citicorp's success was that it didn't immediately make changes," a former KKB partner says. That reluctance was understandable. German bankers say KKB's loans and services consistently carry higher charges than its competitors impose, and thus it is one of Germany's most profitable banks.

The 291-branch KKB has largely avoided interest-rate battles by competing on service. But its strong appeal among blue-collar workers may pose future problems. Manufacturing's share of the German economy is declining and the population is aging. In the future, fewer traditional KKB customers will need installment loans.

So, KKB is going after German yuppies needing investment services. Its bankers also are making house calls to customers

in the evenings; they offer, at no extra charge, a full range of banking services, including checking and savings-account deposits and withdrawals, insurance policies, and applications for mortgages, installment loans and credit cards. And it is changing its advertising, offering new products, installing the latest automated tellers and trying to get debt-wary Germans to accept credit cards in place of charge cards, on which balances have to be paid monthly.

Despite the successes, Citicorp's global strategy is fraught with risks. The most obvious is political risk.

China's recent turmoil, for example, is casting a shadow over Citicorp's highly profitable, 21-branch Hong Kong system, which is second in size only to Hongkong & Shanghai Bank's. If residents flee en masse in anticipation of Hong Kong's reversion to Chinese control in 1997, Citicorp could start losing money there.

In Panama, Citicorp's seven branches have been hurt by U.S. economic sanctions and an economic slump stemming from Gen. Manuel Noriega's refusal to recognize the 1988 presidential-election results. Yet Mr. Chia says, "Our commitment to Panama is still there. We're not there as a bunch of barracudas—to be there in good times and leave in bad times." And Mr. Braddock adds philosophically: "You take a hit every once in a while. That's why we're in 40 countries."

In its rush to grow, Citicorp also risks making an ill-advised acquisition—as it did in France. About four years ago, Citicorp bought a small Paris bank, Compagnie Generale de Banque, hoping to serve medium-sized French companies. That strategy flopped. Now, Citicorp is trying to reposition the 12-branch Compagnie Generale as a consumer bank. But the French have been unimpressed, and the bank, having attracted only 3,000 consumers, continues to hemorrhage red ink.

Why can Citicorp reinvigorate a sick Spanish bank but not a solvent French one? Ricardo Angles, a Uruguayan who ran Citicorp's Spanish bank and now runs the French one, says, "The French banks are very good, and we haven't put a clear strategy together there." Mr. Vienot of Societe Generale comments, "Paris has been very difficult for foreign banks. In Spain, except for Banco Santander, banking was in the Middle Ages until recently."

In the years ahead, Citicorp faces diffi-

cult choices. Some current and former Citicorp executives see its international consumer business at a crossroads. They say some foreign operations are too narrowly focused; in Britain it only makes mortgages and offers credit cards. Such niche banks must grow in size and product array if they are to compete effectively. But growing by a branch at a time will take too long. So Citicorp is shopping, thus far unsuccessfully, for big acquisitions.

In 1987, Citicorp came close to making such an acquisition. Well-placed executives say Citicorp seriously considered an offer to buy Midland Bank, one of Britain's four large clearing banks. That year, however, Brazil declared a moratorium on interest payments to Western banks. That chilled investors in Citicorp and Midland, both big lenders to Brazil, as well as Citicorp's interest in Midland.

Some Other Strategies

But these executives say even Citicorp, with $10 billion in shareholder equity, lacks the resources to simultaneously build banks in 40 countries into significant market shares and expand its U.S. branch network to 2,000—its stated goal—from 600 now. Some say Citicorp should forgo big, costly acquisitions in developed markets such as Japan and Britain and focus on about a dozen or so countries where economic prospects, market inefficiencies and Citicorp's technological prowess promise rapid growth.

And some contend that Citicorp should concentrate on U.S. acquisitions. Mr. Theobald, the former vice chairman, argued that the stock market discounts foreign earnings, lumping such local-currency businesses together with bad loans to developing countries. Better for Citicorp's stock, he added, to buy a U.S. bank.

Mr. Braddock agrees that in the past, Citicorp's overseas expansion hasn't done much for its stock. "The market tends to reward acquisitions where the benefits are obvious and immediate," he concedes. But he and others argue that many leading U.S. corporations, such as International Business Machines Corp., make 50% of their sales overseas and that the contributions of overseas profits are evident.

"We're going to have some difficult choices to make," Mr. Braddock says, "but it's not an either/or situation. We have priorities, and we'll be doing things in phases."

Bright Idea

How Williams Cos. Turned Oil Pipelines To Conduits of Data

In the Process It Has Become Very Big in Fiber Optics And a Threat to AT&T

A Glitzy New Marketing Blitz

By CALEB SOLOMON
Staff Reporter of THE WALL STREET JOURNAL

TULSA, Okla.—Williams Cos. has always been interested in getting from here to there.

It started out building sidewalks. It built pipelines. Later, it bought pipelines and pumped petroleum. Along the way, it also got into fertilizers, gas and coal.

Nothing glamorous, but staying down to earth it became, in 1986, a $1.9 billion business.

That year, a bunch of pigs with rope on their tails marched through 1,000 miles of unused Williams pipe, and now the pipes are transmitting messages from here to there.

Pipeline "pigs" are plastic balls just a bit smaller than a pipe's diameter. They are pushed along, squeezing out remnants of crude oil, gasoline or liquid fertilizer—whatever it was that last oozed through the system. The pigs that Williams turned loose pulled behind them sheaths of fiber-optic cable. Thus, pipes that once moved crude oil at three miles an hour would henceforth carry dots of information at the speed of light.

Suddenly, Williams was in the high-tech, $50 billion telecommunications business—the fourth-largest purveyor of long-distance service in the country, competing with the likes of AT&T, MCI and US Sprint. "They pulled off a neat trick," says Jack Grubman, a PaineWebber securities analyst.

Now, just as suddenly, the 81-year-old company is at another crossroads, facing a test that confronts many companies trying to break out of hard-hat industries: It must make the transition from tangibles to in-

tangibles, from delivering products to selling services.

Marketing Push

In marketing, Williams has no special advantage.

So it is hustling, ripping up everything from office carpets to corporate culture. Though stodgy pipeline operations still generate 90% of its volume, the company is spending heavily on what it sees as its future. Williams Telecommunications Group Inc., a company division, now has 900 employees, about a quarter of Williams's total employment. Only about 10% of these people were already working for Williams, mostly as executives. "All our salespeople come from other companies," says Dean Cary, the head of commercial sales for the communications unit.

No one at Williams is looking back. "In five years, you'll see telecommunications

Joseph Williams

clearly the largest part of our business," predicts Joseph Williams, the company's chairman. Though the unit is a relative infant, it already makes money—$20 million last year. In contrast, Sprint, the industry's No. 3 company, has yet to do that well for a full year.

Wall Street also seems to approve. Williams shares have risen in price about 25%, to $39.125, over the past two months. (But that may have something to do with the fact that Carl Icahn, who has held about 4% of Williams for more than a year, is walking around with $2 billion to spend right now.)

"Our area of risk is in marketing," acknowledges Mr. Williams. Roy Wilkens, the former pipeline executive who conceived the scheme and now heads Williams Telecommunications, agrees: "The biggest frustration that we've had is getting away from the image that we're an oil company just toying with telecommunications."

But then, even Mr. Wilkens was dubious about the scheme when he dreamed it up early in this decade. Mr. Williams had sent out an SOS for ideas—"conventional or unconventional." Mr. Wilkens looked around. American Telephone & Telegraph Co. was about to be broken up. Fiber optics that could carry far more data than regular phone lines were becoming practical. Williams had empty pipeline. Bingo!

It seemed to make sense, but he didn't

know what kind of reaction to expect from Mr. Williams, the 56-year-old son of one of the firm's founders and an up-through-the-ranks pipeline builder. So Mr. Wilkens "softened up" Vernon Jones, the silver-haired company president. Which seems to have been a smart move. "Vernon tiptoed in and told me, 'This is a kooky idea,'" recalls Mr. Williams. "With Vernon, I took it seriously. I might have thrown Roy out."

Williams started with a small, $30 million experimental network in the Midwest. Next, it headed west, stringing cable in its own out-of-service pipelines and buying other pipe when it could. Where there was none, it bought 8,000 parcels of land and laid cable in the traditional manner, four feet underground. In 1987, it acquired a company in the fiber-optic-cable business for $95 million plus stock so as to lengthen its north-south route, and this year it bought another concern for $365 million, giving it cable up and down the East Coast.

Of course, Williams's operations remain tiny compared with the Big Three. AT&T has 26,000 miles of fiber-optic cable; Williams has 11,000. A Sprint spokesman tells a reporter inquiring about Williams: "You're the first one who has ever asked." Williams doesn't market to residential customers and doesn't advertise on television. It leases lines to other long-distance outfits and "big pipes," or private lines, to companies that run their own communications networks. That $5 billion market niche is expanding—"growing like a weed," Mr. Williams says.

Taking On AT&T

Such fiber-optic networks have become lifelines for many companies. American Airlines, for example, budgets almost as much for communications as for fuel and airplanes. Private lines link its computer reservations network with travel agencies, 14 "hub" sites across the country and parent AMR Corp.'s computer center in Tulsa.

Williams gets less than 10% of AMR's coveted volume—which illustrates one hard truth of the business. Most of it goes to giant AT&T, because it "has provided us good service over the years," says an AMR communications manager. That's undoubtedly true. But, as Williams salespeople are fond of saying, "Nobody ever got fired for choosing AT&T." Says Mr. Wilkens: "If AT&T's system goes down, it's an act of God. If our system goes down, it's a mistake."

Williams markets its cable-in-the-pipeline trick heavily because a broken fiber-optic line, carrying far more data than a

(cont.)

regular phone line does, is a big disaster. Williams can brag that its line from the Midwest to the West Coast is the only one in the industry never to have been cut.

Even Williams cable laid alongside working pipelines is more secure than rivals' lines, Mr. Wilkens says, because "Danger" signs posted on the right of way tend to keep vandals and builders away. Also, Williams continues its old gas-pipeline practice of regularly patrolling its line. In risky areas, such as a 40-mile stretch around Los Angeles, employees walk sections of the line every two hours.

Speed of Delivery

The giants nevertheless have been chipping away at Williams. With recent Williams acquisitions, they note, more than half of Williams's cable is just like theirs. Williams once also could claim speed as a selling point; indeed, just a few years ago, AT&T sometimes needed 18 months to set up a customer's lines. Now it's just a month, contends AT&T, and time is "no longer an issue."

"Price is No. 1" today, declares Nick DiCerbo, whose job at AT&T is to evaluate rivals. Many customers agree. "It's a commodity service," says Rod Baxter, who helps manage Mitchell Energy & Development Corp.'s communications. "And we're very cost-conscious." He keeps a mental list of carriers he views as virtually interchangeable, and last month switched one of four lines from Williams to a smaller competitor, primarily for price reasons.

Williams once was able to undercut AT&T's prices by 30% to 40%, but as industry capacity increases, prices are falling. Now Williams makes more-modest claims, closer to a 10% price advantage.

As it revs up its selling efforts, however, that is useful enough—particularly in the Southwest and Midwest. "The best markets we can deal in are in financial distress," where price means the most, Mr. Wilkens says. One big Houston customer is recently bailed-out First City Bancorp. of Texas. (Cut-rate prices, on the other hand, flopped with certain unnamed rich California companies, Mr. Wilkens says. "We offered them discount facilities, and they wanted premium facilities.")

Williams salespeople are aggressive. In the Southeast, "We do a lot of presentations for people who have never heard of us," says Mr. Cary, the marketing official. In Houston, Mary Goudreault, a Williams account manager, recently beat out AT&T, MCI, Sprint and a company called Cable & Wireless for the Texas account of Coca-Cola Enterprises. "It took me six months to get that contract," she says.

How did she prevail? Answer: "Knock out the competition one at a time" by carefully matching what the customer has said it needs. Security was big with Coca-Cola, for example. Its automated system tells Atlanta headquarters what Texas supermarkets are selling and sends back instructions on how many cases of what soft drink to hoist onto delivery trucks. "If the line goes down, they can't get their trucks loaded," Ms. Goudreault says. Coke won't abide communications failures.

Now she is working on Texaco. After a year she has sold it some services and is negotiating for other contracts. "Texaco wasn't going to talk to us until we had credibility," she says.

To find this kind of dogged sales force, Williams goes outside the ranks of its pipeliners, who are still having trouble adapting to rapid change in the natural-gas business. "We lure them away from our competition," says Mr. Cary, who came with

The Largest Fiber-Optic Networks

Ranked by miles of fiber-optic cable

AT&T	26,000
US Sprint	23,000
MCI	16,000
Williams	11,000

Source: Industry reports

LDX Net Inc., acquired by Williams in 1987. Ms. Goudreault was at LDX and before that was a sales rep for Alka-Seltzer. A Houston colleague used to sell Mary Kay cosmetics.

Some customers came along with firms Williams acquired and then stayed. Amoco Corp., one of Williams's biggest customers, could have pulled out of its contract with LDX when Williams came in, but "we've had no reason to leave," says K. Bruce Fingerly, Amoco's telecommunications network manager.

Williams woos big potential customers with a guided tour of its high-tech Tulsa national control center. There, three giant TV screens monitor the fiber-optic network and the nation's weather. Six-inch-high blue neon lights across the front demand "Zero Tolerance," a promise of perfectionism.

The equipment is impressive. Sitting at a large computer screen, senior technician Todd Shildt contrives a problem. A thousand miles of cable on the network map goes red. He moves a computer "mouse" to the line and hits a button. The screen shows a smaller part of the red line. Successive maneuvers isolate one circuit at a certain "regen" station. These are facilities that *regenerate* signals in the cable every 22 miles or so.

But marketing, not hypothetical problem solving, is "80% of it," says one official, touting the art of salesmanship. "We probably average three tours a day," says another. That is why an interior designer coordinated everything from the layout of the control center to the beige, blue, purple and aqua file cabinets. All in all, it's a far cry from what pipeline customers see and company employees endure elsewhere in the same building: dingy beige cubicles, fading wallpaper and carpet somewhere between maroon and orange.

To clinch deals, Williams salespeople take customers to the teleconference center, a board room with a full-time demonstration TV hookup with Williams's St. Louis operation. Officials say the "close rate" on a sale is 90% once customers get the full on-location treatment, compared with 15% to 20% in the field. It isn't that they need or want the ability to teleconference, says Mr. Wilkens. "It's that we show them we can compete with AT&T."

Nonprofits' bottom-line:

They mix lofty goals and gutsy survival strategies

by Karen Schwartz

Karen Schwartz is a free-lance writer based in Elmwood Park, Ill.

High ideals, mission statements, and dedicated volunteers may not be enough for nonprofit organizations in the 1990s.

Faced with pursuing lofty goals and paying the rent in a crowded world of service, charitable, and educational groups competing for the same dollars, many nonprofit organizations—without marketing plans—soon may be taking unwelcome baths in vats of red ink.

Addressing a board retreat of the San Fernando Valley Unit of the American Cancer Society on what he called a "crisis time for the nonprofits," Frank W. Wylie, a public relations professor at California State University, Long Beach, said, "Marketing, a word once never heard in the health services field," is "now the No. 1 buzzword."

"In the older days, and in an ever expanding economy, there was room for growth for everyone. Now we have a static economy, and very finite resources," said Wylie, who serves the Van Nuys-based unit as a volunteer on its Marketing Communications Committee. "The total is fixed. Our economy barely grows enough to pace inflation.

"Therefore, when a new force such as AIDS comes along, our share of the resources is diminished," he said. "Marketing presents the sensible alternative, the most plausible of the solutions."

Wylie said marketing forces nonprofits to focus on what they're all about, determine their specific needs, and decide which groups and persons can help them to achieve their goals.

"It means we substitute research for guessing, and that we pay attention to what the research tells us," he said.

"It means that we learn to plan ahead effectively, dealing with the realities rather than favoring traditional preferences," he said. "It means that marketing communication must become an integral part of the research, planning, execution, and evaluation of every activity."

Although marketing and its associated research costs still scare some

Photo courtesy WTTW/Chicago

Chicago's WTTW not only plays the marketing game, it's winning. As volunteers answer pledge calls, on-camera host Marty Robinson displays a premium gift—a recipe book by Jeff Smith, "The Frugal Gourmet." The station produces the popular show, which it markets to other public TV stations.

groups, others are hiring savvy marketers and developing well-planned strategies to ensure their survival.

■ **A good example of making ends meet** while still meeting organizational goals is the Chicago-based American Dental Association, "an organization that took marketing by the horns and really moved with a marketing concept," according to Max Russell, president of Max Russell and Associates, a marketing consulting firm in Chicago that works with many major nonprofit health care groups.

■ **Public TV station WTTW/Channel 11 in Chicago** not only plays the marketing game, it's winning. According to A.C. Nielsen figures, WTTW is the most watched viewer-supported station in the U.S. In the 17 years since president and general manager William J. McCarter took over the helm, the number of subscribers has increased from 21,000 to 225,000 families that contribute some amount to the station's revenue.

■ **The New York-headquartered Girl Scouts,** which claims the honor of being the world's largest voluntary organization for girls, is exploring ways to generate additional income. Although it may not use the term marketing, when its executive director talks about "reading demographics"

and "responding to trends," Scout's honor, she's talking the language of research and marketing.

■ **Although the 5,000-member Retail Council of Canada,** Toronto, doesn't consider itself a marketing-driven organization, Mel Fruitman, council vice president, said, "We're putting more emphasis on the marketing of our events and activities." It's doing so to ensure financial growth to enable it to provide services to members.

The profession of dentistry, consultant Russell said, needed to convince consumers of the continuing need for dental care throughout their adult years. So the ADA launched what he called "one of the most professional approaches to marketing I've seen in an organization."

The ADA started with some high-level marketing research, then developed a national ad campaign and a marketing strategy that could be used at the state association level, so that individual members could better market their own practices. But not all health services nonprofit organizations are as aggressive or sophisticated in their marketing approach as the ADA.

"There's still, especially in health care, a reluctance to say the word 'marketing.' And many nonprofit organizations are scared off when they see the

cost involved in doing market research, even when the benefits pay off down the road."

In counseling nonprofit groups, Russell emphasizes the importance of linking marketing directly to the mission of the organization. "When I go into an association, that's the first thing I look at: the mission statement and the bylaws and what the organization's doing in terms of marketing and communications to support the objectives of that mission."

Exchange of value

Russell views marketing in a much broader sense when applied to nonprofit organizations. Rather than "an exchange of money for goods sold," he sees marketing as "an exchange of things of value, and in a nonprofit organization those things are not necessarily products. Many times, it's goodwill, professional respect, information, and educational opportunities."

He asks association leaders not just to look at what is considered classic competition from other associations with similar missions. "When you're trying to reach the general public, you are competing with every other advertiser out in the universe," he said.

"Many times, associations think their message is going to stand out because it's a good message, but they for-

(cont.)

get there's a lot of sophisticated communication going on out there in organizations," Russell said. "If they're going to play in the ballpark, they've got to be a major player."

A major player in the public TV game, WTTW's viewer subscriptions represented 48% of all its 1987 income, production contracts contributed 25%, governmental sources contributed 6%, and the rest came from foundation grants, underwriting grants, and endowments.

To obtain subscription dollars, the station conducts an extensive direct mail campaign tied in with a sweepstakes that offers company-donated prizes, including around-the-world vacations, cars, and clothing.

It also usually holds three pledge drives a year, though in 1988 only two were held. Subscription dollars are vitally important because they are often matched three- or even fourfold by corporate donations.

"Though we only use 1% of all of our yearly air time for subscription drives, we're very sensitive to the fact that people don't like them," said William Natale, director of publicity and promotion. "Maybe at some point we can get it down to one pledge drive a year."

In addition to buying quality programs, the station creates TV pilots and markets them to Disney and HBO, and produces programs such as "The Frugal Gourmet" and "Sneak Previews," which are seen nationally on public TV.

Asked who the competition is, Natale replied, "Everyone. Your commercial stations are trying to buy the same product, and a program like 'National Geographic' that only used to

be on our station is now being shown on independent stations.

"Our strongest competition now for the subscription dollar is cable," he said. "They're aggressively out there, and frankly, they have more money. With one wrestling match, they make $50 million-$60 million."

Though operating in the black, "it's a constant struggle to try and get the money we need to put programs on," Natale said. "A lot of people watch

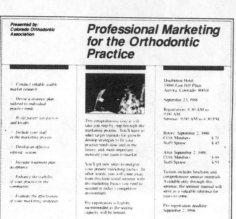

Professional Marketing for the Orthodontic Practice

The American Dental Association's current strategy features a series of seminars to help its members learn how to market their individual practices.

us and don't feel obligated to pay for the programming.

"And we have the same costs that other stations have. Our technicians are unionized, our talent is AFTRA [American Federation of Television and Radio Artists], and we buy the same light bulbs as anyone else. However, we squeeze more out of a buck than any other TV facility."

Although WTTW has a strong track record in marketing, other non-

profit groups have just begun to adopt it. The Girl Scouts organization consists of more than 3 million girls and 700,000 adult volunteer leaders, consultants, board members, and staff specialists.

According to Frances Hesselbein, national executive director of the Girl Scouts, the organization has two missions: address the needs of girls growing up in a changing society and obtain the funds to reach those goals.

Girl Scout troops are organized by 355 local councils. The councils' funds are derived from product sales, including cookies, 47%; local chapters of the United Way, 25%; and gifts, grants, and bequests, 28%.

The national group gets about 35% of its income from dues, 37% from equipment sales (uniforms, books, etc.), and the rest from investments, gifts, grants, and governmental and miscellaneous sources.

In a 1987 article published in *Management Review*, Hesselbein said, "From now until the year 2000, we need to become more expert in reading demographics, responding to trends, and appreciating the differences as this country grows exceedingly diverse. Attracting support so we can meet the needs of this rapidly growing society is becoming more of a priority for us."

The Retail Council of Canada has coast-to-coast representation of about 65% of all Canadian retail store sales. The trade association lobbies and provides cost-saving educational services to all types of retail operations.

According to its mission statement, the council's goal is "to enhance the Canadian retail trade in all provinces

and territories, influencing public policy and providing services to members." The council's Fruitman said an emphasis on financial growth is also part of the organization's overall plan.

"We can provide services to our members, but do it in a way that is cost-effective for them but provides revenue to us, as long as we don't lose sight of the fact that we are a service organization," he said. "We have to be very careful not to cross the line into becoming a commercial entity; that is, putting on activities solely for the purpose of obtaining revenue."

Reduce member fees

To reduce reliance on membership fees in generating revenue, the organization, Fruitman said, is investing more time and energy in obtaining top-notch speakers for its annual conference and trying to take its programs on the road to reach members throughout Canada.

As he pointed out, as nonprofit organizations increasingly employ sophisticated marketing techniques to generate additional revenue, they need to keep the main mission of the organization in mind, because it too is a "bottom line."

"Marketers untrained in how to apply their skills in nonprofit environments may go in and feel they should have a very visible and strong role, whereas they really should take on the role of understanding the mission of the organization," according to Jeffrey Heilbrunn, American Marketing Association executive vice president and publisher.

"Understanding that will lead to an understanding of marketing's role to teach others within the organization about marketing," he said. "If marketing doesn't understand its role as a teacher, a struggle for power could eat up the organization." *MN*

Karen Schwartz, "Nonprofits' Bottom-line" reprinted from the February 13, 1989 issue of *Marketing News*, published by the American Marketing Association, Chicago, IL 60606.

Finding Target Market Opportunities

TWO BIG MACS, LARGE FRIES —AND A PEPPERONI PIZZA, PLEASE

Now, McDonald's wants to cut itself a piece of the pizza market

TESTING GROUND: EVEN IF THE PIZZA IS A HIT IN EVANSVILLE, McDONALD'S WILL MOVE SLOWLY

PHOTOGRAPHS BY DAN DRY

It's all happening just outside of Evansville, Ind., at the McDonald's restaurant over by the Sun Set Motel on U. S. 41. There, curious locals gather as the No. 1 hamburger chain dishes up—guess what—pizza. The McDonald's Corp. experiment, unveiled on July 10, made front-page news in this Bible Belt city of 130,000 in the rural southern part of the state. It has also put the fear of God into pizza marketers nationwide. "Our people have been all over it," says a Pizza Hut spokesman.

You may think the last thing the world needs is another pie monger, but the pizza market may be too mouth-watering for McDonald's Chief Executive Michael R. Quinlan to pass up. Americans wolfed down $20 billion worth of pies last year, and pizzeria sales have grown at an 11% annual clip over the past five years. By contrast, the $31 billion burger business is growing only 8% a year. With its global reach and $1 billion annual marketing budget, McDonald's could quickly grab a big slice of the action.

TOUGH FIGHT. Besides giving McDonald's a new growth market, pizza could fill a gap in the company's business. Its evening trade is fairly light, so McDonald's will po-

sition the pie as a dinnertime meal available only after 4 p.m. The fresh, 14-inch, 8-slice pizza comes in four varieties—cheese, sausage, pepperoni, and deluxe—and the price ranges from $5.84 to $9.49. At those prices, pizza and soft drinks for four cost about the same as burgers and such for the same crowd.

McDonald's won't comment on test re-

sults so far. It's holding off until late August, by which time about 20 stores in Evansville and nearby Owensboro, Ky., will be peddling pizza. But even if the offering is a hit, McDonald's is likely to move cautiously. The reason: Its pizza gambit will surely meet fierce opposition. Pizza Hut Inc., the top pie chain, plans a tough ad campaign to keep McDonald's out of its turf. Two years ago, Pizza Hut blasted the single-serving, frozen pizza product tested under the Golden Arches in Charleston, N. C., and Salt Lake City. Pizza Hut's TV ads featured an icy McPizza thudding onto a store counter. McDonald's ditched the idea of selling pizza by the slice.

Besides fighting off angry rivals, McDonald's will have to be sure its pizza doesn't cannibalize nighttime sandwich sales. And it must maintain its legendary efficiency with a new and different product. Says Mike Raymond, Domino's Pizza Inc.'s vice-president for marketing: "This will be a real challenge for them."

QUICK TURNAROUND. That might be wishful thinking. Pizza-making used to be a tricky art: Chefs had to maneuver the pie slowly around the hot and cold spots of traditional deck ovens. Now, speedy conveyer ovens blast hot air evenly over the top and bottom of the dish, leaving little room for error and producing a fresh-cooked pizza in about five minutes. That kind of turnaround, coupled with McDonald's drive-through capacity, could augment the restaurant's in-store sales and could lure carry-out customers from Pizza Hut and Little Caesars Pizza, as well as from Domino's delivery business.

With its 10,500 outlets, McDonald's also boasts strength in numbers. Even Pizza Hut, the industry's big cheese, has only 6,000 stores. So in smaller markets, giant McDonald's will be competing with the tiny, mom-and-pop pizzerias that still make up about 40% of the industry, according to Chicago food consultant NPD-Crest.

For now, Evansville seems tickled that the fast-food colossus chose the town as its testing ground. "We pretty much represent the country as a whole," crows Evansville Mayor Frank McDonald. If so, executives at Pizza Hut and the other major chains had better hope that McDonald's new pizza lays an egg in Evansville. If it doesn't, Mickey D's rivals are heading for a real case of heartburn.

By Brian Bremner in Evansville, Ind.

McMAMMA MIA, THAT'S A PRETTY GOOD PIZZA

Does McDonald's pizza have pizzazz? To find out, BUSINESS WEEK treated the Piper family of Evansville to a couple of pies. Tom and Brenda Piper are confessed pizza freaks: They pick up one or two pies a week from Pizza Hut, Domino's Pizza, or Noble Roman's, a regional chain.

Overall, the Pipers were impressed with the McDonald's sausage and deluxe pies they tried. They liked the healthy assortment of fresh ingredients and voiced just a few minor complaints. Tom, an affable service technician with Digital Equipment Corp., found the seasoning a bit timid. Brenda

thought McDonald's was rather stingy with the tomato sauce but preferred its crust to Domino's "cardboard" version.

The Piper boys didn't carp. After three slices, Chris, 9, bestowed the coveted thumbs-up award, while

TOM PIPER: A BIT TOO MILD

Brandon, 2, merely waved a slice of pepperoni. Later, after painting his face with vanilla ice cream, Brandon rendered his verdict on the pizza: "I like, too."

Tiny Leasing Firm Bests a Giant With Focus on Market Segment

By Stephen P. Galante
Staff Reporter of The Wall Street Journal

MAJOR LEASING INC. of Atlanta is a small fry as vehicle-leasing companies go. But the concern, less than two years old, is beating leasing giant Gelco Corp. in competing for the business of the independent dealers who drive through America's industrial parks each day selling Snap-on Tools Corp. products from the backs of leased trucks.

The Snap-on dealers' business, to be sure, is only a tiny fraction of the overall vehicle-leasing market. But it has given Major Leasing a strong foothold from which to expand. A look at how Major Leasing has bested Gelco so consistently in even that small segment illustrates the ability of a highly focused entrepreneur to outmaneuver a large company.

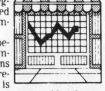

More significant, perhaps, the story behind the formation of Major Leasing also demonstrates the risks a large corporation runs in relying upon an independent-minded entrepreneur to help it enter new markets. That is because the man behind Major Leasing—a 55-year-old Atlantan named Woody Briscoe—is the same man Gelco brought aboard in 1979 to help broaden its leasing business. After a honeymoon that lasted several years, Mr. Briscoe quit Gelco in frustration in December 1985. He formed Major Leasing the following month to challenge Gelco on its own turf.

MR. BRISCOE IS a short, scholarly looking man with gray eyes and a wreath of light-brown hair. "I knew this part of the leasing business honestly better than anybody at Gelco," he says. "Gelco is oriented toward big fleets. They're not oriented toward giving the personal service needed" to deal with small-business people, such as Snap-on dealers.

Mr. Briscoe's association with Gelco began in 1979, when he and co-investors sold an Atlanta company called Leasing International Inc. to Gelco for $3.5 million. Gelco, already a major lessor to large corporate fleets, wanted to get into Leasing International's niche, leasing vehicles to individuals and small commercial fleets.

Gelco retained Mr. Briscoe to head the operation as a Gelco unit and initially gave him free rein to run it as he always had. But in 1984, Mr. Briscoe says, executives at Gelco headquarters in the Minneapolis suburb of Eden Prairie, Minn., began pushing the Atlanta group to go after large corporate accounts. He says Gelco also began centralizing functions, such as credit reviews, that had allowed the Atlanta office to respond quickly to customers.

"They lost sight of their goal, which was to saturate the U.S. with strategically located leasing companies and to concentrate on leasing to individuals and small fleets," Mr. Briscoe says.

GELCO DENIES requiring the Atlanta operation to seek large corporate accounts. "Our customer mix hasn't changed," says Senior Vice President Kevin R. Mitchell.

However, Lloyd McPherson, who retired as a Gelco executive vice president in 1985, confirms Mr. Briscoe's account. Both men attribute the shift in strategy to a change in the management of the Gelco division to which the Atlanta unit reported.

Mr. Briscoe, in any case, decided to quit. "I said, 'OK, I'm going to do what I do best, which is work with the small lessee.'" With him went eight people from Gelco's Atlanta office, including Foy Thompson, who was in charge of Snap-on truck leasing.

The decision to bring Mr. Thompson along was significant. Mr. Briscoe's plan was to build a customer base for Major Leasing from among the more than 3,400 Snap-on tool dealers in the U.S. Most of these dealers lease their trucks, which cost upward of $45,000.

From the beginning, Major Leasing enjoyed several advantages over Gelco in bidding for the Snap-on business. For one thing, Mr. Briscoe and Mr. Thompson were the center of Gelco's Snap-on expertise, and their departure, by most accounts, severely disrupted the Atlanta office.

MOREOVER, MR. THOMPSON, an affable white-haired Georgian, enjoys a favorable reputation with Snap-on dealers in a business where the personal touch is important. "Foy is a hell of a nice guy," says Scotty Nipper, a Snap-on dealer in Macon, Ga., who moved his business to Major Leasing from Gelco after Mr. Thompson showed him how he could afford a new truck by skipping some optional equipment.

Mr. Briscoe and Mr. Thompson also have cultivated ties with people who bring them Snap-on business. While Snap-on scrupulously avoids steering dealers to any particular financing source, other companies that supply Snap-on vendors are under no such constraint. By recommending Major Leasing most of the time, "we have a lot of control over where leasing gets done," says David Krause, general manager of Lynch Display Vans Inc., Burlington, Wis., a major builder of vans leased by Snap-on vendors.

These advantages have allowed Major Leasing to finance approximately 400 Snap-on trucks so far, accounting for about half of the $33 million in leases the company has written since its formation in January 1986. Major Leasing's assault has been so effective, in fact, that Gelco has temporarily stopped writing new Snap-on leases, according to a Gelco executive.

The official says Gelco will be back in the market, but only after it gets rid of more than 50 used trucks it got stuck with when Snap-on dealers traded them in for new ones during Major Leasing's initial sales blitz. "Woody is very good competition," the Gelco official says. But, he adds, "Starting fresh in the same business is an enviable position to be in."

National Firms Find That Selling To Local Tastes Is Costly, Complex

By ALIX M. FREEDMAN
Staff Reporter of THE WALL STREET JOURNAL

In the 1960s, national marketers lumped consumers by age and income. In the '70s, they divided them up by life style and attitude. Now the buzzword is "regional," and the pitch is to local taste.

Consumer-goods makers of everything from coffee to cars are attaching new importance to the old idea of different strokes for different folks, supplementing or replacing mass-market strategies with custom-tailored approaches. These include not only specially targeted ads and promotions but also new products—or new versions of existing ones—that cater to regional preferences.

Experiences so far, however, suggest that this latest way to segment the population can be a risky undertaking. Product tinkering often invites production headaches. Marketing efficiency is apt to erode. Regional campaigns can provoke local producers to become more aggressive, or can blur a brand's national identity, weakening hard-won customer loyalties. And regional marketing doesn't come cheap.

As Thomas W. Wilson Jr., a director of the New York-based consulting firm McKinsey & Co., puts it, "Breadth of choice equals complexity; complexity equals increasing cost."

Zeroing In

The national companies experimenting with regional marketing hope it will help them win competitive advantages in a slow-growth environment. In large part, the shift has been accelerated by sophisticated technology, such as scanners at the checkout counter, which enable marketers to analyze the buying habits of specific groups, even down to neighborhoods.

Ogilvy & Mather, for instance, provides its national advertising clients with detailed consumer profiles for eight U.S. regions. The New York-based ad agency's research concludes that the Midwest is filled with "belongers"—members of the traditional middle class. By contrast, the Pacific Northwest is heavily populated by aging, inner-directed flower children. In the Rocky Mountain region, men outnumber women—which Ogilvy says may explain why oatmeal sales are booming there while bubble bath takes a soaking.

Regionally focused national marketers are also motivated by the example of what happens when local preferences are misread or ignored. General Motors Corp.'s Buick division did some research two years ago to try to understand its lackluster sales performance in California. The company discovered, among other problems, that its sales practices could use a tune-up. Since many Buick dealers were closing their service facilities as early as 5:30 p.m., Southern Californians, who are used to long commutes and later service hours, were going elsewhere. (The company is working to address the problem.)

Still, regional marketing often seems easier in theory than it is in practice. Campbell Soup Co. recently got a taste of the challenges involved when it decided to make a spicier version of its Nacho Cheese Soup, which would be available only in the West and Southwest. The recipe called for more jalapeno peppers—lots more.

"When we first put them in the soup in large quantities, it created almost a gas cloud—it was virtually impossible for the workers to work with," recalls Larry A. Carpenter, Campbell's senior marketing manager for soups. "At one point," he adds jokingly, "we were considering gas masks." Instead, Campbell got its supplier to provide pureed peppers.

Although Campbell remains a big booster of the regional approach, it isn't prepared to make more than two Nacho Cheese soups. "Beyond two, it gets a little too complex," concedes Mr. Carpenter. "You run into production problems and the risk of something going wrong."

There is also the risk of losing efficiency on the marketing side. As a rule, specialists say, orchestrating a host of products and promotional strategies drains talent and budgets. "The major disadvantage is that you used to have to do things only once for the nation, but now you may have to do it 20 or a hundred times," says John M. McCann, a marketing professor at Duke University's Fuqua School of Business. "This is a major aberration in the way these companies do business."

To put its program into effect, Campbell last year divided the country into 22 regions and promoted 88 employees, mainly from its sales force, to "brand sales managers." The company also had to retrain its sales force—accustomed to executing a largely homogeneous national plan—to perform as much more autonomous regional marketers.

As many companies have learned, regional marketing also carries a high price. General Foods Corp., for example, recently sponsored a series of regional events—such as rodeos in Dallas and a show at New York's Radio City Music Hall—to promote its Maxwell House coffee brand. The company estimates that such disparate efforts cost two to three times more than a single national promotion.

For many marketers, the hardest step is developing the right product for the right province. A few years ago, Chrysler Corp.'s California K car stalled because the company assumed that Californians would be more interested in appearance than in performance. The 1982 model was essentially the same as the K car sold elsewhere in the U.S.—except for blackwall tires, some stripes and special paint.

"It wasn't what California is all about," says Clark Vitulli, regional sales manager for Chrysler in California. "It was a surface treatment for trying to have a car that looked like a California car." The company hoped to sell 500 of the cars statewide in the three months after their introduction; it sold only 100.

By contrast, when Chrysler introduced an all-white Dodge Lancer Pacifica especially for California last year, the company steered clear of fancy stripes. Instead, by offering such things as better suspension and a high-performance radio—items that Californians apparently do care about—the company exceeded its sales projection of 300 cars by 200 over the first six months.

But even if the product is right for the region, national marketers can encounter strong retaliation from local competitors, who have more at stake. That happened when Campbell introduced its spicy Ranchero beans in the Southwest. The local biggie, Ranch Style Beans, now owned by American Home Products Inc., suddenly sprang to life with heavy advertising and promotion, blunting the Campbell rollout.

Indeed, local brands often have a home-turf advantage over such regional items introduced by national companies. "Consumers develop a strong loyalty to home-grown," says William E. McLaughlin Jr.,

(cont.)

marketing manager in Campbell's grocery-business unit.

Conflicting Messages

In regionalizing goods or promotions, companies may give consumers around the country conflicting messages about the product. Marketers warn that this can undercut loyalty to a brand whose image has been nurtured by expensive national advertising. Some companies are wary of regional marketing for this reason.

Domino's Pizza Inc., for instance, offers different toppings in different regions but doesn't publicize it. Instead, the chain's national campaigns focus on its speedy home delivery. "That's what distinguishes us, not pineapples in Hawaii or anchovies in Texas," says Douglas J. Dawson, a Domino's vice president. "We're in the pizza business, not the pineapple business." Besides, he adds, regional efforts "would blow our whole advertising budget."

Thomas J. Lipton & Co. is another holdout. Lipton already knows a lot about how regional differences in taste and habit apply to its products: Northerners sip more hot tea than Southerners, who tend to guzzle more iced tea; New Englanders prefer their instant tea presweetened, while Midwesterners like theirs unsweetened. But the company believes it's better to keep using the same advertising themes and tea blends all over the country.

"Even if consumption varies, consumers everywhere want the same tea flavor," contends Ted Labiner, Lipton's director of creative services. "The economies of scale you get make it much more efficient to market nationally than regionally."

Evaluating Opportunities in Uncontrollable Environments

COVER STORY

Name is hot; marketing lacks spark

Lighter sales zip

Since Zippo started making lighters in 1932, 210 million have been sold.

Number of lighters sold by Zippo

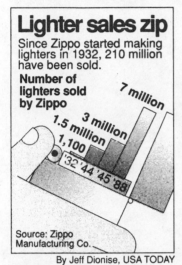

Source: Zippo Manufacturing Co.

By Jeff Dionise, USA TODAY

By Lisa Collins
USA TODAY

BRADFORD, Pa. — When U.S. soldiers and sailors came home at the end of World War II, they brought back a huge sentimental attachment to four key brand names: Jeep, Coca-Cola, Camel cigarettes and Zippo lighters.

Only Zippo has failed to cash in.

Today, Jeep is more than military vehicles. Its Cherokee wagon, which now accounts for more than half its sales, is a favorite among yuppies. Coke has evolved into a diversified international food company. Camel has gone beyond its harsh, macho filterless smokes to filtered "light" cigarettes popular with young smokers. All three are part of publicly owned powerhouse corporations.

But Zippo Manufacturing Co. had just $50 million in revenues last year, a pittance compared with what its war buddies rack up in a year. It's owned by Sarah Dorn and Harriet Wick, middle-aged daughters of founder George G. Blaisdell. The publicity-shy sisters — who declined to comment on their company — set a conservative tone for Zippo, which is run day-to-day by President Michael Schuler. The company, nestled among the rolling hills near this northern Pennsylvania oil refinery town of 18,000, cranks out 9 million of its famous lighters a year and several lines of executive gadgets. "We're alive and doing well," says Schuler.

Zippo is the story of a little company that could — but for the most part hasn't. Marketing experts say the Zippo reputation for quality and reliability is a huge, untapped brand gold mine.

"They are an enormously valuable property that is extremely underexploited," says George Rosenbaum, president of Leo Shapiro & Associates, a Chicago market research firm. "The Zippo name is known for two promises — convenience and reliability. Often to get convenience, you pay a price in reliability, so Zippo has something unusual going for it."

But Zippo's name must be exploited quickly before the generation that made Zippo a legend fades away.

"Zippo is frozen in time," says Clive Chajet, chairman of Lippincott & Margulies Inc., consultants in identity and image management. "If all Zippo wants is nostalgia, that's terrific. But ... their image will eventually die as their audience ages."

Without World War II, Zippo lighters would just be another brand of lighters. War correspondent Ernie Pyle brought the lighters fame when he wrote to founder Blaisdell and asked him to send lighters to the front. Blaisdell sent thousands of lighters free to Pyle, and Pyle, Santa Claus-style, handed them out to soldiers. Pyle wrote of soldiers heating soup in steel helmets with Zippos and lighting campfires in swamps.

Zippo hasn't just been sitting on its laurels since the war. Here's what it's trying to do to keep up with changing times:

▶ Diversify its specialty advertising products — key tags, golf balls and pocket knives with clients' logos stamped on them. But none of those can be bought in retail stores. The company sells them directly to clients. A butane lighter called Contempo, the regular liquid-fuel lighters and a pen-and-pencil set are the only Zippo products you can buy. Basic lighter models run up to $20; there are 200 models of Zippos.

▶ Globalize by selling its name to Japanese licensees that make wallets.

▶ Automate and expand. A new $1.5 million machine will increase production from 45,000 to 70,000 lighters a day.

But marketing experts say Zippo needs to temper its caution with calculated risks to take full advantage of its name.

In an era when thousands of new products are introduced each year, a well-known name is invaluable. "It's such a truly terrific word," Chajet says. "It's not a dictionary word, so it can be made to mean anything."

It also sounds great. Here's how it came to be: In nearby Meadville, the zipper was invented. Blaisdell was fascinated by the gadget and thought an offshoot of the name, "zippo," might be a catchy, snappy name for his new lighter. He was right.

"That is their No. 1 asset," Chajet says. "It is truly priceless."

To keep its flame from fizzling, Zippo should make products that would benefit from the company's reputation for reliability: flashlights, battery-operated tools, shaving accessories, automobile batteries, car wax and antifreeze, Rosenbaum says.

"The name has a macho and masculine image," Chajet says. "If I could buy a Zippo aftershave, there is no question in my mind I would. And Zippo jogging shorts."

As long as the sisters run the company, Zippo jogging shorts — or any of the experts' other suggestions — aren't likely to materialize. They aren't people who relish controversy, says Bill Jones, Zippo's vice president for advertising.

A major sticking point: The company wants to offer the same guarantee on new products that it always has on lighters: "Works ... or we fix it free."

Jones says the company has considered launching into all kinds of new products before, but backed away. In most cases, a well-known brand already dominated that market. "We can't carry our other gift items over into retail because there's so much competition."

If Zippo is unwilling or unable to pull itself into the present and future, perhaps it should consider selling out. A new parent company would provide money for a big advertising campaign — the company now spends only $3 million a year on ads.

Rosenbaum says Zippo could fetch three or four times its annual revenues, or up to $200 million.

"There is not a month that goes by without an offer on this company," Jones says. "But it's simply not for sale, and the two

(cont.)

women who own it are very satisfied. And their children rely on it for their livelihood, so it will be at least another generation before they would even consider selling it. In fact, the shoe is on the other foot. We would be interested in buying someone to pursue our diversification."

But the clock is ticking: 1991 is the 50th anniversary of Pearl Harbor, marking the end of an era.

"They may have waited too long to capitalize on a great reputation," says Jim Julow, a marketing executive at the Jeep division of Chrysler Motors. "Eventually, only a very small portion of the general public knows who you are and what you're about, and once they're gone, it's a very difficult process to get back in the public eye. The world may have passed them by."

THE PORTABLE EXECUTIVE

FROM FAXES TO LAPTOPS, TECHNOLOGY IS CHANGING OUR WORK LIVES

Meet Lionel Goetz, portable executive. Chairman of Pan Atlantic Re Inc., an insurance underwriter and reinsurer with operations in Britain, Ireland, Bermuda, and the U.S., Goetz is rarely in his White Plains (N.Y.) office. But with electronic mail, facsimile machines, a personal computer at work, another at home, and a laptop for travel, the 45-year-old lawyer is always in touch. He can read and answer electronic mail from anywhere. For the latest headlines, he logs onto a news service. To buy or sell stock, he enters his orders by computer. "When the IBM PC came out, I bought one right away," Goetz says. "I decided that I was going to move forward with the technology—or I was going to be obsolete."

Or take Clifton E. Haley, president of Budget Rent a Car Corp. in Chicago. Back in 1986, a cellular conference call he made to two executives on their way to separate golf outings in Tokyo helped him get the financing Budget executives needed to do a leveraged buyout from Transamerica Corp. Since then, Haley has made advanced technology a way of life, a tool to help him "run the company 24 hours a day, seven days a week."

The electronic society that futurists began predicting 20 years ago seemed as if it might never come. For much of that time, the tools were too crude or too expensive—or just didn't exist. But now they're here, they're cheap, and they work. Computer technology has become an indispensable part of nearly every product, every job, every trivial pursuit. And it's becoming portable as well. Suddenly, with little real fanfare, the electronic revolution has arrived.

Personal computers. Cellular phones. Voice mail. Electronic mail. Faxes. These electronic tools are catching on rapidly—and they're spreading beyond the traditional office. They are letting people organize their lives in new ways by loosening the confines of time and space that dictated 9-to-5 days in downtown offices, bracketed by a lengthy commute. Initial versions of drawings on this page arrived by fax from Malden Bridge, N.Y., 135 miles north of Manhattan.

Weaned on VCRs, the U.S. is also becoming a nation of "time-shifters." Instead of waiting until they can meet face-to-face or connect on the phone, millions of Americans now use fax, electronic mail, and voice mail to deposit messages for one another to be picked up when it's convenient.

NEW STRESSES. These people are pioneering a lifestyle that can liberate individuals, spark their creativity, and make businesses far more efficient. Working across time zones and continents, users of the new electronic tools are prompting corporations to consider reorganizing their structures. If employees can operate with equal efficiency from office, home, or a ski chalet—and be happier doing it—why shouldn't they?

The new lifestyle creates new problems and stresses, too. Since the Industrial Revolution lured Americans off the farm, there has been a clear separation between work and home life. When the office comes home, what happens to the family? And if home becomes the locus of work, how does one replace the social interaction of the office? "Serendipitous, spontaneous contact is crucial to getting work done," says Robert E. Kraut, a social scientist at Bell Communications Research Inc.

A few companies are testing the limits of how the electronic corporation will work. The Discovery Channel acquires, packages, promotes, and transmits 200 television programs a month to 34 million homes in the U.S. To do this, many of its 105-member staff are constantly traveling. But they run the company with 40% fewer employees than the Arts & Entertainment Channel, a comparable operation, says Discovery President Ruth L. Otte. Discovery's advantage: a sophisticated communications system that delivers to Otte an average of 100 electronic memos a day—either in her Landover (Md.) headquarters or anyplace there's a phone jack to plug in her laptop PC. "I feel like I'm never out of the office," she says.

For some, the electronic lifestyle means leaving the office for good. With data lines instantly feeding trading information from world markets to his mountaintop home above Lake Tahoe, economist Robert A. Jones seldom travels to his office near San Francisco. From what he calls "Wall Street in a most unlikely location," the chairman of MMS International Inc., a $29 million research firm, broadcasts interest rate forecasts to traders over the Telerate wire. When he's on the lake, he uses a ship-to-shore radio. On the ski slopes, he keeps a cellular phone in the lodge.

Electronic gadgets are even invading the lives of executives who can't tolerate computers. They won't be able to escape voice mail—essentially, an answering-machine service built into the phone system for receiving, leaving, and broadcasting messages. Fax machines are also ubiquitous: They're even being installed in the homes of key executives so that important documents—and decisions—can be handled immediately. Budget Rent a Car's Haley even has a fax at his retreat in Northern Michigan.

CLOSED DOOR? As this electronic lifestyle spreads, it will undoubtedly alter the social and economic landscape. Satellite communications and computer networks already have made it easier for a corporation such as J.C. Penney Co. to abandon the canyons of Manhattan for the flatlands of Plano, Tex. And with a nationwide, digital phone network, which will vastly improve computer communications and have the capability of trans-

(cont.)

mitting full-motion video, it will be possible to imagine electronic corporations made up of individuals and groups scattered all over the country. Such networks could be available by the year 2000. At that point, corporations could leave the cities entirely. Experts doubt they will do so en masse: For one thing, it may be decades, if ever, before electronic communications can duplicate the interplay of face-to-face meetings. But, inevitably, the electronic lifestyle encourages economic decentralization.

Some social outcomes of the electronic revolution are already clear—and they're not all positive. For example, it seems that the disadvantaged may wind up more isolated than ever (page 106). Even if offices remain in the inner city, many of the low-level clerical jobs that once gave minorities an entrée into office work will be automated out of existence. Other jobs, such as data-entry work, are being shifted offshore. "There will be fewer opportunities in major organizations for people who don't have high literacy skills and aren't trainable to do analytical work," says Shoshana Zuboff, author of *In the Age of the Smart Machine.*

DRIVE AND DIAL. Meanwhile, the shift to an electronically assisted lifestyle is gathering momentum. The cellular phone shows how quickly and completely such changes are occurring. Only three years ago, it was an expensive toy for gadget-happy technophiles. Now it's a necessity in elite business and social circles. In Knoxville, Tenn., Chris Whittle, chairman of $150 million publishing empire Whittle Communications, says his cellular phone "has probably added 7 to 10 hours per week of productive time to my schedule." Whittle used to have little time to return calls. "Now 80% of my calls are made in my car or on a portable phone," he says.

Nowhere is the cellular boom more apparent than on Southern California's clogged freeways. Real estate developer William A. Burke, founder of the Los Angeles Marathon, says he conducts 30% of his business on the freeways over the two cellular phone lines in his Mercedes. Despite the cost—about $1,200 for the equipment and 45¢ a minute for local daytime calls—plenty of or-

dinary Angelinos use cellular to make drive time more productive. With nearly 200,000 customers and 8,000 more signing up each month, Los Angeles is the biggest cellular market in the U.S. Worldwide, sales of cellular phones will nearly double this year. By 1990 there will be 7 million in use, says economist Herschel Shosteck of Herschel Shosteck Associates in Silver Spring, Md.

Europe's Asea Brown Boveri Ltd., an electrical equipment maker, has come up with perhaps the ultimate in ride-and-work convenience. Headquartered in Västeras, 75 miles northwest of Stockholm, it was having trouble finding professionals who would make the 85-minute trip twice a day. It took Ann Larsson, a Stockholm MBA, only a few months of getting up at 5 a.m. for the commute by car to suggest an alterna-

BELESKEY AND HIS "OFFICE": THE GMC VAN IS RIGGED WITH PHONE, FAX, AND PC

SIBBALD/PICTURE GROUP

tive: a railcar outfitted with phones, faxes, and personal computers. Now about 40 Asea white-collar employees begin their workday as the 7:40 for Västeras pulls out of Stockholm. "I wouldn't still be with the company if it weren't for the train," says Larsson.

In Canada, Bernie E. Beleskey has rigged his own office on wheels in a 1984 GMC van, complete with phone, fax, and laptop computer. He racks up 3,700 miles a month as a marketing director for Investment Center Financial Corp., a seller of financial services. Beleskey likes his setup so much that he hopes to sell the same package to some of the 180 agents he supervises.

The next step is skipping the trip to work altogether by "telecommuting." The idea arose nearly 20 years ago with Jack Nilles, an engineer who wanted to curb auto pollution in Los Angeles by reducing commuting. He proposed set-

ting up satellite offices in the suburbs, near the homes of clerical workers. Instead of driving downtown, clerks would use computer terminals in the regional offices.

In a six-month experiment in 1973, Nilles says, turnover among suburban data-entry clerks dropped to zero from 33% downtown. Office rental costs fell, and productivity rose 18%, thanks to fewer absences. But the employer, an insurance company, decided to stick with the traditional arrangement—pink-collar factories of 1,000 workers or more. "They suffered from an edifice complex," Nilles says. He went on to found Jala Associates, a Los Angeles telecommuting consultant.

Across the country, there still are only about 20,000 full-time telecommuters, says Gil Gordon, a consultant based in Monmouth Junction, N.J., though Nilles thinks as many as 2 million employees telecommute occasionally. His 1986 survey of 900 middle managers in large companies found that 3% spent more than eight hours a week using a home PC on company work, and 50% spent at least one hour a week. "Not one of those companies had a formal telecommuting program," he notes. Gordon thinks 5 million workers could be telecommute frequently by the mid-1990s.

In Los Angeles, there's renewed interest in telecommuting—as an alternative to spending $42 billion to $110 billion on new roads and mass transit to relieve traffic and pollution problems. Meanwhile, stiff new California laws require private employers to cut the number of car trips made by workers. That should give telecommuting a push—and perhaps set a pattern for other gridlocked cities such as Boston and New York.

But what really could make telecommuting click is labor shortages. With the Baby Bust generation entering the job market, "the U.S. is going to have a real crunch, particularly around 1995," says T. Travers Waltrip, telecommunications vice-president for Travelers Corp., the Hartford insurer. "By then we won't be able to persuade a highly skilled person living in California to move to Hartford. Telecommuting is going to become a very important alternative."

In some places, it already is. When

(cont.)

Pacific Bell moved 2,000 jobs from its San Francisco headquarters 40 miles to San Ramon in 1985, many employees looked for other work. Telecommuting helped Pac Bell to keep hard-to-replace marketing managers, accountants, and programmers. Up to 1,000 of the company's 17,000 managers now work at home part-time. Hedi M. Hesse, a systems analyst, spends four days at home and one in the office, 50 minutes away. Working in spurts or at night, she now has the time to pursue a psychology degree at the University of California at Berkeley.

Telecommuting has its limitations. Initially it was used to farm out routine clerical work, such as processing insurance forms. Such piecework has "a lot of potential for exploitation," says Lotte Bailyn, a professor in the "Management in the '90s" research program at the Massachusetts Institute of Technology's Sloan School of Management. Two years ago telecommuters sued California Western States Life Insurance Co. in Sacramento. The company had denied them vacation, health, and retirement benefits, claiming they had become independent contractors. Last January the company dropped its telecommuting program, and in May the employees settled out of court for an undisclosed sum.

Employers can't regard telecommuting as a cure-all for the child-care crisis, either. "You can't do any kind of work that requires concentration and simultaneously watch children," says Kathleen Christensen, author of *Women and Home-Based Work.* She says that two-thirds of mothers who do professional work at home have full-time child care. The exception may be when the kids are older. When her two sons get home from grade school, says Jill M. Horan, an Old Saybrook (Conn.) computer analyst who telecommutes for Travelers, "it's wonderful being here."

'ORIGINAL SIN.' If telecommuting is so ideal, why don't more companies try it? "The clash with the corporate culture is the biggest problem," says David Nye, a former Sohio Chemical Co. executive and author of *Alternate Staffing Strategies.* Employers cling to an industrial-age view, says Alex Malcolm, director of software services for John Hancock Mutual Life Insurance Co.: "It's the idea that people were born with original sin—unless you watch them, they won't work."

FOR MORE WORKERS, THERE'S NO PLACE LIKE HOME

MILLIONS

'87   '88 EST.   '89 EST.

WHITE-COLLAR WORKERS OPERATING OUT OF HOME OFFICES
□ FULL-TIME (MORE THAN 35 HOURS/WEEK)   ▨ PART-TIME
■ PCs USED IN HOME OFFICES, EXCLUDING THOSE USED BY TRADITIONAL OFFICE WORKERS AT NIGHT

DATA: LINK RESOURCES INC.

FAX MACHINES USED IN HOME OFFICES

'87   '88 EST.   '89 EST.

INSTALLED BASE IN THOUSANDS

But managers who have escaped corporate Calvinism report good results, not the least being improved managing techniques. Supervisors "tend to give more quantifiable, results-oriented direction," says William J. Benham, a manager of telecommuters at U. S. West. And that spills over to the rest of the work force. "You start managing by results, not surveillance," notes David Fleming, a telecommuting consultant who is running a 150-employee project for the State of California. "Staffers turn in much better work because they are less distracted by being watched over," adds Paula K. Norwood, a manager of telecommuters at RW Johnson Pharmaceutical Research Institute in New Jersey. Consultant Gordon claims that telecommuting can lead to productivity gains of 25% or more.

An increasing number of workers aren't waiting for their bosses to reach this enlightened conclusion. According to market researcher Link Resources Inc., some 4.7 million Americans operate full-time businesses from their homes—up 35% from 1987. There are probably as many reasons for this as there are people doing it, but most have one thing in common: a computer. "It's simple: It lets them do the work of more than one person," says Thomas E. Miller, director of Link's Home Office Research Program.

Six years ago, Raymond M. Jassin hit a dead end in his career. After 20 years as a librarian for the Association of the Bar of the City of New York, he interviewed for other jobs only to realize that "things wouldn't get much better." He started moonlighting on the hunch that he could sell his skills part-time to law firms and corporate law departments. It worked. Today he and his wife, Marjorie, run Law Library Management Inc. out of an apartment in their Huntington (N. Y.) home.

Although he didn't use a computer at first, Jassin says, "within a year I saw I couldn't do more without one." Now he has three PCs to track invoices, payments, and interlibrary loans and requests for his clients—just as any in-house law librarian would do. He also peruses data bases to do client research. A fax machine exchanges messages with clients, and Jassin uses beepers to dispatch a staff of 20 helpers to perform such tasks as updating loose-leaf binders of periodicals for clients. During his occasional hour-long drives to Manhattan, he uses a cellular phone.

Displaced executives also are becoming computer-assisted entrepreneurs. When RCA Corp. sold its record division

GOETZ VOWED EARLY ON TO MASTER COMPUTERS—"OR BE OBSOLETE"

(cont.)

in 1987, it left Don L. Ellis, senior vice-president of classical marketing, out of a job. Wanting to stay in England, the 50-year-old American set up shop as an international trader of branded consumer goods, including sportswear. At first, he says, new technology "was all mumbo-jumbo to me." But now, using an IBM PC clone and a fax machine, he brokers deals among a far-flung network of buyers and sellers. Ellis has become a master time-shifter. With a fax, he says, "it's possible for me to be in touch with Japan, Africa, Latin America, and the U.S.—all in one business day."

There are obvious pitfalls to the home-entrepreneur concept. A former middle manager may be able to find a buyer for his skills, but he may also take a financial drubbing. According to Bell Communications' Robert Kraut, home-based workers earn about 70% of what their full-time office counterparts make. Link's Miller says that a "significant number" of home-based entrepreneurs are just "passing through" until they find another full-time job.

There are other stresses. Jassin is finally earning what he might have gotten at a top law firm, but he still works long hours and hasn't had a vacation in 18 months. Home workers often find that their jobs begin consuming their lives. To survive, they must consciously plan activities away from home. "They soon realize that they can burn out just as quickly at home as in the office," says Julian Cohen, former chairman of the American Home Business Assn., which sells group health insurance and other services to home business owners.

Burnout can occur faster at home. "It used to be if you woke up at 4 a.m. with an idea, you'd roll over and go back to sleep," says Roberta A. Shecter, a psychologist at the Postgraduate Center for Mental Health in New York. "Now you can go to your PC and start working."

Still, aficionados of the electronic lifestyle claim that it can be liberating. "When I was in my 20s and early 30s, I had no time for a personal life because I was always working," says publisher Whittle. "Now I have a personal life because of the machines around me."

Reprinted from the October 10, 1988 issue of *Business Week* by special permission copyright© 1988 by McGraw-Hill, Inc.

QUALITY TIME. Nicholas Negroponte, founder of the Media Lab think tank at MIT, has lived the electronic lifestyle for years. He insists that in the long run his high-tech tools give him more out of life. "I work substantially bigger work weeks than most people, but I still get six or seven weeks off a year," he says.

One of the hottest technology markets is for after-hours home workers—often parents of young children who leave the office at five and finish work on a PC after they put the kids to bed. Paul S. Goodman, a professor of industrial administration and psychology at Carnegie-Mellon University in Pittsburgh, surveyed the region's 50 largest employers and found that only a few had full-time telecommuters. But more than half encouraged after-hours telecommuting. Employees say that shifting the extra work hours to the home reduces stress and improves morale.

Carried to their logical conclusion, the trends of the late 1980s could reshape countless jobs—and corporations. Travelers' Waltrip expects his company to use more teams of relatively autonomous information workers who meet most often electronically. Most workers will come to the office, but "I see more and more people working for Travelers living in different places," he says. "It won't make any difference where."

Companies with the nerve to try this could become far more competitive, says William L. Bramer, a director for Arthur Andersen & Co.'s consulting practice. He notes that in factory automation, corporations hit a snag a few years back: They had bought all the machinery that could boost productivity by eliminating jobs. Then they looked at how the remaining employees worked. After retraining and cross-training, these workers developed the communications skills to solve complex problems. Many work in close-knit teams, every member able to do every other member's job. Bramer is working on ways to make the same thing happen in offices by helping clients redesign organizations so that computer technology extends the abilities of employees, rather than replacing them. Improvements in technology will help.

One of the next important innovations in software, for example, is called "groupware." At Discovery, Ruth Otte and her colleagues use a package called "The Coordinator." It categorizes electronic messages—requests, proposals, offers, responses—and notes what action needs to be initiated. At any point, Otte can see what commitments she has made in her communications to others and what commitments are due her. Everyone in the company is on the system.

ELECTRONIC SECRETARY? Such departures from the attitudes and structures of the industrial age tend to flatten an organization, eliminating the hierarchy that gave only those at the top a view of the entire corporation. Starting six years ago, Cummins Engine Co. in Columbus, Ind., began using electronic mail. Now 14,000 employees, including factory workers, are on the network. "It has broken down a lot of the formal communication processes that built up over years," says Jane Kennedy, lead information center analyst. By opening up communications, management learns faster what is going on throughout the company, she notes.

That free flow of electronic information "poses some serious control issues that many corporations find difficult to deal with," notes Alan Kay, an Apple Computer Inc. research fellow. Kay, whose ideas helped inspire the Macintosh, says that the technology is becoming available to see his 20-year-old dream come true: a truly personal computer that will work as an individual's able assistant—to automatically gather the information he needs, make the right phone calls, keep track of appointments, and switch back and forth between different jobs effortlessly. There are few technical reasons why this electronically assisted lifestyle should not reach full flower in the next few years. Only humans remain as obstacles.

By Geoff Lewis in New York, with Jeffrey Rothfeder, Resa W. King in Hartford, Mark Maremont in London, Thane Peterson in Paris, and bureau reports

Critical Condition

Generic-Drug Scandal At the FDA Is Linked To Deregulation Drive

Agency Treated the Industry As 'Partner,' Critics Say; A Cut in Staff Also Hurt

An Official's Free Trip Abroad

By Bruce Ingersoll
And Gregory Stricharchuk
Staff Reporters of The Wall Street Journal

WASHINGTON — The conditions were ripe for a regulatory disaster at the Food and Drug Administration.

The agency, which regulates a hefty 25% of the nation's consumer economy—from kumquats to cosmetics—has been lurching from one crisis to another in recent years, trying to meet mounting de-

Problems at Lilly

U.S. inspectors find widespread quality-control problems at an Indianapolis plant, causing the firm to halt distribution of all drugs made at the facility and to recall 10 drugs. Story on page A6.

mands with a shrinking staff. There were product tamperings to contend with, a blood-bank emergency triggered by fears of AIDS contamination, a panic over cyanide-laced grapes from Chile and ever-increasing pressure to speed new life-saving drugs through the approval process.

So it was that disaster followed.

In the last two months, a drumbeat of disclosures has revealed a widening scandal involving the agency's generic drug program—a five-year effort to bring to market cheap alternatives to brand-name drugs. Three FDA employees already have pleaded guilty to taking illegal gratuities from generic-drug makers. Two generics companies have admitted duping the agency with falsified data. And the FDA has found manufacturing and record-keeping problems at nearly all of the 12 generic-drug makers it has investigated so far.

"I would hang them if I could," says FDA Commissioner Frank Young.

But the generic-drug scandal, unlike the grape scare or the epidemic of acquired immune deficiency syndrome, is a crisis largely of the FDA's own making—and a crisis in which many feel Dr. Young played a prominent role. "He was in his own world, whether it was chasing grapes or problems concerning Social Security programs," contends Roy McKnight of Pittsburgh-based Mylan Laboratories Inc., a generic-drug maker. It was Mylan's complaints about the FDA's generic-drug practices that spurred investigations of the agency by the House Energy and Commerce Committee's investigative panel and the U.S. attorney in Baltimore. And it was these investigations that brought to light the FDA's raft of troubles.

There were policy issues, too, that led to the scandal. The FDA's current problems are a legacy of the Reagan administration's push to deregulate. By scaling back their enforcement actions while publicly embracing the generic-drug industry as a "partner" rather than an adversary, the FDA created "an atmosphere of lawlessness," says Sidney Wolfe, head of the Public Citizen Health Research Group. "It isn't surprising that the generics companies pulled these shenanigans."

Some notable shortcomings within the agency aided in the scandal. Five years after Congress ordered the FDA to speed the approval of generic drugs—as part of the 1984 Waxman-Hatch Act—the agency has yet to issue specific rules for the process. Indeed, officials are still soliciting public comments on the proposed package of regulations. In the meantime, the agency has been operating under guidelines that have fostered arbitrary, case-by-case decisions on generic-drug applications, creating opportunities for favoritism and fraud.

Petty internal squabbles have worsened things. FDA policy forbids the approval of

Frank Young

a new generic drug if inspectors have found manufacturing problems at the drug company's plant. Yet officials in the plant-inspection office have refused to provide inspection reports to other FDA officials reviewing new-drug applications; instead, the new-drug department has had to file for the reports under the Freedom of Information Act—an almost unheard of practice. And when the documents were turned over, much of the information had been blanked out.

The generic-drug division is also se-

verely prone to losing paper work—so much so that some industry officials fear they are the victims of deliberate sabotage. For instance, the disappearance of documents filed by Biocraft Laboratories Inc. delayed a new-drug application by that company for at least a year. Internal investigators from the Health and Human Services Department, of which the FDA is a part, are looking into the possibility that an FDA drug reviewer intentionally mislaid the documents as a favor to a rival company.

After presiding over, from a regulatory standpoint, the rise of generic drugs from a cottage industry to a multibillion-dollar business, Dr. Young generally defends his agency's actions. But he admits that the scandal may devastate the industry he befriended: "There's a real possibility that the generic-drug industry may be totally discredited," he says.

That, in turn, would deal a severe blow to the government's efforts to bring down health costs with generics. Specific generic-drug regulations still haven't been issued, leading one senior FDA official to conclude: "If we find out many more things that are wrong, we will have to re-evaluate" the agency's pending generic drug regulations.

The generic-drug scandal is far from the only problem plaguing the agency. Consumer advocates complain that food safety—in particular, the growing problem of bacterial food poisoning—has been given short shrift. The FDA inspects only a dribble of the swelling tide of food imported into the U.S. Critics fault the agency for relying too heavily on state authorities to ensure the safety of shellfish and milk supplies.

At the same time, the agency is being faulted for not cracking down on medical-device manufacturers for failing to report malfunctions that result in deaths and injuries. Some manufacturers see disturbing parallels between regulation of this area and the generic-drug mess. In a lawsuit, closely held Clark Research & Development Inc., which makes dialysis-related devices, accuses the agency of losing documents and of pursuing a "pattern of harassment" after Clark complained about a competitor being allowed to make misleading claims. "We want that company subject to the same regulations we're subject to," says Michael Pearl, a Clark officer. "We want a level playing field."

A Question of Health

The FDA's defenders, while not playing down the seriousness of such allegations, say the current controversy obscures the agency's positive accomplishments. "Don't focus on the glitches that occur periodically," says Sanford Miller, a former FDA official, who is dean of the University of Texas Graduate School of Biomedical Sciences. "Take a look at the overall health of the American people.

"Doing everything people want the FDA to do would require an FDA the size of the Defense Department," he says. But over the last decade the agency has instead shrunk—to 7,400 employees from 8,100. The Bush administration is seeking a budget authorization of $570 million for the next fiscal year, a 5% increase.

Although some AIDS activists depict him as an uncaring paymaster of a sluggish bureaucracy, Dr. Young insists he has made new drugs for the desperately ill a top priority: The average time to approve such critical drugs is 4.2 years; the average for most other drugs is 7.8 years. The FDA approved an anti-viral drug, AZT, in 107 days—a record. The new medication slows the progression of AIDS in individuals showing early symptoms.

The generics scandal, in Dr. Young's view, is the fault of an unrealistic Congress, which five years ago saw generics as a way of reducing prescription-drug costs for constituents. The Waxman-Hatch Act generated thousands of applications to market generic duplicates of brand-name drugs on which 17-year patents had expired. The law spared companies the cost of time-consuming clinical tests to prove the safety and effectiveness of their copycat products. Instead, the companies merely had to show the FDA that their products were "bio-equivalent" to the brand-names they mimicked—that they performed in the bloodstream in about the same way.

Feeding Frenzy

As patents expired, companies scrambled to be the first to win FDA approval for their products. Typically, the first on the market could count on capturing a lucrative share of total sales by undercutting the brand-name price.

In view of the high stakes—and the FDA's practice of accepting bio-equivalency test results on faith—the scandal shouldn't have caught the agency completely off-guard. As early as December 1985, middle management at the FDA began receiving reports of drug reviewers favoring one company over others in return for "some quid pro quo," according to a Congressional investigation. There was even a tip telephoned to the FDA about a romantic entanglement between an agency drug reviewer and a woman executive from a drug company that was seeking his approval of its product. The tip wasn't acted on.

At the very least, critics say, officials should have been suspicious of the phenomenal success of two small generic-drug makers in beating their competitors to market. Par Pharmaceutical Inc. and its Quad Pharmaceuticals Inc. subsidiary received a stunning 77 drug approvals in 1986, almost twice as many as any other company. The companies pleaded guilty earlier this year to dispensing illicit gratuities to speed their drug applications through the FDA bureaucracy.

In time, other companies complained about bureaucrats deviating from the FDA's first-come, first-served policy on new generic-drug applications.

The FDA "engages in nothing short of market manipulation" as it decides on applications, H. Lawrence Fox, an attorney for Barr Laboratories Inc., asserted in Congressional testimony, adding: "The FDA has told us, 'We screwed you on this one, so we'll take care of you on the next one.'"

The untimely disappearance and destruction of documents at the FDA further fueled suspicions of favoritism. At the same hearing, a Congressional panel embarrassed the FDA by producing the original copy of a generic-drug application that had been found, torn in half, in the trash of Charles Y. Chang, a former FDA branch chief, who pleaded guilty in a federal court in Baltimore to two counts of interstate travel in aid of racketeering.

Specifically, the charges involve his accepting a paid, round-the-world trip totaling more than $3,000 that a drug industry consultant offered him at the direction of the president of American Therapeutics Inc., a generics maker based in Bohemia, N.Y. The president of American Therapeutics also purchased furniture and computer equipment for Mr. Chang totaling almost $8,000.

In return, Mr. Chang allegedly took steps to get American Therapeutics drug applications through the process more quickly by assigning the applications to speedy reviewers, among other things.

Neither American Therapeutics nor its officers have been charged with a crime. The company denies any wrongdoing.

Harold Snyder, chief executive officer of Biocraft, says he "went into orbit" when he learned that part of his company's application had been mysteriously misplaced. "They lose samples, they lose this, and they lose that," he says. But out of fear of retaliation, Mr. Snyder won't accuse the agency of playing favorites.

Taking most of the flak for the agency's failings is Dr. Young, a Bible-quoting biotechnology specialist who previously served as dean of the University of Roch-

ester medical school. Many in industry doubt that he will survive the scandal as head of the FDA. One view is that the 58-year-old Dr. Young is exhausted after five years in the job and about to resign. The other is that his ouster is imminent. But Dr. Young, seemingly upbeat, says he "has the best job in town," while administration insiders say he still has the confidence of the White House and Health and Human Services Secretary Louis Sullivan.

There are doubts, too, whether Dr. Young is tough enough for the battle ahead. Says one industry executive: "He's not a street fighter; he's a pussy cat." But Dr. Young, decked out in the summer whites of the U.S. Public Health Service's officer corps, aggressively defends his agency's performance.

"Here you've got an industry," he says, "that would stoop to giving gratuities to federal employees, that would stoop to falsifying data and submitting false data to the FDA.

"Could we have designed the system [to catch] that? Yes, we could have." But, he adds, "What was Congress telling us to do? 'We need to get generic drugs on the market. We're going to give you four months, agency, to get your act in order.'" The solution: to use "the procedures that were tried and true in the past."

Although there is no evidence yet that shoddily made generic drugs have gravely injured anyone, Dr. Young vows that within three months he will be able to conclusively answer every consumer's question: "Doc, are the drugs safe and do they work?"

FDA officials are conducting top-to-bottom inspections at more than 30 generic-drug makers, and scrutinizing the paper work and pre-marketing test results on some 200 generic drugs to see if there are more instances of companies falsifying data and, as was the case with some companies, substituting brand-name products as their own to win approval for their generic copies. So far, the inspections have resulted in 128 product recalls and suspensions. FDA chemists are also testing the potency of the 30 top-selling generics on the market.

The agency, asserts Mr. McKnight of Pittsburgh-based Mylan Laboratories, "is doing what they should have been doing five years ago—they're now off their derrieres."

The FDA's efforts to get to the bottom of the generic-drug scandal further overextends an agency long on mandate and short on money and manpower. "The bottom line is, routine work doesn't get done,"

(cont.)

says a senior FDA official. "Surveillance inspections of other drug and food companies don't get done." Gavin Meerdink, a veterinary toxicologist at the University of Arizona, for example, says he recently tipped off a local FDA official to illegal over-the-counter sales of oxytocin, a prescription-drug for livestock. "He just didn't have the manpower to do anything about it," says Dr. Meerdink.

Though he got blind-sided by the generic-drug crisis, Dr. Young runs the FDA bureaucracy like a chief executive officer specializing in crisis management; he plans for emergencies. But sometimes the challenges may simply be too overwhelming for the FDA. Take the grape scare. At its peak, the FDA threw 650 investigators and lab technicans into the fray. Though they worked night and day, they managed to inspect less than 5% of the fruit unloaded off nine freighters.

—Sue Shellenbarger in Chicago contributed to this article.

17

FIGHTING BACK

THE RESURGENCE OF SOCIAL ACTIVISM

At first, Phil Sokolof must have seemed like just another one of those crank-letter writers that companies often brush aside. Crusading against fat-laden tropical oils that have been linked to heart problems, Sokolof wrote about his own heart attack and pleaded with cookie and cereal makers to dump the oil. But Sokolof didn't stop there. In all, the 66-year-old Omaha millionaire sent out 11,000 letters. Then the full-page newspaper ads started, $200,000 worth, with offending Hydrox cookies and Cracklin' Oat Bran cereal pictured under the stark headline: "The Poisoning of America."

That was six months ago. At the time, Kellogg Co., maker of Cracklin' Oat Bran, called the ad "irresponsible." Yet within a month the giant food processor decided to take the coconut oil out. Most of the packaged-food industry's other players have done the same, along with several fast-food chains.

Many of the companies say they reacted to the general public's concern about diet, not Sokolof's blitz. But whether by design or by chance, Sokolof won. And he's not alone. In recent months, environmental and consumer groups, virtually ignored for most of the Reagan years, have notched victories over insurance underwriters, cigarette companies, gunmakers, and even producers of racy television shows.

DECADE OF WAITING. It's not a return to the 1970s, when left-wing protest groups staged mammoth political marches and national boycotts. Yet the evidence seems undeniable that grass-roots activism is back. Does it all add up to a full-fledged backlash against business, which fared so well politically in the 1980s? Probably not. Still, more often than not business is the target—and will pay the price.

The situation is different this time around partly because the cast of characters has changed. Many activists, such as Sokolof, president of a company that makes metal parts, come from the other end of the political spectrum. Even those with '60s credentials have emerged, after a decade of waiting, more sophisticated in their methods and savvy about how business operates. "We're no longer able to simply beat up on business," says Bill Zimmerman, the 48-year-old Los Angeles-based political consultant who helped mastermind last November's California vote to roll back both auto and home insurance rates. "The arguments need to be sharper and better documented."

Brandishing reports that it said showed insurance companies making handsome profits on their investments while increasing individual rates, the consumer group Voter Revolt last November won narrow passage in California of Proposition 103. The measure would roll back auto and home insurance rates by 20% and impose a one-year freeze on new rate hikes. The victory marked the return to the national limelight of consumer advocate Ralph Nader, the proposition's most

> Environmental and consumer groups, virtually ignored during the Reagan years, are winning victories again

visible supporter. Now, say both Nader and Zimmerman, the consumer movement intends to strike while the iron is hot.

"A new brand of citizen activism is under way," says Nader, who this year bested Congress over its plan to give itself a pay raise. Just days after California's Supreme Court upheld the major elements of Proposition 103, Nader unveiled a plan to seek similar relief in several other states. He figures that the savings could run as much as $23 billion annually. And farther down the road, Nader says, he intends to work on methods to combat rising health care costs, ozone depletion, and indoor air pollution.

With a mailing list of 200,000 as one prize from its Proposition 103 win, California-based Voters Revolt also is making big plans. Zimmerman says the group is looking at ballot initiatives to deal with crime, poverty, and medical insurance. The organization's most likely target in 1990, however, will be some of the tax breaks given to business by California's Proposition 13 in 1978. Reducing them could raise around $10 billion annually, he says, and some of that money would be channeled toward low-cost housing. Local governments would get the lion's share to fund education, police, and other services cut after Proposition 13. Households would get rebates.

The insurance initiative took months of planning. Environmentalists, in a backhanded sort of way, plain got lucky. The Exxon Valdez oil spill yielded nightly TV footage of blackened beaches and oil-soaked birds that rallied the faithful. Disk

(cont.)

jockeys around the country urged Exxon Corp. credit-card holders to relinquish their cards, and more than 10,000 did. Legislation allowing oil exploration in the Arctic National Wildlife Refuge, ready for a Senate vote, was put on hold.

Such groups as the Sierra Club, which raised $115,000 to aid the cleanup, saw their membership rolls swell. And suddenly, Big Oil finds itself back in the villain's role it occupied as oil prices spiraled upward in the 1970s. Executives at other oil companies worry that they, too, will soon become targets. "Environmental groups just see a window of opportunity" to score points with the public, fumes consultant Herb Schmertz, a former Mobil Oil Corp. vice-president for public affairs. "They're professional attackers."

But you don't have to be an oil giant to feel the heat. And the speed with which some companies react shows that after years of being left alone, many are uncomfortable with public scrutiny. When the American Nurses Assn. wrote to express dismay this April over how nurses were portrayed in the NBC television show *Nightingales*, sponsors Sears, Roebuck & Co. and Chrysler Corp. quickly backed out. A spokesman for Procter & Gamble Co., which argued that Sokolof's ad was misleading, nonetheless says it is taking palm oil out of its Crisco shortening "to remove it from all that confusion."

POISONED GRAPES. Those reactions are typical, says University of Southern California marketing professor Ben M. Enis. "A company is only going to look like a bad guy if it picks those kinds of fights," he says. "There's always another TV show to sponsor." But Enis, an economist, also notes that such attacks are more frequent now. "For years, people have been worried about the economy—where interest rates are going, the unemployment rate," he says. "For the last few years, things have been doing well with the economy. Now, they're looking around at other things that may affect their lives."

Indeed, there's a wide range of new concerns popping up almost daily on the evening news. The scare about poisoned Chilean grapes is over, but concern about chemicals sprayed on apples lingers on. In Detroit, Nader's lawyers joined local citizens in a lawsuit to stall a three-year plan to merge the business operations of the city's two daily newspapers. Seattle voters are expected on May 16 to approve a ban on high-rise development. Jay D. Hair, president of the National Wildlife Federation, says people are also reacting to the huge amounts of toxic pollutants emitted daily. "They're angry, and they want to exert some sort of control," he says.

Such exertion takes many forms. There are still some old-style guerrilla tactics. To save trees in the Northwest, environmentalists booby-trapped some with foot-long metal spikes that would spew shrapnel if struck by a logger's chainsaw. Animal-rights groups have sprayed red paint on New Yorkers wearing fur coats, and others have stolen into a hospital lab in Loma Linda, Calif., to free animals earmarked for research.

With so many issues upsetting the public, environmental and consumer groups have no lack of causes around which to rally. "It's going to happen as long as there is an absence in leadership by our elected officials and corporations," proclaims Voter Revolt President Harvey Rosenfield. Though it may not be a backlash, business had better get used to taking the heat.

By Ronald Grover in Los Angeles, with bureau reports

18

Despite Skepticism, a Once-Lowly Bran Now Aspires to the Level of Oat Cuisine

By ALECIA SWASY

Staff Reporter of THE WALL STREET JOURNAL

It's as bland and gritty-tasting as sand, but suddenly oat bran is appearing in everything from cereals and bread to pasta, pretzels and potato chips.

The appetite for oat bran, a nutritious grain long fed to horses, was triggered last year by health studies linking it to lower cholesterol. Now a marketing battle has emerged among big and little food companies eager to snare health-conscious consumers.

Demand is such that "it's become a feeding frenzy," says David Liederman, founder of New York-based **David's Specialty Foods**. Sales of his company's oat-bran muffins have soared to 75,000 a week from 300 when they were introduced last May.

Companies are so eager to capitalize on the demand that they would be willing to market "toilet paper impregnated with oat bran," says Joseph Smith, a consumer psychologist who heads Oxtoby-Smith Inc., a New York consumer-research firm.

Mr. Smith recently surveyed 1,000 consumers nationwide and found that 60% believe oat bran is healthful for them. Those who've tried it say they now eat oat-bran products three or four times a week in an effort to lower their cholesterol levels. He notes that some physicians are feeding the demand, advising patients to eat more of the fiber.

But some food-industry consultants and others are skeptical of oat bran's benefits or lasting appeal. Nutritionists charge that the amounts added to foods aren't nearly enough to lower cholesterol significantly—and that oat bran can't make junk food healthful. It can be a taste-bud turnoff: Mr. Smith, for one, stays away from oat-bran muffins. "They're like inflated hockey pucks," he says.

Yet food companies say they can't move fast enough to keep oat-bran products on grocery shelves, and they're betting on sustained appetites. **Quaker Oats** Co. and others, for example, are investing in new plants to churn out greater amounts and varieties of oat-bran-enriched foods.

The biggest oat-bran marketing battle is in the cereal arena, where companies will spend millions of dollars this year introducing an array of new products. **General Mills** Inc., Minneapolis, is test-marketing Benefit, an oat-bran cereal that it says it will soon distribute nationally. Quaker plans to offer a cold version of its hot Oat Bran cereal, featuring what the Chicago company claims will be the highest amount of oat bran per serving of any cereal: 20 grams an ounce. **Kellogg** Co., Battle Creek, Mich., is offering $5 rebate coupons for cholesterol screening tests on the back of its Common Sense Oat Bran cereal boxes.

Other breakfast foods are becoming part of the fray. A Kellogg subsidiary, Mrs. Smith Frozen Foods Co., has added oat bran to one line of its Eggo waffles. **Procter & Gamble** Co., which learned from calls on its toll-free consumer telephone line that muffin lovers were grinding up oat-bran breakfast cereals to make their own homemade mixes, has introduced two Duncan Hines oat-bran muffin mixes.

And oat bran isn't just for breakfast anymore. It's in fettuccine and rotelli made by **Edward & Sons Trading** Co., Union, N.J., and is expected to help almost double the company's revenue this year to $8 million.

For snack time, **Robert's American Gourmet**, Roslyn Heights, N.Y., offers oat-bran-enriched pretzels, potato and tortilla chips. For the potato chips, "I did it to solve a problem," says owner Robert Ehrlich, a former gold trader on Wall Street. When the chips are dusted with oat bran, he explains, "they're less greasy."

But there's a catch, Mr. Ehrlich concedes: Most of the oat bran settles to the bottom of the bag of chips. That's not a problem, he says, with the pretzels and tortilla chips because the oat bran is baked into them.

But health specialists say consumers are only fooling themselves if they wolf down bags of oat-bran tortilla chips, cookies and muffins as a means of helping their hearts. "You can put oat bran into almost anything, but is it worth eating?" asks Bonnie Liebman, director of nutrition at the Center for Science in the Public Interest, a Washington, D.C., research center. She adds: "This craze has gotten a bit out of hand."

Moreover, oat bran may only help lower cholesterol levels if it is ingested in large quantities. Ms. Liebman's group estimates that to lower cholesterol by just 3%, a person must consume 35 grams of oat bran daily for a month; a two-month study found no additional improvement. To get 35 grams of oat bran from Robert's American Gourmet chips, a person would have to eat about nine ounces—1,225 calories.

Consumer enthusiasm about oat bran may stem partly from misleading ads, Ms. Liebman suggests. Some Quaker ads last year "exaggerated the drop in cholesterol you could expect from oatmeal," she asserts. A Quaker official says the ad was accurate but has been replaced because "it didn't test well with consumers."

There is one important constraint on the oat-bran boom: The grain is in short supply, making oat-bran products more expensive than alternatives. A 100-pound bag of oat-bran flour, for example, costs about $130, compared with about $18 for the same amount of white flour, says Helmer Toro, manager of **H&H Bagels**, New York, which now offers oat-bran bagels.

Last summer's drought has kept U.S. oat supplies tight, forcing companies like Quaker to import the grain from Argentina, Canada and elsewhere. Quaker also is expanding capacity at its milling plant. "We need all we can get," says an official.

Getting Information for Marketing Decisions

19

What Do People Want, Anyway?

Researchers are fighting it out: Can computers replace humans in consumer studies?

By CLAUDIA H. DEUTSCH

THE Campbell Soup Company, like most consumer products companies, has always asked its customers lots of questions. Last year alone, its field researchers contacted close to 110,000 people to talk about food — taste, preparation, nutritional value, the works. On the basis of what they said, Campbell changed the seasonings in five Le Menu dinners and introduced a line of low-salt soups called, appropriately enough, Special Request.

Both the new and the reformulated products are selling well, so the survey techniques clearly gave Campbell's a good reading of consumer preferences. But could Campbell's have gotten the same information more easily — say, from finding out how similar products were selling? Put another way, could knowing what consumers buy today give Campbell's, or any consumer products company, a good idea of what they will buy tomorrow?

These are by no means simple questions. At least since the days of Sigmund Freud, psychologists have been debating the best ways to predict human behavior. But now that debate has spilled onto Madison Avenue and into board rooms. It lies at the heart of a controversy that is pitting computer specialists against pollsters, market researchers against marketing executives, and psychologists against each other. The outcome could affect not only how companies make marketing decisions but what products people will get to buy.

In one camp sit the behaviorists, who believe that the best indicator of how people will act in the future is how they act now. Opposite them is the cognitive camp, which says people operate from an endless array of motivations and that the only way to predict what someone will do is to figure out what is going on inside his or her mind.

In practical terms, the two sides are debating whether computers can replace people as the linchpins of consumer research. And the behaviorists are winning converts.

"The role of the consumer as the party giving answers and opinions will be significantly less," said Jagdish Sheth, a consumer psychologist at the University of Southern California. "It will be replaced by measuring his behavior, not his opinions."

"We are heading to an age where most information can be captured electronically," said George S. Fabian, an executive vice president at Backer, Spielvogel & Bates, a New York advertising agency. "It is unavoidable. And it is welcome."

Is it?

Until recently, that would have been a moot question. There were few electronic data sources, so companies had little choice but to plumb the collective consumer mentality through surveys. Ask enough people enough questions, the theory went, and some semblance of truth will emerge. According to Diane Bowers, executive director of the Council of American Survey Research Organizations, companies spend nearly $1 billion each year to ask more than 50 million consumers their opinions on products and services.

Even proponents of surveys concede that the companies are not buying absolute truth for their money. "Consumers say they are eating fewer snacks, yet the snack food industry has record sales; they say they are on a diet, yet everyone seems to be more overweight," said Anthony J. Adams, director of marketing research and planning for Campbell's.

Similarly, Lynn R. Kahle, associate professor of consumer psychology at the University of Oregon, cites a recent survey in Detroit in which people were asked what they thought of the Metallic Metals Act. The legislation was purely fictitious; about a quarter of the respondents had an opinion on it anyway. "People hate to look foolish or uneducated, even to strangers," he said. "They lie all the time to make themselves look good."

STILL, until recently, consumer surveys were the only research game in town, and companies designed countless products, packages and services around them. "Almost every one of our major product innovations was inspired by something consumers told us," said Jonathan B. Sims, manager of media planning and research at the General Foods Corporation.

But in the last few years, technological and demographic trends have converged to make the validity of surveys suspect. At the same time, alternative ways of gauging consumer preferences have emerged. Scanners in supermarkets and people meters in homes can now electronically record consumer buying and television viewing patterns. That makes it possible for a company to learn overnight how well its product is selling, how competitors are doing and how commercials affect sales.

Moreover, consumers have systematically been weaning themselves from surveys. In the 1960's, the halcyon days of consumer research, people cheerfully participated in most any question-and-answer exercise that came their way. But that was before many women pursued careers outside the home, before computer-generated phone calls and salesmen masquerading as researchers made many people hostile to surveys, and before banks, insurance companies and other service organizations adopted survey techniques that simply led to survey overload.

There are even surveys about how people feel about surveys, and they are turning up some discouraging results. "People are getting burned out on surveys," Professor Kahle said. Indeed, studies show that over the last few years, the amount of time it takes an interviewer to get an hour's worth of usable survey data has increased to eight hours, from five.

And that hour's data are not likely to represent a random sample of the public. Interviewers report little trouble reaching retired people and full-time homemakers. But they have a

---

> 'High tech will never replace high touch,' one marketing expert insists. But others argue otherwise.

---

hard time pinning down working women, city dwellers, young people, families without children and high-income people — often, the very groups that marketers want to reach.

"No matter how good your sampling method is, as soon as people start refusing in large numbers to participate, your random sample has become a convenience sample," said Mr. Sims of General Foods.

Not surprisingly, companies that sell electronically generated information say computers provide an adequate amount of data on consumer behavior. The small companies and solo practitioners who make a living from field surveys contend that computers simply disgorge information on what is happening without showing why it happens. Such data, they say, cannot provide the basis for a rational marketing decision.

Neither side is painting the picture all black and white. But each is quite adamant about where the preponderance of evidence falls.

"Of course we must avoid the arrogance of saying, 'I know you well enough to know how you'll react without asking you questions'," said Lorraine C. Scarpa, vice president of customer information marketing at the Dun & Bradstreet Corporation, whose A.C. Nielsen unit is a leader in electronically provided data. "Still, the real energy in the business is going to the quantitative side."

"Those who still rely on talk rather than scanners for descriptive information are anthropological artifacts," said Joseph G. Smith, a consumer psychologist who is president of Oxtoby-Smith Inc., which does field research. "But what people do does not say anything about why they do it. There is no surrogate available for talking to the consumer."

Corporate annals are rife with stories that support Mr. Smith's contention. Perhaps the most famous is that of the Pillsbury Company's cake-mix fiasco of 30 years ago. Pillsbury came up with a mix that required cooks to do no more than add milk. It yielded a great-tasting cake, yet it bombed in the marketplace.

Pillsbury failed to ask a key question: How do cooks feel about the time they spend in the kitchen? The company found in a later study that cooks wanted to feel they were "adding value" to a packaged product. It reformulated its mix so the cook had to add an egg. Sales took off.

ATTITUDINAL research helped Mr. Fabian of Spielvogel avoid a similar failure when he designed an ad campaign for an automotive client. He already knew that price was a major factor when people bought cars. But later research "showed that people will only buy a low-priced car if they feel smart about the purchase," he said. Thus, Mr. Fabian designed his campaign around the idea that the best and the brightest were gravitating to his client's low-priced car.

General Mills has used a similar combination of descriptive and attitudinal data to design a restaurant chain. A few years ago, responding to figures showing that Italian food is the most frequent choice of those who eat out, the company opened its Olive Garden Italian restaurants. But, because attitude data showed that many people felt that Italian food had

(cont.)

too much garlic and basil, the company reformulated Olive Garden recipes to make them less authentically Italian but more palatable to diners. As Lawrence D. Gibson, the recently retired director of market research at General Mills, put it: "Simply tracking what's going on in the world is never going to tell me how much spice to put in my product."

Still, only the biggest — and richest — companies are willing to spend the hundreds of thousands of dollars that it takes to do both descriptive and attitudinal surveys. And many chief executives are more comfortable with hard data generated by computers and are skewing research budgets toward computerized methods.

"I'd hate to see us become slaves to computer printouts, but managements want to hear what's happening, not what consumers say is happening," said Mr. Adams of Campbell's. "So the data on actual behavior are beginning to push out a lot of the survey data on attitudes."

PARTICULARLY troublesome to many researchers is that their companies maintain the illusion of continuing direct consumer research by using more focus groups. These are groups of 10 or 12 people who are paid an average of about $50 each to sit for a few hours with a mediator and discuss a product, commercial or concept. The sponsor generally sits apart, often behind a one-way mirror, taking notes.

Focus groups are easy to fit into squeezed marketing budgets. But they use too small a sample that they are not representative of much of anything. "Sure, you can get a few perceptions from a focus group, but nothing I would want to build a $10 million factory around," said Mr. Adams. Nor should companies build a multimillion-dollar ad campaign around them, said Mr. Fabian of Backer Spielvogel. "Focus groups can only be an add-on to solid qualitative research," he said.

Researchers have a bit more faith in mail surveys. In fact, marketers are making far more use of direct mail than they have in the recent past, betting that hard-to-reach people will respond when they can do so at their own convenience, and that they are less likely to try to impress a sheet of paper than an interviewer.

Companies are offering incentives in mailed questionnaires. Although some offer contests with expensive prizes, most just offer token payments. "It's amazing what a nice crisp dollar bill in an envelope will do," said Mr. Gibson, the former General Mills executive. "People feel guilty if they take the dollar and don't fill out their questionnaires."

Market research companies have mounted an ad campaign, using the slogan "Your Opinion Counts," to woo consumers back to surveys. "People used to feel that surveys were a way to tell manufacturers how to serve them better," said Frank Walker, chairman of Walker Research and the man who spearheaded the campaign. "We're trying to get them to again believe that their participation will come back in better products and services."

Mr. Adams of Campbell Soup is thinking along a similar vein. He wants to advertise the reasons behind the changes in Le Menu and the introduction of Special Request. "We're considering a campaign saying that last year, we talked to 110,000 of you and here's what we've done," he said. "To keep consumers interested, we have to communicate some of the action that's been taken on research."

General Foods has already started doing that. "You talked — Post listened," the company says on cereal boxes, referring to the new Zip-Pak resealable packaging that it re-

cently started using.

Computers, meanwhile, are taking some of the drudgery out of the interview process — automatically calling up Question No. 7 for a telephone interviewer, for example, if the survey requires her to skip questions 4 through 6 for any respondent who said "no" to question 3.

Several researchers are trying Conjoint Analysis, a program developed by Sawtooth Software Inc. that helps figure out how important different product attributes are to different people. A participant in a survey on cars, say, might be asked: Would you rather have a two-door blue car or a four-door red car? The next question would be based on the answer to the first.

"You wind up with a tradeoff analysis," said Richard M. Johnson, Sawtooth's president. "You find out not only someone's favorite color or favorite number of doors, but whether he would sooner give up his favorite color or his door count."

Normally, researchers who use such computerized surveys ask participants to do their own keypunching. "There's a whole body of research that says that people will answer emotional questions more honestly if they do not have to verbalize their response, but just have to punch in an answer," said Diane Schmalensee, vice president of research operations for the Marketing Science Institute.

Still, computerized interviews are no panacea. They are impractical for national surveys, they are expensive, and they may turn out to be a fad.

"Computer questioning has a lot of novelty," said Professor Kahle. "But by the 24th time they are asked, people will not find it all that attractive."

The whole business of market research seems in for a bumpy few years. When the dust settles, many companies will no longer be around. Others will have found special niches — for example, working with manufacturers whose products are not sold in supermarkets, or with small manufacturers who cannot afford to subscribe to electronic data services that can cost upwards of $500,000 a year. Still others will have been gobbled up by the giants in the research field.

The consolidation has already started. In August, Dun & Bradstreet bought Information Resources Inc., one of the fastest-growing firms in market research. SAMI, Time Inc.'s market research arm, bought Burke Marketing a few years ago. And last month, the Control Data Corporation, whose Arbitron Ratings Company is a major purveyor of local television and radio ratings, announced that it will buy SAMI/Burke.

No one is predicting that old-style consumer surveys will ever be easy or inexpensive again. But no one predicts their demise, either. "High tech will never replace high touch," said Dun & Bradstreet's Ms. Scarpa.

Indeed, although getting a representative sample of people to sit still for an interview will keep getting harder and more expensive, most experts say there will always be enough companies willing to foot the bill. Backer Spielvogel certainly is one. "People today are marketing me-too products," said Mr. Fabian. And that, he says, makes it doubly important to insure that advertising takes into consideration what motivates consumers. "We will find the money, our clients will find the money," he said. "We can't afford not to." ∎

20

Advertisers Put Consumers on the Couch

Research Probes Emotional Ties To Products

By Ronald Alsop
Staff Reporter of The Wall Street Journal

A few months ago, researchers at the McCann-Erickson ad agency were baffled after interviewing some low-income Southern women about the insecticide brands they used. The women strongly believed a new brand of roach killer sold in little plastic trays was far more effective and less messy than traditional bug sprays. Yet they had never bought it, sticking stubbornly with their old sprays.

To try to understand this contradiction, the researchers asked the women to draw pictures of roaches and write stories about their sketches. What McCann-Erickson hoped to do was probe the women's subconscious feelings about roaches. Before advising a client on developing a new insecticide, the agency wanted to know how people really relate to roaches.

According to Paula Drillman, the agency's director of strategic planning, the roaches in the pictures were all male, symbolizing men who the women said had abandoned them and left them feeling poor and powerless. "Killing the roaches with a bug spray and watching them squirm and die allowed the women to express their hostility toward men and have greater control over the roaches," Ms. Drillman says.

McCann's figure drawings are a sign of advertisers' growing use of research techniques borrowed from psychology and other behavioral sciences. To sell products in the 1980s, people on Madison Avenue increasingly feel they must put consumers on the couch and play shrink.

Seeking a New Edge

"We're using a whole battery of psychological techniques—some new and some old—to understand the emotional bond between consumers and brands," says Ms. Drillman. "You have to sell on emotion more than ever because it's a world of parity products out there. The days of having a competitive edge and a special product benefit are long gone."

The disastrous failure of new Coke in 1985 also has spurred advertisers to pay more attention to consumers' emotional

The Mind of a Roach Killer

The McCann-Erickson ad agency asked women to draw and describe how they felt about roaches. The agency concluded from the drawings that the women identified the roaches with men who had abandoned them and thus enjoyed watching the roaches-men squirm and die. That's why, the agency figured, that women prefer spray roach killers to products that don't allow the user to see the roach die.

"I TIPTOED quietly into the kitchen perhaps he wasn't around. I stretched my arm up to the light. I hoped I'd be alone when the light went on. Perhaps he is sitting on the table I thought. You think that's impossible? Nothing is impossible with that guy. He might not even be alone. He'll run when the light goes on I thought. But what's worse is for him to slip out of sight. No, it would be better to confront him before he takes control and 'invites a companion'."

"ONE NIGHT I just couldn't take the horror of these bugs sneaking around in the dark. They are always crawling when you can't see them. I had to do something. I thought wouldn't it be wonderful if when I switched on the light the roaches would shrink up and die like vampires to sunlight. So I did, but they just all scattered. But I was ready with my spray so it wasn't a total loss. I got quite a few...continued tomorrow night when night time falls."

"A MAN LIKES a free meal you cook for him, as long as there is food he will stay."

ties to products and rely less on standard focus group interviews and taste tests. "Brands are not just commercial products we buy and use; they're our companions in life as well," declares Rosalinde Rago, director of advertising research at the Ogilvy & Mather agency.

The Foote, Cone & Belding ad agency is using picture-sorting studies more often nowadays. What researchers do is give consumers stacks of photographs of people's faces and ask them to sort out who might be the typical users of certain brands. Each face represents a different emotional reaction to a product.

In addition to figure drawings, McCann-Erickson also is asking consumers to write newspaper obituaries for brands. The agency's researchers say they learn a lot about a product's image depending upon whether people describe the brand as young and virile and the victim of a tragic accident, or as a worn-out product succumbing to old age.

Advertising researchers are especially fascinated with the right brain/left brain concept. For instance, the N.W. Ayer agency tells people to draw shapes with their left hands to show their reactions to new product ideas. "Since the right hemisphere of the brain is visual, symbolic and emotional and it controls the left half of the body, this technique taps into perceptions better expressed as images rather than words," says Fred Posner, a senior vice president at Ayer.

All this psychological analysis harks back to the 1950s, when ad agencies first became enamored of social scientists and motivational research. Back then, it seemed quite sinister. In his book "The Hidden Persuaders," Vance Packard cautioned: "With all this interest in manipulating the customer's subconscious, the old slogan 'let the buyer beware' began taking on a new and more profound meaning."

Today, ad agencies' psychological research is even more pervasive and sophisticated, but not nearly as controversial. What criticism there is comes mostly from within the advertising business itself. "The subconscious techniques of clinical psychologists have yet to prove their utility," says Peter Kim, the head of the consumer behavior department at the J. Walter Thompson ad agency. "I'm really skeptical about these psychoanalysts who talk about people's phallic stage in relation to their car purchases."

But other agency research executives insist that verbal techniques alone simply aren't sufficient. They maintain that people aren't able to express many of their feelings in words, either because they're not conscious of them or because they're uncomfortable sharing them with a stranger conducting the interview.

That's why the McCann-Erickson ad agency resorted to stick-figure sketches in research on its American Express Gold Card account. Focus group interviews hadn't made clear consumers' differing perceptions of gold-card and green-card holders.

The drawings, however, were much more illuminating. In one set, for example, the gold-card user was portrayed as a broad-shouldered man standing in an active position, while the green card user was a "couch potato" in front of a TV set. Based on such pictures and other research, the agency decided to market the gold card as "a symbol of responsibility for people who have control over their lives and finances."

While psychologists on McCann's own staff analyze consumers' drawings, some agencies prefer to consult with psychoanalysts in private clinical practice. "We don't want psychologists who specialize in market research," says Penelope Queen, director of planning and research at the Saatchi & Saatchi DFS Compton agency. "We prefer practicing doctors who do true psychoanalysis with patients and really know what makes people tick."

Saatchi recently brought in therapist Samuel Cohen to tap people's innermost feelings about cold medicine. The agency expects the psychoanalysis to inspire it when it creates ads for a new over-the-counter medicine. Part of Mr. Cohen's session with a New York City travel agent went like this: "I see a gurgling waterfall and hear a woman's voice saying, 'You're safe from the pain,'" the man says, describing an imaginary dream to Mr. Cohen. "It's a sensual, mysterious voice, not like my mom's. Mom was always there for me, but I didn't crave her as a child."

And just what do the shrink and the agency's researchers make of the travel agent's imaginary dream about cold medicine personified as an alluring siren? The waterfall, it seems, represents the soothing effect of the cold medicine, while the seductive woman reflects his desire to be coddled by someone. The woman, however, can't be his mother because he doesn't want to regress to his childhood.

This doesn't exactly rank up there with Sigmund Freud's "The Interpretation of Dreams." But Saatchi believes so strongly in psychoanalysis that it keeps seven practicing clinical psychologists on retainer to study consumers' emotional responses to the brands it advertises—everything from Wrangler jeans to Molson beer.

Saatchi credits the psychological research with helping to inspire one of the agency's funniest, most talked about campaigns—its Philips light bulb commercials. The light bulb is an undeniably boring product. But the agency's consulting psychologists found much more there than meets the eye.

"When a bulb burns out, it is far more than a momentary annoyance," says Regina Kelley, a research executive at Saatchi. "For that instant when the switch is hit and nothing happens, the consumer is reminded briefly but powerfully about how much he depends on his light bulb to meet his security need." Thus were born some comical Philips ads in which the light bulb fizzles at particularly awkward moments.

Pitching the Concept

Saatchi also used its psychological probe last year to try to win some new business—the $200 million Burger King ad account. In the presentation to Burger King executives, Ms. Queen, Saatchi's research director, certainly embellished the hamburger eating experience. She discussed how fast-food restaurants fulfill basic human needs for immediate oral gratification (especially important to demanding baby boomers), regression to a carefree, childlike state, and dependency on someone else. ("People look to fast food almost as a surrogate mom," she says.)

She further noted that McDonald's, through such marketing gimmicks as the Ronald McDonald clown and kiddie playgrounds, created a nurturing atmosphere that satisfied many of those needs. Burger King, on the other hand, came off as aggressive, masculine and distant in the agency's psychological research.

For example, when a psychologist asked a female bank employee to describe the two fast-food chains as animals in cartoons, she characterized McDonald's as a cute, friendly baby chick and Burger King as a sly, unfriendly cat. The woman also proposed that a Burger King ad might feature aliens from outer space, an image the psychologist found rich with subconscious meanings. "The alien suggests that she feels a certain distance from Burger King," the psychologist says. "It's not a fun place, not quite like home like McDonald's is for her."

But Burger King executives didn't buy the psychoanalysis: The account went to N.W. Ayer, not Saatchi.

WHEN J.D. POWER TALKS, CARMAKERS LISTEN

Companies swear by his market research—and sweat over it

Ford Motor Co. is upset. It claims that Chrysler Corp.'s current ads falsely imply that buyers rank Chrysler No. 1 in quality among U.S. makes. But Ford also blames J. David Power III. His automotive market-research firm, J. D. Power & Associates, approved the ads, which are based on a customer satisfaction survey Power released last month. The survey did put Chrysler first among domestics—but that ranking was based more on dealer service than on car quality.

Ford might be less angry if Chrysler's ads didn't trumpet the J. D. Power name. Dave Power, a tall, genial researcher, has become the oracle of how Americans feel about cars. He has achieved that status partly through promotional headline-grabbing that bothers some of his clients, of which Ford is one. But carmakers increasingly think the imprimatur of his Los Angeles firm amounts to an automotive version of the *Good Housekeeping* Seal of Approval. "Buyers know J. D. Power—his customer satisfaction index has crept into the parlance," says Mary Treisbach, Subaru's U. S. market-research manager.

More and more, carmakers are using the power of Power in their marketing. American Honda Motor Co. splashes the J. D. Power emblem across new ads proclaiming its Acura division the overall winner in this year's customer satisfaction survey. Power's research can sting, too: In April his firm announced that Honda's U.S.-built cars lag behind its Japanese autos in quality. While Honda has previously denied any difference, it now promises to do better. "We take his research very seriously," says American Honda Chairman Tetsuo Chino.

QUICK STUDY. Power's high profile is unusual among market researchers, whose clients usually prefer to keep data private. "We like to stick our necks out, to take a stand," says Power, 57. He does so by paying for the splashiest studies himself and selling them to carmakers. His top clients are Jaguar, Chrysler, GM, and BMW. But almost every carmaker buys some of the 200 reports cranked out yearly by his staff of 100.

Some do so grudgingly. "I really dislike paying Power to do research that my competitors can use in their advertising against me," says Martin Schwager, U.S. consumer-research manager for Nissan Motor Co. He buys Power's data anyway—and particularly likes the quick study of new-model quality, which lets Nissan correct problems early in production. Another popular service is Power's five-year forecast of car sales, model by model. One current prediction: The Japanese will capture 20% of the U.S. luxury-car market by 1992, up from 3% now.

Most of Power's studies are based on questionnaires mailed to car owners. Some clients occasionally criticize them as superficial: Ford division general manager Thomas J. Wagner complains that many of Power's opinion samples aren't big enough to support the broad conclusions he draws. Power admits that his methods were sometimes sloppy a few years ago but claims to have improved—and most clients agree.

Power's top competitor, Maritz Inc., hasn't discussed research with the press or allowed its use in advertising. As a result, few car buyers have heard of the company—even though it will bill $14 million for auto research this year, compared with J. D. Power's $10 million. But Maritz says it now plans to fight Power more openly. "You're going to hear more from us," promises James M. Stone, a Maritz research manager.

That doesn't worry Power, who expects to double revenues in 18 months. Car dealers are one target: He has launched seminars to explain his research to dealers, and he plans to train their employees to avoid the kinds of customer complaints revealed in his surveys. This summer he opened research offices in Britain and Japan. He expects Japanese car companies to make a big push into Europe—and to buy lots of market research. "It will be just-like the Japanese coming to the U.S. 15 years ago," Power predicts.

BLAND LOYALTY. That onslaught built his company. A Wharton MBA, Power held research jobs with General Motors, Ford, and chainsaw-maker McCulloch Corp. He opened his firm in 1968 to do broad consumer-products work. But Japanese carmakers hired him to help plan their U. S. entries. Now auto work represents 95% of revenues.

Power visits clients constantly, spending about 70% of his time on the road. What kind of car does Power drive on that road? At the moment, an Oldsmobile sedan. But he switches every six months, usually picking a bland model with a middling rank in his satisfaction index. That's partly to avoid suggestions of conflicts of interest. But there's another reason: This arbiter of automotive passions says cars just don't excite him very much.

By Stewart Toy in Los Angeles with James B. Treece in Detroit

HOW TO OUTSMART AUNT JANE

*Because her teenagers eat so much of it,
Aunt Jane claims teens eat most of the ice cream
consumed in the U.S.*

by Doris Walsh

Almost anyone you ask would say that teenagers eat the most ice cream, but this is what is called an "Aunt Janeism"—a personal observation that may or may not be true. How can you determine whether personal opinion is true or false before you make a marketing mistake? Try analyzing syndicated survey results. Companies such as Mediamark Research and Simmons Market Research Bureau conduct large surveys of American consumers each year, asking about their use of a broad range of consumer products.

Using Mediamark's data as an example, you too can outsmart all the Aunt Janes out there by making sure that your marketing plans are based on fact, not fiction.

Doris Walsh is the publisher of American Demographics.

There is no doubt that ice cream is a popular food. Three-quarters of the "female homemakers"—the women who do the household shopping—surveyed by Mediamark say they bought ice cream in the last six months. Regular ice cream, the most popular type of product in this category, is purchased by two-thirds of the homemakers. Sherbet—the next most popular type—is purchased by 11 percent of homemakers, while only 7 percent buy ice milk, 3.5 percent diet or low-fat ice cream, and 3 percent fruit sorbet.

Both Simmons and Mediamark divide consumers of specific products into heavy, medium, and light users. Mediamark defines heavy users as those who purchase four or more pints of ice cream a week. About 16 million households—or 27 percent of all ice-cream buyers—are heavy users, but they account for 70 percent of all ice-cream

buying. In other words, one-quarter of the customers buy more than two-thirds of the product. Medium users—those who buy two or three pints of ice cream a week—are also 27 percent of households, but they buy only 23 percent of ice cream. The light users, buying one pint or less a week, are 46 percent of households, but they represent only 8 percent of the market.

Demographically, the heaviest users are households with children. Households with children are 33 percent more likely to be heavy users of ice cream than the average household, and households with children between the ages of 12 and 17 are 56 percent more likely to be heavy users of ice cream than the average household.

Because teenagers are so important to the ice-cream market, it is not surprising that homemakers aged 35 to 44 are the ones most likely to be heavy users of ice cream—since they are likely to have children in this age group. The group next most likely to be heavy users of ice cream are homemakers aged 45 to 54—again, people likely to have teenagers in their households.

THE CUSTOMER OF THE FUTURE

Once you know not only who your customers are, but who your best customers are, you can identify the best ways to reach them. Also included in the Mediamark and Simmons surveys are the media that consumers use—the television shows they watch, the magazines they read, and so on.

The homemakers most likely to be heavy users of regular ice cream, for example, are avid TV viewers, according to Mediamark. To increase your share of the ice-cream mass market, a television campaign may be the best route. But to turn light ice-cream users into heavy users, a print campaign might be better, since light users are less likely to watch TV and more likely

(cont.)

to read magazines than heavy users. With this type of demographic, purchasing behavior, and media-use information, businesses can develop effective marketing strategies.

Businesses can also go one step farther by projecting the growth of their markets. Heavy users of ice cream are middle-aged Americans, for example. This fact should warm the hearts of the nation's ice-cream makers, because the number of middle-aged Americans is growing rapidly. The number of households headed by 35-to-44 and 45-to-54-year-olds will increase by 28 and 59 percent between 1988 and 2000.

And now back to Aunt Jane and those teenagers. Her instincts were right in this case. Teenagers are the most important demographic influence on the purchase of ice cream. The number of households with teenagers should grow impressively in the 1990s, as the baby boomers' children grow up. Although the presence of children is important to the ice-cream market, ice-cream makers whose entire marketing campaign depends on households with children may overlook other opportunities. When the baby boomers move out of their child-raising years, and the number of households with children begins to decline around the turn of the century, ice-cream manufacturers could see a decline in sales. Now is the time to develop a marketing strategy that will sidestep such a decline.

By knowing who is buying your products and how much they buy, and by comparing this information with population projections, businesses can create new strategies to increase market share. Businesses can also plan new products that will target untapped consumer niches. ●

Reprinted with permission© *American Demographics*, July 1988.

23

Brother Nielsen Is Watching

A TV monitoring device will keep a close eye on viewers

It seems like something out of George Orwell: television sets souped up so they can watch viewers watching them. Last week Nielsen Media Research, purveyor of the make-or-break TV ratings, announced plans to develop just such a gizmo. The "passive people meter," a computerized camera system, would sit atop sets in thousands of households, keeping an eye on every move that viewers made.

The purpose of the system, which will not be ready for deployment for at least three years, is to get a more objective, precise measure of who makes up the TV audience. In the past, viewers in Nielsen homes either filled out diaries or identified themselves by pushing buttons on hand-held consoles. With the new system, a computer would simply spot individual household members as they came into view and record them, second by second, as they faced the TV, read newspapers or merely turned their heads.

The soul of the new machine, developed in conjunction with the David Sarnoff Research Center, is the same basic technology used by U.S. missiles to distinguish between Soviet and American warplanes. A sensor scans the space in front of the TV searching for patterns of light and dark—the shine of a nose, the line of a mouth—that suggest the presence of a face. A computer then makes more detailed scans at higher and higher resolutions, trying to match facial features to those of family members stored in its memory. (An unfamiliar face would be recorded as a "visitor.") When the machine makes a match, the information is sent by phone lines to Nielsen's central ratings computer, and then to subscribers.

So far, the reaction of advertisers and broadcasters to Nielsen's new meter has been generally positive. With $25 billion in annual ad revenue at stake, the industry has an interest in accurate audience measurements. The one uncertainty, assuming the system works, is how viewers would react to the presence of a camera-like device in their homes. Nielsen officials take pains to point out that the machine would not transmit pictures—only data about who is watching what.

NBC's Barry Cook, who heads a group that analyzes rating methods for the networks, is concerned that the sight of a camera on top of their

TVs might make people self-conscious, affecting their viewing habits and skewing the results. And some would be sure to see in the new device a computer-age version of Big Brother's telescreen—the two-way television that monitored the citizenry in Orwell's *Nineteen Eighty-Four*. ■

Buyer Behavior

At OshKosh B'Gosh, Childhood's Magic Days Are Past

Clothier for Tots Makes Plans for a Future in Which the Kids Are Grown

By Andrew Patner
Staff Reporter of The Wall Street Journal

OshKosh B'Gosh Inc. is learning that success can make a company grow too big for its britches.

After years of go-go growth in sales, the Wisconsin maker of children's clothing is facing some obstacles. Expansion has brought coordination problems, excessive inventories, and increasing vulnerability to the whims of fashion. Last year, earnings fell 12% to $19 million, even though sales rose 12% to $252 million.

All of which has caused some soul-searching among the tightly knit senior executives, who look back almost wistfully on the seemingly effortless expansion of the previous decade. "We thought those were like magic years," says the company's president and chief executive, Charles P. Hyde. "It just seemed to be so easy."

It isn't so easy anymore. As such, OshKosh's situation offers a glimpse of why its sales growth has caused some problems. But OshKosh is also a case study of how one company is trying to deal with the situation. Among tactics are these four: teaming up with a big retailer (**Sears, Roebuck & Co.**), searching for overseas markets, maintaining a conservative balance sheet and adhering to quality.

Started as a Novelty

Actually, OshKosh's main problem would appear an enviable one—dizzying sales growth. The company's pint-sized overalls started out as novelty versions of work clothes for dairy farmers and workers on the railroads when the firm itself was tiny. Then, almost by accident, the tykes' trousers made a national splash in the 1980s, propelling the family-run company to its position as a leader of the children's apparel industry.

As OshKosh overalls became the uniform for children of baby boomers, annual sales rose more than tenfold in less than a decade. The product mix also shifted drastically—going from 85% work clothes to 85% children's apparel.

To keep up with the skyrocketing demand, the company added 15 plants in the South to its sole Oshkosh, Wis., facility. Coordination and timing of deliveries lagged sharply. As the company expanded into multiple-piece children's wear, tops would arrive in stores before bottoms, or, worse yet, only one piece would arrive at all. In the rough and tumble world of apparel merchandising, retailers can usually cancel all orders with a manufacturer if schedules aren't met. "We were not keeping our promises, and we were failing our customers," Mr. Hyde says.

When an overdue warehouse consolidation took place last year, OshKosh executives found themselves with $6.7 million in obsolete fabric and trimming materials, inventory adjustments, and other unanticipated costs. William P. Jacobsen, chief financial officer, foresaw a $4 million writedown for 1988, but the larger charge was hard to swallow. Between canceled contracts, inventory adjustments, and excess write-downs, Mr. Hyde says, "We were lucky that we did not fall on our faces."

As it looks toward the future, OshKosh also faces a problem of demographics. Trends show the so-called echo baby boom falling off after 1991—and with it the centerpiece of OshKosh's market, children's sizes zero through seven. So the logic might seem to dictate a shift in manufacturing to follow this market. But fashion-conscious children start thinking for themselves in the eight-to-14-year-old range that OshKosh would like to have. And when kids hit that stage, they want to put away childish things in favor of what the older teen-age set is wearing.

As the market for higher-priced children's clothes becomes more fashion-conscious, manufacturers have had to conform to the vagaries of seasonal lines. After experiencing record returns from stores the past two years, OshKosh realized that it faced vulnerability to fashion, and began looking to diversify and to give its current lines more support. Retailers are now consulted in advance on new styles, and spring sales this year are promising.

"OshKosh always tried to adjust production to match an ever-increasing demand. That was probably the main culprit in their setbacks," says Steven Ashley of Blunt Ellis & Loewie in Milwaukee. "Now they've made one of their most significant marketing moves in trying to match demand to production plans."

OshKosh is looking for other markets, and analysts agree this is the best hope for the future. OshKosh hopes to lure back adult customers through a licensing agreement with Sears Roebuck. The big retailer will make and distribute some of the company's casual and work wear. The company has already been increasing its exposure in adult markets through its 13 Genuine Article stores in outlet malls.

Even more important are untapped European and Far East markets. But OshKosh is wary of letting its junior overalls become the superannuated Izod alligator of the next decade, and so it is moving deliberately and preparing to enter the European market by 1992, when European trade barriers are to be relaxed.

Deeply Conservative

Company executives say such conservatism is a hidden strength that will help see them through the transition. Few would quarrel with the statement that OshKosh management is deeply conservative. Voting stock and management are still concentrated in family hands. The 68-year-old Mr. Hyde joined the company 40 years ago after marrying the boss's daughter. Mr. Hyde's son, Douglas, 38, is the vice-president for merchandising, and his son-in-law, Michael D. Wachtel, 35, is operations director. Many other top executives have been there for 20 years or more.

Another strength, say insiders and outside analysts alike, is a strict adherence to the same standards for quality that went into the company's work wear—even with a large amount of work done through outsourcing to other firms. That adherence has inspired consumer confidence and shored up the loyalty that parent-buyers have shown in the brand.

The cautious approach has left OshKosh with a strong balance sheet. It carries less than $6 million in long-term debt against $60 million in working capital.

"OshKosh is still the quintessential name in children's clothing," says Blunt Ellis's Mr. Ashley. "But just as OshKosh previously moved beyond farm clothes, so its future problems may go beyond mere fashion marketing and distribution. According to Jay E. Van Cleeve of Robert W. Baird in Milwaukee: "Some of the fallout from OshKosh's structural changes will only become apparent over the next couple of years. They have become a large textile company, and they face some of the same problems as any other large textile company trying to turn itself around."

Marketers Err by Treating Elderly as Uniform Group

By RICK CHRISTIE

Staff Reporter of THE WALL STREET JOURNAL

E.J. Moore gets livid when he sees ads depicting older people "looking so dopey and scared."

"I'm in my 70s and traveled to Europe [recently]. And no way am I going to act like some I see in TV ads," says the Glastonbury, Conn., resident. "I also will not buy from companies if they make fun of older people."

Mr. Moore's frustration is a reminder of how far marketers have to go to win over the nation's richest consumer group. Just how far is reflected in three new studies that examine the buying behavior of the 55-and-over age group. They conclude that this group isn't nearly so uniformly stingy and narrowly focused as current marketing efforts indicate.

"We were stunned at the high percentage of older consumers who felt that their needs were not being met," says George P. Moschis, author of a study by Georgia State University's Center for Mature Consumer Studies.

The study, based on a national survey of 1,000 older consumers, found that about 80% of the respondents were dissatisfied with the way companies market their products and services to them. For example, 70% said they found packages and bottles difficult to open, while nearly 60% said the lettering on labels is too small to read.

And these consumers are recognizing the influence of their huge buying power. While only 23% of American consumers are 55 or older, they control 75% of the nation's wealth and about half of the discretionary income.

The elderly "are realizing they don't have to take anything, even advertising, lying down," Mr. Moschis says. Nearly one-third of those he surveyed have boycotted products and services because of inappropriate age stereotyping in their ads.

And 75% let others know when they are unhappy with products and services.

The other two studies come from Grey Advertising Inc. and Ogilvy & Mather Inc., ad agencies based in New York. They warn marketers that overlooking the 50-and-over market could be a strategic disaster.

While some pharmaceutical, financial-services and housing companies have marketed aggressively to older people for years, most other consumer-product businesses have been slow to catch on. And many of those, Mr. Moschis says, still base their marketing strategies on the false assumption that everyone over 55 is sickly or inactive, financially strapped and stingy with what money they do have.

Older people "are markedly absent from commercials, or at best portrayed as ancient or infirm," says a Grey Advertising spokeswoman. "Where there should be an advertising explosion, there is instead an advertising void."

Marketers are missing out, Mr. Moschis says, partly because they often segment older consumers by age. "We found that age didn't make a whole lot of difference in their buying habits," he says. Rather, the Georgia State study determined that people age along what Mr. Moschis calls biophysical and psychosocial lines in different ways. Thus, he was able to divide older consumers into four categories according to their needs and concerns:

• Healthy hermits, who made up 38% of the survey respondents, are in good health but have little interest in staying active or making social contacts. They are an especially good market for tax and legal advice, home entertainment, do-it-yourself products and domestic services. They can be reached most effectively through direct mail and print media.

• Ailing outgoers, about 34% of the respondents, are in poor health but are still socially active and health-conscious because of an unwillingness to accept "old-age" status. This category would be the target of planned communities, medical and health services, and leisure marketers. The best ways to reach them are through cross-selling (pitching related products at the same time), sales promotions and special services.

• Frail recluses, about 15%, are also in poor health but are socially and psychologically withdrawn. They make good targets for home health-care marketers, medical services and home entertainment concerns, and are best reached through mass media and cross-selling.

• Healthy indulgers, the remaining 13%, are outgoing and in good health; they still want to live well, see new places and do new things. Consumers in this category are ripe for financial services, travel and entertainment, clothing and high-tech products. The best ways to reach them: in-store special promotions, specialized print media and direct mail.

The Ogilvy & Mather and Grey studies agree that older people should be grouped by attitude more than age. Ogilvy found two distinctly different groups of older consumers: those who spend and those who save. People in the latter group still have Depression-era fears and are viewed as more skeptical or just plain stingy.

Indeed, according to the Georgia State study, about 70% of people 55 and over would rather save than spend. In addition, 73% of those surveyed said they use coupons, while 57% said they would switch brands to save money.

Consequently, Mr. Moschis says, identifying and understanding the different types of older consumers is only half the battle. The other half: persuading them to part with both their fears and their money.

Five digits tell all about what we eat, drive and watch

By DEBBIE MOOSE
Staff writer

If you leave the country club in time to pick up your teenage daughter at her piano lesson, mail your donation to the Sierra Club, stop by the gourmet grocery to pick up a case of wine and ingredients for the recipe you clipped from Bon Appetit, load it all in the BMW and pull up in front of your two-story Colonial just in time for "Masterpiece Theater," that can mean only one thing:

Your Raleigh ZIP code is 27615. And you're a resident of "Furs and Station Wagons," according to a marketing system that's the subject of a new book, "The Clustering of America."

The system, as explained in Michael Weiss' book, works on the theory that we are what we buy, and that consumers of a feather flock together.

Claritas Corp., a consulting firm in Alexandria, Va., uses the system, called PRIZM (Potential Rating Index for ZIP Markets). PRIZM uses census characteristics and consumer surveys to analyze the nation's 36,000 ZIP codes and divide them into 40 neighborhood types. The types are matched with media and product surveys to create lifestyle profiles. Claritas says those profiles can tell business people where residents are more likely to buy grits than croissants and let political campaigns know who is more likely to vote Republican than Democrat.

They also cover everything from work and family patterns to political leanings. The system works because people tend to live with others of their ilk, and although households in a cluster differ, clusters differ more.

According to "The Clustering of America," North Carolina overall falls into the "high" category in several clusters. The western half of the state scores high in "Mines and Mills" (Thomasville is cited as a sample town). The whole state is either high or above average in "Back-Country Folks" (Mount Airy, for example). The whole state rates high for "Norma Rae-Ville" (Burlington and Tarboro). The eastern part of North Carolina rates high in "Tobacco Roads" (Warrenton).

The details of each cluster vary, but the ones just mentioned are all lower-middle-class mill towns populated by people who have high-school educations and work at blue-collar jobs. They have deer heads on their walls and watch "Dallas" and the soaps instead of "Night Court" or "The Today Show." They consume canned spaghetti more than twice as often as they do whole-wheat bread. They buy pickup trucks instead of convertibles.

According to the book: "Back-Country Folks discuss stockyards as animatedly as city dwellers debate stock markets." And "Norma Rae-Ville is the kind of southern outpost where the good ol' boys chew tobacco, watch wrestling and install shock absorbers on their cars — all at rates above the norm. And the women are heavy purchasers of hair-styling combs, home permanents and feminine hygiene deodorant sprays."

Before people in Beemers begin howling protests, those are broad categories.

"One lesson you learn from that is you can't make broad inferences. You'll miss some communities," says John McCann, associate professor of marketing at Duke University's Fuqua School of Business.

Systems like PRIZM are popular in marketing today, Dr. McCann says, although Claritas has taken it further than most companies. Direct-mail marketers and other target advertisers use them.

The thought that a computer knows that your idea of a good time is driving to a Tupperware party in your Dodge with the latest copy of True Story in the back seat ["Back-Country Folks"] may be Big Brotherlike to some people. Dr. McCann thinks it's a route back to personal service, as in the days when you called the grocer, placed an order, and it appeared at your door.

"They know about you statistically, but not individually," he says. "It's been around a long time, with finer and finer gradations. Someday they may have you personally in the database, if you agree to it. I don't think it's scary. It may be better. I'd like to tell someone what I'm interested in. If I'm interested in buying a CD player, send that information to me. If I could get a two-way system and punch in a code, that would be nice. And it may not be far down the road."

The computers know a lot already — even about the Triangle. Claritas provided cluster compositions for three Raleigh ZIP codes, and one each for Cary, Durham and Chapel Hill.

■ ZIP code 27615, North Raleigh: It's 45 percent "Furs and Station Wagons." It's the kind of place where mom throws on a fur coat to ferry the children around in the station wagon. It's new money, parents in their 40s and 50s, sprawling homes with six-figure price tags that are filled with teenagers. They belong to country clubs, read Forbes, eat rye bread and watch "60 Minutes." They don't own motorcycles, read Outdoor Life, use non-dairy creamers or watch "Wheel of Fortune."

■ ZIP code 27608, Hayes Barton area: It's 47 percent "Gray Power," the cluster of active, well-to-do retirees. These social animals cruise to dinner parties (which they host more often than the general population) in Lincoln Continentals or Cadillac Sevilles. They buy movie projectors, read Architectural Digest, eat canned corned beef hash and watch "Good Morning, America." They don't go hunting, read True Story.

■ ZIP code 27601, downtown Raleigh: It's 78 percent "Public Assistance," the cluster of the poorest people on welfare, the working poor and destitute elderly. They buy corner-store items like cold cuts, malt liquor and soft drinks. Since many can't afford doctors, they purchase over-the-counter health treatments like laxatives and cough syrup.

■ ZIP codes 27511, Cary; and 27712, Durham's Croasdaile area: Both are predominantly "Young Suburbia" (88 percent in Cary, 79 percent in Durham). These folks fill their grocery carts with pretzels, frozen waffles and copies of "World Tennis," stash the bags in the Nissan 300ZX (next to the hedge clippers) and zoom from the mall in time to hit the garage-door opener and unload before "Cheers" starts. It's today's version of Ward, June and the boys, in cookie-cutter subdivisions. They're 40 percent more likely to buy lawn mowers.

ZIP code 27514, Chapel Hill: More than 50 percent are "Young Influentials," the prototype yuppies. "Young Influentials is more than a neighborhood type; it's an adjective that qualifies the trendiest habits and purchases," the book says. They have two incomes, no children and high-tech jobs. They spend their weekends speed-walking to the sushi bar. You might find them listening to jazz, reading Sea & Pacific Skipper, driving Alfa Romeos, eating yogurt and watching "At the Movies." They wouldn't be caught dead with a bowling ball, reading The Star, driving a Chevrolet Impala, eating white bread or watching "Knots Landing."

Reprinted by permission from *The News and Observer* of Raleigh, NC, December 30, 1988.

Hispanic Supermarkets Are Blossoming

Familiar Foods, Lively Decor Draw Shoppers

By ALFREDO CORCHADO
Staff Reporter of THE WALL STREET JOURNAL

LOS ANGELES—It's Sunday and time for Alicia Maruffo's weekly grocery shopping. So she and her family hop in the car and motor some 65 miles from their home in Oxnard—past at least 30 other grocers—to get to a Tianguis supermarket here.

As the Maruffos, originally from Mexico, stroll down aisles stocked with such items as *empanadas* and handmade tortillas, so does a group of mariachi singers.

"Normally, we don't drive this far for groceries," says Mrs. Maruffo, after run-

Hispanic Media Blitz

Univision Holdings Inc. is planning Spanish-language TV shows modeled after mainstream hits and a glitzy People-type magazine. Story on page B9.

ning up a $130 bill in five hours of shopping. "But I like the people here, the products and especially the music." Besides, adds her husband, Pablo, "everyone speaks Spanish."

Hispanic supermarkets such as Tianguis, a three-store Southern California chain launched two years ago by **Vons Cos.**, are hotter than jalapeno peppers. Flourishing primarily in the West and the Southwest, where the bulk of the U.S. Hispanic population is concentrated, they are changing the way many grocers in the region—and beyond—are operating in a crowded business.

'Special Needs'

"Hispanics represent a foreign consumer market within the U.S.," explains Henry Adams-Esquivel, vice president of Market Development Inc., a San Diego-based marketing-research concern. "They have special needs."

All kinds of businesses are trying to cash in on the Hispanic market, and it doesn't take a genius to figure out why. The U.S. population of Hispanics has grown 34% since 1980, four times the country's overall growth rate during the same period. There are now nearly as many Hispanics in the U.S. (about 22 million) as

A Strong – and Concentrated – Market

The growth in overall Hispanic purchasing power
(In billions of dollars)

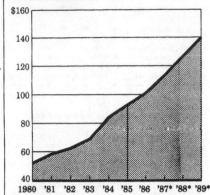

*Estimate

Geographic distribution of the Hispanic population as of March 1988
(In percent)

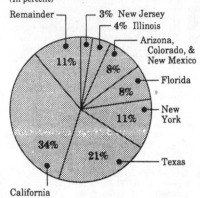

Sources: Census Bureau; Hispanic Business Magazine

there are Canadians in Canada (25.3 million). By 2015, there will be—by conservative estimate and excluding the huge numbers of illegal immigrants—some 40 million Hispanics in this country, making them the nation's largest minority group.

Although the Hispanic market is made up largely of families with meager to modest incomes, those families' overall purchasing power is an impressive $140 billion a year. So it's perhaps no wonder that **Fiesta Marts** Inc., begun in the early 1970s and one of the first chains to cater to Hispanics, has become the fourth-largest grocer in Houston. Its 15 stores—some in black and Anglo neighborhoods—generated an estimated $400 million in sales in 1988, and three more will be added this year, including a 200,000-square-foot giant.

Since the early 1980s, **Danal's Food Stores** Inc. has opened a half-dozen Hispanic-oriented stores in Dallas and is now eyeing sites in nearby Fort Worth. In Los Angeles, Alfredo Brener, a Mexican businessman, has recently acquired 50 supermarkets, most of which he intends to convert into Viva stores. What's more, Vons recently acquired 170 Safeway stores in the region and plans to transform several of them into Tianguis outlets.

"We didn't build Tianguis as a social cause or out of charity," says William Davila, president of Vons. "We did it because it's good business, big business."

Tapping into that business takes work, however. The Hispanics shopping at such

stores are mostly recent immigrants who seek the familiar sights, sounds and smells of their native land. And to reach this market, grocers must provide special training to employees, find ways to lure shoppers who don't necessarily read the daily newspapers (where grocers traditionally advertise) and carry products that most U.S. supermarkets have never heard of.

Distributors say that in some Southern California stores, for example, Ariel laundry detergent, made by Procter & Gamble Co. for the Mexican market, outsells the company's Tide 5 to 1. Before grocers north of the border started stocking it, Ariel was in such demand in Hispanic communities that some individuals made a business of bringing it up from Mexico.

Hispanic shoppers are also more comfortable speaking Spanish than English, and they expect services seldom seen in U.S. stores, including gold-and-silver exchanges and Western Union booths where they can wire money home to Mexico.

To identify its customers' needs, Tianguis—the name is a Spanish adaptation of an Aztec word for "marketplace"—spent two years and $2.5 million researching the market. Store operators have made dozens of trips to Mexico and to cities in the Southwest with large Hispanic populations in their search for the right atmosphere and product mix. They consulted small Hispanic retailers and visited Mexican museums, supermarkets, cantinas and restaurants. Some prospective products were rig-

(cont.)

orously test-marketed in Mexico.

Tianguis also worked closely with Aurrera, Mexico's largest diversified chain. Aurrera specialists trained Tianguis personnel in Los Angeles for a month, drilling them on how to cut meats, make *ceviche* (a fish dish) and bake breads and tortillas. In exchange, Aurrera was briefed on the latest store technology.

One important lesson gleaned from all this research: Most Hispanics view shopping as an eagerly awaited social event. They want to spend hours browsing and chatting; they want to eat while they shop and listen to music that reminds them of home. In short, they want a fiesta.

Tianguis obliged. The stores set up stands serving a wide variety of Mexican foods and added outdoor patios for dining. They splashed the walls with festive colors and designs and hung dozens of *pinatas*—crepe-paper sculptures filled with candy—from the ceiling. They now feature live mariachi music four days a week and piped-in Spanish music at other times.

Hispanic grocers have also learned that staffing is critical. Recent immigrants have enough problems adjusting to a new culture and language; they want to feel comfortable at the grocery store. "Almost everyone here, from the shopper to the employee, is an immigrant," says one Fiesta employee. "We speak each other's language, and we understand each other's fears of being in a new country—including shopping. Here, we feel at home."

Attention to such details has paid off. In two years, Tianguis has become one of the most profitable chains in Southern California, according to industry analysts, raking in nearly $1.7 million in sales weekly. And weekly sales at Top Valu in Torrance, Calif., have doubled to about $260,000 since it introduced Hispanic decor, services and products several months ago.

Growing Pains

As their numbers and profits grow, Hispanic grocers are also facing new problems. Under the 1986 immigration law, for example, many employees have become newly legal residents—and have grown more vocal about wage demands. Competition is also getting stiff. Mr. Brener's Viva stores have developed into a major headache for Tianguis, which says it has had to cut costs to meet the challenge. "No doubt, they're our biggest threat," says Christopher Linskey, vice president and general manager of the Vons division.

Even the mom-and-pop Hispanic grocers, who once controlled the market, are feeling the pressure. Steve Soto, the president and chief executive officer of the Mexican-American Grocers Association, says that when Tianguis asked for advice, he quickly obliged. The result: One of his three stores closed because of competition from the chain, to which he also lost three employees. "I always thought I was picking their brain," he says. "It turns out they were picking mine."

The association's 10,000 members are fighting back, which has further intensified the competition. Many have increased workers' salaries by as much as 10%, hoping to keep them from moving to the big chains. Many, too, have added products and tried to improve service, urging employees, for example, to address regular customers by their first names.

Meanwhile, business at the chains keeps growing. Crowds at a Houston Fiesta Mart have even outgrown the store's parking lot. "Many of our customers park there," a Fiesta official notes, referring to the lot of a Safeway store across the street.

They're like us, except they're rich

Down-to-earth, well-to-do

Wealthy value traditions: Family, home, hard work

By Martha T. Moore
USA TODAY

He's 48 years old, self-employed, politically conservative. He's married, put his two kids through college with sheer hard work. He can't imagine retiring. He has no use for fancy cars, exotic vacations — what's important is family. Call him the very portrait of a solid middle-class citizen.

There's just one catch. He's rich. Very. He's part of the thinnest economic upper crust: households with incomes of more than $100,000 a year. Only 1.2 million households in the USA have that kind of dough, 1.9% of the population.

With apologies to F. Scott Fitzgerald, the rich are not different from you and me, says a Louis Harris & Associates study released Thursday. They may be the "upper affluent," but when it comes to hearth, home, the flag and the work ethic, they're just folks: hard-working, family-oriented and mainly in business for themselves.

"If you stopped the average person on the street and asked them what they think of wealthy people, they think J.R. Ewing and Wall Street inside traders," said Charles M. Finn, vice president of CIGNA Individual Financial Services Co., which commissioned the survey of 500 families with more than $100,000 in annual income or $500,000 net worth (excluding their homes). Questions covered not only money matters but personal priorities — a rarely studied subject, Finn said.

"A major surprise is the traditional values," Finn said. Not to Anthony Autorino, who fits the survey's statistics to a T-bill.

"The harder I work, the luckier I get," says Autorino, 48, of Wethersfield, Conn., chairman of Shared Technologies Inc., breeder of Arabian horses, and partner with son Anthony Jr. in a firm that provides transportation for schools. "You can do what you want to do, but you've got to work at it."

CIGNA, a Bloomfield, Conn., financial planner, studied the lifestyles of the rich-but-not-famous to find out more about its own clientele — whose median net worth is $1 million-plus — and pick up some marketing information along the way. Its findings:

■ **They're male, married, middle-aged.** Median age is 48, a whopping 83% are married and 85% have children, mostly grown. The main income producer was a man in 75% of the households. Their occupations run from educators to athletes, scientists to sales reps. Among business owners, company size is "medium," Finn said. How rich is rich? The majority pull down $100,000 to $200,000; 21% have less income and only 11% say they have more. In net worth — including their homes — 20% are millionaires.

■ **Family ties are strong.** 85% rated as "important" or "essential:" making sure their families are provided for if anything happened to them. 75% gave the same high ranking to sending their children to private schools and colleges.

■ **Hard work pays.** 87% work; 84% said being able to apply their talents and energies to the maximum is essential or important, and 82% said their money came from their own hard work. Spouses work, too, in 56% of the married households.

■ **Many work for themselves.** 42% are self-employed or own an incorporated business. 45% work for a corporation. But the richer they are, the more likely they work for themselves: 68% of the millionaires are their own bosses.

■ **They invest cautiously and are confused by the new tax law.** Most shun risky "junk" bonds or commodities for real estate, stocks and money market funds. "They're not high fliers," said CIGNA's Finn. "They're not trading pork bellies.

Tax-free bonds are becoming somewhat more popular in response to tax reform, which has left 51% convinced they'll pay more taxes. (They're right, says Finn.) But not enough are making the changes that they should, Finn said. "People intellectually understand that they have to change behavior, but emotionally they haven't made the change."

"They're totally unremarkable as far as their investment strategy. They're totally baffled by the (new) tax law," said Louis Harris Senior Vice President Merl W. Baker, who ran the survey. "These aren't Wall Street types."

Sound familiar? Then how come they're rich and we're not?

Shared Technologies Inc

THE AUTORINO FAMILY OF CONNECTICUT: Back, from left, Lynn, Anthony — who fits the statistics from the survey of the rich, Carol and Fred; front, Anthony Jr. and Andrea

"They're workaholics," Baker said.

Ah, yes. They make money the old-fashioned way.

"My relaxation is work," said Autorino, who put in 25 years at United Technologies Corp. before buying out the company that became Shared Technologies. "The biggest complaint my wife has is that she never sees me." Autorino, who says his income exceeds $100,000, is a CIGNA client; Louis Harris would not release the names of survey participants.

In fact, the richer they are, the harder they work. Overall, 16% of those questioned said they would never retire. But among the millionaires — net worth of $1 million or more — 26% didn't plan to retire ever. "These people never want to give up control," Finn said. "They don't go fishing."

So much for the idle rich. Only 1% said they were "not working but not retired." The stereotypical silver spoons were also scarce — only 6% said they inherited most of their money. Selfish? 77% give to charity; 41% participate in public affairs. Shallow? 61% say they've made a religious commitment. Insular? "Once they agreed to be interviewed they were quite forthcoming," Baker said. Dilettantes? Owning art and antiques was rated important by a mere 11%. Snobs? Only 11% valued owning an expensive car and only 7% belonging to a prestigious club.

"I didn't get a feeling of (the) 'Me Generation,' " Finn said.

Scott H. Smith, a CIGNA client, who runs his insurance brokerage in Hartford skipped vacations for six years after starting out on his own. Now, he owns three cars, a summer house, plays tennis and sails.

"The fruits of success are delicious," said Smith, who at 35 is on the young end of the age spectrum. . Nonetheless, "I find the time with my children to be the most gratifying thing I do."

Though they have a lot to look after, the upper affluent don't necessarily delegate their financial affairs to the hands of trust officers or investment bankers. 71% said they manage their finances themselves. For help, 61% turn to certified public accountants, 47% to stockbrokers, and 36% to lawyers. Only 32% cited financial planners, but that was enough to please CIGNA, especially since the youngest of the "upper affluent," those under 45, used financial planners the most — 37%. "Ten years ago, the term was virtually unknown," Finn said.

Despite their down-home values, the rich still manage to live like the rich: 53% own expensive cars anyway, 35% belong to those prestigious clubs, 43% own art or antiques, 36% own a second home, and 79% say they've provided their families with the "very finest" home and clothes.

That disparity didn't bother Baker. "I couldn't find a thing in this entire data set to dislike about these people. And I was kind of looking for it," he said. "They're just a nice bunch of people."

Upheaval in Middle-Class Market Forces Changes in Selling Strategies

THE SHATTERED MIDDLE CLASS

LAST OF A SERIES

By John Koten

Staff Reporter of The Wall Street Journal

First, there was Tide, the Chevy, the gray flannel suit, and Coke. They were the material symbols of the great middle class, and they defined the American mass market.

Today, though, the traditional middle-class consumer is an endangered species. No longer is there such a large group of buyers that can easily be identified by their common goals, motivations and values. Instead, companies have had to learn how to cater to consumers in ever-smaller market niches. So now there's all-temperature Cheer, the Eddie Bauer-style Ford Bronco, Levi's with a "skosh more" fabric for men and diet Cherry Slice.

For manufacturers and retailers, the decline of the once-reliable middle market has been one of the most wrenching developments of the past two decades. It has slowed the growth of such giants as Procter & Gamble Co. and Sears, Roebuck & Co. And it has forced a rethinking of marketing strategies at companies ranging from breweries to auto makers.

'Can't Sell to Middle America'

"You can't sell to middle America" anymore, says Dannielle Colliver, an advertising manager at General Motors Corp.'s Chevrolet division. Adds Ray Ablondi, a marketing research director at Ford Motor Co.: "We don't recognize something called a middle class. We work across demographic, psycho-graphic and life-style lines. If we want to, we can use 200 or 300 different measuring points to identify our customer."

Some of that, of course, merely reflects an improved ability to identify differences among consumers. But few marketers would deny that the psychology of their customers has also changed drastically since the banner years of the middle class.

One of the most sweeping differences has been the decline in the number of Americans who aspire to the mainstream. In the two decades that followed World War II, people generally seemed happy to embrace the symbols of their new-found prosperity as more and more entered the middle class.

"There was the hierarchy of automobiles to show when you were making it. You started drinking scotch. You had children, saved money . . . and moved to the suburbs. You conformed," says Ann Clurman, senior vice president of Yankelovich Clancy Shulman, the research firm.

The consumer's desire to fit in provided corporate America with a platform for building huge brands. Coca-Cola found it could sell soda using such appeals as "Along the highway to everywhere." Advertisements for Admiral televisions in the 1960s could feature a married couple called "the Happy Mediums." Sears became the top retailer by catering to young families with a phalanx of new suburban stores and sturdy, no-nonsense merchandise. The range of acceptable tastes in the late 1950s was so narrow, in fact, that Hart, Schaffner & Marx prospered in men's tailored clothing despite offering only three styles of suits in its best lines.

An 'Umbrella Brand'

But today the range is much wider and many companies can't succeed unless they offer a broad choice. While Chrysler Corp. sold 10 basic car models in 1965, today its dealers stock 25 models. Coca-Cola has gone from a single product to what its maker now calls an "umbrella brand," with permutations that include Coca-Cola Classic and Diet Cherry Coke, each aimed at a different type of consumer. Hartmarx has expanded the three basic suit styles in its Hart, Schaffner & Marx line to 15. And Levi Strauss & Co., which produced one uniform for an entire generation, now sells more than 5,000 styles of apparel.

Companies today even think twice before broadcasting that they sell the leading brand—an image many people might construe as a negative. Marketers say many baby boomers today are especially put off by threats to their individuality. "They don't want to be perceived as ordinary," says Mandy Putnam of Management Horizons, a retail consulting firm. Thus, while they might help fuel the initial success of a new ice cream or fashion, many stop buying when one of those products becomes too commonplace.

The disdain for the average has helped polarize the marketplace. Today, the fastest-growing retailers either sell image-oriented merchandise (The Limited) or offer the consumer a good price (Wal-Mart). Shoppers see less value in anything in between. The consumer "has a burning desire to beat the system," says Carol Farmer, who owns a New York retail consulting concern. It's harder to do that at traditional middle-market stores.

The middle market has also been eroded by the increased tendency of people to buy outside of class boundaries. In the past, people's shopping decisions were restricted partly by their limited familiarity with what was available. But mass communication has since spread tastes and wants across social and economic lines. Baby boomers today are far more familiar with many of the accoutrements of wealth and status than their parents were. As a result, a lower-income buyer today might be as much a candidate to purchase a top-quality brand as someone with a much higher income. "A life style that once was known only to the leisure class has become an equal-opportunity aspiration," says a report published by Grey Communications Inc., a New York ad agency.

Piling Up Bills

Increasingly, consumers today are apt to behave like Kevin Ellis, an Eagle Rock, Calif., computer consultant who, with his wife, spent $6,000 on clothes, vacations and fancy dinners last year despite modest incomes. Why? "I want everything, and I want it now," says Mr. Ellis, who says he avoids middle-market stores like Sears and J.C. Penney.

Indeed, market researchers say as many as half of the 76 million baby boomers consume products of a price and quality far beyond what might be expected

(cont.)

for their means. That's one reason why Chevrolet, in recent advertising for its Nova model, uses the theme, "If your standards are higher than you think you can afford, look at Chevy." Similarly, J.C. Penney has added designer names like Alan Flusser, Lee Wright and Halston to its stores. The Northern Trust Bank in Chicago recently ran an ad advising that "Anyone who lives within his means suffers from a lack of imagination."

Today's more splintered life styles also dictate more varied consumer wants. While Procter & Gamble could once satisfy a large segment of the population with sound value, the company sees an emerging threat to such leading brands as Tide detergent because of fragmenting consumer wants. P&G's response: offer more options. Now there's regular Tide, liquid Tide, Tide in 10-box "Redi-Paks," and—now in test markets—Tide in "multi-action sheets." In a slightly different vein, Coca-Cola is experimenting with a new marketing campaign aimed at getting more people to drink Coke at breakfast.

With fewer people living in families and more mothers working, an increasing number of people are also making their own shopping decisions. Now women buy their own cars and coats, men do more of the grocery shopping, and children purchase many of their own clothes.

Avoiding Department Stores

"Before the kids started to know what they wanted, I shopped at stores like Sears," says Jane Boxell of Western Springs, Ill. "Now, general stores don't fit our individual needs." That's why on one recent outing, the Boxells avoided department stores, buying instead at specialty outlets such as The Limited. At such stores, "You can get the brand names that kids go for," explains Kathy Boxell, 13 years old.

For marketers, the result of all these changes is a less-homogenous, more-confusing marketplace that defies simple definition. Increasingly, companies say they have to target smaller and smaller fractions of the population to succeed. Columbia Pictures, for instance, now finds it advantageous to offer sneak previews of movies by invitation only. The reason: The public is so fragmented that the old-fashioned sneak preview won't draw enough people who are "predisposed to like the movie," thus reducing the preview's usefulness in word-of-mouth advertising.

Today, Ford finds that it can so narrowly define its audience that the character of its products changes in the process. Its Bronco four-wheel-drive utility vehicle was gentrified years ago with the Bronco II's nicer interiors. Five years ago, the vehicle was yuppified with the two-tone, big-engined Eddie Bauer model, designed to appeal to urban cowboys and cowgirls. For 1987, Ford added a two-wheel-drive version of the Bronco. "It's for people who say, 'I don't need a four-wheel-drive, I just want to be different,'" says John Tighe, Ford's North America automotive customer research manager.

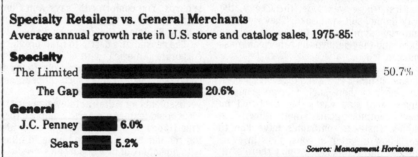

D ISDAIN for the average has helped polarize the marketplace. The fastest-growing retailers either sell image-oriented merchandise or offer low prices.

Specialty Retailers vs. General Merchants
Average annual growth rate in U.S. store and catalog sales, 1975-85:

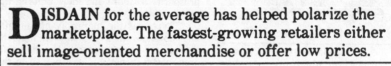

Specialty
The Limited ████████████████████████ 50.7%
The Gap ████████ 20.6%
General
J.C. Penney ████ 6.0%
Sears ███ 5.2%

Source: Management Horizons

30

WHY ALL THOSE CITY FOLKS ARE BUYING PICKUPS

Changing lifestyles bring a boom in sales of light trucks

The auto market may be soft right now, but one new luxury import is doing just fine. It has a $30,825 price tag, and its initials are RR—but it's not what you think. It's a Range Rover, a boxy-looking, four-wheel-drive "sport/utility vehicle." That's a fancy name for a glorified truck.

Trucks are hot. Over the past 10 years, sales of light trucks, which include pickups, vans, and sport/utility vehicles, have shot up 65%, while car sales have risen only 10%. Truck sales this year have continued to cannibalize weak car sales.

Once the workaday tools of Wyoming ranchers, trucks have become trendy, thanks to a combination of changing lifestyles, new products, and refocused marketing. Some truck models are still marketed to rural buyers, hunters, and fishermen. But light trucks are also attracting city denizens, women, and "a lot of guys who've never owned a truck in their lives—who've gone to work in a shirt and tie for 35 years," says John D. Rock, general manager of GMC Truck at General Motors Corp.

It all began with the full-size pickup. Some full-size models are fancy and expensive—so-called Georgia Cadillacs with all the options for wealthy, rural buyers. But the market changed in the early 1980s when the Japanese brought over the compact pickups they'd been making for Japan's narrow streets. These small, low-priced trucks drew young buyers away from subcompact cars. Even today, a compact pickup with two-wheel drive costs about $7,900, compared with $8,600 for a subcompact car. "People will gag when they see the price of a small car, and a smart salesman will walk them over to a truck," says Jerome B. York, truck operations vice-president at Chrysler Corp.

Detroit countered with its own versions of the light pickup—and got lucky. The domestic trucks hit the market at about the same time as smaller family cars designed for the energy crunch. Suddenly, people who wanted to tow boats or campers found that new cars were too small to do the job. "What emerged is the ability to sell compact trucks to people who didn't even know they wanted to buy trucks," says Raymond B. Pittman, director of the compact truck business at Ford Motor Co.

That has been a boon for Detroit. The American reputation for building high-quality, durable, full-size pickups has rubbed off on their smaller trucks. As the rising yen has forced up prices of Japanese compact pickups, Detroit has gained market share. In the first five months of 1987, domestic sales of compact trucks rose 21% while imports fell 17%, giving U.S. auto makers 56% of a market the Japanese created.

'PHENOMENAL.' Ford sold more trucks than Ford cars in the U. S. in 1986. GM, which will shut nine plants by 1990, was considering dropping the second shift at its Moraine (Ohio) factory. Instead, that shift will make a sport/utility vehicle. And at Chrysler, Chairman Lee A. Iacocca cites Jeep, which has 4% of the truck market and "the best-known automotive brand name in the world," as the main reason he's buying American Motors Corp.

Following up on its success in small pickups, Detroit is aggressively selling vans and utility vehicles to distinct markets. Minivans have replaced station wagons as second vehicles for families. Women drive half of all minivans and often choose which model to buy. To appeal to them, ads stress "garageability" and low step-in height. "Demand is phenomenal," says Chrysler's York. With no buyer incentives and minimal advertising, Chrysler's new Grand Voyager minivan is selling at full production capacity.

Four-wheel-drive utility vehicles are aimed at young, outdoorsy buyers. With a base price of $7,500, the Suzuki Samurai minijeep is the hottest set of wheels among California teens. But not all utility trucks are aimed at kids. Almost 45% òf the buyers of Chevrolet's $11,588 S-10 Blazer earn $50,000 or more. "In California, the S-10 Blazer is a Mercedes-driver's second vehicle," says George R. Hanley, manager of marketing information and research for Chevrolet Trucks.

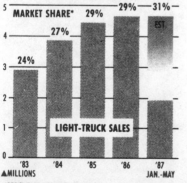

FOR FOUR-WHEEL-DRIVES AND PICKUPS, SALES JUST KEEP ON TRUCKIN'

MARKET SHARE*

LIGHT-TRUCK SALES

'83 24%
'84 27%
'85 29%
'86 29%
'87 JAN.-MAY 31% EST

▲MILLIONS

*PERCENTAGE OF COMBINED SALES OF PASSENGER CARS AND LIGHT TRUCKS

DATA: *WARD'S AUTOMOTIVE REPORTS*, MERRILL LYNCH

PAUL GRANGE

"It's marketed as a car alternative. It's not really labeled a truck."

Many other models aren't really advertised as trucks either. With about 600,000 buyers a year switching from cars to trucks, truck ads are emphasizing lifestyle and image rather than durability and toughness. GMC Truck has led the way, with such campaign themes as "A truck you can live with." Ads showed trucks on tony Rodeo Drive and in front of the Mark Hopkins Inter-Continental hotel in San Francisco. GMC Truck even considered an ad theme of "How to live without a passenger car."

GMC Truck's new campaign shows an actor strolling past his car collection, including a Porsche and a Corvette, before he stops at his new GMC Sierra pickup. "There's a fantasy element in trucks," says Garry G. Nielsen, vice-president at McCann-Erickson/Detroit, GMC Truck's ad agency.

Ads also emphasize how trucks can be customized, using options that, not coincidentally, have boosted manufacturers' margins to roughly the same as those on cars. A truck "becomes an extension of you, where, with a Porsche, you become an extension of it," says Jim L. Driver, national advertising and sales administration manager at Suzuki of America Automotive Corp. "People can do a lot to tailor a truck to themselves," says Ford's Pittman. "There's a perception that you can't do so much to a car."

MACHO LOOK. Because most buyers are male, customizing often means adding a macho look. This year, Chrysler's Detroit dealers asked the company to produce a special-edition pickup for them. Chrysler added special lights, oversize tires, and other extras, slapped on a decal branding the truck the "Defender," and sold 2,000 more trucks than usual in three months. Dealers who normally sell 5 pickups a month sold more than 40. Special editions have since been created for Kansas City and the Northeast.

The real test for truck marketing will arrive over the coming year. After nearly five years of steady growth, annual truck sales could plateau soon at about 5 million units, industry officials say. Already, pickups aren't capturing as many former car buyers as they used to, and first-time truck buyers are declining as a percentage of new pickup buyers.

That means that the market isn't luring as many new customers as it once did. And there are growing worries about the customers it already has. The compact-pickup owners who bought trucks in the early 1980s are due to trade in their vehicles in the next 6 to 12 months. The big question: What will they buy as a replacement? Will they trade up to a full-size pickup? Will they switch to a van, to a sport/utility vehicle, or maybe back to a car?

The compact-pickup owners who bought their vehicles because of low prices are unlikely to trade up to bigger or fancier trucks, says Jan Leon Woznick, senior vice-president and director of research at McCann-Erickson/Detroit. Instead, they'll probably go back to cars. But drivers who chose pickups for camping or hauling peat moss are likely to remain in the market. Still, the young, single driver who bought a light pickup a few years ago may now have a wife and children. That means he could well switch to a van.

Such doubts about trade-in patterns leave future production and marketing plans in question. But in an increasingly segmented market, how those questions are answered will be critical to the sales and profits of Detroit.

By James B. Treece in Detroit

31

SHAPING UP YOUR SUPPLIERS

It's survival time. And to make the cut yourself you've got to get real tough with your vendors. Innovative programs can teach them how to deliver.

■ *by Joel Dreyfuss*

SMALL manufacturing companies are in crisis. Their main customers, the big boys of U.S. industry, have been humbled by global competition and are seeking their salvation in higher standards of quality and productivity. The big companies can't find redemption alone. So, like passionate converts, they are spreading the gospel of efficiency to their suppliers. Suddenly, small companies whose greatest concern was once to simply get the product out the door are under pressure to adopt the latest technologies, use quality control methods, *and* slash prices.

The suppliers often do not understand the new processes and management techniques their customers want them to embrace. Says L. Joseph Thompson, professor of manufacturing at Cornell's Johnson School of Management: "Small companies are less likely than large companies to have made improvements for productivity. They're concerned about meeting the payroll and not about the longer term." Besides, if the suppliers do manage to come up to their customers' idea of quality, they expect to be paid more, not less. They're not the world's best experts in management.

Suppliers had better learn fast. Most large U.S. manufacturers are reducing their number of vendors in order to control quality. Says Charles E. Lucier, a Booz Allen & Hamilton vice president: "Most want two or three suppliers instead of ten or 12." They will give preference to those close to home. Russell W. Meyer, the chairman of Cessna Aircraft, the small-plane manufacturer headquartered in Wichita, says: "We spend a lot of time with subcontractors. It's a lot easier to work with someone in Wichita than with someone in Los Angeles."

To make the cut, suppliers will have to go through a rigorous survival drill. Buyers routinely send inspection teams to rate a small company's plants. They want to see Japanese-style just-in-time manufacturing and delivery techniques, statistical process controls that identify causes of defects, and the ability to handle data electronically.

Some small companies resist, either from ignorance or from fear. Says Joseph A. Bockerstette, a manufacturing specialist at consultant Coopers & Lybrand: "Many suppliers feel just-in-time is a way for FOR-TUNE 500 companies to dump on them." When a large company begins asking for three deliveries a day, a small supplier may end up stockpiling the goods the customer wants. Craig Skevington, president of Factory Automation & Computer Technologies, a consulting firm near Albany, New York, that specializes in manufacturing, says, "Just-in-time becomes just-in-case."

The stringent requirements could bring a wave of restructuring among little manufacturers as wrenching as the one the large companies went through. Because the small fry are great sources of innovation and new jobs, Skevington and others worry that a weakened small manufacturing sector could chill entrepreneurship and hurt the ability of the U.S. to generate new products.

Help is on the way. New organizations, sponsored by government and private companies, are coming to the rescue of manufacturing's embattled little guys. Among them:

■ The Cleveland Advanced Manufacturing Program, one of nine technology research centers financed by the state of Ohio's $250 million Thomas Edison Program, provides a free assessment of a manufacturer's production line and recommends improvements.

■ In New York and Michigan, state-employed manufacturing experts roam industrial areas, offering small companies that can't afford consultants new ways to improve their manufacturing processes.

■ On Massachusetts's Route 128, Coopers & Lybrand has started a manufacturing center to help local outfits solve their production-line problems.

■ In Cleveland, Troy, New York, and Columbia, South Carolina, regional manufacturing technology centers have sprung up. Funded through the National Institute of Standards and Technology (formerly the Bureau of Standards), they aim to transfer advanced manufacturing technology developed in government labs to smaller companies.

■ In Pennsylvania, government and corporations are raising $60 million for nine Industrial Resource Centers that help the state's small manufacturers by providing consultants on technology, management, and marketing.

■ In Wichita, the Center for Technology Application—financed by local companies, a regional economic development agency, and Wichita State University—offers training classes for computer machine tool operators, provides engineering advice, and promotes closer ties between large and small companies.

WICHITA'S technology center provides some fascinating insights on how such programs help small suppliers. The flat plains spreading to the horizon and the big open sky around Wichita suggest God had flying as much as farming on his mind when he created the vast Midwest. A fortuitous combination of air pioneers and willing investors made Wichita a wellspring of aviation activity. Wichita is home to Cessna, Beech Aircraft, Gates Learjet, and the military aircraft division of Boeing. Hundreds of high-tech machine and tool-and-die shops grew up around the aircraft business. Other major manufacturers include NCR (computers) and Coleman (camping equipment). Among the wheat fields, manufacturing generates 20% of Kansas's output of goods and services.

In 1986, when Wichita's most important

Toolmakers talk of reducing from weeks to days the time it takes to translate a customer's design into a finished product. Says Tomison: "If you want to compete, you're going to have to work fast."

industries—aircraft, farming, and oil—slumped at the same time, the area's most prominent executives and politicians launched a major development program. The WI/SE Partnership for Growth, named for Wichita and surrounding Sedgwick County, decided that the usual efforts—lure new companies, revitalize the downtown, and get more direct flights from major cities—would not be enough. The group also wanted to help small manufacturers. So it started the Center for Technology Application at Wichita State University, whose large engineering department has long provided support to the aircraft industry.

The center asked more than 400 small manufacturers what their needs were and created programs to meet them. When the companies complained about a lack of skilled workers, the partnership organized classes in machine tool programming and shop math at the regional vocational school. When tool- and die-makers said they wanted to receive manufacturing data electronically, the center set up a task force to find inexpensive ways of transmitting data by modem between the large contractors and their suppliers.

Knowing how vulnerable they are, many small manufacturers eagerly supported the program. "The smaller you are, the better you have to be," says Willie F. Tomison, co-

owner of NC Machine, a tool-and-die shop (1988 sales: $310,000) whose customers include Boeing, Bell Helicopter, and General Dynamics. "It's obvious we're going to have to be able to meet new manufacturing requirements." The shelf outside Tomison's office is lined with familiar products his company has helped produce. Among them: a styrofoam container for a McDonald's hamburger, the handle for a Sears Craftsman wrench, and the plastic holder for a Toyota auto seat belt.

Tool-and-die shops like Tomison's must translate the designs of engineers into products or the molds to make them. The job combines brute strength and incredible delicacy: carving a block of metal to accuracies far finer than a human hair. Traditionally, big companies prepare blueprints for a part and send them to the tool shops, where the drawings are measured by hand and converted into movements on a milling or drilling machine. Now, computer-controlled milling machines and computer-aided design offer another option: direct transmission of an engineer's concepts by tape or modem to the sophisticated tooling machines.

TOOLMAKERS talk of reducing from weeks to days the time it takes to translate a customer's design into a finished product—and of eliminating most errors in the process. Says Tomison: "If you want to compete, you're going to have to work fast." He is working with the Wichita partnership to test equipment and transmission standards for speedier design and production.

Why is the Wichita program a good model? First, WI/SE got off to a fast start because organizers immediately recruited 32 important leaders of business, government, and academe. The heavyweights raised a quick $9 million, eliminating lengthy fund-raising drives.

Second, the attempt to help small companies was part of an overall economic development plan and thus could command lots of community resources. To compile a directory of companies with electronic capability, the partnership enlisted an organization of retired engineers. Wichita State's Institute for Aviation Research and its Composite Materials Laboratory willingly diverted their focus from large avi-

(cont.)

ation companies to small manufacturers.

Third, everyone bought into the program. The large companies' need for better suppliers meshed with the desire of the small companies to sell more. Both groups have enthusiastically supported the training classes and the data transmission project. But few small manufacturers have joined the university-sponsored quality council, perhaps because their customers are just starting to demand perfection.

One of the most controversial aspects of WI/SE was a proposal to transfer technology from large to small companies. The notion was that the big guys develop and discard many new technologies because they offer no immediate practical value. But smaller companies could devote the energy needed to bring them to market. So far, only NCR has agreed to participate in the transfer program. The company came up with 14 items that Colin Isenman, NCR's director of engineering in Wichita, describes as "mostly half-products: more than a concept but pulled from development." In January, NCR invited 17 local companies to a presentation of the "half-products." So far none have decided to ask NCR for a license and no other large manufacturers have followed NCR's lead. They cite restrictions in government contracts and argue that their neglected ideas would require too much capital investment for small companies. Perhaps they are also worried about competition.

WHAT hath Wichita wrought? Small manufacturers report they feel less isolated because large companies and the university are involved in their problems. For that reason, Bill J. Pritchard, president of Wichita Tool, says he canceled plans to move his company to Texas. The meetings have fostered a new spirit of cooperation among the minimanufacturers, who now talk of joining forces to bid on projects no one could handle alone.

Closer ties between large and small companies have also flourished. Excel Manufacturing, a maker of precision machine parts and a supplier to Boeing, McDonnell Douglas, and General Dynamics, worked with Cessna for the first time in the partnership test of an electronic data transmission system. Impressed by Excel's work, Cessna invited the company to bid on contracts worth $30,000 for wing fittings on the Citation III corporate jet. Excel won the contracts and is now bidding on several other Cessna jobs.

Beyond Wichita, there are other success stories. When the Cleveland Advanced Manufacturing Program offered a free plant inspection to members, Cleveland Machine Controls, a $40 million manufacturer of industrial controls, signed up and came away with ten recommendations. President William N. Jones adopted suggestions for scheduling work flow and using more efficient machines for high-volume work. Says he: "There's no question we've reduced inventory and the time a work or-

A pilot system enabled a book manufacturer to shorten the design-to-delivery cycle from 14 months to six.

der is in our shop." In New York City, Ed Lewison, one of the state's ten technology extension agents, has helped small manufacturers upgrade their technology inexpensively by finding sources of rebuilt equipment. Lewison also brought two companies together to develop a metal stamping business; the heads of both say the joint enterprise will eventually produce $2 million in revenues.

Consulting firms are getting in on the action. Recently, Coopers & Lybrand's Center for Manufacturing Technology in Massachusetts developed a pilot computerized system to help a small company design and test manufacturing procedures for book and magazine production. The test enabled the company to shorten the design-to-delivery cycle from 14 months to six months.

Small manufacturing companies are perhaps the most dynamic part of American industry. In the decade from 1976 to 1986, they created 1.4 million jobs while the big manufacturers lost 100,000. Many large companies are shifting to what the management experts call distributed manufacturing. That means treating their factories like small companies and farming more work out to suppliers. There's plenty of business for small manufacturers, and plenty of reason to help them do it better. After all, says Booz Allen's Lucier: "They are the future of manufacturing in the U.S." **F**

32

U.S. Car-Parts Firms Form Japanese Ties
Quality Is Big Issue in Opening Doors to Orient

By Joseph B. White
Staff Reporter of The Wall Street Journal

DETROIT—For years, there's been little love lost between Japanese auto makers and U.S. parts suppliers. The Japanese thought the Americans peddled junk. The Americans, in turn, believed the Japanese didn't like them, much less their wares.

But now, the two sides have begun an elaborate, and often awkward, mating dance. The Japanese are deploying teams of engineers, who are pushing U.S. factory managers to adopt new methods to boost quality and cut costs. The Americans, in turn, are filling flights to Tokyo, and changing many longstanding practices to suit the Japanese.

All this is happening because Japanese auto makers and American parts suppliers have concluded that, while they might not trust each other, they do need each other. The Americans know that by 1990 the Japanese will be building as many cars in North America as **Ford Motor** Co., and see Japanese parts makers—140 so far—setting up shop in the U.S. The Japanese know that the cost of shipping parts from Japan is rising with each new surge of the yen.

"A year and a half ago there was no incentive for (Japanese car makers) to talk to us," says Neil Feola, president of **Wickes** Cos.' automotive group. "The circumstances are different today." So different, in fact, that a Japanese auto maker recently gave Chicago-based **Borg-Warner** Corp.'s automotive unit a surprise, cold-call order for 150,000 solenoids valued at a total of more than $1 million.

The Japanese say they want to buy more from Americans. **Honda Motor** Co. has announced a goal of 75% U.S. content for its Ohio-made cars by 1991, up from 63% today. But achieving those goals won't be easy because the two sides have different expectations.

Building Relationships

U.S. parts makers typically want contracts. But Japanese buyers want to build "relationships" that go beyond a purchase order. **Toyota Motor** Corp. even grades suppliers on their attitude. U.S. firms like privacy. The Japanese like to get close to their suppliers. "They want to know everything," says William Dugan of **Admiral Tool & Mfg.** Co., a Chicago metal-stamping concern. "We aren't used to that."

U.S. suppliers also aren't used to being lectured about their quality problems. But Japanese auto executives feel obliged to lecture. **Nissan Motor** Co.'s Tennessee assembly plant still junks U.S. parts at a rate more than double that for Japanese parts. And Mazda's top U.S. manufacturing executive says he has similar woes.

"It often seems that if something is 90% right," complains Osamu Nobuto, president of Mazda Motor Mfg. (USA), a unit of **Mazda Motor** Corp., "there is a tendency to believe that further improvement is either unnecessary or not worth the extra effort." American suppliers sometimes adopt a take-it-or-leave-it attitude, he adds, that "is disturbing, and quite astounding, to us."

American suppliers concede the Japanese obsession with detail surprises them. When Michigan-based **Van Dresser** Corp. produced a prototype part to be used at Toyota's new Kentucky plant, a Toyota engineer got "down on his hands and knees measuring the gap" between the car's steel door frame and Van Dresser's interior door panel, says Van Dresser manager Douglas G. Kruse. "He was saying, 'Look, the gap is a millimeter too wide.'" Van Dresser reworked the mold.

No Apologies

At Honda, officials make no apologies for being perfectionists. Parts quality department manager George West regularly subjects American parts to "zenbara," which means tear apart and analyze, and

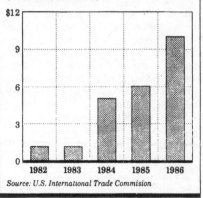

U.S. Trade Deficit In Auto Parts
(In billions of dollars)

Source: U.S. International Trade Commission

"higahikaku," or comparison, usually to Japanese parts. The two Japanese terms are Honda shorthand for the exhaustive testing U.S. suppliers' wares undergo before Honda buys them. "A lot of vendors really want to do business with Honda," says Mr. West. "But after that, comes reality."

Reality, as **Capitol Plastics of Ohio** Inc. discovered, can mean working for three years to ship a $216 batch of parts to Honda's Ohio motorcycle plant in 1978. Even now that Honda is one of Capitol's two largest customers, the small, closely held Bowling Green, Ohio, concern has to run full speed to keep up with Honda's demands.

On a recent Thursday, Honda told Capitol to start shipping parts on pallets arranged to match perfectly the color sequence of cars on Honda's assembly line. By the way, Honda added, do it by Monday. With more than 100 different parts to repackage, says Capitol President William E. Taylor, "it was a horrendous thing to get a handle on." But Capitol complied.

Shipping procedures are just the start. If a supplier's factory operations seem inefficient, Japanese auto makers will press for change—and for a share of the savings. At Van Dresser's plant in Westland, Mich., for example, advice from Toyota led the company to switch a door-panel assembly operation from a traditional straight line to one shaped like a tight U. That way, one worker can operate two stations when production volume is low.

Joint Ventures

Sometimes, meeting Japanese quality demands isn't so simple. **Inland Steel** Corp. spent $460 million between 1984 and 1986 to overhaul its plants and keep its status as the main steel supplier to Honda's Marysville, Ohio, plant. And a year ago Inland formed a joint venture with **Nippon Steel** Corp. to build a $400 million facility in New Carlisle, Ind. That plant will turn out the same steel in one hour that Inland needed 10 to 14 days to make, says T. Andrew Ellwein, Inland's general manager for sales.

Joint ventures such as this are becoming increasingly common, as Americans see alliances with Japanese firms as the only way to get a share of the business of Japanese auto makers. But some specialists warn that joint ventures also can be dangerous.

(cont.)

"Although the joint venture may be profitable for the American partner in the short term, in the long term it may leave the American partner vulnerable," says Robert B. Reich, professor of political economy at Harvard's Kennedy School of Government. "It may give the Japanese a significant beachhead in the U.S. market."

But going it alone is risky, too, as **AES Interconnects** of Avon, Ind., can attest. The small maker of electrical wiring assemblies has tried to sell to three Japanese plants in the U.S. The results to date: zero. Says Dan Sirotin, AES's sales manager, "I've spent 36 of the most frustrating months of my life doing this."

CAN REYNOLDS WRAP UP THE KITCHEN MARKET?

The aluminum giant bolsters its stake in plastic packaging

When Reynolds Metals Co. decided to roll out a new line of colored plastic food wrap in transparent shades of red, green, yellow, and blue, it faced a marketing challenge. Research showed women loved the stuff, but men didn't see the point—and the purchasing staffs of supermarkets are mostly men. So Reynolds sent samples to the buyers' homes, hoping their wives' reactions would convince them the product would sell. The strategy helped. After 10 weeks, colored Reynolds Plastic Wraps are in stores in 75% of the country, and sales are exceeding expectations.

If the name Reynolds Metals brings to mind a boom-and-bust aluminum company, look closer. The Richmond (Va.) company is turning into a savvy consumer products marketer as well. While the bulk of its $5.6 billion in sales comes from the aluminum used in cans and buildings, Reynolds has built a thriving $500 million sideline in products used to cook today's turkey and wrap yesterday's pot roast.

The most recent addition to the Reynolds family is a line of plastic resealable food-storage bags introduced in April. The company already has leading market shares in wax paper, cooking bags, and aluminum foil. Now, Reynolds is considering brand-name trash bags, plastic cups, and utensils. "We want to own that aisle" in the supermarket, says Chairman William O. Bourke.

Bourke's strategy is to rely on consumer goods to smooth out the inevitable earnings swings in metalmaking. Sales of packaging products tend to rise during economic crunches because consumers are more likely to prepare their own food. And Reynolds' wraps, bags, and foils carry pretax margins as high as 40%, compared with 7% to 12% for aluminum. Consumer products contributed only 12% to Reynolds' $482 million in earnings last year, estimates J. Clarence Morrison, aluminum industry analyst at Dean Witter Reynolds Inc. But he forecasts that net profits from consumer products, including bulk sales to food-service businesses, will increase 330%, to $196 million, or 26% of total earnings, by 1992.

For Reynolds to realize such results, it must open markets that are under pretty tight wraps. In the $350 million reclosable plastic bag business, Dow Chemical Co.'s Ziploc has a 75% share, and First Brands Corp.'s Glad claims most of the rest. To defend their products, Dow and First Brand offered discounts and rebates weeks before the Reynolds brand hit the stores.

BASHED BORSCHT. Reynolds budgeted $60 million to develop its triple-seal bags, including about $20 million for ads. TV spots that highlight their strength show how to make such concoctions as "bashed borscht"—put beets in a bag and smash them with a bat.

Reynolds is no newcomer to the supermarket. Former Chairman David P. Reynolds virtually created the aluminum foil business—and one of the most durable brands in Reynolds Wrap—by spending heavily on national TV advertising in the 1950s. But the company didn't put its name on another consumer product—plastic wrap—until 1982, a year after Bourke arrived from Ford Motor Co. Seven years later, Reynolds commands 19% of the $250 million plastic wrap market. With the colored wrap, Bourke vows, Reynolds will vault into the No. 1 spot, ahead of Dow's Saran Wrap, which has 26%. Bourke's goal: to reach $1 billion in consumer product sales by 1992.

Bourke frets that investors haven't recognized the value of Reynolds' consumer businesses. The company's stock, at around 56 a share, has been trading at only six times earnings, half the average for the Standard & Poor's 500 industrial companies. "I guess the market won't be convinced until the next recession," Bourke says. If profits hold up, there can be little doubt Reynolds Metals means more than just aluminum.

By Michael Schroeder in Richmond, Va.

REYNOLDS' CONSUMER PUSH

1989 REVENUES: $6.5 BILLION

1989 NET INCOME: $620.5 MILLION

☐ ALUMINUM ■ GOLD
■ CONSUMER PRODUCTS

'88 '89 '90 *ESTIMATES
▲ PERCENT OF NET INCOME
DATA: DEAN WITTER REYNOLDS INC.

Battle of telephone titans

Bidding war

The new USA government phone system will:

▶ Be the world's largest private phone system when installed in the '90s.
▶ Link 1.1 million government workers in 1,311 locations across the USA.
▶ Transmit voices, information and pictures over a single cable.
▶ Handle 1.6 million calls a day, 26 million a month, 320 million a year.
▶ Save taxpayers an estimated $100 million a year in government phone bills.
▶ Rack up $25 billion in sales over 10 years for the winning bidders.

Competing for the contract:
▶ **Team 1:** Martin Marietta; MCI; Bell Atlantic; US West; BellSouth; Pacific Telesis; NYNEX; Ameritech; Southwestern Bell; Northern Telecom
▶ **Team 2:** AT&T; Boeing
▶ **Team 3:** Electronic Data Systems; US Sprint Communications

By Tim Dillon, USA TODAY

THAMES: Martin Marietta vice president says bidding has been an 'emotional roller coaster,' but firms keep at it.

Phone deal is line to confusion

Delays plague companies seeking $25B contract

By Mark Lewyn
USA TODAY

CHANTILLY, Va. — Gerald Thames doesn't look like a general in his white shirt and steel-rimmed glasses. But the Martin Marietta Corp. vice president is marshalling an army of engineers in an attempt to win one of the largest government contracts in USA history.

At stake: $25 billion in the next 10 years to replace the government's 25-year-old phone system. It will be the world's largest private telephone network.

Some of the USA's toughest corporate warriors are trying to slice off the biggest piece of that contract. Martin Marietta, MCI Communications Corp., Northern Telecom and the seven Bell operating companies are one team; AT&T and Boeing Co. on another; Electronic Data Systems Corp. and US Sprint Communications Co. are the third.

But backroom politics, corporate foot-dragging and alleged criminal misconduct are shaping the battle into the business equivalent of chemical warfare. The Justice Department, Senate, General Services Administration and a federal grand jury are investigating whether GSA officials leaked confidential AT&T information to competitors in a separate but related contract. The investigations could delay installation of the Federal Telecommunications System 2000, or FTS-2000, into the 1990s, although the GSA said this

(cont.)

week it is proceeding with the FTS-2000 on schedule. But the investigations haven't cooled the competitive fire of Martin Marietta or its rivals.

"We're going to bust a gut to win it," says AT&T Chairman James E. Olson, pounding his fist into his hand. "If that sounds a little emotional, that's because it is."

Each side has assembled an army working 12- to 15-hour days to put together its bid and do whatever else it can to win the contract — from lobbying Congress to wooing the press.

The Martin Marietta team's "war room" here has cubicles for each member of its team, coded locks on all doors to keep out spies, and a padlocked blue drum for sensitive documents.

AT&T and Boeing have their own nerve center in nearby Vienna, Va. A battalion of several hundred engineers sport special security badges. "We wanted to go as far as we could to make sure there were no leaks" from this building, says Louis C. Golm, the vice president heading the project for AT&T.

But security may be the least of his problems. The deadline to get bids in to the GSA is March 31. The winner will be announced Sept. 30 — assuming all goes according to plan, which may be a big assumption the way things have been going. Says Thames: "This has been an emotional roller coaster."

"The situation is really screwed up," AT&T spokesman Herb Linnen says. "It has been just fraught with confusion."

Contributing to the confusion:

▶ A criminal investigation: The government says that a GSA engineer, Sureshar L. Soni, handed secret AT&T pricing information to two competitors (BellSouth Corp. and Bell Atlantic Corp.) on a related phone contract to replace 12 AT&T phone switches. Last week, BellSouth offered to give up one of the two contracts, saying secret AT&T information was used. This week, AT&T said more than one GSA official might be involved. All this raises the question: Is the GSA process for handling large contracts tainted? The grand jury is looking into that.

▶ A rule change: GSA Administrator Terence C. Golden said Oct. 29 there would be two winners instead of one. The players then scrambled to redo their bids, which are about the size of telephone books and — at least for the Martin Marietta team — have cost up to $100 million. The other two teams won't comment on their costs.

▶ Deadline changes: The deadline for submitting bids has been changed from June 30, 1987 to Aug. 24 to Sept. 30 to March 31. Reason for the delays: haggling between the GSA and Congress over how the contract should be structured.

▶ Waffling by bidders: The EDS team dropped out, frustrated by the delays. Now that two winners will be named instead of one,

it says it probably will get back in this month.

▶ Threats and counterthreats: AT&T has threatened to use the 1984 court order that broke up Ma Bell to help bludgeon the Baby Bells from Martin Marietta's team. Martin Marietta has threatened to throw in the towel because two winners will be crowned.

Delays play to AT&T's advantage, competitors argue. Handling 50% of the government's phone calls boosts AT&T sales by $225 million a year. (Profits from individual contracts are proprietary information.) By slowing the process, competitors say, AT&T makes money and keeps everyone else off balance. Consider:

▶ AT&T last year asked U.S. District Court Judge Harold H. Greene to get Martin Marietta to dump the regional Bell companies as partners. The company argued the 1984 agreement that broke up Ma Bell barred the offspring companies from providing interstate switching for Martin Marietta. Ironically, if AT&T wins the contract, it's expected to use the Baby Bells in the same way.

▶ AT&T asked the GSA to delay the original June 30 deadline, arguing that the fine print in the contract didn't allow a regulated company such as AT&T to participate in the bidding.

▶ AT&T unsuccessfully tried to force Martin Marietta to rewrite its bid by asking the Federal Communications Commission to classify Martin Marietta as a "common carrier" — a phone company — because of its link to MCI and the regional Bells.

AT&T denies charges of delay. "It's a bum rap," Linnen says.

Thames has a hard time swallowing that. But Martin Marietta plans to persist. If it wins the contract for FTS-2000, the company hopes to use it as a showcase of the world's first entirely digital phone system. The way it's planned, the system will send voices, computer data and pictures over a single phone wire. It will also have standard phone features such as call forwarding and call waiting. Installing and operating such a huge system would be one way for Martin Marietta to sell itself as an "integrator" of phones and computers to companies, a business that's expected to grow at a healthy clip. Beyond that, money is to be made from government workers' toll calls. While the winner will have to undercut AT&T's present charges, modern equipment should still mean substantial profits for the winners.

Martin Marietta's Thames and AT&T's Golm often run into each other at the GSA. Despite the competition between their companies, the two — who used to be colleagues at AT&T — are still friendly. At one meeting, Golm noticed Thames had a cast on his foot. When he asked how Thames broke it, Thames couldn't resist saying, "You got me so mad the other day, Lou, that I kicked a can, and broke it."

Product

35

Supermarkets Push Private-Label Lines

They Upgrade Brands, Launch New Products

By ALIX M. FREEDMAN
Staff Reporter of THE WALL STREET JOURNAL

You're in the supermarket staring at a blizzard of premium ice-cream bars. "If you like Haagen-Dazs, you'll love me," blares the not-so-fine print of the Gourmet Bar.

This pushy pitch doesn't come from Haagen-Dazs's snooty rivals like Dove, Frusen Gladje or Ben & Jerry's. It's from Pathmark, the grocery chain that makes and markets the Gourmet Bar.

The hard sell is beloved neither by **Pillsbury** Co., parent of Haagen-Dazs, nor by the slew of other companies whose coattails Pathmark rides. But like many supermarkets, Pathmark is turning somersaults to give its store brands an image beyond cheap and chintzy.

Promotional Blitz

For years, store brands and marketing were mutually exclusive concepts. Supermarkets simply plopped their store brands on the shelves, hoping that their price tags alone would attract penny-pinching shoppers. And, in fact, for years that worked.

No longer. As the high-inflation days of the late 1970s and early 1980s fade from memory, price by itself doesn't sell. So private labels are moving uptown to attract new customers. Some supermarket chains are revamping the packaging and quality of their products. Others are courting consumers with every marketing gimmick—"buy one, get one free," trial sizes, cents-off coupons—perfected by the packaged-goods giants whose brands they have always sold.

Still others are going beyond product knockoffs to innovate and beat the national brands at their own game. The first ketchup in Chicago available in a squeezable bottle came from **Jewel** Cos. The first low-calorie yogurt with Nutrasweet in the nation came from **Kroger** Co. And while **RJR Nabisco** Inc. has low-salt Ritz Bits crackers, **Supermarkets General** Corp.'s Pathmark is about to roll out its own *no*-salt version.

"Private label is going past the stage of

Private Label's Declining Share

Private-label sales in supermarkets totaled $16.4 billion in the 12 months ended Oct.7, 1988 — 12.6% of the stores' $130 billion total sales. Here's how that share has changed:

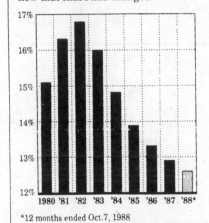

*12 months ended Oct.7, 1988

Top 10 private-label food categories for the year ended Sept. 9:

	SALES (millions of dollars)
Natural and processed cheeses	$1,547.9
Frozen and refrigerated orange juice	699.5
Granulated sugar	676.6
Regular soft drinks	538.0
Lunch meat	520.8
Butter	342.9
Bacon	309.6
Regular coffee	213.1
Peanut butter	207.6
Canned tuna	200.4

Source: Sami/Burke

saying, 'Here it is—it's cheap,' " says John Huffman, senior vice president of **Fleming** Cos., a wholesaler of store brands. "It's becoming more consumer-driven."

Shoppers' confidence in private-label goods certainly appears to be growing. In May, 60% of consumers polled by the Philadelphia-based Consumer Network "strongly disagreed" with the statement that "store brand quality is generally inferior to national brands." Mona Doyle, the firm's president, says, "The second-rate quality image once associated with store brands is being overcome."

But many people in the industry fret that the changes may undermine the brands, whose credo has been better value for less money. Mark Hansen, vice president of **Federated Foods** Inc., which develops store-brand programs for supermarkets, says, "If private label doesn't maintain an unwavering commitment to best value, it will enter the danger zone and become a national brand"—thus diminishing its very appeal to consumers.

Grocers have a clear incentive for upgrading their own offerings: Private-label goods typically cost consumers 10% to 20% less than other brands, but their profit margins typically run 10% to 15% higher. Although store brands have declined to just 12.7% of total supermarket sales from 16.8% in 1982, profit-minded retailers want

to hang on to their remaining share—and perhaps even expand it.

Another force behind the private-label overhaul is cutthroat competition for shelf space. Supermarkets that once let their own brands stagnate for years now kill them outright. Pathmark used to give its private-label items as much as three years to win a following. Now the chain reviews them after six months, the same as national brands. Similarly, **Stop & Shop** Cos. recently introduced and eliminated its version of Gatorade, called Thirst Quencher, in one year. "In the old days we would have hung on for ever and ever," says Richard Ponte, a vice president.

The remaking of store brands also reflects the changing American consumer, whose focus has turned from price to prestige. Black and white generic goods are dying. In one sign of the times, retailers are replacing them with a new breed of products that falls between the old generics and mainstream store lines. These have brand names, more consistent quality and, often, rainbow-colored packaging.

In fact, glitzy packaging has become a key consumer selling point for those store brands that compete head-on with national ones. Several years ago, **Grand Union** Co. hired the design firm of **Milton Glaser** Inc., which will soon complete the overhaul of its store-brand packaging. "We

(cont.)

want to bring private label up from being a poor second cousin compared to national brands to being on a par—not just a cheap imitation," says David Freedman, art director of the Glaser firm.

Indeed, many supermarkets are trumpeting in every way they can that their main store brands are equal, if not superior, to nationally advertised lines. Pathmark now prints nutritional claims on its cereal boxes that precisely emulate those made by leading cereal makers. "Since we have duplicated the ingredients, we're entitled to duplicate the claims," says a spokesman for Supermarkets General.

To build consumer confidence in their brands, private-label purveyors also are going to great lengths to mimic the sometimes expensive marketing techniques of their national rivals.

Fleming is hardly a household name. But not to be outdone by the packaged-goods giants, who pride themselves on being just a phone call away from the nation's shoppers, Fleming is now considering putting an 800 number on all its packaging to field consumer inquiries and complaints. **Spartan Stores Inc.**, another private-label supplier, is embracing a tactic long used by the big boys: "100% satisfaction guaranteed or your money back."

Above all, store brands are wooing the traditional consumers of national brands with all manner of "buy me" incentives. Coupons are just the tip of the iceberg. For example, **Shurfine-Central** Corp., one of the largest suppliers of private-label products, is handing out cookbooks (with recipes featuring Shurfine products) to customers at the 8,500 stores that buy its private-label products.

But the new approaches have perils. Federated's Mr. Hansen worries that the costs of heavy promotions will be passed along to consumers. Others fear that supermarkets will get so carried away with pushing their own store brands that they'll crowd national brands out. (No one knows the hazards of that strategy better than **Great Atlantic & Pacific Tea** Co. When store brands soared to 35% of A&P's sales mix in the 1960s, shoppers, perceiving a lack of choice, defected to competitors.)

Some people in the industry also wonder if supermarkets' newly aggressive approach to their private labels will provoke a backlash from the very giants whose brands they sell. Publicly, most big packaged-goods companies are keeping quiet for fear of straining relations with their retail customers. But privately, there is griping. For example, some argue that Pathmark's unflattering comparisons are misleading. Says a Pillsbury spokesman, "Whatever claims Pathmark may make, we have serious doubts they can meet the quality of Haagen-Dazs."

The biggest risks are with a new generation of premium store lines that are even more upscale than national brands. Several years ago, Grand Union, witnessing brisk sales of specialty imported foods, introduced Laurent, its own line of fancy fare. But selling, not marketing, is a retailer's stock in trade, and the chain has faced a steep learning curve. Initially, Grand Union narrowly avoided a big blunder: It was tempted to induce consumers to try the expensive new imports by offering them at bargain-basement prices. And because Grand Union hasn't hired any Madison Avenue image makers, communicating with consumers about Laurent has been an uphill struggle.

Communication Hurdle

Instead, purchasers of Laurent products draw their own conclusions from point-of-sale materials that read, "Imported Directly for You by Grand Union." Brooke Lennon, a Grand Union vice president, concedes: "We really aren't marketing like a branded company, so it's hard to get the message across to consumers."

Nevertheless, with profit margins higher on upscale than mainstream store brands, many chains are following suit. A&P got into the act this summer when it started rolling out a line of jams, pastas and other foodstuffs called Master Choice, an effort to fill what the company sees as a price gap between costly imported brands and mass-market national lines.

But will consumers pay for the difference? While some shoppers are receptive to the idea, consumer trust in store brands is far from universal. Shopping at an A&P-owned Food Emporium in New York City, Martin Lomazow, a real-estate consultant, says he eschews all private labels because they aren't "appealing to the eye." He adds: "I'm sold on the advertising of the national brands."

Wary, too, is Pat Kotnour, who would seem like an ideal candidate for Master Choice's jams. She doesn't like Smuckers but finds imports too costly. "I would love something that's as good as top quality and costs less," she says. Then, she quickly puts a jar of Master Choice strawberry jam back on the shelf. "But I have been burned by store brands so many times."

36

WHEN QUALITY ISN'T EVERYTHING

What do you do if you build a better mousetrap and no one cares?

BY PAUL B. BROWN

Let's pretend.

Say you and your friends find yourself in a place where there are lots of mice, but not enough cats. What do you do?

Why, you build a (better) mousetrap, of course.

Now that's simple to say, but hard to do. After all, you don't know much about mice and even less about building traps. But you keep at it. You're confident that if you succeed, the world will reward your ingenuity, even though you're out in the middle of nowhere—say, Fairfield, Iowa, a city of 9,200 people who live a good hour and a half from Cedar Rapids.

So you keep fiddling with springs and types of bait, until you finally think you have THE ANSWER. And maybe—in our fantasy, anyway—you do. We'll say *People* magazine hears about your work and calls it the "Best Mousetrap in America."

Heck, let's keep the dream going. Why not have *Playboy* write that in a world of imitation, your mousetrap is the real thing. And as long as we have gone this far, let's go all the way. Let's imagine that while still President, Ronald Reagan—a good midwestern boy himself, after all—discovers your mousetrap and mandates that from now on, yours will be the only mousetrap used in the White House.

If it all came true, it would be better than a Frank Capra movie, wouldn't it? You'd appear on magazine covers; folks would ask you for your autograph; and you'd be frolicking with Robin Leach on "Lifestyles of the Rich and Famous."

Well, if you substitute ice cream for mousetrap you have the oversimplified story of The Great Midwestern Ice Cream Co. *People* did say it made the best ice cream in America. *Playboy* was even more effusive, and President Reagan did serve it at the White House. (Despite reports that he loved the blueberry, here's the real scoop. "Dutch" is a vanilla man.)

So with all this by way of background, you're prepared to hear about how The Great Midwestern Ice Cream Co.—a 12-person manufacturing operation started when the founder couldn't find any decent ice cream in Iowa, a state with more cows than people—rose from rags to riches. From laughingstock to ice-cream laureate, from . . . well, from however else those clichés go.

And Lord knows, we'd love to tell you all about it.

But we can't. By the time you read this, it will be virtually impossible to buy a pint of Great Midwestern. The company is now making ice cream for other people. Out of necessity, it has gone into private labeling.

"What happened was we built our whole marketing campaign around our quality; we put the quotes from *Playboy* and *People* on everything that came out of here, and we discovered quality is just not a positioning statement," says company president Josh Roberts, 33.

That's a bit harsh, but Roberts has a point, one applicable to everyone who knows they have a better product, but are still waiting for the world to beat a path to their door. First off, the word "quality" has been so debased as to be meaningless. Absolutely everyone today promises quality. Second, Roberts's industry makes competing on quality particularly difficult. If people are going to pay $2 a pint for gourmet ice cream—which, roughly defined, has a lot more butterfat and a lot less air than the half gallon you buy down at the supermarket—quality is a given, and rightly so. Häagen-Dazs, Ben & Jerry's Homemade, and Frusen Glädjé all make good ice cream.

So Great Midwestern's sales plan was doomed from the start. "We were coming late to market with what consumers saw as a me-too product," says Roberts. Distribution had been locked up. Häagen-Dazs (owned by Pillsbury Co.) and Frusen Glädjé (Kraft Inc.) had no problems getting shelf space. And after Ben & Jerry's won its highly publicized distribution dispute with Häagen-Dazs, many grocers were willing to stock it, too. But then they shut the freezer case. After all, how much superpremium ice cream could they sell?

Repositioning Great Midwestern was a possibility, but the good images were taken. Häagen-Dazs ads imply that the product is elitist. Serving Ben & Jerry's after dinner tells friends you're hip.

Other options? "Well, given that they make a good ice cream, especially in some unusual flavors like blueberry, I'd forget about national distribution. They don't have the capital," says Mark Stevens, president of The Häagen-Dazs Co. "I'd concentrate on the Midwest, and I'd become a strong regional player."

That, says Jamie Vollmer, Great Mid-

President Josh Roberts, left, and VP Jamie Vollmer
'We were spending all our time on distribution.'

(cont.)

western's executive vice-president, won't work. "If you look at where the superpremiums are strong, it is basically on the two coasts. People in the Midwest are just not going to spend $2 a pint on ice cream. We could own the Midwest and still not have a business."

So we're back to square one, with Great Midwestern finding itself trapped in a box that contains many small companies. The product is fine—maybe even better than the competition's—but not enough people care. There isn't money for a massive advertising campaign, which might help. And selling out is no longer an option. As demand for superpremium ice cream cools, thanks to concerns about cholesterol and the widespread introduction of frozen yogurts, the days of hypergrowth are over—and interest in buying small ice-cream companies melts.

So what do you do?

Turn your marketing plan on its head, say Vollmer and Roberts.

Instead of trying to get people to recognize the name Great Midwestern, they plan to spend the rest of their days hiding their light under a bushel.

It is, they say humbly, a perfect solution.

"We have a great product, but instead of concentrating on that, we were spending all our time trying to get distribution," says Roberts. "By concentrating on the private-label business, we won't have to get distribution. The supermarkets will give it to us, since we will be making the ice cream for them. We won't have to market, because the stores will do that for us, and we won't have to worry about building up a name, because there won't be a name to build up. All we have to do is make great ice cream. The plan capitalizes on our strengths and eliminates our weaknesses."

True. And it would be true for anyone with a great product who is finding sales hard to come by.

Well, maybe almost anyone. At first blush, private-label superpremium ice cream sounds like an oxymoron, something along the lines of cut-rate caviar or no-name champagne. As with any quality product, part of the allure of gourmet ice cream is its snob appeal. The names of Häagen-Dazs and Frusen Glädjé, both made in the United States, were fabricated with just that in mind. How much appeal is something called Acme's superpremium ice cream going to have?

Probably not much, says Roberts. But, he adds, nobody ever said you have to use the store's name. "There are some places—like Marks & Spencer, in London—where everything in the store is private label. There the expectation is since the product carries the store's name, it's the best there is. In supermarkets that are known for having excellent private-label products, we will use the store's name. In places where the store's name is not as good, we'll make one up."

And Roberts has a third option. He's willing to give the store the exclusive use of the Great Midwestern logo within its selling area. In addition to capitalizing on whatever equity the name has, that will allow Great Midwestern to use up all those pint containers it has sitting in the backroom.

If you look at the numbers, the idea of selling private-label superpremium ice cream makes sense for both Great Midwestern and the supermarkets. Let's deal with the company first.

Despite the wonderful reviews, Great Midwestern, founded in 1979, hasn't been profitable since it expanded beyond Iowa. In 1987, its best year—in terms of revenues, anyway—the company had sales of $2.7 million and lost $1.2 million. Last year, Great Midwestern lost $400,000 on about $2 million in sales. By going private label, the company should be profitable, because almost all marketing costs will be eliminated. And without those costs, the company can offer the supermarkets a better price.

Supermarkets like the fact that they can buy cheaper and that there is no middleman to deal with. Those savings should allow stores to make 10% to 15% more on their private-label line, even though it will be sold at a slight discount (see box, "The Private-Label Route," page 119). And as Roberts points out, falling into his sales pitch, the supermarkets can use Great Midwestern's ice cream as the cornerstone for upgrading the image of the rest of their store brands. So far three supermarket chains have signed contracts, although none will talk about its deal.

Will the idea work? Well, there is precedent. Recently department stores have taken to aggressively promoting expensive private-label brands in an effort to increase margins and customer loyalty. But it's one thing to outline the economics of the arrangement; it's another to convince consumers to buy a luxury item with a name no one has heard of.

Still, people keep flying out to Fairfield to talk, and as of this writing Great Midwestern seems confident of signing at least three more contracts by year's end. If that happens, the company expects to show a $20,000 profit on $2 million in sales in 1989. While a 1% margin is not something that causes you to send up fireworks, it sure beats losing money.

But what of the loss of ego involved? After all, the initial dream was to make the name Great Midwestern as famous as Coca-Cola. Under the new plan, the name is guaranteed to remain only in Iowa, where the company expects to continue selling ice cream on its own.

"I never lost a minute of sleep over it," Roberts says. "I want to build a successful company. Selling under our own name, we couldn't do it. This way, we think we can." □

NESTLÉ: New bags push candy in stores; boxes usually are on higher shelves.

Right package is vital to wrap up more sales

By Susan Spillman
USA TODAY

V-8 Juice long has been one of Campbell Soup Co.'s best sellers. But one conspicuous crop of shoppers — yuppies — weren't among those stocking up on the stuff.

Company research turned up that this health-conscious group simply doesn't shop the canned-goods aisle. So Campbell did the only prudent thing: It put V-8 juice in cartons. The cartons, so far available only in the East, got V-8 a coveted spot in the refrigerator section. The results: a 15% jump in sales.

Campbell isn't the only one wooing new customers to old products by putting them in different packages. In fact, says Eric Larson, an analyst at PaineWebber Group Inc., "The way package goods are packaged has never been more important, and smart companies know that."

The reasons: Consumers are demanding more convenience. Today the average supermarket boasts 18,000 brands, all vying for shoppers' attention and money. In addition, since 1980s' consumers are busier,"50% of them will encounter products for the first time on the supermarket shelf without ever having seen any advertising," says Alvin Schecter of Schecter Group, a leading package-design firm.

Among the successes:

■ H.J. Heinz Co. put its ketchup in squeezable bottles 18 months ago and has

> **"** Packaging has become almost as important as the product itself. **"**
>
> **— Campbell Soup Co. spokesman James Moran**

sold more than 70 million.

■ Noxell Corp. brought out its 71-year-old Noxzema skin potion in a pump late last year and found a new market: working women with long fingernails, who don't like opening jars.

■ Nestlé Foods Corp., as part of an overhaul of its Raisinets and Goobers lines, introduced the candies in bags. The famous treats still are available in boxes in movie theaters. But "we put them in bags for stores so that stores would move them lower down on the shelves where people can see them. Boxes get stored on higher shelves," says John Lister, a co-owner of Lister Butler Inc., the New York firm that designed the new bags.

Expect more. Campbell soups in microwave bowls are being tested in Philadelphia, and Swanson TV dinners in plastic microwave trays are being phased in.

"Packaging has become almost as important as the product itself," says Campbell spokesman James Moran.

The Truth About Fats on the Label

SUMMARY: Two lawmakers want to take the food labeling bull by the horns and bring truth to packaging cholesterol and fats. Their bill seeks to clarify the use of saturated fats, a recognized dietary hazard, and to make sure the full nutritional story gets told.

Federal guidelines recommend that Americans lower their cholesterol intake by reducing the amount of saturated fats in their diet, and yet the Food and Drug Administration allows food producers to disguise the amount of those fats their products contain. Packaging labels boasting 100 percent pure vegetable oil suggest the products are healthy, lacking the cholesterol found in animal fats, but some processed foods bearing that claim are made with cheap, artery-clogging tropical oils that contain more saturated fat than does pure lard.

Palm kernel and coconut oils, in fact, contain more than twice the amount of saturated fat found in equal portions of lard. But under current law, those oils can be classified simply under the words "vegetable oil," which may be viewed as a healthier alternative by consumers who do not understand that saturated fat, and not so much dietary cholesterol, is the greatest culprit in raising cholesterol levels in the blood.

Nutrition labeling appears on about 55 percent of all foods found in the grocery store. But even when it does, the information does not necessarily tell consumers what they want to know. As an example, American consumers, who are generally unfamiliar with the metric system, may not understand the amount of ingredients listed in grams or milligrams, says Bruce Silverglade, legal affairs director at the Center for Science in the Public Interest, a nonprofit consumer advocacy organization. Adds El-

len Haas, executive director of Public Voice for Food and Health Policy, "Current food labels not only can promote consumer confusion but at times perpetrate fat fraud."

Pending legislation by Sen. Tom Harkin of Iowa and Rep. Dan Glickman of Kansas, both Democrats, would help end such confusion. The measure would require that "if a food label includes a statement that the food contains a vegetable oil or a statement regarding cholesterol content, then it must provide nutrition information (including, but not limited to, the amount of fat, saturated fat and cholesterol contained in the food) elsewhere on the package."

The bill is the result of the growing concern among consumers, health officials and legislators that the labels on a number of food products do not tell the whole truth. "Manufacturers mislead or unintentionally mislead consumers because some products are marketed on the pretense that they are healthy — using photographs or other images of healthy foods," says Glickman's press secretary, Scott Swenson. "Lots of consumers read labels, but more don't. The thrust of advertising campaigns is health-oriented because manufacturers know that people are increasingly health-conscious."

The American Heart Association has determined that more Americans die of heart disease than of any other cause and has advised that cutting back on salt, fat and cholesterol can have tangible health benefits. "The scientific evidence is very clear," says Virgil Brown, president and chief executive officer of the Washington-based Medlantic Research Foundation and chairman of the association's nutrition committee. "Saturated fat, more than any other single substance in our diet, is clearly linked with hardening of the arteries, the underlying process that results in heart attacks and strokes. We definitely need to reduce the saturated fat intake in the Amer-

ican diet, but we cannot do that unless consumers have all the information about the products they purchase."

By using the vague label, which often lists vegetable oils that may have been included but is not specific, producers also are able to take advantage of price fluctuations in tropical oils. The legislation would require manufacturers to change labels to specify exactly which oils their products contain as well as the share of saturated fat.

Though the FDA has not taken a position on the bill, spokesman Chris W. Lecos says the agency believes current labeling requirements are somewhat outdated and that the agency needs to take a closer look. "The agency's present position is to encourage the voluntary declaration of cholesterol and fatty acid content on labeling," says Lecos. "If a manufacturer decides to state the cholesterol content of a product, the label would also have to tell the amount of polyunsaturated fat and saturated fat."

But urging voluntary declarations is not enough, the lawmakers insist. "Some manufacturers will volunteer because, more and more, they find out that truth in labeling is good business," says Swenson. "But that is by no means an industrywide practice. While some manufacturers may decide that it's good business, the bill would make it mandatory."

Some, however, see the bill as merely a first step and are pushing for the consideration of legislation establishing stricter requirements for the listing of a broader range of ingredients on labels later this year. "We're looking at much broader legislation to cover sodium and fiber labeling because we recognize problems other than just animal fats," says Scott Ballin, vice president and legal counsel for the American Heart Association. "But until then, the Harkin-Glickman approach is a good start."

— *Kristin R. Kurtenbach*

Guarantees at fever pitch

From appliances to antifreeze

By SARA E. STERN

Consumers are basking in a new wave of "satisfaction guaranteed" marketing efforts.

Companies such as First Brands, Whirlpool Corp. and Domino's Pizza are offering free repairs or replacements to dissatisfied customers. While not a new marketing tool, it's a newly popular one.

The latest examples:

Wilson Foods Corp., the largest U.S. seller of boneless hams, next week starts an ad campaign that vows to refund customers' money if they can find a leaner, better-tasting ham.

Next month, Northwest Airlines will guarantee on-time arrivals for flights on its most popular business route—between Minneapolis/St. Paul and Chicago. If flights between the cities don't arrive on time during November (with certain conditions), passengers get a free one-way ticket for their next such trip.

Offering guarantees is a way to set apart products that differ little from competitors' goods, said Donald Schultz, professor of advertising at Northwestern University, Evanston, Ill. Also, it is one way U.S. companies can "emulate the Japanese," who are known to stand behind their products.

"It's become obvious to the American manufacturer that in order to solidify existing position and strengthen itself from the competition, it not only has to talk about quality but offer quality," said Herb Rose, national advertising manager at Whirlpool, Benton Harbor, Mich.

That strategy worked for Victor Kiam, who in his role as TV spokesman for Remington shavers repeatedly has underscored the confidence that led him to buy Remington Products by also guaranteeing customer satisfaction with its products.

Chrysler Corp. Chairman Lee Iacocca also embraced the "personal guarantee" approach as the cornerstone of his efforts to rebuild the automaker.

Some observers credit Mr. Iacocca with helping spur the product-guarantee boom.

"A consumer's perception of a company depends on how the company is marketed," said Remy Fisher, appliance industry analyst at Irving Trust Investment Management, New York. "Because most consumers buy big-ticket appliances from a discount warehouse instead of a brand-specific dealer, they rely on such promotions to distinguish one company from another."

In June, Whirlpool introduced its 100% Consumer Commitment program. It offers a full-year, free-replacement guarantee on any Whirlpool major appliance, including dishwashers, dryers, refrigerators and washers.

Whirlpool is supporting the program with a print ad campaign via D'Arcy Masius Benton & Bowles, Bloomfield Hills, Mich.

Simultaneously, General Electric Co.'s appliance division debuted its Satisfaction Guaranteed program, which gives dissatisfied customers a 90-day refund or exchange option on most of its major appliances.

"We're either very foolish or very confident," GE's print ads from BBDO Worldwide, New York, declare. The campaign stresses that the Louisville, Ky.-based division is not satisfied until its customers are, and says any major appliance can be returned for up to 90 days after purchase, no matter what the complaint.

"We saw a trend in this type of marketing that not only reassures the customer about the product, but at the same time increases sales," said Richard Smith, advertising manager of Eureka Co. The Bloomington, Ill.-based vacuum products company introduced a Double Buyer Protection Offer that allows a consumer to get a free repair or free unit for up to two years after purchase.

"The program hopefully will convince the consumer to spend money on a product that lasts," Mr. Smith said.

Eureka is backing its program through December with a $2 million print and TV campaign from Keller-Crescent Co., Evansville, Ind. The campaign broke in late August.

Because of the low turnover rate for purchases, the appliance industry in particular has embraced the guarantee pitch.

"The key to our offer [is to] differentiate the Whirlpool brand from the competition. And to get there,

(cont.)

we must enhance the consumer's perception of our quality," Mr. Rose said.

Of course, the spell is broken once the competition offers similar guarantees.

"Offering a guarantee is consistent with Maytag's philosophy," said Mr. Rose, who suspects Maytag Corp. is watching the GE and Whirlpool programs in anticipation of starting its own.

A spokesman for Maytag, Newton, Iowa, said there are no plans for a similar program.

There are marketers who are guaranteeing the very products they are supposed to protect.

Danbury, Conn.-based First Brands last month broke a $20 million campaign for its Prestone antifreeze, promising that if the product fails, the company will pay for ra-

diator repairs. **The ads, from Young & Rubicam, New York, announce "the antifreeze so good it actually guarantees your radiator."**

Domino's Pizza has taken to guaranteeing its delivery service. The Ann Arbor, Mich.-based company has broken a TV spot that promises a money-back refund or replacement pizza to any dissatisfied customer and $3 off the price if delivery takes more than 30 minutes (AA, Sept. 7). Group 243 handles.

The new TV spots for Oklahoma City-based Wilson Foods emphasize taste and quality but also mention the money-back offer.

A Sunday newspaper supplement in an undisclosed number of markets nationwide will highlight the guarantee and include a 50¢-off coupon.

"Our emphasis is on taste, but we demonstrate to the consumer that we back up the taste and quality with this money-back guarantee," said Mike Mitchell, account representative at Wilson's agency, Campbell-Mithun, Chicago.

As for St. Paul, Minn.-based Northwest Airlines, its on-time guarantee on flights between the Twin Cities and Chicago applies to both Chicago airports. The program coincides with the start-up of a new hourly shuttle service from O'Hare.

United Airlines, which begins an hourly shuttle between the same cities Oct. 31, has no plans to match Northwest's guarantee promotion.

Saatchi & Saatchi DFS, Minneapolis and New York, handles Northwest.#

Curt Autry in Oklahoma City contributed to this story.

40

What's in a Lifetime Guarantee? Often Value, Sometimes a Catch

By JEFFREY ZASLOW

Staff Reporter of THE WALL STREET JOURNAL

If you bought an L.L. Bean shirt back in 1932 and now realize it's "not you," just return it. Everything the company sells carries a lifetime guarantee.

Customers bring back boots from the 1940s, camping gear from the '50s, duck decoys from the '60s. Not long ago, a man even brought back nothing—and still got a refund.

"All he had was his sales slip," says Kilton Andrew, L.L. Bean's spokesman. "The store's supervisor told him, 'Sorry, if we're going to give you a refund, we'll need the merchandise.' The guy looked him square in the eye and said, 'Sir, that's my problem. What I bought here was a boomerang.'"

The lifetime guarantee is one of the marketing world's strangest, smartest and most enticing inventions. Your Cross pen, Zippo lighter, Fuller brush, and Midas muffler are good for a lifetime. But whose lifetime? Yours? Your children's? The company's? The product's? It's usually open to interpretation, and plenty of businesses close down and disclaim their lifetime promises.

Building Good Will

Still, many companies spend millions of dollars each year making good on their pledges of eternal satisfaction—and they say it's money well spent. Lifetime guarantees breed good will and good publicity. They often increase market share or, when used defensively, stave off competitors with similar promotions. And more companies are discovering that lifetime guarantees can bring in business for other product lines.

The North Face, a maker of outdoor gear and apparel, has a staff of 11 handling about 18,000 returns a year, including tents torn apart by grizzly bears, ski suits damaged in avalanches, and thousands of zipper repairs. "We'll fix someone's old backpack and win them as a customer for life," says Mary Scott, a North Face spokeswoman.

Midas International Corp. dealers don't mind when customers drive up waving their guarantees. After replacing a muffler, "we check the shocks, the brakes, the coil springs—and that often leads to additional work," says John R. Moore, president of Midas. About 17% of the company's repair jobs are to honor lifetime guarantees.

Few consumers hold companies to their lifetime guarantees—especially if products put in enough years of useful service. "If everyone took advantage of our guarantee, we'd probably go broke," confesses William Jones, a vice president of Zippo Lighter Manufacturing Co., Bradford, Pa. As it is, about 250,000 lighters are sent back to Zippo each year for free repair.

If a museum were ever established to recognize the lifetime guarantee, it would feature a devastated assortment of returned products. Norwich, Conn.-based Thermos Co. could donate thermoses flattened by trains or dropped from skyscrapers. Zippo could display the lighter that stopped a bullet from killing a man or the lighter that was swallowed, digested and disposed of by a pig. And A.T. Cross Co., the Lincoln, R.I.-based pen maker, could donate the pen that spanned four of a man's ribs during a head-on auto accident, helping to protect his heart.

In this age of planned obsolescence, lifetime guarantees are refreshing reminders that quality products still exist. But often such guarantees are mere hype, or contain fine-print caveats.

Why spend $1 for postage and handling to send back a Hoan Products nutmeg grater that sells for $1.29? How can the $1 Etona Disposable Stapler be disposable and still come with a lifetime guarantee? What if you move far away from a muffler company that offers a world-wide lifetime guarantee, but only has outlets in one

> **S**OME FIRMS have contingency plans in their guarantees. The president of a toy company advertises a lifetime guarantee—'my lifetime.'

state? And what of the lifetime memberships in home video or health clubs? "A lot of them are fly-by-night," says David Berliner, assistant director of Consumers Union, publisher of Consumer Reports magazine. "You come back a few months later and the video club has become a delicatessen."

Last year, a company making computer paper offered a 400-year guarantee "under archival conditions." Mr. Berliner muses: "If the paper falls apart, your great-great-great-grandchildren can return it." But now, the paper company itself is nowhere to be found. Its competitors, officials in its town and an industry trade group say they don't know what became of it.

Actually, the company may have disappeared just in time. "Under the best conditions, most computer paper starts falling apart after five years," says an executive at a major paper maker.

More durable companies can run into troubles with lifetime guarantees, too. New owners of Gerry Sportswear Corp. must cope with the lifetime guarantee offered by previous owners on sleeping bags and other products that Gerry no longer makes. "It's a continual, complicated situation," says Tim Reed, marketing administrator of Denver-based Gerry. "We do what we can, and we ask people to have equipment fixed elsewhere and we'll reimburse them."

Smart companies have contingency plans in their guaranteees. A Dutch maker of toxic-waste containers offers a lifetime guarantee that would be voided after an atom bomb attack. And the president of a small toy company advertises a lifetime guarantee—"my lifetime."

Learning Annex, an adult-education business in several big cities, is careful which courses get a lifetime guarantee. Its "How to Stop Smoking" and "How to Lose Weight" courses carry the guarantee "for backsliders." Others don't. "A 'How to Find a Lover' course with a lifetime guarantee might have everyone coming back month after month," says Bill Zanker, founder of the Learning Annex.

Inflation muddles some guarantees. Anne Nixon recently found good-for-a-lifetime gift certificates from Marshall Field's, the Chicago department store, in her late mother's old handbag. The certificates—one for $10, two for $5, and five for $1—dated back to about 1942. Ms. Nixon jokes that she hoped the certificates, when adjusted for inflation, would be enough for a new fur. Instead, with just $25 in 1987

(cont.)

funds to spend. she had only enough for a few boxes of her favorite mints.

For a company, one obvious hazard of a lifetime guarantee is that it may limit future sales. Why buy more pens, lighters or umbrellas if the ones you have can always be fixed or replaced? Well, companies aren't foolish. They tend to guarantee products that disappear long before a lifetime has passed. "You keep track of your car, but not your thermos," says Donald Maurice, customer service manager for Thermos Co. "You loan a thermos to someone or you give it to your child, and you never see it again. So you have to buy a new thermos."

Of course, there are always consumers who figure out ways to abuse the privilege of lifetime guarantees. Consider the fisherman who returned a Zippo he found inside a fish. Consider, too, the people who misuse Sears, Roebuck & Co.'s Craftsman tools, then return them.

'It's Going to Break'

"When you're under a car, you use whatever you've got—screwdrivers as pry bars, ratchets as hammers," says Steve Glusman, an engineer from Springfield, Pa. "And if you use a tool the wrong way, eventually it's going to break. So you return it. But I'm not as bad as the people who go to garage sales, buy old Craftsman tools, and take them back for new ones."

Coffman Shenk, 96 years old, knows well the lure of lifetime guarantees. As the world's oldest Fuller Brush man, he first touted Fuller's guarantee in the 1920s. "There are a few people who abuse our company's generosity," he says from his home in Gettysburg, Pa. "They have us replace brushes that are actually completely worn out. I don't argue with them. But if I can't work with them on a reasonable basis, I stop calling on them."

Leonard Dunlap, president of Fuller Brush Co., tells of a woman who recently sent back brushes. "She wrote that the brushes were showing signs of wear and she wasn't happy about it—so what did I intend to do? I didn't recognize the brushes. So I checked and found out that the last time we made them was in the 1920s."

Mr. Dunlap replaced the brushes, but didn't get a thank-you note. "She probably thought I owed it to her," he says, adding that he sometimes gets nervous talking about Fuller's guarantee.

"We'll take returns, no matter how old they are," he says. "But please, tell your readers not to go into their closets and get out all their old brushes."

41

GM Seeks Revival Of Buick and Olds

New Models, Marketing Unveiled In Bid to Redefine Units' Images

By JACOB M. SCHLESINGER
Staff Reporter of THE WALL STREET JOURNAL

"They keep calling it a 'luxury car' and all it is, is a Mercedes. Christ, a Mercedes is like a Buick used to be."
– Sherman McCoy, the bond-trader protagonist of Tom Wolfe's novel "The Bonfire of the Vanities"

DETROIT — Of all General Motors Corp.'s recent problems, perhaps none ranks larger than losing the broad American middle- to upper-middle-class market. Almost all of GM's lost sales in the past three years—one-fifth of its base—have come from its two big aspiration nameplates, Buick and Oldsmobile.

So this year the two divisions are launching high-stakes, high-profile comeback campaigns. Both have sleek new models as part of GM's most expensive new-product program in its history. The cars are accompanied by sophisticated marketing intended to create distinct images out of the haze that now surrounds the brands: Oldsmobile is steering itself toward aging baby boomers tempted by imports and intrigued by technology, Buick toward people who are somewhat older, richer and more traditional.

Halting Reverses

There's a lot riding on these tires. "The turnaround of Buick and Olds is crucial to the future of GM," says William E. Hoglund, the company's vice president for large cars.

If success means simply stemming further sales erosion, the Buick-Olds efforts are likely to reach that goal. Dealers say the cars are higher quality and better designed than anything they've seen from the company. Also, dealers say, GM has become much more responsive to their complaints and suggestions.

But big hurdles remain. In some ways, the new models muddy rather than clarify the divisions' images. The new cars miss much of the family market because they don't yet have four-door versions. And they aren't as technologically advanced as their advertising suggests. The result: Winning back lost territory will be tough. Early sales figures, in fact, are mixed.

The divisions are "now clearly focused on what we want to do," says John R. Dabels, a Buick marketing official. But, he adds, "not all the products and merchandising have been changed yet to be consistent with that focus."

Digging a Hole

GM dug a hole for itself, as company officials see it, by blurring the distinction between Buick and Oldsmobile, and between those cars and other GM lines. "We offered luxury cars, sports cars, compacts that were sporty, compacts that were conservative," says Darwin E. Clark, Buick's marketing manager. "We were almost trying to be everything to everybody."

That wasn't how GM grew to dominate the industry. For a half-century, the company's divisions formed a progression: A customer started with a Chevrolet, switched to a Pontiac if he was flashy, progressed to a more conservative Oldsmobile, and then a more opulent Buick, and finally, if he made it big, landed a Cadillac.

Then came the look-alike era of the early 1980s, when GM downsized its model lines and cut costs by sharing many basic parts across divisions. The changes hurt Buick and Olds more than other GM nameplates. That's because they're supposed to represent status, while Chevrolet is merely efficient transportation.

Not too long ago, "people who had arrived in the middle class bought a Buick or an Olds," says Michael T. Marsden, professor of popular culture at Bowling Green State University in Ohio. Today, he adds, "if someone wants to demonstrate arrival, they'll reach out for different symbols: a BMW, a Mercedes, a Saab, a Volvo."

Buick and Olds together once accounted for nearly half of GM's sales. Now their portion is down to one-third. Their combined share of the U.S. market plunged to 12.4% last year from 20.2% in 1984; in this year's first quarter, as the new marketing effort gained momentum, their combined share edged up to 12.9%.

So, the divisions are trying to modernize and move apart. Oldsmobile is courting the middle-class family that considers itself trendy. It is sponsoring promotions in conjunction with McDonald's and the Star Wars ride at Disneyland. Seeking to reduce its average buyer's age to 45 from 51, it is running ads with the singing group the Four Tops and the slogan: "This is not your father's Oldsmobile."

Buick, meanwhile, mounted a last-minute drive to give its 1988 cars more luxurious details, such as wire wheels on the new mid-size Regal. Its marketing will be "more actively involved with golf," says Mr. Clark. It wants to increase the portion of buyers with annual incomes above $40,000. (The goal is 65% in that category, up from 40% in 1986, the most recent year for which figures are available.)

So much for the promotions. What about the products?

Similar to Taurus?

The Olds Cutlass Supreme and Buick Regal have gotten good reviews from car-buff magazines, and both mid-size coupes differ markedly from their boxy predecessors. In their sleek styling, however, they aren't clearly distinguished from each other—and also seem quite similar to Ford Motor Co.'s Taurus and Mercury Sable models, which were launched two years ago and have hurt GM in the mid-sized market. Another potential problem is the lack of a four-door version in either model—a gap that leaves Ford officials openly relieved. Two years ago, GM decided to delay the sedans' introduction to save money.

Then there's the Buick Reatta two-seat coupe. It, too, has gotten good reviews, and its innovative rounded design attracts attention on the road. But while it carries a Buick price tag, at $25,000, its design seems to fit Olds's "expressive" image rather than Buick's "traditional" one. At a recent internal meeting, workers at GM's Buick-Oldsmobile-Cadillac group headquarters asked why the Reatta is a Buick and not an Olds. Lloyd E. Reuss, GM's executive vice president in charge of cars and trucks responded that "it has a couple of elements that appeal more to luxury. . . . It has a large trunk for a two-seater. It also has a nice ride."

As for Oldsmobile, its promise of high-tech innovation isn't yet fulfilled. It trails competitors on such technologies as anti-lock brakes. A 16-valve engine is optional only on the 1988 Olds Calais and isn't even

(cont.)

available on any other Oldsmobiles; the same type of engine is standard on several Japanese cars.

GM officials acknowledge these obstacles but say the comeback drive could take up to five years. By the early 1990s, Oldsmobile officials say, they expect to be back to a 10% market share, up from 7% in 1987, and Buick officials want to return to 8% from 5.4% last year.

So far, Buick is faring better than Oldsmobile. In the first quarter, Buick was GM's hottest division, with sales growing from the year-earlier quarter at nearly double the industry rate. But Regal sales have been lukewarm, and Buick began offering incentives on the model only five months after it was introduced.

Oldsmobile was GM's slowest division in the first quarter, gaining sales at about one-third the industry pace. But its new Cutlass Supreme is just coming out, so it's too early to tell how that model will fare and how it will affect the division.

Attentive to Dealers

Buick and Oldsmobile dealers are encouraged that the divisions' declines have humbled GM's management into listening to them. The name for the Gran Sport variation of the Regal came from dealer suggestions, as did the decision to give the Reatta all-leather seats.

And Buick officials vow never to repeat a disaster like the 1986 Riviera, which was released even after extensive market research predicted a flop. "Rather than trying to teach customers to buy the cars that we build, we're building cars that the customers want," says Buick General Manager Edward H. Mertz.

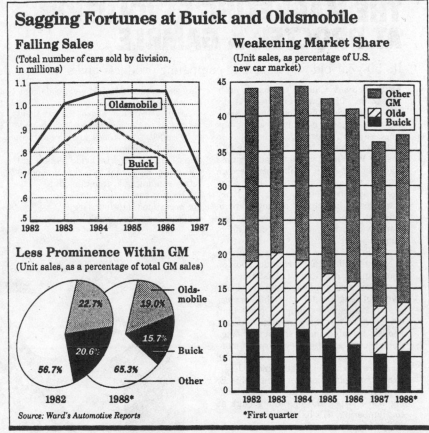

Sagging Fortunes at Buick and Oldsmobile

Falling Sales
(Total number of cars sold by division, in millions)

Less Prominence Within GM
(Unit sales, as a percentage of total GM sales)

Source: Ward's Automotive Reports

Weakening Market Share
(Unit sales, as percentage of U.S. new car market)

*First quarter

An example of both the progress GM has made and the distance it has yet to go comes from Nathan McDowell, a cashier at the Metropolitan Parking garage in San Francisco. He sees many cars every day, and the Reatta clearly sticks out on first sight. "It looks real nice," he says. But when asked if he would recommend buying the car, he responds, "Twenty-five thousand for a Buick? Forget it."

42

THE MARKETING REVOLUTION AT PROCTER & GAMBLE

Its 50-year-old way of selling competing products gives way to a new concept: The category

Procter & Gamble Co. had a problem. Its new, perfumed Camay soap was languishing in the shadow of Ivory, the company's oldest and most successful brand. So in 1931 an executive outlined what became the P&G gospel: Why not pit the brands against one another? Each would have its own internal advocate, and the Camay manager would compete against the Ivory manager as fiercely as if they were in different companies. The brand-management system that grew out of that notion has since been copied by almost every U. S. consumer-products company.

Now the outfit that wrote the book on marketing is rewriting it. Last October, P&G reorganized along category lines. Even reticent Procter calls this the biggest management change in more than 30 years. The reorganization doesn't abolish brand managers, but it makes them accountable to a new corps of minigeneral managers with responsibility for an entire product line—all laundry detergents, for example. President John E. Pepper's goal is to quicken decision-making and sharpen the marketing edge at the lumbering, $19 billion giant.

By fostering internal competition among brand managers, the classic system established strong incentives to excel. But it also created conflicts and inefficiencies as brand managers squabbled over corporate resources, from ad spending to plant capacity. And it often meant that not enough thought was given to how brands could work together.

HOT TOPIC. "That was fine when markets were growing and money was available," says A. Courtenay Shepard, president of Colgate-U. S., which began moving toward a category-management system about four years ago. But now most packaged-goods businesses are growing slowly if at all, brands are proliferating, the retail trade is accumulating more clout, and the consumer market is fragmenting. "There is a growing feeling that marketing needs an overhaul" to cope with this bewildering array of pressures, Shepard says. Adds Andrew J. Parsons of McKinsey & Co.: "Is this a hot topic? You better believe it is. Over the next 5 to 10 years, you're going to see some radical changes in the

way the traditional packaged-goods company organizes itself."

Amid a growing sense that the old approach no longer works, many consumer-goods companies are already reexamining their management structures. Pepsi-Cola Co. used to divide its national soft-drink marketing by sales channel—retail, vending, and fountain. But it recently carved its marketing operations into four large regions with responsibility

for selling to all customers. Campbell Soup Co. hopes that focusing its efforts on ever-smaller geographic targets will give its marketing more punch. "You see a whole series of different ways to cut the job—by menu segment, franchise, category, geography," says Marc C. Particelli, a senior vice-president at Booz, Allen & Hamilton Inc. "Everyone's

ROBERT DE MICHELL

BEFORE AND AFTER

ADVERTISING
P&G advertises Tide as the best detergent for tough dirt. But brand managers for Cheer started making the same claim in ads that were pulled after the Tide group protested. Now a category manager decides how to position Tide and Cheer to avoid such conflicts

BUDGETING
Brand managers for Puritan and Crisco oils competed for a share of P&G's ad budget. But a category manager might decide that Puritan could benefit from stepped-up ad spending to publicize its new formula, while Crisco can coast on its strong market position for a while

(cont.)

searching for the way right for their business."

Under P&G's new approach, each of its 39 categories of U. S. business, from diapers to cake mixes, will be run by a category manager with direct profit responsibility. Advertising, sales, manufacturing, research, engineering, and other disciplines will all report to the category manager. The idea is to devise marketing strategies by looking at categories and fitting brands together rather than coming up with competing brand strategies and then divvying up resources among them. And instead of having managers from the different functions work together only on special projects, the system should allow for more coordinated marketing on a regular basis.

The move stems in part from a continuing drive by Pepper and Chairman John G. Smale to streamline the management of a company notorious for its memo-passing bureaucracy.

P&G officials won't discuss the reorganization, and its final shape is just now emerging. But interviews with former executives and company-watchers reveal that the measures reflect a growing sense of uneasiness. As Smale told employees in a P&G newsletter, "our historical way of managing Procter & Gamble's business no longer fits well the company that we are today nor the business environment in which we must compete."

The company that sold the first heavy-duty synthetic laundry detergent (Tide) and the first fluoride toothpaste (Crest) is finding it harder to come up with true product innovations. Now, says one former P&G executive, "you can't rely on product news to provide growth." At the same time, a torrent of competing new products is hitting supermarket shelves. Since 1979, for example, the number of detergent brands has increased from 27 to 46, while unit sales

are up just 17%, according to SAMI/Burke, a market researcher.

Instead of simply demonstrating a performance edge, such as less dandruff with Head & Shoulders or drier babies' bottoms with Pampers, P&G must hone its marketing strategies. Now one experienced category manager will follow each line of business and decide how to coordinate each brand.

The approach is already resulting in some sharp breaks with P&G orthodoxy, under which minor line extensions were heresy. Now, if there's a marketplace gap in mouthwash, for example, the response might be the quick launch of a peppermint-flavored Scope. Such flexibility, notes Gordon Wade, a Cincinnati marketing consultant, contrasts with the old approach of "having brand managers competing for positionings, and some guy up the line refereeing." That referee might well be overwhelmed with personnel issues, environmental matters, and any number of other responsibilities.

'LUNACY.' The managers of P&G's eight bar soaps, for instance, squabble over who gets to use the word "clean" in ads. "You're apt to get better marketing by saying 'How am I going to separate these brands?' as opposed to arbitrating these disputes," says one ad-agency executive on P&G accounts. Under the new structure, P&G can also recognize more easily that all its brands aren't equal and marshal resources accordingly. In the past, says Donald Baker, Procter's retired package-design chief, brand managers for Tide, Cheer, and Era might all come to him at the same time wanting a new package right away. "It's a costly thing," he says. "Nobody gets a good job."

Perhaps most crucial, P&G's shift to category management, by easing the fierce internal rivalry among brands, should refocus its marketers' attention on what other companies are up to. While that might seem elementary, P&G has suffered some of its worst reverses because it didn't pay enough attention to its rivals. Most notable was the flop of Encaprin, a coated aspirin P&G launched in 1984, just as consumers were blitzed with new, nonaspirin painkillers.

There's plenty of skepticism about P&G's moves, of course. The company has long been infamous for its slow, centralized decision-making. A former brand manager for Prell, for example, says it took a year and $50,000 in market research before he was able to get approval for a flip-top cap on the shampoo. Critics suggest that the creation of category managers will further clog an already slow-moving system. "It's lunacy," says one former P&G executive. "Every other company is reducing man-

P&G'S MARKETING SHIFT

PACKAGING

Brand managers for various detergents often demanded new packages at the same time. Designers complained that the projects were hurried, and nobody got a first-rate job. Now the category manager decides which brand needs a new package first

MANUFACTURING

Under the old system, a minor detergent such as Dreft had the same claim on P&G's plant as Tide—even if Tide was in the midst of a big promotion and needed more supplies. Now a manufacturing staffer reports to the category manager, helping to coordinate production

(cont.)

agement levels. Procter is going in the opposite direction."

But the company hopes that the category approach, together with some other, little-noticed management changes, will help shift decision-making down the ranks. In the wake of disappointing returns on some of its investments in the 1980s, such as troubled forays into cookies and orange juice, P&G has recently been trying to make its managers more accountable for profits. Category managers will be paid in part on the basis of their financial results. That marks a distinct change from P&G's long-held credo that if managers concentrated on gaining volume and market share, the profits would surely follow.

And on July 1 the company took decision-making authority away from its highest-ranking body, the administrative committee, which numbers about 40 people and met every Tuesday at 10 a.m. to ratify all significant promotions and spending plans. Instead, a 20-member executive panel will meet weekly to deal with only the most important issues. Other decisions, probably including some expenditures that the administrative committee would previously have had to approve, will be made by lower-ranking staff, including category managers.

INSTANT RESULTS. It's still too early to tell how well the shift will work for P&G. But similar moves at Colgate already are paying off. After adopting its category approach, for example, Colgate decided that the company had more detergent brands than it needed and reduced the number it sold from seven to four. Instead of overlapping, each brand now has a distinct market position, Colgate's Shepard says.

Because its marketing managers now have some control over other functions, such as finance, research, and manufacturing, Colgate says the new system promotes better-planned, faster new-product launches. "By surrounding the marketing people with these multidisciplinary skills, we make them instantly effective," says Shepard, a former P&G executive. Colgate recently went national with one result: its Fab 1 Shot detergent and fabric-softener packet. The product "went from my head to a national launch in 11 months," Shepard says. "We accomplished something in a time frame we never could have in the past."

It seems unlikely that Procter's new structure will have quite as many imitators as its pioneering brand-management system did. For one thing, rivals have discovered in recent years that they sometimes can outfox the Cincinnati giant. But if P&G succeeds, their huge competitor will be a lot more agile.

By Zachary Schiller in Cincinnati

43

New Kinds of Beer to Tap a Flat Market

Brewers Hope Niche Products Will Buoy Sales

By Marj Charlier
Staff Reporter of The Wall Street Journal

Once upon a time there was beer, plain and simple. Then Miller Brewing Co. introduced Lite, and the industry hasn't been the same since.

Now, the market is being flooded with new products—dry beers, draft beers, light beers, red beers, seasonal beers and pale ales. And, brewers say, the rising tide isn't expected to ebb any time soon.

"Until recently, the brewers' attitude was 'if God wanted us to brew a different beer, Granddaddy would have done it,'" says Robert Weinberg, professor of marketing at Washington University and a former Anheuser-Busch Cos. executive. Now, he says, beer makers are acting more like packaged-goods companies, constantly developing new products to try to lure young consumers and keep older ones.

This new look is a response to a stagnant market, which has turned beer selling into trench warfare. In the past year, per-capita consumption of beer declined while the overall market, which totals about $16 billion, rose a scant 0.6%. "In a flat market, we have to do what we can to keep our own drinkers and steal someone else's," says Craig Guthrie, brand-development manager for Adolph Coors Co.

The 'Family' Approach

Recognizing that consumers want choices, brewers are expanding product lines as never before. Instead of fretting that new labels will cut into old brands, they are focusing on their overall "family" of labels. Some are even dabbling in non-alcoholic drinks to hedge their bets.

"We believe that a national brewer needs to have a brand out there for every consumer," a Miller spokesman says.

Anheuser-Busch, the nation's largest brewer, is testing Budweiser Dry in six markets and O'Douls, a no-alcohol beer, in five markets. It is also introducing a combination draft-light beer, Busch Light, in three states. G. Heileman Brewing Co., a unit of Australia's Bond Corp. Holdings and the fifth-largest U.S. brewer, is testing

the waters for dry malt liquors with its new Colt 45 Dry and will add Lone Star Dry to its list of dry regional beers soon.

Miller, a unit of Philip Morris Cos., is trying out Miller Genuine Draft Light in a few cities. Corona drinkers soon will be able to squeeze limes into Corona Light. And while it won't be specific, Coors said it has a couple of new brews slated for test markets shortly. The company already has extended its line with Coor's Extra Gold draft, George Killian's Irish Red and a new super-premium, Herman Joseph's.

The new-brand trend started in 1973, with the runaway success of Miller Lite, which lifted Miller from the seventh-largest brewer to a strong No. 2 spot. Other brewers then sought superstars in a cluttered market. The hottest newcomers: draft beers, which are cold-filtered instead of pasteurized, and dry beers, which have less sugar and less aftertaste.

The overnight success of some new labels has brewers fantasizing about catching lightning in a long-neck. Rainier Dry, Heileman reports, has captured an astounding 4% of the Seattle beer market in just five months. Frank Walters of Impact International, which publishes industry magazines, says he "wouldn't be surprised" if dry beers corral nearly 5% of the U.S. market in the first full year.

The product craze also comes from a packaged-goods credo that brewers have begun to accept: that a brand can be hot for only so long before consumers get bored. "It's true with most consumer products and certainly true with beer brands," says Mr. Guthrie of Coors, which has seen its once-highflying flagship beer slide for the past several years. "It may even be true of Budweiser," he says.

Indeed, while Budweiser accounts for one in every four beers consumed in the U.S., the beer's annual growth slowed to less than 2% last year from 5% in 1986, analysts estimate. That's one reason the brewer is introducing Bud Dry, analysts and competitors say. "They are realizing Budweiser is reaching a plateau," says Mr. Walters of Impact. "They also realize the dry category is going to boom."

Anheuser contends Budweiser isn't in trouble. "It not only dominates the premium segment, it's damn near all the category," says Budweiser group brand manager Tom Sharbaugh.

Regardless, dry beer is helping Anheuser-Busch steal some thunder from Miller's hot new draft category. "They took the top spin off [Miller] Genuine Draft," says Ian Crichton, senior executive vice president at Heileman. Now Miller must decide whether to follow Anheuser

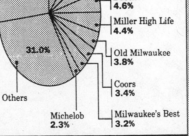

Battle of the Brewers

The Top Brands
Share of U.S. beer market in 1988

Budweiser 27.0%
Miller Lite 10.3%
Bud Light 5.1%
Coors Light 4.9%
Busch 4.6%
Miller High Life 4.4%
Old Milwaukee 3.8%
Coors 3.4%
Milwaukee's Best 3.2%
Michelob 2.3%
Others 31.0%

Per Capita Consumption
In the U.S.; in gallons
(chart from 1960 to '88, ranging 14 to 26 gallons)

Source: Impact American Beer Market Review and Forecast 1989

(cont.)

with a dry. A Miller spokesman says the company is studying dry beer. "We're not sure it's a lasting segment," he says.

Likewise, Anheuser says it doubts packaged drafts will become a strong category. Yet draft sales have been hefty enough that the big brewer is testing its own incarnation, Busch Light, in Missouri, Illinois and Longview, Texas. The company is playing down the draft aspect of the beer and emphasizing instead that it is a light version of its popular Busch, the nation's fifth-largest-selling beer.

Up until now, breweries would never have marketed two premium beers whose appeal might overlap, much as Bud Dry might appeal to Budweiser drinkers. But today, brewers don't see that as cannibalizing established products, they see it as modernizing them, says Mr. Weinberg. Miller, he says, brought out Genuine Draft in 1986 to pick up slack from its sagging premium brand, High Life.

Brand extensions are also a way for brewers to reach out to younger consumers, who drink more and aren't yet set in their ways. Mr. Crichton says that in Chicago, Heileman's Old Style Dry is bringing a new cachet to the company's Old Style beer, which is struggling to hold on to its market lead there as young people move to imports and trendier light beers. Some 70% of 21- to 25-year-olds there have tried dry beers, while only 40% of those over 25 have, surveys show. "We're all looking for that edge over the competition to penetrate the young-adult market," Mr. Crichton says.

Despite the success of drys and drafts, some think the new-product strategy has its limits. Brand proliferation will continue, says Emanuel Goldman of Paine-Webber Inc. in San Francisco, but there are only so many varieties on a theme. "Now you've got Bud Dry, you aren't going to get barbecue-flavored Bud Dry," he quips."

Furthermore, Mr. Goldman notes, it's very expensive to brew new brands. Brewmasters aren't cheap; neither are the package development, equipment, advertising and marketing needed to develop a new beer. "What we do is very capital-intensive," says Coors's Mr. Guthrie.

Giants Have an Edge

For smaller brewers, "it's not much fun" to compete in this new environment, Mr. Goldman of PaineWebber says. Miller, for instance, budgeted $37 million in 1986 for ads to introduce Genuine Draft, dwarfing the $4.2 million that Pabst Brewing and the $14.6 million that Heileman spent on all their advertising that year.

Some brewers are looking elsewhere for growth. Coors plans to test-market a bottled water soon, and the company is putting more emphasis on its ceramics business. **Stroh Brewery** Co. has come up with a successful alcohol-free fruit and sparkling water mix called Sundance.

Within the beer market itself, brewers don't predict any slowdown in new-product proliferation, at least for a while. But if consumption stays flat, each new brand will split the market into tinier segments. "Most brewers have tremendous unused capacity," says Budweiser's Mr. Sharbaugh. "Any new brand that can help fill that volume will be looked at, and that means smaller and smaller niches."

44

Fast Game

Intel Introduces a Chip Packing Huge Power And Wide Ambitions

It Hopes New Microprocessor Can Keep Firm Dominant Amid Swarms of Rivals

Its Lawyers Guard the Fort

By Brenton R. Schlender

Staff Reporter of The Wall Street Journal

SAN FRANCISCO—Things move fast in the world of high technology, even when you're on top.

Intel Corp. held a glitzy coming-out party yesterday for its latest gee-whiz product—a thumbnail-sized sliver of silicon called the 860. Packing a million transistors and crunching data five times faster than its nearest competitor, the 860 is, for now at least, the world's most powerful microprocessor chip.

It also is Intel's belated entry into a new high-tech sweepstakes to supply the chips that act as the brains of technical workstations, the fastest-growing and most performance-hungry segment of the computer industry. Originally designing a chip simply to help personal computers draw three-dimensional graphics, Intel in less than two months repackaged the product as a general-purpose microprocessor and, in the process, took back the high ground in the performance battle. Intel was in such a hurry to announce the 860 that Andrew Grove, its chief executive, wasn't on hand because of a previous commitment.

Still a Horse Race

Intel's scramble to unveil the 860 is but the latest example of how the microprocessor business is still a horse race even for the company that dominates it. Although the Santa Clara, Calif., company has methodically built a lucrative near-monopoly supplying the chips that act as the brains of most personal computers, it has been beset recently by a swarm of newer, faster chips that threaten to supplant Intel's as the industry's technological pacesetters.

Meanwhile, an army of Intel lawyers is struggling to protect that near-monopoly, by going to court to prevent other chip makers from illegally copying Intel's most popular circuits and by trying to cut short longstanding technology-sharing agreements enabling other competitors to make them legally. Moreover, Intel is still smarting from a stumble late last fall, when it realized too late that it had built too many of its most profitable chip, the 80386. The miscalculation has stalled Intel's growth for two quarters now and has led some analysts to grumble that it got carried away in its aggressive drive to dominate the microprocessor business.

"The big question is, 'Can Intel maintain its monopoly when it is the nature of the marketplace to attack monopolies?'" says Richard Shaffer, a computer industry analyst who publishes Technologic Computer Letter. "It's a difficult job, and to do it Intel has to keep its foot on its competitors' throats."

Noting the turmoil, Mr. Grove says: "We're in a key technological position, and all this conflict is a sign of that. People don't attack a loser, do they?"

Intel is in that key position largely because of Mr. Grove's efforts. A Hungarian emigre and a chemical engineer by training, he was the architect of Intel's audacious strategy to dominate the industry. He also is the driving force behind Intel's other controversial strategy of competing directly in the markets of its own best customers, by selling add-in boards and complete computer systems as well as chips. In the process, Mr. Grove, who has been known to publicly excoriate employees, has reshaped Intel as a reflection of himself—very quick and very aggressive.

Not long ago, Intel was the chip industry's biggest loser. For 1985 and 1986, it reported operating losses totaling nearly $200 million amid the industry's worst slump and deep price cutting by Japanese memory-chip companies.

Major Turnaround

Since then, however, Intel has been anything but a loser. It has been perhaps the biggest beneficiary of a boom in computers and chips. It earned $452.9 million last year, up from $248.1 million in 1987. Revenue last year more than doubled to $2.87 billion from $1.27 billion in 1986. (The stock rose 50 cents yesterday to $25.50.)

Intel rebounded by getting out of the memory-chip business that it pioneered in the 1970s and concentrating on making microprocessors. It had a head start. In 1980, in what Mr. Grove calls "earned luck," International Business Machines Corp. chose Intel's 8088 microprocessor to serve as the heart of its new line of personal computers and, by mid-decade, the PC industry had standardized around IBM's design. Even during the slump, Intel and several chip companies licensed by it to help it establish the 8088 as a standard were cranking out microprocessors by the millions.

Recognizing that the PCs would continue to be the fastest-growing segment of the computer industry, Mr. Grove and his top marketers in 1985 hit upon a strategy of developing more powerful versions of its standard chip, versions that only it could make because it held the patents and copyrights. That so-called sole-sourcing strategy would enable Intel to reap all the profits from its technology and enable it to dictate the direction of future computer designs.

So, in 1985, Intel developed the 80386, a chip that until recently was the most powerful microprocessor around. Designed to be compatible with Intel's earlier models, yet novel enough to avoid being covered by previous licensing agreements with other chip makers, the 80386 would allow Intel to, in effect, corner the market for high-performance microprocessors. That, in turn, would allow it to charge as much as customers would pay—more than $250 a chip, against the $50 to $75 commanded by its previous-generation 80286 chip.

"Sole-sourcing has been absolutely the key to Intel's success," says Drew Peck, a Donaldson Lufkin Jenrette analyst. "Without sole rights to the 80386, Intel would look just like Advanced Micro Devices Inc. and National Semiconductor Inc.," two big Silicon Valley chip makers that never fully recovered from the 1985-86 slump.

Also benefiting from sole-sourcing was another big microprocessor maker, Motorola Inc. It has a similar, though smaller, monopoly supplying the 68000 family of microprocessors, which power Apple Computer Inc.'s Macintosh personal computers and a variety of engineering workstations made by Sun Microsystems Inc., Hewlett-Packard Co., Apollo Computer Inc. and others.

But however lucrative, sole-sourcing causes problems. It puts a lot of pressure on the manufacturer to be able to provide adequate supplies of reliable chips. It also requires that the manufacturer assiduously protect its design with patents and copyrights so competitors can't easily copy the chip. Finally, a single supplier has difficulty judging the size of the market.

Although 80386 chips were hard to come by in 1986, Intel managed to build up its production quickly enough to hold onto its customers. And Intel appears to have locked up the design of the chip well enough to discourage the quick cloning of the 80386. But last year, it did have trouble discerning true demand for the chips.

(cont.)

As Intel's chip plants finally hit full stride last fall, it abruptly found itself with a glut of 80386 chips. Apparently, wary customers had ordered too many chips, just to be sure of having enough. Once it became clear Intel could meet demand, they quit ordering so many.

"What were we supposed to do, second-guess our customers?" Mr. Grove asks. "I'd a lot rather have too many chips than turn customers away. Besides, these things don't rot on the shelf." Now, he says, orders have picked up, and the glut is easing.

Price Umbrella

Sole-sourcing creates another anomaly. Although the lack of competition enables Intel to hold its prices higher longer, it also creates an artificial price umbrella that beckons rivals to come in with competing chips—either clones of Intel's or others that may not be compatible with Intel's but are cheaper and/or more powerful.

So far, rivals haven't found a legal way to copy the 80386, but several, including Advance Micro Devices and Chips & Technologies Inc., apparently are trying. Other companies, however, are striving to leapfrog Intel.

In 1987, Sun Microsystems, with the help of Fujitsu Ltd.'s U.S. chip subsidiary, introduced the SPARC chip, which incorporated a new chip design called reduced instruction set computing (RISC). The new chip promised three to five times the processing power of the 80386 at a comparable price. To help it sell the chip to other computer manufacturers, Sun lined up five other chip makers, including Texas Instruments Inc., Cypress Semiconductor Inc. and LSI Logic Corp.

At about the same time, MIPS Computer Systems Inc., another tiny Silicon Valley chip company, introduced its own RISC chip, which will be made by various companies. And shortly thereafter, Motorola weighed in with its 88000 RISC chip. Both chips could calculate circles around the 80386. The only handicap the three upstart chips faced was that they couldn't run software written for computers using Intel's chip; instead, they used American Telephone & Telegraph Co.'s Unix operating system.

Nevertheless, Intel found itself upstaged. At first, Intel reacted by calling RISC microprocessors a passing fad and said its next-generation conventional chip, called the 80486, would hold its own. (The 80486, another impressive, million-transistor chip compatible with the 80386, will be introduced this spring.) But after computer-industry heavyweights such as IBM, Digital Equipment Corp. and Hewlett-Packard Co. announced RISC-based computers, Intel's arguments didn't hold up.

A Change in Plans

Since 1986, Intel's own engineers had been working on a specialized RISC processor to be used as an "accelerator" to plug into PCs alongside its conventional 80386 to boost its number-crunching capacity and improve its graphics. Then called the N10, the new chip would be the most complex, most powerful processor chip ever built, but Intel didn't plan to sell it as a general-purpose microprocessor.

Not until last December. Then, Intel started showing the chip to its best customers. "We had our own marketing story for the chip, but our customers changed it," Mr. Grove says. "They said, 'Listen, this isn't just a coprocessor chip. This could be the central processor of a super-technical workstation.'"

By mid-January, Intel officials concluded that the N10 gave them a chance to charge into yet-another new market for Intel microprocessors, the fast-growing workstation arena. So, they abruptly junked their original marketing plan for the N10, ordered development of support chips and software necessary to make it a general-purpose processor, and started planning yesterday's big announcement to position the N10—now called the 860—to compete with the other new RISC chips.

"You've got to hand it to Intel, once they decided to go ahead with a RISC microprocessor, they went all the way," marvels Michael Slater, a chip-industry consultant in Palo Alto, Calif., who publishes Microprocessor Report. Although he says programming the chip is so difficult "it would be a great challenge for puzzle fanatics," he concedes that the 860 will help Intel "regain respect" as a maker of high-performance microprocessors.

Intel's new 860 is a big threat to competing RISC chips designed by Sun Microsystems and MIPS Computer Systems, which are manufactured by a variety of American and Japanese chip makers. Indeed, several Japanese companies have licensed either the Sun or the MIPS chips in hopes of gaining a foothold in the microprocessor business, a market in which, so far, they haven't done well. To a lesser extent, the 860 also competes with Motorola's RISC chip.

Legal Battles

Meanwhile, Intel lawyers may well have their hands full battling chip makers trying to clone the 80386. A recent federal-court ruling in Intel's bitter, five-year battle with Japan's NEC Corp. resulted in a split decision, upholding Intel's copyright of crucial features of its microprocessors but conceding that there are legal, albeit dauntingly difficult, ways to replicate those features.

"It definitely can be done," says Thampy Thomas, the president of Nexgen Microsystems, a San Jose, Calif., company trying to build a seven-chip processor set compatible with the 80386 for use in its own computers. "But it will be extremely difficult to make a compatible chip that costs as little to produce as Intel's chip."

Mr. Grove professes unconcern. "I never said it couldn't be done, but if somebody does come out with a compatible part, our lawyers will be all over it."

Earlier this month, Intel's lawyers got a temporary restraining order against ULSI System Technology Inc., of San Jose, after a police raid turned up confidential Intel documents that Intel contends were used to illegally design a popular support chip for the 80386. ULSI denies any wrongdoing, but the police investigation is continuing, and the court order effectively halted ULSI's plans to market the chip.

Officials of both NEC and ULSI accuse Intel of using litigation to unfairly thwart competition, a charge that riles Intel's chief counsel, F. Thomas Dunlap. "We flatly do not use litigation as a marketing tool," he says. "My job is to get an appropriate return for Intel's intellectual property rights, every last one of them. If we develop it, we should profit, and nobody should be able to simply copy it."

—Peter Waldman contributed to this article.

45

Small Pioneers In HDTV Bet On a Head Start

By Jeffrey A. Tannenbaum
Staff Reporter of The Wall Street Journal

NEW YORK—The prospect of high-definition television conjures up images of giant corporations, billions of dollars and global battles. But the nascent HDTV industry consists of little companies as well as big ones.

Unlike **Sony** Corp., **Hitachi** Ltd. and the other major players moving into the field of super-clear video, these small companies are mostly in the U.S. And more important, unlike the Japanese giants, the small, specialty companies are betting everything on a single technology previously untested in the marketplace.

"The major risk is that if you've hung your career and reputation on an idea that sinks, you may sink with it," says David Niles, the president of **Eleven Twenty Five Productions** Inc., a New York pioneer in high-definition programming.

At least three other companies also have jumped into the HDTV business as niche players. **Rebo Studio**, based in Manhattan, is typical. The company has invested more than $4 million in HDTV production gear, says Barry Rebo, president. With 40 employees and about $3.5 million in annual revenue, Rebo produces HDTV programming and is developing a line of specialty equipment for HDTV production. Other entrants include **Zbig Vision** Ltd. of New York, and **Powder Moon Productions** in Provo, Utah.

These little entrants are a reminder—a disturbing reminder, perhaps—that large U.S. companies have been slow to take up the potential HDTV challenge posed by Japanese electronics firms. Moreover, the smaller firms are welcomed by the Japanese players, because several of them are working on programming, or so-called software, which nicely complements the television sets and studio hardware that the large producers are focusing on.

As such, the smaller companies offer a look at the symbiotic relationship between big companies and start-ups that often characterizes the early stages of development in a new technology.

"These companies have taken significant risks in order to become front-runners," says Jeff Cohen, the product manager for high-definition video systems at Sony Corp. of America, a unit of Tokyo-based Sony. These pioneers, Mr. Cohen says, are valuable Sony customers not only because they buy its production equipment, but also because they promise to be effective "ambassadors" in introducing the technology to others.

The potential rewards for such ambassadors are huge: big reputations, rapid sales growth and the chance to make a mark in business history. High-definition television, an infant industry today, could become a major source of consumer entertainment, industry growth and jobs in the 1990s, with revenue from such things as TV sets and video production equipment totaling as much as $20 billion a year by the turn of the century.

But the risks are also great when a small company stakes its future on costly new technology. If a company chooses the wrong technology, its money will be wasted. Even if it picks the right technology, timing is crucial: Early entrants may still be struggling to pay for their equipment when much better models hit the market, giving later competitors an edge. "We may end up as the pioneers with the arrows in their backs," quips Denis Bieber, Rebo's chief executive officer.

Eleven Twenty Five says its HDTV business moved into the black recently, after a two-year start-up. But because of the high cost of entry to HDTV, Rebo—which turned to the technology in 1986—is still in the red and says it expects to stay there at least two more years. The technology is developing so fast that much of Rebo's HDTV equipment, which it had initially planned on amortizing over five years, grew obsolete in less than two years. Now Rebo must lay out money for a newer, even costlier generation of equipment.

"We don't regard this as losing money," says Mr. Bieber, who owns the company along with Mr. Rebo and Tomio Taki, a Japanese investor. "We regard it as investing in the future."

So-called high-definition TV sets—with a screen shape and picture quality akin to movies—are still far from the consumer market in this country; industry predictions place their arrival anywhere from three to 10 years in the future. By investing heavily in the new technology now, Eleven Twenty Five and Rebo aim in the short term to win production contracts—for making movies, music videos, TV shows and commercials—that might otherwise go to companies still wed to older technologies. The two companies also are building libraries of their own HDTV programming. They hope to be sitting on a trove of such programming when HDTV

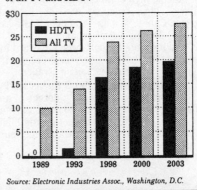

Video Forecast
Estimated retail value, in billions of dollars of all TV and HDTV

Source: Electronic Industries Assoc., Washington, D.C.

sets finally reach consumers' homes.

Rebo, which was founded in 1975, "has always been involved in the newest video technologies," Mr. Rebo says. "You have the greatest competitive advantage if you move in first and move in quickly."

At Eleven Twenty Five, Mr. Niles says he has risked his future on new technology several times. In 1977, for example, he embraced a tape format not widely adopted until about four years later. He was also a pioneer in special-effects equipment and computer graphics. With an initial 1985 investment of $900,000 that has since grown to more than $4 million, HDTV is his biggest gamble, he says.

A payoff is beginning to materialize, the companies say. With limited success, they have persuaded Madison Avenue and other clients to produce HDTV programming now, even though consumers wouldn't benefit yet. The advantage in picture quality is lost when high-definition programming is "down-converted" for showing on ordinary TV sets. The plus side is that these HDTV tapes wouldn't become obsolete when consumers switch to high-definition sets.

Meanwhile, with HDTV, shooting costs are reduced at least 15% to 20% compared with film—more if there are a lot of special effects, for which HDTV is especially useful. In one Rebo demonstration tape, the sexy woman on the video monitor appears to be dancing through a spacious art gallery with paintings nearly as big as she is. In fact, she was standing on a 15-square-foot mat inside a studio. The "gallery" consisted of postcard-size pictures tacked onto cardboard.

To hold down their risk and keep income flowing, both Rebo and Mr. Niles have continued to operate facilities for conventional TV programming. Mr. Niles

(cont.)

says he will sell his conventional facilities, based in Paris, this year, with proceeds to be invested in HDTV operations.

Rebo's high-definition work began with music videos, such as one for the rock group Cameo's song "Candy." More recently, Rebo's "Performance Pieces," a 10-minute comedy short, won an award for best fiction short at this year's Cannes International Film Festival in France.

To find new applications for its HDTV technology, Rebo is working dozens of angles—trying, for instance, to persuade museums to record their collections on high-definition tape for insurance and other purposes.

Increasingly, Rebo is also focusing on HDTV-related hardware as well as programming. It is taking various manufacturers' equipment, such as Apple computers, and customizing systems of its own. At the National Association of Broadcasters show in Las Vegas, Nev., in April, Rebo showed off four innovative products: a camera-control system, an optical transmission system, a computer-based "framestore," for isolating single frames of programming, and a down-converter for changing high-definition computer graphics into conventional TV format. Rebo has begun to sell some of these.

As Rebo sees it, these smaller companies are getting in on the ground floor of what will be a gigantic industry. Rebo's picture of the future is much wider, after all, than just the wider TV sets. Rebo also foresees, for example, high-definition picture telephones and high-definition computer peripherals.

In the absence of short-term profits, Rebo for now, is settling for recognition. In beating others to the trade show with such products, Mr. Rebo says, the company "showed up a lot of much bigger American companies. We even showed up some bigger Japanese companies." A wide, clear and bright future, he reasons, is sure to follow.

P&G Moves To Revamp Its Pampers

By ALECIA SWASY
Staff Reporter of THE WALL STREET JOURNAL

The diaper that made disposable a household word is about to be changed.

Procter & Gamble Co., keenly aware that Pampers has lost a startling chunk of market share, isn't talking. But people close to the consumer-products company say a new, improved Pampers—along with an expensive ad campaign—will come before year end.

"They say they have to do something," says Bonita Austin, analyst with Wertheim Schroder & Co. "Pampers isn't No. 1 anymore," adds Hugh Zurkuhlen of Salomon Brothers, "and that disappoints them."

Pampers is now the underdog, and making a comeback will be tough. Its share of the market has eroded to about 26%—down from 59% in 1980 and down from 75% in the mid-1970s. Huggies, meanwhile, the rival brand made by **Kimberly-Clark** Corp., has grabbed 31% of the market, up from a mere 9% in 1980.

Some analysts claim that P&G, after making early improvements in super-absorbency, essentially ignored Pampers. Kimberly-Clark, meanwhile, hasn't stopped tinkering with Huggies in recent years. Both products are about the same price, but Huggies has been aggressive in making changes such as softer elastic and in advertising those improvements.

"Procter fell asleep too long with Pampers," Mr. Zurkuhlen says.

Yet another reason for Pampers' decline is a sibling rivalry with Luvs, also made by P&G. Luvs' share has grown to 24% from 11% in 1980, largely at the expense of Pampers. Luvs Deluxe, diapers with strategic lining designed in a boys' version and a girls' version, has been particularly successful. But in bringing out Luvs, the company wanted to create a premium segment; it hadn't intended to rob Pampers of sales. And even with Pampers and Luvs together, P&G's diaper market share isn't what it used to be.

On top of everything, the diaper market is relatively flat, with sales steady at about

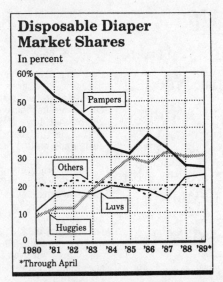

Disposable Diaper Market Shares

In percent

Pampers

Others

Luvs

Huggies

1980 '81 '82 '83 '84 '85 '86 '87 '88 '89*

*Through April

$3.5 billion a year.

The new Pampers is likely to include one or more improvements. It may be thinner or have better-sticking tape fasteners. Or it may include "cuffs" that block leakage around the leg openings.

Cincinnati-based P&G already sells cuffed diapers in Japan, but Huggies has beat them to the U.S. Earlier this year, Dallas-based Kimberly added a strip of cuff-like material inside the leg openings of its Huggies Supertrims. The material acts as a dam to stop leakage. The diaper, available in a few Western states, is expected to be launched soon nationwide.

The new Pampers is bound to trigger a diaper battle. "We'll probably get another marketing war," with both P&G and Kimberly-Clark advertising heavily and offering lots of coupons, says Jack Salzman, analyst with Goldman, Sachs & Co. Prices could also come down.

Kimberly-Clark won't comment, but marketing specialists say Huggies isn't going to yield ground easily. "Huggies has got a lot of momentum going already," and that will only increase with the new cuffed product, predicts Lynne Hyman, analyst with First Boston Corp.

Meanwhile, both Pampers and Huggies face the challenge of coming up with biodegradable diapers to answer growing environmental concerns. **RMed International** Inc. of Sedona, Ariz., claims its diaper is more than 90% biodegradable, compared with 60% for most disposable diapers.

P&G disputes RMed International's claims of a superior product. Still, it may soon begin test marketing in Europe a diaper that has corn starch, an ingredient found to speed disintegration of plastic.

Speeding Up

Manufacturers Strive To Slice Time Needed To Develop Products

They Cut Bureaucratic Cycles And Use Suppliers More To Compete With Japan

Honeywell Inc.'s 'Tiger Team'

By John Bussey
And Douglas R. Sease
Staff Reporters of The Wall Street Journal

A few years ago, Xerox Corp. executives were stunned to learn that Japanese competitors were developing new copier models twice as fast as Xerox and at half the cost. Its market share eroding, Xerox faced a painful choice: either slash its traditional four- to five-year product development cycle or be overtaken by more nimble competitors.

Today, after a sweeping reorganization and millions of dollars of investment, Xerox can produce a new copier in two years. But that still isn't as fast as some of its Japanese competitors, who have also quickened their pace. "We'll be 30% more efficient by 1990," promises Wayland Hicks, Xerox executive vice president.

Quality in U.S. industry may be up and costs down, but American companies like Xerox are still getting sideswiped by foreign competitors who get new and improved products to market faster. The edge those competitors get from shorter development cycles is dramatic: Not only can they charge a premium price for their exclusive products but also they can incorporate more up-to-date technology in their goods and respond faster to emerging market niches and changes in taste.

'The Next Battlefield'

"It's the next battlefield," says Vladimir Pucik, a University of Michigan business professor who has studied product cycles in the auto industry. "The game the Japanese [auto makers] are going to play is to leave the Americans [building] well-engineered but boring and obsolete cars."

Now, U.S. manufacturers of all stripes are scrambling to shorten their development cycles and be the first to market at home and abroad. To do that, they are attempting to break out of old, stratified ways of developing new products—methods that, up to now, have left them uncompetitive. The Big Three auto makers, for instance, all recently formed task forces to cut ponderously bureaucratic development cycles that have swollen to nearly five years. The Japanese, by comparison, can design and build a new car in a little over 3½ years.

Some of the "innovations" U.S. industry is using to close the gap are really just common sense by any other name. A couple of years ago, for example, General Motors Corp. management was puzzled by a huge testing backlog at its Milford, Mich., proving grounds. The backlog was delaying entire car projects, so GM called in consultants. They found that drivers were completing a full test cycle to check just a handful of parts. Why not double the number of parts tested on each run? the consultants asked. That done, the backlog quickly shrank.

'Business Discipline'

"We're not talking about rocket science here," acknowledges James Rucker, who heads a GM group searching for ways to trim lead-time. "We're talking about business discipline."

Similarly, Allen-Bradley Co., a unit of Rockwell International Corp., recently abandoned its old, "sequential" method of developing new industrial controls. Under that approach, the marketing department handed off an idea to designers, who drew up concepts they then passed on to product engineers. The engineers, working in virtual isolation like everyone else, built a batch of expensive prototypes and then handed one off to the manufacturing department, which had to find a way to build the new product.

Now, all of Allen-Bradley's departments work together to find—from the start—a design that fits both the customer's demands and the company's manufacturing capability. Results have been striking: Allen-Bradley recently developed a new electrical contactor in just two years. It would have taken six years under the old system.

Honeywell's 'Tiger Team'

It is often desperation, not enlightened planning, that drives U.S. industry to shorten development cycles. Until recently, Honeywell Inc. required four years to design and build a new thermostat. Then a customer, worried about the delay, threatened to take its request for a new climate-control device to a competitor. In response, Honeywell set up a special "tiger team" of marketing, design and engineering employees and gave it carte blanche.

"We told them to break all the rules but get it done in 12 months," says John Bailey, a Honeywell vice president and general manager. The team did.

Such innovations can turn old-line companies upside down. The Big Three auto makers, for example, have all adopted "parallel engineering" programs similar to Allen-Bradley's, scrapping their traditional sequential approach. "It's a whole change in philosophy," says Donald Mullaney, the manager of development of medium and large four-wheel-drive cars at Ford Motor Co. "We've got to teach our engineers to get involved upstream, to learn to be predictive."

Indeed, the auto companies provide a good case study of how U.S. industry is tackling the development-cycle problem. For years, the car companies decreed public taste, often cranking out one million cars of a single design in a year. Management regularly changed designs at the last minute—incurring huge retooling costs—and let stylists run free.

In one moment of excess, the Chrysler Corp. design shop ordered up a fin for the middle of the trunk lid on an early 1960s Plymouth. "It was a magnificent fin, a fin like this," recalls Stephan Sharf, former head of manufacturing, running his hand high into the air. There was just one problem: No stamping machine could press it, so factory workers would have had to weld the fin by hand onto each car. At the last minute, recalls Mr. Sharf, Chrysler scrapped the idea.

Such reverses were common. Until 1981, in fact, Chrysler's manufacturing group wasn't even represented on its product-design committee. That might explain why, in the past, the company regularly raised program budgets by 25% to 40% to cover expected midstream changes.

By contrast, Japanese auto makers have long designed with an eye toward production. At Honda, for example, stylists generally don't craft door panels that require more than four operations by a stamping press to shape them. (In the U.S., intricate designs often require six, seven or eight operations.) And at Honda, the concept of all departments working together is old hat. The company even has a nickname for the resulting discussions—"wai-gaya," loosely translated as "hub-bub."

Japanese Firsts

The benefits of this approach: Up to

(cont.)

now, Japanese auto makers have needed only half to two-thirds the number of engineering hours that U.S. companies require for comparable car projects, estimates Kim Clark, a professor of business administration at Harvard University. Consumers in the U.S. have seen the difference in Japanese firsts—for instance, 16-valve engines offered as standard equipment.

Now, rapid market segmentation is forcing auto companies to design more cars than ever, making speedy development cycles increasingly critical. Ford, Chrysler and GM are responding with strategies of their own, and all essentially incorporate the same truth: A lot of headaches can be prevented by planning ahead, sticking to decisions and working as a team.

The push for shorter cycles is evident in each phase of the development process. In design and engineering shops, engineers are building early "math models" of vehicles on computer-aided design systems. This reduces the need for laboriously crafted clay mockups and the construction and testing of dozens of prototypes. Now, says Donald Atwood, GM vice chairman, you, "in effect, only build a clay model to validate your aesthetics."

These computer designs—which contain detailed specifications—also help the factory get a head start on tooling production equipment. (Previously, it had to wait for design engineers to take measurements from clay mockups and pass those specifications on to manufacturing.) Simultaneous, or overlapping, engineering like this, for example, recently saved Chrysler two weeks in the tooling stage of a new midsized car program, according to John D. Withrow, executive vice president of product development.

Problems With Bumpers

Americanized "wai-gaya" also is helping save time on the factory floor. A few years ago, for example, Chrysler suppliers ran into problems making the complex three-tone bumpers the auto maker wanted on its cars. That quickly backed up manufacturing, so Chrysler management handed down an edict: no more car designs with bumpers in more than two tones. To avoid such problems in the future, the company is increasingly moving manufacturing personnel into offices with the engineers designing the product, instead of having the two groups work in isolation.

At the same time, the auto makers are awarding more contracts to trusted suppliers without a lengthy bidding process. These suppliers, in turn, are doing more design work for the Big Three, speeding information over common computer systems rather than waiting for dog-earred blueprints to arrive in the mail.

In another effort to streamline production, Ford has halved the number of suppliers it uses in North America, keeping only the ones who don't pose quality problems. It, like other auto makers, is also relying more on suppliers to do time-consuming assembly work. A Dana Corp. division, for example, now delivers "subassemblies" of an entire power system—including axles, drive shafts and transfer cases—for Ford's Tempo and Topaz four-wheel drive models. Before, it just sent axles.

The auto makers claim such changes have pushed development cycles below five years, and some say that segments of the cycle are now comparable to Japanese efforts. GM's Chevrolet-Pontiac-Canada group, for example, has squeezed 14 weeks out of its cycle by getting the finance and engineering departments to review designs at the same time, instead of sequentially, says Gary Dickinson, the director of engineering. He contends efforts like this already have helped cut engineering costs on an average project 35% since 1986.

Beautiful But Inefficient

Faster isn't always better, of course. GM got its Fiero to market ahead of other low-cost, two-seat sporty cars, but with an engine prone to bursting into flames. And the new gospel isn't yet fully reflected in products now on the road. At Chrysler, Richard Dauch, the head of manufacturing, taps a pointer impatiently against a photo of one of the company's 1988 luxury cars on his office wall. It takes 10 separate stamping operations to form the car's intricate fender, which complicates the manufacturing part of the development cycle. "That design is beautiful, but it's inefficient," Mr. Dauch says. "We can't live with that in the future."

Clearly, the pressure is on the auto industry in general to fix this sort of problem quickly—and find other ways to catch up with the Japanese. Donald Smith, an auto-industry expert at the University of Michigan, says the world's inefficient car companies will have to cut current development-cycle time by a further 25% to 33% and development costs by 50% to keep pace with the top auto makers five years from now.

"Whenever the last bell rings and we've fought the last round," he says, "this is going to determine who won and who lost."

Place–Channel Systems and Physical Distribution

Recording Firm Makes a Name With the State of the Art

Telarc's Success Shows the Benefit of Turning to a Different Distribution System

By PETER PAE

Staff Reporter of THE WALL STREET JOURNAL

After seven years of making "vanity" records financed by star-struck amateur musicians, Jack Renner launched his own recording company. His aim: using technical innovations to snare serious audiophiles.

But Mr. Renner immediately hit a snag. "Record stores wouldn't touch an unknown label," he recalls. In many industries glutted with small independent brands, newcomers face agonizing obstacles to winning precious shelf space in established outlets.

Mr. Renner's response shows how an entrepreneur can solve this problem by exploiting his company's special strength—in this case, using state-of-the-art technology—and turning to a different distribution system. In the end, the entrepreneur even won over the record stores.

Mr. Renner's strategy helped make his privately held Cleveland concern, Telarc International Inc., a leader in high-quality recordings of classical music, now mainly on compact disks. Started in 1978, the company says its sales reached $1 million a year in 1982, and have soared to $20 million a year since. Earnings are also rising, the concern adds.

Lost in the Shuffle

But it wasn't a soaring success as it tried to peddle its wares through standard record stores 11 years ago.

Record stores tend to buy CDs and LPs from major recording companies, which act as distributors for most of their own labels. Smaller independent labels must rely on an independent distributor that may be pitching several dozen other companies.

"It's difficult for small labels to break into record stores," says George Balicky, vice president of National Record Mart, a record chain in the Midwest and East. "There is a glut of small labels, so they are more likely to get lost in the shuffle."

Therefore, Mr. Renner turned to another channel: audio equipment stores. There, the high-end Telarc records met a marketing need. Audio stores sold expensive audio equipment but could point to few records that could take full advantage of the equipment's capabilities. Many gladly stocked Telarc records along with their fancy equipment. "We put audio stores in the software business," says Mr. Renner.

Grammy Awards

The audio stores didn't offer a huge mass market, but they did allow Telarc to sell records and develop its reputation year by year. Telarc has won 17 Grammy awards since 1980. Last February, the company captured four of five awards in the classical field including classical producer of the year. In the process, it beat out recording giants Polygram Records, owned by N.V. Philips, and CBS Records, a unit of Sony Corp. Indeed, audiophiles happily fork out an extra dollar or more per recording for Telarc's premium image.

The technical reputation helped Telarc sign up some of the most famous orchestras, such as the Berlin Philharmonic and the Boston Symphony. Telarc President Robert Woods says the company constantly scouts the electronic industry for cutting-edge recording equipment. "We're fanatical about it," adds the 54-year-old Mr. Renner.

Telarc introduced digital recordings of symphonic music in the U.S. in 1978, was a leader in offering CD titles in 1983, and issued the first CD with music not released initially on a long-playing record.

The emphasis on technical quality paid off handsomely in 1983. Sony, with its new product—the compact-disk player—asked Telarc to produce CDs to be distributed with the equipment.

"It was very important for the launch that not only did we have the hardware but the software to demonstrate and impress the listener of a CD system," explains Marc Finer, who was a Sony official involved in launching the CD player in the U.S.

Telarc's Mr. Wood adds: "Sony helped by getting Telarc's name out there. By the time the CD was established in the U.S., we had established good customer recognition." Compact disks now constitute 34% of all recordings sold, while long-playing records make up only 8.5%. (LP singles, cassette tapes and CD singles represent the rest of the market).

Telarc is still small by recording-industry standards. It records only a dozen or so new titles each year. Of 10,500 compact-disk classical recordings on the market, only about 100 carry the Telarc label.

(Among its more popular titles: "Beethoven or Bust.")

Yet, the company has snared more than 8% of the classical-recording market. "Our strategy from the beginning has been to get right in there and compete with the major recording companies," says Mr. Renner. "But there is a danger of getting too big, so we are careful to control the number of titles we put out each year."

Betting on DAAD

While working on the cutting edge of technology obviously has paid off, it has a drawback: Competitors eventually catch up and the company must take new risks to stay ahead. Now the company is sticking its neck out with a major venture: producing cassette tapes with a new recording technique called DAAD (for digital audio analog duplication).

The move involves a significant risk because DAAD competes with another technology, digital audio tape or DAT, which has been touted as the next-generation audio system. But the recording industry, concerned that DAT technology will encourage pirate recordings, has threatened to sue DAT manufacturers if their equipment intended for consumers is sold in the U.S. No manufacturer has yet challenged the threat and DAT equipment is available to consumers only on the "gray" market.

While DAT equipment uses smaller tapes than those found in standard cassettes, a DAAD tape doesn't require new equipment; it is a regular cassette tape that integrates a new recording technique. Telarc began limited introduction of DAAD tapes last year. They now contribute about 10% of the company's revenue.

"Our typical CD buyer is a cassette user," explains Mr. Renner. "Many of our customers now record material from CD on blank cassettes. With DAAD tapes we're providing the same customer a cassette source similar to CD."

Still, some industry experts say DAT will eventually make its way to the U.S. and make regular cassettes obsolete, a prospect that could hurt Telarc.

Whether or not DAT is introduced in the U.S., Telarc doesn't seem worried. "I don't think the DAT is a threat at all to the cassette tape," Mr. Renner maintains. Anyhow, he adds, "we can always enter that medium if it becomes a viable product here."

Coke Unveils Compact Dispenser, Hoping To Sell More Soft Drinks in Small Offices

By BETSY MORRIS
Staff Reporter of THE WALL STREET JOURNAL

ATLANTA—Coca-Cola Co. is mounting an assault on that venerable office institution: the water cooler.

Coke, naturally, would rather see employees gathering and gossiping around a Coca-Cola dispenser. So the company is introducing a compact machine, called BreakMate, that chills water, carbonates it, mixes it with Coca-Cola syrup and dispenses it into a 6½-ounce cup.

The soft-drink giant has been test-marketing BreakMate in small offices in 30 U.S. cities and overseas. It is now starting a national rollout of the machine, to be completed by the middle of next year. Coca-Cola won't say how much it has spent on BreakMate, the result of a project that started nearly 20 years ago. The company says only that the machine is one of the most expensive research and development projects it has ever undertaken.

'Giant Leap'

W. Andrew Harvill, director of packaging and distribution development for Coke's fountain-sales division, says BreakMate "takes a giant leap forward" by enabling the company to reach places that are too small or unprofitable for a regular vending machine. "This could do for Coke what the microprocessor did for computers."

That's a grand vision, but some competitors aren't overly concerned. "It's interesting," says an executive at another big soft-drink company. "We're watching it. But it isn't something I ask my guys to report on every week."

Although Coca-Cola denies it, some soft-drink specialists believe BreakMate is a forerunner of a dispenser that will one day provide Coke, like tap water, in the home. "This is a Mr. Soda unit," says Jesse Meyers, publisher of the trade publication Beverage Digest. Mr. Meyers says he knows of five other big-name companies currently developing similar machines. "This is the opening salvo in home soft-drink distribution—Cola Wars III."

BreakMate is part of Coca-Cola's age-old strategy of making its soft drinks available in every possible nook and cranny of the world—"within arm's reach of desire," as the company's longtime chief executive officer, the late Robert W. Woodruff, used to say. The theory behind the strategy: If it's there, people will drink it.

"With soft drinks, there is no pucker factor, as there is with juice," says Mr. Meyers. "And there are no ill effects, as there are with alcohol. If it is available, it will be consumed." As evidence of this

strategy's success, soft-drink consumption surpassed water consumption in the U.S. two years ago and now stands at about 45 gallons a person per year, according to some industry estimates.

But many workplaces have been largely untapped by soft-drink companies. A soft-drink vending machine is only profitable where there are at least 45 employees, according to Coca-Cola's research. As a result, the more than one million offices around the country with fewer than 45 workers have no ready access to soft drinks. Even in many big offices, vending machines are a long walk or an elevator ride from many departments. But Coke says BreakMate can be profitable in offices or departments with as few as five workers.

Coke isn't the first soft-drink company to try to reach smaller offices. Two years ago, PepsiCo Inc. introduced 24-can mini-vending machines that can be mounted on a wall or sit on a countertop. "It has been a healthy business for us," says a Pepsi spokeswoman. But it hasn't exactly run away with the market. The small ma-chines have increased by 10% Pepsi's overall vending business, which itself accounts for 10% of the company's total soft-drink business.

Pepsi says it hasn't tried to introduce an office fountain machine such as Break-Mate because of "issues of sanitation, service, mixing and maintenance," the spokeswoman says. "How will you get over those hurdles of having volunteers operating that equipment?"

Attempts by several other companies to crack the market have failed either because they required office workers to mix their own syrup and water or because distribution of just a few cans to many places was too cumbersome, recalls John Farquharson, president of Araserv, a food service concern that distributes coffee and refreshment services to offices.

Syrup Canisters

Coca-Cola believes it has solved those problems. BreakMate, which is about the size of a microwave oven, contains three disposable canisters of syrup, each with enough for about 31 drinks. The machine also holds a cartridge of carbon dioxide good for about 250 drinks. These containers, which snap into place, can be replaced by office workers when they run out.

If the machine can't be connected to an outside water supply, it can be fitted with a water tank. BreakMate does all the measuring, mixing and dispensing. Workers either put coins into the machines or have the soft drinks paid for by their employers.

The machines are made by a West German appliance company, a joint venture of Robert Bosch G.m.b.H. and Siemens AG, and Coca-Cola provides the soft-drink syrup. BreakMates are being distributed by BreakTime Enterprises, a Coca-Cola spinoff, through office coffee services, bottled-water operators, vending companies and bottlers, who regularly visit offices.

Araserv, one of its largest customers during the test-marketing, says its customers have been pleased. They've even accepted what might not fit into every office decor: the bright red Coke logo.

Little Publisher Has Big Ideas on Where To Sell His Books

* * *

Chain Stores Aren't the Place For Nick Lyons's Wares; Try the Auto-Parts Store

By Sanford L. Jacobs
Staff Reporter of The Wall Street Journal

For Verlyn Klinkenborg it was a dream come true. The New York Times raved about his first book, "Making Hay," a 160-page paean to family farming in the American heartland. It was the kind of review that sends people flocking to bookstores. But in this case, few would-be readers could find it.

"Making Hay" was published by Nick Lyons Books in New York, the type of small specialty publishing house that is all but ignored by the nation's big retail book chains. But Nick Lyons, the company's founder and president, has a knack for finding other outlets for his books.

Take the NAPA Auto Store in Rock Rapids, Iowa. Why an auto-parts store stocks a stack of books on hay farming is easily explained. "Verlyn is a nephew of mine, of course," says the store's owner, Kenneth K. Klinkenborg. To give folks in Rock Rapids an opportunity to buy the book, Mr. Klinkenborg used to drive 32 miles to Sioux Falls in his pickup truck to buy copies, paying the full $14.95 retail price. It didn't bother him that he didn't make a cent reselling them to his customers. "I'm just trying to get as many books sold as I can," he explains.

Fishing for Profits

When Mr. Lyons got wind of this, he offered to sell Mr. Klinkenborg copies at 40% off the cover price, even if he ordered only six books. The arrangement pleases the author's uncle, who says, "We sold about 10 or 15 already, and they let me make a little money, too."

So it goes in the backwaters of book publishing, where 15,000 small publishers stay afloat, or even turn a comfortable profit, by catering to quirky or limited interests and doggedly pursuing every last sale. They operate with a gritty resourcefulness unheard of—and unnecessary—at the 300 or so big trade-book publishing houses that produce roughly 60% of the 50,-000 new titles appearing each year.

"The most serious problem for a small publisher is persuading the chains to open an account," Mr. Lyons says. But chain stores have little incentive to buy 50 or 100 copies of a single title from outfits such as his. John Dessauer, the director of the Center for Book Research at the University of Scranton in Pennsylvania, explains: "The cost of opening an account for one title is going to be more than any profit from the book."

Nick Lyons

Yet small publishers provide a rich variety, printing books on odd subjects, giving unknown authors a voice and resurrecting out-of-print titles. Howell Book House Inc. of New York has been successfully publishing books about dogs for 26 years. Its mainstay is a line of 60 books, each devoted to a different breed. "We are the Tiffany of dog publishing," says Sean Frawley, the president.

A Rare Blockbuster

Occasionally, a tiny publisher hits pay dirt. Ten Speed Press in Berkeley, Calif., published "What Color is Your Parachute?" in 1972. The career-planning book became a runaway best seller a few years later and still sells briskly.

Nick Lyons Books hasn't yet produced a blockbuster. But then, most of the roughly 20 new titles it brings out each year concern fishing or the outdoors—books that, Mr. Lyons concedes, "few others are interested in publishing."

The people who publish Sidney Sheldon or Judith Krantz aren't gnawing their knuckles because Mr. Lyons beat them to "Angling Entomology: A Primer for Fly Fishermen." But Mr. Lyons has been successfully publishing such fare for more than 20 years, first for other publishers and, for the past four years, as head of his company. Though revenue was a meager $447,000 for the year ended last March 31 and is headed toward $800,000 in the current fiscal year, his company hasn't run in the red or needed to borrow.

For Mr. Lyons fishing is more than a publishing specialty, more than a pastime he writes about gracefully in a column in Fly Fisherman magazine. When it comes to fishing, he says, "I am a lunatic."

The $100,000 seed capital to start his company came from seven well-heeled fishing cronies who are minority stockholders. Mr. Lyons owns 51% of the stock; ac-

tive partner Peter Burford, 31, who joined him after a stint at Crown Publishers Inc., also holds an interest.

Publishing so-called backlist books that are kept in print for years on end has some advantages over publishing best sellers. A good fishing book will never match a Jackie Collins novel in total sales. But it will outlive her racy fiction, with its fickle readers. Publishers will dump most of this year's best sellers on "remainder" tables next year, where they may fetch as little as $1 apiece.

Nick Lyons doesn't put any of his titles on the remainder heap because most just keep on selling. A number of Nick Lyons books have sales increases each year "without any work on our part," he says. He adds, "It's like having an annuity, and each year's new titles are added to the income stream."

Occasional clinkers do creep in. A $5.95 paperback parody of university literary reviews has sold a paltry 250 copies since 1984, leaving 3,250 unsold and about $3,500 in unrecovered costs. "This isn't the kind of mistake we could afford to make every day," says Mr. Burford, who is responsible for production.

Small publishers can turn a profit selling as few as 1,000 copies of a book. They operate with a frugality unknown at big publishing houses, whose annual lunch tabs could keep a small firm going for a year. The printing and promotional budget for all 16 new books in the Nick Lyons spring catalog is only $65,000. A big house spends that for one book deemed to have modest sales potential, and spends millions more for a blockbuster.

A typical author's advance from Nick Lyons Books is $1,500, a sum that "would embarrass a big house," Mr. Lyons says. But it means the writer is eligible for royalties that much sooner. "Our authors earn money as their books earn money," he says.

Mark Sosin, the author of more than a dozen fishing books, says that although he has received heftier advances for books published by big houses, they didn't sell as well as those published by Nick Lyons. "Anybody can publish," Mr. Sosin says. "Marketing is another story. Nick has come up with some unusual marketing ideas."

The University of Scranton's Mr. Dessauer, a veteran industry observer, agrees. "The trade-book publishers don't know what to do with specialized books," he says. "Often they only market to the bookstores, and if the stores don't buy a book, the hell with it."

(cont.)

It is not in Nick Lyons's nature to shrug off sales. Twenty years ago, while working at Crown Publishers, he realized that bookstores weren't the best outlets for fishing books. As a result, 95% of the books bearing his logo (a trout leaping over the firm's initials) are sold elsewhere: in fishing-tackle stores, mail-order catalogs, and, of course, that auto-parts store. The "L.L. Bean Fly Fishing Handbook," which has sold some 30,000 copies and is in its 12th printing, is his best-selling title.

"We try to use common sense," Mr. Lyons says. "We ask ourselves who will be interested in these books." For "Grizzly Country," it was readers of Bear News, a publication of the Great Bear Foundation in Missoula, Mont. The foundation used an excerpt of the book in its newsletter, which has 3,000 subscribers. Later, Mr. Lyons arranged for the foundation to buy the book at wholesale to resell to its members. Lance Olsen, the foundation's president, says: "It sells good. It's a classic."

At times, Mr. Lyons departs from formula, as when he published actress Rita Gam's memoir, "Actress to Actress," last fall. The manuscript, rejected by other publishers, found its way to him at a time when he was seeking something different. "I think you can do too many fishing books," he says.

Miss Gam made the rounds of the talk shows, including the "Today Show," to plug the book. And it became the first Nick Lyons book to be carried by the B. Dalton chain. It has sold more than 3,000 copies, is in its second printing and has made money for both publisher and author.

Miss Gam is happy. Of Nick Lyons Books, she says: "They did anything a larger publishing house could do for me." The book, she adds, led to her first movie role in years, in the upcoming thriller "Twisted," starring Sally Kellerman.

But with hindsight, Mr. Lyons thinks the book was too far afield for his company. "We don't have the flash to do justice to this kind of book," he says. "And we don't want to have the flash."

51

WHY SOME BENETTON SHOPKEEPERS ARE LOSING THEIR SHIRTS

With the Italian manufacturer expanding so fast, its U.S. licensees' problems are multiplying

Alex Robertson, Liliane Scallan, and Nita C. Fanning are not Benetton success stories. In February, Robertson closed his two Benetton sportswear shops in Bend and Medford, Ore., after struggling for more than two years to turn a profit. Scallan was forced out of business after a competing Benetton store opened across the street from hers in Hartford. Fanning was unable to make money because Benetton's representative insisted on locating her outlet in a Waco (Tex.) mall that didn't attract an affluent clientele. "They grossly oversold us and then put us in the wrong location," she says.

These experiences are the first public signs of trouble in the U.S. for the fast-growing Italian chain. Since Benetton owns few stores, it relies on independent licensees to sell its merchandise. But as the company has steamrolled its way across the U.S., some store owners have prospered while others have been crushed.

Dissatisfied licensees complain that Benetton has stuck too many stores too close together, that U.S. operations are poorly organized, and that it is difficult to reorder goods once a selling season begins. Company officials admit problems exist—caused either by inexperienced licensees or normal growing pains.

LITTLE ITALY. The tale of how Luciano Benetton and his three siblings built their worldwide fashion empire from a small town near Venice is the stuff of business legend. Since 1965, more than 4,500 Benetton stores have sprouted up around the globe to sell the Italian manufacturer's colorful brand of knitwear and cotton apparel. For 1987, Benetton Group is expected to report a 20% increase in profits, to $108 million on roughly $1 billion in sales, up 16% over 1986. The growth of Benetton in the U.S. has been no less spectacular. In eight years the company has expanded from 2 to 730 retail outlets, which produce 15% of the company's total sales.

Benetton's licensees pay no fees or royalties. Instead, they agree to sell only Benetton-made goods through one of several standard store formats. Startup costs can top $200,000, and a store can make a nice profit if its sales volume exceeds $200,000 a year. Licensees are selected by one of Benetton's 14 U.S. agents. These company representatives show new collections to store owners every six months and earn a 4% commission on orders they place.

The agents have been crucial to Benetton's rapid expansion in the U.S., its most important market outside Europe. But some store owners say the agents are also part of the problem. Linda N. Dossey, a commercial real estate broker in Boise, Idaho, is in litigation in Superior Court in Seattle, with Benetton's Minneapolis agent, Azzurra Corp., over four Seattle outlets. In a counterclaim to a suit brought against her by Azzurra, Dossey alleges the agent misled her about the profitability of the already existing stores. Only after she took possession, she says, did she discover those outlets were losing money. Azzurra sued her for $200,000 in inventory it claims she sold but never paid for. Dossey counters that the losses she incurred as a result of misrepresentations by Azzurra exceeded that amount.

'GREEDY.' Other licensees complain that some Benetton representatives are hard to reach when problems come up. "It was as if they were on the moon trying to run this business," says Scallan, the former Hartford licensee whose agent worked out of Boston. They also fault the quality of cotton merchandise from Benetton's year-and-a-half-old factory in Rocky Mount, N.C.

But the biggest gripe among Benetton licensees is that stores are located too close to one another. Benetton clusters shops on the theory that the more there are, the larger the market they create. But it doesn't always work that way. Scallan maintains that her sales in downtown Hartford were good until another Benetton store opened in the mall across the street. "Our business was almost cut in half," she says. "Had we not sold out, right now we would be filing for bankruptcy."

A LOT OF BENETTONS	
	U.S. stores*
1983	250
1984	307
1985	393
1986	564
1987	731
1988**	758

*Includes Canada and Caribbean **Estimate
DATA: BENETTON

ILLUSTRATION BY MIKE BARTALOS

Says Erica Healy, a West Hartford licensee: "I believe in Benetton, but I think they're greedy. All these stores are not good for the image. Instead of being exclusive, it gets too popular."

With 28 Benetton shops, Manhattan is a particular trouble spot. Because rents are steep and shoplifting is a big problem, New York stores must generate sales much higher than average to be profitable. Danny Markowitz, three of whose 26 Benettons are in Manhattan, says the company has been "supporting stores by easing up payment terms."

BACK TO BASICS. Aldo Palmeri, managing director of Benetton Group in Treviso, Italy, claims the U. S. operation is in good shape. He notes that credit losses from U. S. stores that fail to pay for merchandise—an early indicator of trouble—amount to less than 1%. Still, Palmeri concedes, rapid expansion has produced problems involving "some specific outlets and owners." But he says that's inevitable with a large stable of licensees, some of whom have limited retailing experience. Adds Sanford I. Rosenberg, who owns seven stores in the Chicago area: "It's a very demanding business. The people who tried to do this as a lark, they're the ones having difficulties."

Palmeri admits that U. S. management needed strengthening. "You can't run the U. S. operation from Italy," he says. So in December, Benetton brought in former McKinsey & Co. consultant Federico Minoli to head U. S. operations and organize Benetton USA as an autonomous New York company. "Our incredible growth has stretched the organization," he says. "The emphasis is now shifting to consolidation and service."

Minoli is evaluating store sites, with a mind to converting some to larger United Colors of Benetton superstores that carry the full line of products. The company will open fewer traditional Benetton shops, concentrating instead on expanding its children's division. Minoli says recent changes at the U. S. factory have resulted in better-quality clothes for spring. The factory supplies goods accounting for 20% of U. S. sales. Minoli wants to increase that to 50%.

Minoli also wants to strengthen relationships with licensees. He agrees that some stores need more hands-on guidance. To make things easier, he wants to focus the apparel collections better by reducing the number of styles offered. And he has hired a merchandising manager to design clothing displays that store owners can adopt. It may be too late for Robertson, Scallan, and Fanning. But if Benetton is going to continue to prosper in the U. S., it has to take better care of its shopkeepers.

By Amy Dunkin in New York, with William C. Symonds in Rome, Todd Mason in Dallas, and Kathleen Deveny in Chicago

52

Upscale Retailers Head to Enemy Turf

More Now Open Outlets to Rival Off-Price Sellers

By TERI AGINS

Staff Reporter of THE WALL STREET JOURNAL

NEW YORK—Ritzy retailers want to rest assured that their sophisticated customers wouldn't be caught dead rummaging through the racks at discount havens such as **Loehmann's**. But the reality is just the opposite.

Increasing numbers of shoppers are like Ruth Urquhart, a Long Island real estate broker who bypasses the glitzy galleria malls for outlet-store shopping centers. There she regularly finds Calvin Klein fashions and similar designer merchandise at a third of the price department stores charge. "It's a game for me," she says. "You feel so good when you shop discount because it just makes sense."

In an attempt to reclaim those lost customers, a growing number of better retailers are starting to open their own discount stores. In the past year, retailers such as **Neiman-Marcus** Group Inc., **Woodward & Lothrop** and John Wanamaker have opened separate stores stocked with marked-down goods from their regular branches. Other department stores are looking at the idea, including Saks Fifth Avenue, which is negotiating to open a store at the Franklin Mills outlet mall near Philadelphia.

Heading Off Competition

Department stores hope these outlets can help stem the growth of off-price retailers such as Loehmann's and **Filene's Basement**. In recent years, both off-price and traditional discount stores such as Bradlees have been gaining share from department stores in apparel sales. (Traditional discount stores tend to sell lower-end goods, rather than marked-down designer clothes.)

At the same time, some department stores say it's now more profitable to run their own clearance stores instead of selling excess inventory to outsiders. That's partly because of the growth of shopping centers devoted to clearance and factory-outlet stores. George Hechtman, a Richmond, Va., retail consultant, says that

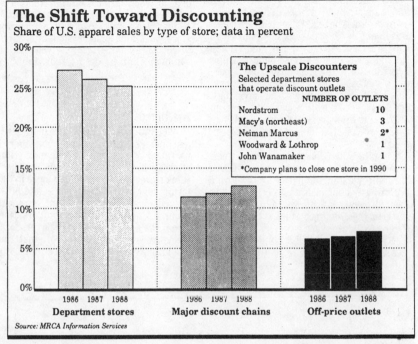

The Shift Toward Discounting

Share of U.S. apparel sales by type of store; data in percent

The Upscale Discounters

Selected department stores that operate discount outlets

	NUMBER OF OUTLETS
Nordstrom	10
Macy's (northeast)	3
Neiman Marcus	2*
Woodward & Lothrop	1
John Wanamaker	1

*Company plans to close one store in 1990

Department stores · 1986 1987 1988
Major discount chains · 1986 1987 1988
Off-price outlets · 1986 1987 1988

Source: MRCA Information Services

rents at outlet malls, which are generally off the beaten path, are lower than at most suburban shopping centers. But outlet malls still attract the big-spending customers department stores want.

The Potomac Mills outlet mall outside Washington, D.C., rivals a traditional shopping mall in size and scope. The mall, which opened last year, has over 200 stores selling clothes, furniture, toys and gifts at prices 20% to 60% off regular retail prices. Most of the stores are operated by manufacturers such as Calvin Klein, Laura Ashley and Nike.

The Franklin Mills mall, which opened in May, claims it will be the largest outlet mall—1.85 million square feet—when fully occupied. The mall's anchor stores include clearance outlets of **Sears Roebuck** & Co. and **J.C. Penney** Co.

Some outlet centers, such as one in Freeport, Maine, have even become tourist destinations, drawing chartered buses full of shoppers who spend an entire day bargainhunting. "As the outlet centers grow in popularity, [department stores] are seeing the cost-efficiencies in getting into that business themselves," says Mr. Hechtman, the consultant.

But some industry executives say department stores may be too eager to get

into the outlet business. They contend that discount retailing is an entirely different business, not just an extension of department-store merchandising. Also, stores risk undermining their high-toned images by venturing into budget turf.

The clearance business isn't entirely new to department stores, many of which once operated bargain basements in their flagship stores. Most of those operations were closed in the 1970s as retailers chased more profitable merchandise. **R.H. Macy** & Co., for example, replaced its bargain basement at its main store in Manhattan with The Cellar, an emporium of kitchenware and specialty foods. Department stores began selling their excess inventory to off-price stores or to middlemen known as liquidators.

Off-price retailing has become a sophisticated business in its own right as it has gained a broad following. This could make it doubly hard for department stores to compete with established operators.

"These stores are tricky to operate," says Mr. Hechtman.

Maintaining a steady inventory of all types of clothes is one hurdle. Also, off-price retailing requires skillful merchandising to make cast-offs look appealing. Sam DeFillipo, senior vice president of marketing and merchandising at Filene's

(cont.)

Basement, cringes at the memory of a recent visit to one department-store outlet where he noticed "100 dresses of one style and one color" lined up in a long row.

Mr. DeFillipo says he isn't worried about department stores taking business away from Filene's Basement. (Filene's Basement is a separate company from Boston-based Filene's department store.) He also says Filene's Basement no longer gets most of its merchandise from department stores, so its sources aren't threatened. Filene's Basement, he says, buys odd lots directly from apparel makers, enabling it to offer fresh, seasonal goods only a few weeks after department stores get theirs.

Despite the challenges, department stores can't seem to resist the thrill of a bargain. Washington-based Woodward & Lothrop says business has been going "extremely well" at its year-old clearance store in the Potomac Mills outlet mall in Prince William, Va.

By shuttling marked-down goods to the clearance store, "we're getting higher profit margins because we are able to turn stock faster and keep fresher [full-priced] goods on the selling floor at our 16 stores," says James Wells, an executive vice president at Woodward & Lothrop. Another advantage, he says is that out-of-season clothes don't look so old at a clearance store, and thus can be sold at a higher price. At an outlet store, "you can sell summer clothes after Labor Day," he says.

A Diluted Image?

Woodward & Lothrop doesn't plan to add more clearance stores, but other department stores are expanding. Nordstrom, which already has 10 Nordstrom Rack stores, plans to add two more in California next year. It expects to add others to accompany its expansion across the country. Unlike some other retailers, Nordstrom has a separate staff of buyers for its Rack stores, which carry original merchandise as well as clearance items from Nordstrom's regular 48 stores.

Retailers say they aren't concerned about diluting their image with clearance outlets. "As a matter of fact, we feel that our image is improved if we don't have deeply discounted merchandise taking up valuable retail space," says a spokesman for Neiman-Marcus Group, which operates one clearance store.

With discount stores and off-price retailers continuing to gain market shares, most industry experts expect department stores to continue to experiment with clearance branches. At the same time, however, some say department stores may be missing the point.

Generating healthy profits at department stores means selling fresh goods at full price, notes Alan Millstein, a New York retail consultant. "Instead of trying to get the last drop of profits out of last season's mistakes," he says, "department stores need to be concentrating on how they are going to sell more goods at regular price."

53

Video chain aims to star as industry leader

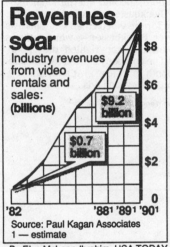

Revenues soar
Industry revenues from video rentals and sales: (billions)

$9.2 billion

$0.7 billion

$8

$6

$4

$2

0

'82   '88¹ '89¹ '90¹

Source: Paul Kagan Associates
1 — estimate

By Elys McLean-Ibrahim, USA TODAY

By Neal Templin
USA TODAY

FORT LAUDER-DALE, Fla. — Wayne Huizenga had never rented a videotape when he was invited to a Blockbuster video store in Chicago in February 1987.

He and his partners spent the next two days poring over the numbers of a fledgling, 25-store chain called Blockbuster Entertainment Corp. By the end of the second day, the group had decided to invest $18.6 million to buy 35% of Blockbuster. Huizenga's biggest worry: "Was this a real industry — or was it like a Hula-Hoop?"

Today, there's no question in Huizenga's mind that the $6.9 billion (sales) video industry is here to stay. Now he's on his way to making Blockbuster the dominant player.

Huizenga, chairman since April 1987, says tape rentals and sales at Blockbuster's company-owned and franchised stores are expected to reach $180 million this year. That edges out its two largest competitors: Erol's Video Clubs of Springfield, Va., and West Coast Video of Philadelphia. Blockbuster revenues will shoot even higher if its acquisition of the 146-store Major Video Corp. based in Las Vegas is approved by Major Video shareholders. By 1990, Huizenga predicts, Blockbuster — which currently has 245 stores — will have 1,000 and systemwide sales of $1 billion. His goal: "We want to be the McDonald's of our industry."

Wall Street loves it. Thursday, Blockbuster — which operates out of a Mediterranean-style building on Fort Lauderdale's chic Las Olas Boulevard — reported net income of $5.2 million for the first six months, vs. $1.4 million in the same period last year. Revenues were $46.8 million, up from $16.3 million in the first six months of 1987. Blockbuster's stock has more than quadrupled since Jan. 1, to $38 a share Thursday, and analysts are touting it as a good buy. Also Thursday, Blockbuster announced a 2-for-1 stock split effective Aug. 10 to shareholders of record as of Aug. 1.

The sudden success hardly fazes Huizenga (pronounced "high-zing-guh"), a bald, craggy-faced man with intense blue eyes. He's been this route before. In 1971, he co-founded Waste Management

Corp., the nation's largest waste-disposal company. Huizenga retired as president of Waste Management in 1984 to spend time with his family. Now the 50-year-old exec brings a team of seasoned managers to a fragmented industry ripe for consolidation.

The video industry, born in the 1970s, came of age in the 1980s when sales of videocassette recorders took off. Annual tape rentals and sales — which didn't hit $1 billion until 1983 — will surpass $10 billion sometime within the next three years. Video rentals have already topped movie box-office receipts.

Despite the industry's growth, small mom and pop stores — each stocking at most a couple of thousand tapes — still predominate. But the trend is toward large stores with a wider selection of films. Blockbuster has the capital to open — at the rate of more than a store every two days — spiffy, spacious stores, each stuffed with 10,000 tapes. The superstore concept is not complicated, but it takes about $550,000 — more than most smaller storeowners can rustle up — to open the typical Blockbuster store.

Analysts don't see any other superstore chains able to raise enough capital to keep pace with Blockbuster. The Erol's Video Clubs chain, which claims 60% of the market in the Washington, D.C., area, is a private company expanding much more slowly than Blockbuster. West Coast Video is concentrating on smaller neighborhood stores. Blockbuster is acquiring the only other publicly held superstore chain, Major Video.

Still, Huizenga fears that if Blockbuster doesn't expand rapidly enough, another company will take the lead. New competition could come from a movie studio or entertainment company eager to break into a lucrative new industry, analysts speculate. Or, like Blockbuster, a competitor could come flying out of obscurity.

Computer expert David Cook conceived Blockbuster and opened his first store in Dallas in 1985. He stocked 8,000 tapes — an enormous selection for those days. Cook sold some franchises, but money wasn't coming in fast enough to keep expanding.

John Melk, an associate of Huizenga's at Waste Management, had invested in a Blockbuster franchise. After weeks of pestering, Melk convinced Huizenga to make that 1987 visit to the Chicago

(cont.)

store. Huizenga was impressed. At first he thought about buying a franchise, but later decided, "Why not buy the whole company?"

Huizenga, Melk and another Waste Management veteran, Donald Flynn, went in as equal partners. Today, they own 29% of Blockbuster stock and hold warrants to buy up to 43%. Each would realize about $60 million if he converted all his warrants and sold the stock.

Cook left in April 1987. The key dispute was over how the company should grow. Cook wanted to concentrate on franchising; Huizenga wanted to build company-owned stores in the major markets and grant franchises in smaller towns.

Huizenga moved Blockbuster's headquarters near his home in Fort Lauderdale, but he has not changed Cook's basic concept. The stores look much the same, and Blockbuster still uses the computer system devised by Cook to track inventory and speed up checkout times for tapes. In May 1987, Blockbuster bought Movies To Go, which had 29 stores in Missouri, Illinois and Texas. This spring, it bought Video Library Inc., a 42-store San Diego chain. This year, Blockbuster will open 100 company-owned stores and 110 franchises. Major Video — the firm Blockbuster has agreed to acquire — is also expanding.

To control the growth, Huizenga has brought in what analysts call the deepest management team in the video industry. He and his partners had no experience in retailing or franchising, so they've lured senior managers from other businesses — mainly the fast-food industry. They also picked up some well-regarded video-industry veterans — like Barry Rosenblatt of Video Library — through acquisitions.

Two key hires rose through McDonald's Corp., the fast-food marketing king. Luigi Salvaneschi, Blockbuster's recently named president, headed real-estate acquisitions for McDonald's. Good store locations are as critical for renting videotapes as they are for selling hamburgers.

Thomas Gruber guided both domestic and international marketing at McDonald's. Now, as Blockbuster's chief of marketing, Gruber is constructing an image for the video chain that borrows heavily from his former employer. Blockbuster — which refuses to rent X-rated films — has already copyrighted the motto: "America's family video store." The company started its first television campaign earlier this month in Chicago, Atlanta and Detroit and eventually plans national television ads.

54

GOING FOR THE GOLDEN ARCHES

By BARBARA MARSH

Staff Reporter of THE WALL STREET JOURNAL

American universities are loaded with people who couldn't get into Harvard. The fast-food industry is filled with people who couldn't make the grade at McDonald's.

Winning a franchise from **McDonald's** Corp. is, in its own way, just as fiercely competitive as getting into an elite college. Well over 2,000 people apply to become McDonald's franchisees in the U.S. each year, but only a tiny fraction succeed. In most years, only about 150 applicants gain admission to the Golden Arches.

With odds like this, there's a lot of heartbreak out there in fast-food land. Those who fail to make the grade at McDonald's often wind up at other fast-food outlets—at Burger King, Arby's, Jack in the Box. Some remember the sting of rejection for years afterward. Terry Jones of Altadena, Calif., even framed his McDonald's rejection letter and hung it above his bed. Now a highly successful Jack in the Box owner, Mr. Jones says he smiles whenever he notices the letter and tells himself, "I'll show those guys."

At the End of the Rainbow

For the winners—survivors of applications, interviews, multiple credit checks, and two years of cleaning toilets and sweeping floors as a McDonald's apprentice—life can be very sweet. The reason McDonald's gets so many applicants is because a McDonald's franchise is about the closest thing to a guaranteed moneymaker. The company doesn't disclose average per-unit earnings for its franchises, but analysts estimate that per-unit sales average about $1.6 million.

Which brings us to the important question of just how, exactly, does one get a McDonald's franchise. McDonald's executives say it requires somebody who is thrifty, clean, hard-working, and so forth. It also requires at least $66,000 in cash up front. And, applicants say, it helps to have something else: pull.

McDonald's officials deny that personal connections are needed to become one of their franchisees, of which there are about 2,000 in the U.S. But many applicants say that knowing a current franchisee or, even better, a regional licensing manager is a gigantic help. Says Gerardo Perez, a Sacramento, Calif., franchisee: Knowing somebody important with McDonald's "will give you an identity."

At a time when some franchise operators are struggling to attract enough franchisees, McDonald's pickiness is something of a luxury. McDonald's is popular in part because of a successful record of good site selection, heavy marketing and management support from headquarters. Another plus is McDonald's practice of working with financially troubled operators—sending in its field consultants, for example, or lowering rent—or buying out those who can't make it.

Nick Mauney, who struggled with two low-performing Sacramento-area stores before leaving McDonald's last year, still praises its system for supporting him in the tough times. "There is no greater corporation on earth for helping somebody who wants to work with them," Mr. Mauney says.

The types of applicants McDonald's rejects out of hand are legion. It doesn't want absentee owners, passive investors, partnerships, corporations or real-estate developers. Aris Mardirossian, chairman of 6-Twelve Convenient-Mart Inc., a food-store chain based in Gaithersburg, Md., says McDonald's turned down his request to start up two McDonald's stores in properties he owns in Maryland. "McDonald's offered to rent the property from me, but they wouldn't give me the franchise," he says.

McDonald's also thinks twice about applications from doctors, lawyers, accountants or any other experts used to having customers come to them. The fear is that somebody like that might be reluctant to circulate during the lunch crunch with a pot of coffee and a ready smile.

People most likely to get interviews are those with "ketchup in their veins"—a McDonald's expression for outgoing, high-energy types who'll devote their lives to the Golden Arches. The company wants only owner-operators committed to working 12- to 18-hour days, seven days a week, personally managing their own stores. Applicants must be content to start with a single store—the company refuses to award territory franchises—and they also must be willing to relocate.

Those who are comfortable handling customers, particularly people with retailing, marketing and sales experience, are more likely to get invited for interviews, even if their backgrounds are weak in other business areas. "A salesman is terrific, a sales manager even better," says Burton Cohen, McDonald's vice president, licensing.

Who Sells the Most

Average 1988 sales per unit of the leading fast-food chains (includes franchisee- and company-owned locations); in thousands of dollars

COMPANY	AVERAGE SALES PER UNIT
McDonald's	$1,600
Burger King	984
Hardee's	920
Jack in the Box	900
Wendy's	759
Arby's	610
Kentucky Fried Chicken	597
Taco Bell	589
Pizza Hut	520
Domino's	485

Source: Technomic Inc.

(cont.)

Minority applicants are also actively courted, now that McDonald's wants to raise the percentage of its franchises owned by minorities above the current 20%. Currently, 31% of the 341 applicants in training are black, 13% Hispanic and 4% Asian.

In general, though, individuals aged between 35 and 45 and with at least 10 years' business experience make the most likely candidates.

Everett Robinson, a 43-year-old black personnel manager at Allstate Insurance Co., figured he fit the bill perfectly. But in 1987 he applied and was turned down without even obtaining an interview with McDonald's. Undaunted, Mr. Robinson figured he'd stand a better chance if he made some contacts. So he went to work at an Oakbrook, Ill., company that provides many McDonald's outlets with restaurant supplies. "To be quite honest, I still had my eye on owning a McDonald's store," says Mr. Robinson. "So I talked to these operators [and] asked them how they went about it." In the process, he also got to know more than 10 store operators. He put several of their names on his new application.

"It's like everything else," says Mr. Robinson. "In an area as competitive as this, you almost have to have an inside track." Mr. Robinson reapplied recently, obtained an interview, and is currently waiting to hear whether he will be called for a five-day tryout at a Chicago-area McDonald's.

While McDonald's officials insist it's unnecessary for applicants to "know somebody" to get in, Robert M. Beavers Jr., a senior vice president at McDonald's, concedes that many candidates "understand the importance of networking."

Applicants must put up an initial equity investment ranging in value from a minimum of $66,000 to more than $200,000, depending on the deal. Those candidates with $66,000 may qualify for a three-year store lease, which carries an option to purchase a store after three years. Those wishing to buy a store outright for, say, $600,000 or more must come up with at least $240,000 in equity and finance the rest through a bank. (Once McDonald's accepts an applicant, bank financing usually comes easily because of McDonald's reputation for aiding troubled franchises.)

Those who get accepted for the two-year training course usually stick it out and wind up with a restaurant. Still, the program is more rigorous and time-consuming than many M.B.A. programs—and some trainees either flunk or opt out.

On the Front Lines

For much of those two years, trainees slave away for 20 hours a week—for no pay—at a local McDonald's restaurant. They do it all—working the counter, flipping hamburgers, cleaning toilets, fixing milkshake machines, and handling the book work—and most continue holding down their regular jobs.

"It's like becoming a Chicago cop. Suddenly you don't see any of your friends," says James Skrypek, a franchisee in Morton Grove, Ill. Looking back on the two-year apprenticeship, Mr. Skrypek says it destroyed his personal life, and by the time the whole thing had dawned on him as a ridiculous amount of time, he was a year into training and "you can't back out."

On top of that, trainees rotate through classes at regional company locations, working their way through a thick four-volume training guide and cramming for periodic exams. The program culminates with a two-week advanced course at Hamburger University, the residential training center at McDonald's headquarters in Oakbrook, where students have to pay as much as $700 a week for room and board.

Even after graduating from Hamburger U., applicants may wait as long as a year for McDonald's to match them up with a location. A few each year get tired of waiting and turn to something else.

But the vast majority of graduates go on to revel in the hard-working ranks of McDonald's elite. Mr. Perez, who waited nine long months to get his own set of Golden Arches, now says, "I couldn't have fallen into taller clover."

55

Retailing Clips Wings of Highflying Mail-Order Firms

By UDAYAN GUPTA
Staff Reporter of THE WALL STREET JOURNAL

Some of the hottest companies in the mail-order business are stumbling as they try to expand beyond catalog sales to retail outlets.

The most recent casualty of an ambitious diversification plan is **Royal Silk** Ltd., once a highflying mail-order supplier of silk blouses and dresses. Last month, Royal Silk filed for bankruptcy protection under Chapter 11, saying its foray into retail stores had been disastrous.

Several other mail-order companies are having trouble becoming storefront successes. **Sharper Image** Corp., originally a catalog retailer, recently announced another quarter of losses—its third in a row. The San Francisco company, which specializes in selling an eclectic array of upscale merchandise—miniature billiard tables, fold-up bicycles and duck-shaped telephones—to the affluent, blamed rapid expansion and greater than expected declines in its catalog sales as two contributing factors.

Still others—such as **Williams-Sonoma** Inc., **Company Store**, **Shopsmith** Inc. and **Brookstone** Co.—also are discovering that moving into retail stores doesn't bring instant riches.

Analysts say successful national mail-order businesses launch retail stores convinced the move quickly will boost sales. Instead, they are confronted with declining sales, rapidly escalating costs and a plethora of new management problems.

'Distinctly Different' Businesses

"Catalog companies get into trouble running retail stores because they don't recognize the two businesses are distinctly different," says Maxwell Sroge, a Chicago-based industry consultant. Adds Janet Kloppenburg, a retail industry analyst with Robertson, Colman & Stephens in New York: "Items that appeal out of a catalog don't always look good on a hanger. A good mail-order business doesn't translate into good retail store sales."

Brookstone, for example, had little success with its first Boston store because "we blindly copied the catalog," says Douglas Anderson, president of the the Peterborough, N.H.-based marketer of tools and gadgets. Shopsmith, Dayton, Ohio, opened retail units convinced they would be ideal outlets for its line of home woodworking equipment. It soon found consumers wanted more. So now Shopsmith stores—in addition to selling the company's own products—sell lumber and a variety of woodworking products from other firms, as well as conducting classes in woodworking.

Successful retail stores need to pay careful attention to store displays, the mix of products they offer and the problem of day-to-day customer needs, notes Ms. Kloppenburg. By contrast, catalogers don't need to pay attention to daily changes. They need a strong and appealing catalog, a fertile mailing list and systems that support timely and efficient servicing of customers. Notes Ms. Kloppenburg, "It's difficult to bring the two businesses together."

Royal Silk tried to do it and failed.

Launched in 1978, the Clifton, N.J., company had developed a strong business selling silk blouses and dresses—in styles and prices that appealed to a wide range of users. By 1983, the catalog concern was on Inc. magazine's list of the fastest-growing companies in the U.S. with sales in excess of $12 million.

The following year, Royal Silk decided to go retail in a big way. The crowds at its one warehouse store in Clifton, near New York City, convinced founder Prakash Melwani that strategically located outlets could prove just as successful. When the Clifton store began to attract customers from all over the Northeast, "We began to wonder if it's so successful here, can you imagine how it will play on Fifth Avenue?" Mr. Melwani says. Besides, with 85% of all U.S. consumers still buying at stores, he adds, "we would eventually have to find a way to reach them."

"But Mr. Melwani underestimated what it would take to run a chain of retail stores, some directly owned, others run by licensees. He hadn't anticipated the costs of developing software to track retail sales or the paper work of running a nationwide retail store and catalog operation."

He found himself intervening to satisfy the demands of his retailers. When some stores wanted a new line of suits that weren't in the catalog, he spent almost $750,000 to design and produce the new line. When a Texas store owner complained that the company should stop mailing its catalogs to Texas, it took days to mediate the dispute. Eventually, Mr. Melwani estimates, the company spent over $3 million in taking over troubled stores in Florida, Hawaii and Colorado and closing down others in New Hampshire and Maine.

Problems Multiplied

By the end of 1987, the problems had begun to overwhelm Royal Silk. Escalating costs had eroded margins of almost 55% in the mail-order business to the low teens. Sales plunged to $31 million from a high of $42 million in 1986 and after an abortive attempt to sell the company, a chastened Mr. Melwani decided to shed the retail business and return to mail order, "the business we know best," he explains.

Despite a similar set of problems, Sharper Image has no plans to cut back on its retail business and return to mail-order sales. "The retail business is giving us all our profits, that's where we want to be in the future," says Richard Thalheimer, the company's founder. The company, which went public in May 1987 at $10 a share is now trading at $5.50 in national over-the-counter trading.

After reaching about $50 million through catalog sales by 1982, the five-year-old company decided to go retail because "we wanted to take advantage of the tremendous advertising we got from our catalogs," Mr. Thalheimer says. But in spite of an initial boost in revenue and high in-store sales—over $1,000 per square foot annually, compared with $200 for retailers in general—the stores seem to have created more problems than benefits.

Critics note that the company's 62 stores are often in expensive urban locations and "cannibalize" the same consumers who buy from their catalog. As a result, catalog sales continue to drift at about $50 million annually. Others say the expensive "toys for big boys" that Sharper Image sells aren't too profitable. "They don't have the exclusive franchise they once had," says Mr. Sroge, the consultant.

Some analysts say the company is still catalog-minded and hasn't expanded management fast enough to cope with store retailing. William Tichy, a retail industry analyst, notes that Mr. Thalheimer continues to own nearly 70% of the company's stock and has done little to attract experienced retailers to senior management.

For his part, Mr. Thalheimer contends that last year's losses are an aberration. "We just lost track of our gross merchandising costs," he says.

Many mail-order concerns get into retail believing that the business can be grown just as fast, says Fred Wintzer Jr., who follows the retail industry for Alex. Brown & Sons. But the nature of retailing forces them to scale back.

Take the example of Williams-Sonoma, which began expanding into retail stores in 1984 but now is pulling back to proceed more gradually. The company opened retail units in 1984 believing it could become

(cont.)

the overnight leader in the homeware market. But it discovered that it would have to revamp its merchandise for the storefront. Moreover, costly investments in systems, the hiring of a slew of new employees and the need to choose new sites carefully has slowed the growth of the company.

A few companies have successfully balanced both the mail-order business and store retailing. Brookstone, for example, after its initial mishaps, has "taken the time to develop a successful retail operation," Mr. Wintzer notes.

The company, launched in 1965, didn't make a serious move into retail until 1982. But after its Boston store flopped, the company recruited experienced retailers to head the move into retailing. Today, Brookstone's 94 stores have a product mix that is radically different from the catalog, noted the company's president, Mr. Anderson. And the company's mail order and retail operations are managed by two different groups. When it comes to finding new sites and negotiating leases, the company uses outside consultants. Says Mr. Anderson: "We know what we are good at and where we need help."

56

Catalog Overload Turns Off Consumers

Some Analysts Predict Demise Of Copycats

By Francine Schwadel
Staff Reporter of The Wall Street Journal

Nan Kilkeary helped fuel the catalog boom of the late 1970s and early 1980s. She preferred shopping by mail because catalogs offered goods she couldn't find in stores, and because she didn't have to fight crowds to buy them.

But these days, the 45-year-old communications consultant from Chicago suffers from what she calls "catalog overload." She receives so many with similar merchandise that she throws many of them away after only a glance. If the cover features "the same old Ivy League blue shirt or cutesy little ducks," she says, "they're gone. Why take your time?"

Catalogs have become the junk mail of today. An estimated 12 billion are likely to be mailed this year, up from 4.7 billion in 1980. This Christmas season alone, catalog shoppers may receive as many as 80 of the books each. But declining response rates to the mailings suggest consumers are throwing away more of them—without ordering a thing—than ever before.

"People are saying they spend a lot less time looking at catalogs than they used to," says Richard Grunsten, a catalog marketer in Chicago who studies response rates and consumer attitudes toward catalogs. "They get so many, they're overwhelmed. The novelty has worn off."

Shake-Out Ahead?

The industry's sales growth has been declining for several years. For 1988, sales are expected to climb about 9.9% to $31 billion, compared with annual increases of 14% to 15% in the early 1980s. At the same time, costs are rising. As a result, some analysts predict a wave of mergers and bankruptcies among smaller companies. The most vulnerable are copycat catalogs—which imitate bigger, more established competitors— or sportswear and traditional apparel, high-tech gadgets, gifts, and children's clothing and toys.

"If we have a soft Christmas, it could shake a lot of them out," says Fred E. Wintzer Jr., an analyst who follows the

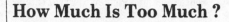

How Much Is Too Much ?

Number of catalogs mailed
(In billions)

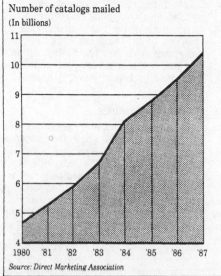

Source: Direct Marketing Association

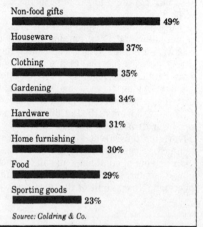

Percentages of surveyed catalog buyers who felt that they get so many of these kinds of catalogs that it's hard to tell one from another

Non-food gifts — 49%
Houseware — 37%
Clothing — 35%
Gardening — 34%
Hardware — 31%
Home furnishing — 30%
Food — 29%
Sporting goods — 23%

Source: Goldring & Co.

catalog industry for Alex. Brown & Sons Inc., Baltimore. Catalog companies typically ring up 40% to 80% of annual sales and profits during the holiday season.

The glut of catalogs has been building for years. The number of competitors in the industry exploded in the 1980s because catalog sales were growing twice as fast as store sales and start-up costs were much lower. Successful companies such as **Lands' End** Inc., which sells sportswear, and **Sharper Image** Corp., which sells high-tech gadgets, attracted imitators hawking similar merchandise and targeting the same customers. Department stores such as Marshall Field's and Bloomingdale's, meanwhile, boosted their mailings.

By the mid-1980s, some weak competitors were beginning to drop out. And in recent months the industry's consolidation has accelerated. Earlier this year, **General Mills** Inc.—which had complained about the high costs of attracting new catalog customers—sold its Talbots clothing catalog and stores to a Japanese retailer and its Eddie Bauer clothing catalog and stores to **Spiegel** Inc. Horchow Mail Order Inc., a gift catalog house, recently agreed to be acquired by **Neiman-Marcus Group** Inc.

As sales growth declines, many catalog companies may find they can't keep up with rising costs. Third-class postal rates rose 25% last spring. Paper prices have risen sharply. And legislation is being dis-

cussed that would increase catalog companies' administrative costs by requiring them to charge the equivalent of the sales tax of whichever state the customer lives in and then distribute it to the states. Currently, catalog companies charge the tax only in states where they operate offices, stores or other facilities.

"The confluence of these two forces [rising costs and slower sales growth] could really put a squeeze on the smaller players," says David Childe, an analyst at Dean Witter Reynolds Inc.

It isn't all bad news for the catalog business. For one thing, demographics continue to be in its favor. More working women than ever are pressed for time. And an aging population is likely to prefer buying by mail to fighting crowds in the mall. Moreover, many catalog companies have raised their stature in the eyes of consumers by speeding delivery and using toll-free numbers to simplify ordering.

The incestuous industry practice of renting competitors' mailing lists to find new shoppers, however, means that too many catalog companies are courting the same customers. Arnold Fishman, president of Marketing Logistics Inc. in Lincolnshire, Ill., estimates that fewer than a third of U.S. households spend more than $750 a year on catalog orders.

The proliferation of catalogs in crowded market niches such as apparel, gifts and gadgets also means that it is tougher for a

(cont.)

catalog to stand out. Because there are so many, people now are "far more blasé" about specialty catalogs than they were when the books started appearing about 10 years ago, says Paul Campbell, a market researcher in Minneapolis who tracks consumer attitudes for retailers. Consumers are still "willing to look through them," he says, "but certainly not as vigorously as they did in the past. It would take a real unusual catalog to make them pore through it."

Christina Joseph, a 35-year-old Chicago homemaker and loyal catalog shopper of cookware retailer **Williams-Sonoma** Inc., rarely peruses the five or six other cookware catalogs she receives. "I'm not interested in trying them," she says, adding that they "just haven't grabbed me."

Even Goldring & Co., a Chicago market research firm that surveyed 2,299 catalog buyers for the Direct Marketing Association last spring and hailed the results as a "strong vote of confidence in catalog shopping," found some evidence of catalog overload. Nearly half of the shoppers who bought non-food gifts through catalogs said they received so many catalogs that it was difficult to tell one from another. More than a third of the people who bought housewares and clothing through catalogs felt the same way.

Ms. Kilkeary, the communications consultant, also complains that stores today carry much of the same merchandise as catalogs. Why "wait six weeks and get something you haven't picked up and touched, when you can get something equivalent or better today?" she asks.

Taking Precautions

Some catalog companies are responding to the slowdown in sales and response rates by—what else?—sending out more catalogs. Lands' End, the Dodgeville, Wis., catalog company that routinely outperforms the industry, said last week that it will take the precaution of increasing its mailings in November and December by about three million catalogs, to a total of about 75 million for the year. Lands' End says its sales growth for the third quarter ending today has slowed to 25% from its first-half rate of more than 30%, and profit margins for the quarter have been squeezed by higher costs. The catalogs' response rate also has been "a little softer recently," a spokesman says.

Other retailers, though, are scaling back their mail-order efforts. The department store unit of **Dayton Hudson** Corp., for instance, decided this year against producing its 64-page Christmas catalog. Instead, the Minneapolis-based chain is spending part of the roughly $1 million it usually devotes to the catalog on a new television ad for the holidays.

"Emotionally it was very difficult" to cancel the catalog, which was mainly an advertising vehicle rather than a money maker, says Jack Mugan, director of creative services. But company officials decided that the TV spot might do a better job of grabbing the attention of customers. Adds Mr. Mugan: "There's an awful lot of stuff coming in the mail."

57

RETAILERS FLY INTO HYPERSPACE

The French created hypermarkets, and U.S. merchandisers wish they had kept them home. But consumers seem to like this jumbo addition to an already overbuilt industry. ■ *by Bill Saporito*

SOMETIME in the mid-1990s Americans will have just two gargantuan emporiums in which to shop. One will be east of the Mississippi River and one west, each extending over hundreds of miles and numerous states. Orange juice? "Just make a left at Wichita, ma'am; it's on the first aisle in Oklahoma."

Shoppers now traveling through the Bunyanesque, get-it-all-here stores known as hypermarkets already have the feeling. Consider: The establishment in northeast Philadelphia run by the French company Carrefour encompasses 330,000 square feet. That's enough for half a dozen football fields, give or take a hockey rink. To march up and down every aisle in pursuit of gro-

REPORTER ASSOCIATE *Mark Alpert*

ceries, apparel, and other general merchandise involves a stroll of a mile or so.

Does retailing really need stores this size? Do we need the exercise? The candid response of most American retailers is "of course not." The amount of retail mall space dedicated to each person in the country has nearly doubled in ten years to about 14 square feet. There are already far too many stores for the available business, but that won't stop the big guys. Once in place, their tactic is to absorb so much business at one location as to prevent anyone else from coming in. There are only half a dozen hypermarkets currently operating and another dozen on the drawing boards. But they have the potential to change the way consumers shop for everything from soup

to tires and to drastically alter the retail landscape in large and small cities alike.

Shoppers stand to gain because the hypermarket is a more efficient retail engine. Since the engine weighs a ton and costs a bundle, hypermarkets play to the strengths of big store operators like K mart, Wal-Mart, and Super Valu. Wal-Mart, run with revivalist fervor by Arkansas billionaire Sam Walton, is now singing hallelujah about the company's two Hypermart USA stores in the Dallas area, run in partnership with Cullum Cos., a well-known Texas grocer. The marts are shoving merchandise through the checkouts at the rate of $130 million to $150 million yearly, double that of any large discount store. "The volume was beyond our wildest expectations," says

(cont.)

Tom Hairston, president of Cullum.

Hypermarkets were created by French merchants after World War II out of a need for efficient distribution among the ruins. Companies like Auchan, Carrefour, Euromarché, Leclerc, and Promodes then expanded across Europe until they ran out of room. Four years ago the French looked west toward the States. A partnership called Hyper Shoppes that includes Super Valu, French real estate developers, and Euromarché opened Bigg's in Cincinnati. "The Europeans see the U.S. as the last oasis of unfettered free enterprise," says Peter Monash, a retailing consultant who has worked both sides of the Atlantic. He expects blood to run in the streets when the giants meet head-on.

Super Valu, the nation's second-biggest grocery wholesaler, initially tried persuading its partners to open a franchise of its low-cost Cub Foods supermarkets. The French

Everything but the kitchen sink

insisted on selling general merchandise, too. *Voilà* Bigg's. Although sales averaged $1.5 million a week, nearly double the volume at a Cub store, profits were nonexistent. Consumers who loved the low food prices weren't buying much else. After the company made adjustments in its general merchandise, consumers adjusted their shopping habits. Now profitable, Bigg's opened a second location in the Cincinnati area this year. Denver is next.

Super Valu, which also owns the ShopKo discount chain, will go solo with its own hypermarket version, called Twin Valu, in northern Ohio next year. K mart will open a hyperstore called American Fare in Atlanta in early 1989 in partnership with a regional grocer, Bruno's Inc. Carrefour, with 115 hypermarkets in Europe and South America, opened its Philadelphia store last February and plans another store on Long Island. Auchan, operator of 50 hypermarkets and other re-

tailing ventures in Europe, will debut in Houston and Chicago.

Until recently Americans have been reluctant players in the hyper competition because of the strong presence here of large supermarkets and discount stores, and even combinations of the two. While hypermarkets also include elements of supermarkets and discount stores, there are distinct differences. The ceilings are high, but in contrast to warehouse stores, the shelves don't rise much beyond seven or eight feet, giving hypermarkets the vast, see-it-all look of a discount store. The grocery aisles are designed for efficiency: Canned goods are usually sold from their cut-open cartons. Along the perimeter, however, shoppers can buy items normally sold in fancier stores: lobsters, croissants, and tortellini salad. A battery of 60 checkout lanes stands in broad testament to the stores' sales ambitions. Many hypermarkets are so big that stock clerks wear roller skates to get around.

The merchandise, market position, and operating economics of hypermarkets are unique and decidedly risky (see table). A typical discount store carries 80,000 items,

These are a few of the 57 registers at a Bigg's hypermarket in Cincinnati. The Franco-American partnership runs two marts and has another planned.

HENRY GROSKINSKY (2)

114

from screws to sledgehammers, and a big supermarket stocks 30,000. A typical hypermarket will lay in a maximum of 50,000 items. The stated strategy is to have on hand the products that represent 80% of consumers' regular needs and to avoid specialty or slow-moving items in all categories. That means, for instance, stocking golf balls but not golf clubs, refrigerators but not trash compactors, and only the six best-selling flavors of yogurt.

No one is sure what combinations of goods and service produce the most sales, and several of the foreign firms have struggled to find out. Bigg's, for example, had too many similar items at different prices. It did not make money until it simplified pricing to help consumers focus on value and discontinued merchandise, like suits, that required a large inventory and personal selling. According to trade reports, Carrefour may be having similar problems.

The distinction that Bigg's and others are trying to draw between themselves and discounters is that hypermarkets are not blue-collar stores. Says Pierre Wevers, executive vice president of Hyper Shoppes: "What one usually calls discount is downscale merchandise. The hypermarket doesn't do that." In fact, the merchandise is distinctly tailored to attract the middle- and upper-income crowd. A discount store's focus on value is represented by an absolute low price: $8 store-brand jeans. Those won't fly in hyperspace. Only brand-name apparel will do—Guess Jeans, for instance, or Arrow shirts, at prices lower than those of any other competing store. At the same time, hypermarkets avoid being too fashionable because the inventory requirements and risks are too large.

Operators of hypermarkets may be cashing in on what some analysts see as a division of stores into two types. The first is the niche store that concentrates on specialized

At Hypermart USA's first store in Garland, Texas, clerks were spending 400 hours a week just collecting carts in the parking lot.

merchandise—say, high-fashion apparel for career women. Typically, the merchandise is expensive and makes a personal statement about the buyer. The second category is ever larger but fewer retail outlets for items that can be classified as commodities: food, basic apparel, housewares. Consultants refer to the concept as "the polarity of retail trade." Linda Hyde of Management Horizons, a Dublin, Ohio, consulting firm owned by Price Waterhouse, says hypermarkets are trying to move more items toward the commodity end of the pole.

THEY ARE also taking the cost structure of big stores to new lows. Their magnet is bargain-priced food. Although it fills only 40% of the space in most hypermarkets, food represents 60% of revenues, mainly because it sells at a gross profit margin of 10%, less than half the figure at a traditional supermarket. The gross profit margin for the entire store is about 15%—ten percentage points below the discount or supermarket range. (An item that costs $1 must sell for $1.18 to achieve a 15% gross.) Similarly, the labor cost must be about 5% of sales, half what a typical K mart spends on labor.

These kinds of operating standards, difficult in their own right, create huge logistical challenges given the size of the stores. Says Larry Parkin, executive vice president

of K mart: "If you blow it, you are going to blow it big." Running 60 checkout lanes—a $600,000 investment—and stocking the floor require a staff of 600 to 700, most of whom are part time. That's a scheduling nightmare only a computer can figure out. And, of course, about 50,000 real live customers stream through the store each week. What a pain. At Hypermart USA's first store in Garland, Texas, clerks were spending 400 hours a week just collecting carts. (The solution: Charge a deposit, payable when the carts are returned to the corral.)

The size-is-all game has implications for the rest of retailing. Supermarket chains such as Kroger, whose standard for new stores was 44,000 square feet in 1983, now go as high as 69,000 square feet. The new stores become profitable in half the time of earlier models. Accordingly, Kroger plans to build fewer but bigger stores. (Those plans may change; see News/Trends.) K mart is launching a sporting goods chain called Sports Giant, whose 50,000-square-foot size will make it a center to the competition's guards.

Even in its traditional discount business K mart thinks bigger is better. On average, an 80,000-square-foot store outperforms one of 40,000 square feet. And in communities where a 40,000-square-foot K mart used to do quite nicely, it will do no more. Says Parkin: "You can have a small store in the right community and have no competition and do gangbusters, but that's not going to continue. Somebody's going to put in a bigger store."

That other somebody might be Wal-Mart. Mr. Sam has signaled his intention in Washington, Missouri (pop. 18,000). Washington used to have a 50,000-square-foot Wal-Mart. This year Sam replaced it with a 120,000-square-foot edifice called Supercenter. It's a hypermarket for Main Street. Wear comfortable shoes. ∎

MACROECONOMICS: HOW RETAILING'S HYPERSIZED LOOK STACKS UP

Store	Size (square feet)	Weekly sales	Items stocked	Gross profit margin	Customers per week	Average purchase	Labor cost (% of sales)	Inventory (annual turns)
Hypermarket	200,000	$1,750,000	50,000	15%	50,000	$35	5.0%	13
Wholesale Club	100,000	$1,000,000	4,500	11%	14,500	$70	4.5%	16
Discount Store	65,000	$150,000	80,000	28%	9,500	$16	10.0%	4
Supermarket	39,000	$250,000	30,000	24%	15,500	$16	12.5%	26

58

For Inland, Moving Steel Is Almost as Big as Making It

Nation's No. 1 Steel Distributor Expands Its Network of Service Centers

By RICK WARTZMAN
Staff Reporter of THE WALL STREET JOURNAL

EAST CHICAGO, Ind.—Mention **Inland Steel Industries** Inc. and inevitably you conjure up images of its mammoth metal-making operations on the shores of Lake Michigan.

Since 1902, the company has fixed its attention on the industrial drama played out here: Nine blast furnaces rise up like battlements, including No. 7, one of the two biggest iron producers in the country. Mill workers move ladles brimming with molten steel sloshing and spitting like hellfire. Hardened slabs are flattened into glistening coils, fit to be shaped into cars or dishwashers.

But these days, Inland is increasingly focused on moving metal, not just making it. Indeed, the nation's fourth-biggest steel producer finds itself, far and away, the nation's biggest steel distributor. And unlike steelmaking, steel distribution enjoys a growing market. Inland's ever-growing network of service centers—which warehouse, process and distribute steel and other goods—is

Robert J. Darnall

expected within a few years to match the company's steelmaking segment in profit and revenue.

In January, Inland continued its expansion into the distribution industry, which is largely populated by entrepreneurial mom-and-pop concerns, with the purchase of two sizable service centers in Minnesota and Louisiana. Terms weren't disclosed. Additional acquisitions are expected. Just last week, Inland said it would expand its three Chicago service centers over the next three years in a $30 million capital program.

"We have a commitment to growth in this area, though we're not going to be drunken sailors about it," says Robert J. Darnall, Inland's president and chief operating officer. "We want to be leaders."

Cheapest Source

Industry insiders laud Inland's distribution units, Joseph T. Ryerson & Son Inc. and J.M. Tull Metals Co., as the most effi-

cient of their kind. "Inland's been smart about it," asserts Don McGill, founding editor of the Metal Center News, a trade magazine. "They've given Ryerson and Tull a lot of autonomy."

In the past, many steel producers set up service centers strictly as convenient dumping grounds for their excess steel. At Inland, though, Ryerson and Tull are encouraged to buy carbon steel and other products—such as stainless steel, aluminum, copper, brass and industrial plastics—from the cheapest source.

For Inland, the interest in service centers has been long and steadfast. Ryerson, more than twice the size of any other service-center company in the U.S., became part of Inland in 1935.

Last year, Inland's service-center businesses accounted for more than a quarter of operating income and 44% of corporate sales, up from just 24% six years earlier. This year, the company predicts, service-center sales will climb 15% to $2.1 billion from $1.82 billion. "There are so many clouds in steel manufacturing that distribution doesn't have," Mr. Darnall explains. "If I only had a buck to spend and I had these two businesses, I'd now probably be interested in spending it on the distribution side."

Growing Segment

His reasoning makes sense. Steelmaking, though riding high for the moment, is more volatile than distribution. Inland's

service-center operations were profitable even when the steel industry went through a recession and the company spilled red ink from 1982 through 1985. While steel consumption is flat, more and more metal is passing through the hands of distributors before being moved on to end users.

At this point, service centers buy more steel from domestic mills than do any other group of customers, save for auto makers. In 1988, the service-center industry shipped an estimated 23.4 million tons of steel, up about 1% from the year-earlier period.

The upward trend is likely to continue as manufacturers seek higher-quality steel that can fit right onto the assembly line. "The guy who makes automobiles is realizing that he just wants to make automobiles," Mr. Darnall maintains. "He doesn't want to have to also be an expert in cutting, slitting and chopping up metal."

Moreover, many manufacturers are trying to keep excess inventory off their own shop floors, finding it more prudent to have materials delivered from a service-center warehouse just before they are needed. This concept, known as "just in time," also promises to keep the service-center industry healthy.

Others Failed

Though the fates of both steelmaking and distribution clearly are tied to the strength of the manufacturing sector, they are, in a sense, countercyclical: Steelmak-

Inland's Profitable Push Into Service Centers

Sales Are Growing...

Sales of Inland's service centers in billions of dollars

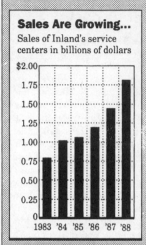

1983 '84 '85 '86 '87 '88

And Profits Jumped...

Service centers' earnings in millions of dollars

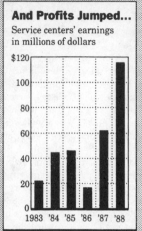

1983 '84 '85 '86 '87 '88

Helping Its Stock

Monthly NYSE close of Inland Steel

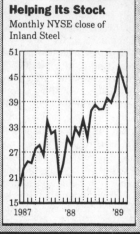

1987   '88   '89

(cont.)

ing is highly capital intensive and tends to eat cash during a recession. Distribution companies, on the other hand, are apt to liquidate their inventories during a downturn, providing good cash flow.

"It's a nice balance," says Michelle Galanter Applebaum, of Salomon Brothers Inc., who has taken a keen interest in Inland's distribution activities.

Still, others have tried and failed. **USX** Corp., the nation's No. 1 steelmaker, got rid of its U.S. Steel Supply Division when it restructured several years ago. **Bethlehem Steel** Corp., desperate at the time for cash, sold Tull to Inland in 1986 for about $100 million. **LTV** Corp. and **National Steel** Corp. have done away with their service-center operations, too. Only **Armco** Inc. continues to flirt with the idea, having bought Southwestern Ohio Steel Inc., a service center, last December.

"Getting into the service-center business is just not an attractive option for all steel mills," says Louis L. Schorsch, who advises steel companies for McKinsey & Co. "The kinds of skills you have at a mill are not necessarily the kind you need in distribution."

In many ways, steelmaking and distribution don't fit together at all. While Inland's sheer size undoubtedly provides its service-center subsidiaries with advantages of scale and extensive research capabilities, distribution demands a nimbleness that few corporate giants can muster.

"The key to this business is to have feelings in your fingertips," says Andrew Sharkey, president of the Steel Service Center Institute, a Cleveland trade group. "A guy might call up during the night and

want metal on his dock by 9 a.m. the next day."

Thus Ryerson and Tull constantly are striving to assure customers that, despite the girth of their Chicago parent, they are flexible enough to deliver metal when it is needed, in the form it is needed.

Consider the scene: In Ryerson's biggest plant, across the Indiana line on the West Side of Chicago, gargantuan metal bars and tubes are stacked 40 feet off the ground. Pieces of metal are sheared on cut-to-length lines or sliced with lasers. Flat-bed trucks are filled by forklifts that scurry around with weighty loads.

On the ground, looking almost out of place, are several small sacks, each no bigger than a hand. Inside are individual metal pieces, each a few inches long. These will be shipped one by one.

59

Fighting Quotas

Independent Farmers Oppose Rules Letting Cartels Decide Output

Fruit, Nut Growers Challenge Depression-Era Legacy; Will Almond Butter Sell?

Repealing Curb on Grapefruit

By Marj Charlier

Staff Reporter of The Wall Street Journal

SANGER, Calif.—Inside a big metal building on the Riverbend International Corp. farm here, shiny oranges bounce jauntily along conveyor belts and down chutes, automatically joining like-sized fruit in boxes bound for Pacific Rim markets.

But outside, in orchards that stretch across the San Joaquin Valley, oranges just as fine plop off trees and rot in the scorching heat. Perry Walker, Riverbend's vice president, says that the fruit wouldn't be going to waste if it weren't for restrictions imposed by a government-backed cartel.

Rotting fruit and lost profits have become a cause. Mr. Walker has joined a growing group of independent fruit and nut farmers and packers who are fighting what they see as 1930s-bred socialism. Fifty-year-old federal regulations allow farmers to form cartels to control supplies, share marketing efforts and allocate production rights through "marketing orders" approved and enforced by the U.S. Agriculture Department. Says one grower: "Even the Communists don't do what we're doing—destroying good food."

Smart and Tough

Using petitions, lawsuits and other legal maneuvers, the farmers and packers are winning some battles. In California, Florida and the Upper Midwest, they have gotten rid of some of the nation's 47 marketing orders and begun to weaken others. "The little guys are starting to get smart and tough," says John Ford, a former Agriculture Department official who works as a consultant for farmers fighting marketing orders.

At stake is the enormous power of huge produce-marketing cooperatives. Because of their big market shares, co-ops like Sunkist, Sun-Diamond and the California Almond Growers Exchange have most of the votes on the committees that administer the marketing orders. Without the protection from competition that the production limits provide, the co-ops might lose farmer members and valuable markets to the independents.

Consumers and many farmers stand to gain if the independents' campaign succeeds. More fruit and nuts on the market would lower retail prices, the U.S. Small Business Administration advocacy office has concluded. And eliminating restrictions would increase farmers' profits 10% to 20% by reducing administrative costs and discouraging imports, among other things, according to a study published recently in the Journal of Law and Economics.

Evening Odds

Back in 1938 when the marketing orders were set up, the co-ops were seeking to even up the odds between thousands of Depression-era small farmers—all trying to sell their produce at the same time—and powerful urban buyers. The law allowed farmers, co-ops and packers to form boards to write and administer marketing orders controlling the movement of produce to market. The lemon and orange orders sought to create "equity of opportunity" in the marketplace for all farmers and packers by letting the boards set weekly quotas for each farmer and packer.

Now, no one is predicting that the marketing-order system will collapse overnight. Indeed, while fruit and nut growers are fighting to eliminate supply controls, Congress is considering mandatory controls for grain farmers. The Save the Family Farm Act, sponsored by Sen. Thomas Harkin, an Iowa Democrat, and Rep. Richard Gephardt, a Missouri Democrat, would have farmers vote to limit their production as a solution to grain surpluses and the nation's farm crisis.

And not all farmers and packers dislike marketing orders. The orders benefit small, part-time farmers who don't have time to vie for market share. And their generic advertising programs and quality standards are universally praised.

A Derailed Crusade

Only four years ago, the Agriculture Department itself wanted to overhaul the system, which it oversees. Under former Secretary John Block, the department pushed to reduce cooperative control and rein in anti-competitive orders. But pressure from Sunkist, the huge Arizona and California orange and lemon cooperative, derailed that crusade, says Mr. Ford, the deputy assistant secretary at the time. (Sunkist officials declined to be interviewed for this story.)

Now, the department has dropped the matter, says Patrick Boyle, who heads the department's Agriculture Marketing Service. "In previous years there was more discussion about that," he says. "But if you look to the department to take the lead, that's not going to happen."

Fine, say the independent farmers and packers; they will do it themselves. And they have become a formidable force. "The system's a house of cards," says James Moody, a Washington, D.C., lawyer who has worked for the growers for the past eight years. "If you keep banging away at it, it will fall."

In the past decade, young, college-educated farmers with marketing expertise have quit the co-ops to pack and market their own produce, capturing profits that used to go to middlemen. Computers, larger farms, better transportation and advance buying by supermarkets have all made that easier. Today, 100 packers process and market almonds, while only 15 did a decade ago.

The new independent farmers and packers like this heated competition. Carl "Skip" Pescosolido, a petroleum marketer and orange grower from Irving, Texas, is one of them. He drove to the San Joaquin Valley for the first time in 1970, bought a farm and in 1979 began funneling his marketing skills into selling oranges. He quickly ran up against marketing-order restrictions—he could sell more oranges than the order would allow—and became an early opponent of the California citrus order.

"I was the only voice of reason in the industry," he says. "Today, it's fair to say 30% of my fellow growers share my views."

What really irks these growers is that the quotas have routinely restricted the sale of oranges in only one of four districts regulated by the committee—the district where most of Sunkist's competitors, the independents, operate. These growers, including Messrs. Walker and Pescosolido, are regularly required to divert about 32% of their navel oranges to lower-profit channels like the export market, charities or juice plants.

The independent growers blame the market restrictions for declining per-ca-

(cont.)

pita consumption of oranges and increasing imports. They also note that farm prices haven't improved despite the supply controls.

'Orderly Flow'

Billy J. Peightal, the manager of the orange marketing committees, concedes that oranges haven't been consistently profitable but says that prices have been higher than they would have been without the marketing orders. "The system creates an orderly flow of oranges to the market," he says. "In the long run, everybody would suffer without this order."

But the only time the orange marketing order was lifted—for five months in 1985 after a severe freeze in Florida and Texas—prices to farmers rose and consumer prices didn't. In a study of that episode, the Agriculture Department's Economic Research Service concluded that most times, grower income would be greater without the restrictions.

Meanwhile, independent almond producers have their own complaints. A major one is that the almond marketing board, dominated by CAGE members, requires co-op and independent packers to spend 2.5 cents on brand-specific advertising for each pound of almonds they handle. If they don't spend it, they must forfeit the money to the almond board.

But independent handlers sell more than 90% of their almonds overseas and as ingredients for ice cream and other foods. Many don't have a brand, and brand advertising won't increase their sales one iota, says Robert Saulsbury of Saulsbury Orchards in Madera, Calif. His 2.5-cent levy over the past seven years has added up to more than $1.4 million.

CAGE, which holds most of the retail market with its Blue Diamond brand, does benefit from brand advertising. The co-op spends its advertising money and doesn't have to pay it to the board.

Generic Ads

The almond board has consistently voted against using the forfeited funds on the generic advertising that many independents would like. "We question if 'go out and eat more almonds' helps sell almonds," says Steven Easter, a CAGE and almond board member.

Mr. Saulsbury and two other almond packers have also filed petitions protesting the board's requirement that producers sell a set percentage of their crop to someone who will make almond butter out of it. The butter is supposed to compete with peanut butter and provide a new market for almonds. But butter makers pay less than market value for the almonds, and many of the independents don't believe that almond butter will sell anyway—especially when it is four times as expensive as peanut butter. "Everybody hates almond butter," says Cloyd Angle, who owns the independent packinghouse Cal-Almond Inc. (Mr. Easter says that the almond-butter program has had significant success in Europe.)

Independent growers and packers are beginning to win some significant victories. In April an administrative law judge agreed with Messrs. Pescosolido and Walker and other orange producers who challenged the navel-orange marketing order. Six years' worth of weekly restrictions on marketing oranges were illegal, the judge said, because the Agriculture Department approved them without adequate review and because they weren't fair to the independent growers. The department has appealed the decision.

Cherries and Hops

Meanwhile, cherry growers in the Upper Midwest gathered enough votes to get rid of their marketing order, and hops growers in California voted to scratch theirs last year. In the state of Washington, spearmint growers are contemplating either a lawsuit or an administrative petition to kill their marketing order. And Florida grapefruit growers voted last month to kill theirs. "As growers realize the marketing orders hinder their ability to satisfy customers, they kill them," says Gregory Nelson, of grapefruit grower DNE Sales Inc. in Fort Pierce, Fla.

The fight against the orders has attracted some colorful warriors. One of them is prune packer Neil Denny of Marysville, Calif., a veteran of battles with the county commission, the state environmental protection agency and the county sheriff. Recently, when the prune marketing board, dominated by the Sunsweet co-operative, proposed a reserve to limit sales and raise prices, Mr. Denny's hackles rose again.

"You don't hide anything from the market anymore," he says. The pools only "keep a small guy who's aggressive out."

While marketing board members flew to Washington at the board's expense to persuade the Agriculture Department to approve the reserve, Mr. Denny and fellow independent grower Neill Mitchell paid their own way and burst into department offices to protest. "We were just two little guys with a big story," says Mr. Denny. But he and Mr. Mitchell stopped the reserve, nonetheless.

60

House calls have found a home

Couch potatoes, busy workers willing to pay for the convenience

By Harriet C. Johnson
USA TODAY

Several times a year, a tailor shows up at investment manager John Crockett's office at Beacon Group in Boston. The tailor, who works for Tom James Co., shows Crockett swatches of fabric and takes his measurements, then returns for fittings and comes back in two weeks with a finished garment. The suits cost $400 to $600 each.

Crockett could find less expensive suits at a store, but then he'd "have to leave the office and kill an hour going to and from some other place," he says.

Convenience. It's one reason the luxury of going nowhere has returned.

Delivery of products and services were nearly wiped out when gasoline prices rocketed in the early 1970s. Gone were the milkman and the housecalling TV repairman. Only florists and a few other businesses held out. But now shops-on-wheels are spreading again — to gourmet dining, videotape movies and oil changes for your car.

A new generation of busy business people and lazy couch potatoes is demanding delivery — and is willing to pay for it. And marketers are learning to use the service to stand out from the pack down at the shopping mall.

Some companies have made delivery their reason for being. That shouldn't be any surprise to a nation that has nearly four times more Domino's pizza drivers (85,000) than physicists and astronomers combined (22,000). Detroit-based Domino's has no dining tables in any of its 4,600 pizza delivery outlets, and its quick, reliable delivery (it promises you'll get your pizza in 30 minutes) by mostly young men driving their own cars is a benchmark for the industry.

In services, Decorating Den is among those leading the way. In the past four years, the network of 700 franchises that brings wallpaper and decorating services to homes has seen its customer list quadruple to 35,000 this year.

Delivery is spreading so rapidly that there's even a directory, *L.A. Delivers*, in Los Angeles that lists more than 100 stores, restaurants and services that bring their goods to your home. A complex map shows who will deliver what to where, and you can get anything from dry ice to health food from Yolanda's, which lists Linda Ronstadt and Bill Murray as clients. A smattering of what's happening elsewhere:

▶ **Food:** In one Atlanta neighborhood, Kroger Co. now delivers groceries. Many small, neighborhood grocers do that, but Kroger is a chain of 1,321 supermarkets in 32 states. Through Prodigy — a joint venture of Sears, Roebuck and Co. and IBM Corp. that allows consumers to shop, bank and read news through personal computers — customers can call up a list of more than 3,500 items. Then they can place an order for a flat delivery charge of $8. Most orders arrive the same day. For now, the system is experimental, designed to test the waters for what Kroger calls "The Electronic Grocery Store."

You can often get a gourmet meal delivered in a major city. But Sundborn Ltd., a unit of Chipwich Inc. (of ice cream sandwich fame), is taking that a step further, delivering to just about anywhere. Say you live in central Kansas, you're planning a big date and you'd like to serve veal chops with prosciutto, fontina and sage. You pick up Sundborn's catalog and phone in your order. Delivery comes within 24 hours; you reheat the meal in your microwave. The veal is $13.75 an order, $2.75 for delivery.

▶ **Other goods:** In Chicago, you can have an evening's entertainment — a video and an Italian dinner — delivered from one of Chicago's four Video Plus stores. The video rental chain has gone into the delivery business with a restaurant. Price: Whatever the meal costs plus $2.50 for the video rental and $1 for delivery. From 25 to 50 customers a week use the service.

In Charlotte, N.C., you can get a book without going to the bookstore. By October, Fort Lauderdale, Fla.-based Books by Wire plans to offer its service nationally. In the test phase in Charlotte, the company says some customers even pay the $5 delivery charge for a single $4.95 paperback. After ordering from a catalog, delivery (by United Parcel Service) takes two to three days.

Sak's Fifth Avenue is seeing its delivery business grow. The company has informally delivered goods for years — in 1980 it started its Executive Service in one store. But now it's in 34 of Saks' 44 stores. For a one-time fee of $50, you can register your sizes at one of the stores. If you spill soup on your tie during lunch, they'll deliver a new one before you meet a client for drinks.

"I think today you really need to be serviced," says Executive Service director Susan Olden. "We're all running in 20 directions to accomplish our workload."

▶ **Services:** In Irvine, Calif., you can get your cleaning picked up at the office. Rainbowman Dry Cleaners picks up your shirts, launders them and delivers them back to you for $1.40 each. A sign of the company's success: Before delivery began last November, Rainbowman's sales were $1,900 a month. Today, sales are more than $20,000 a month.

If you must go shopping, you can even get some services delivered at the mall. For example, while you're strolling, MobiCare, a franchise based in Gettysburg, Pa., will do a 17-point maintenance check on your car for less than $25. The company's 23 vans in 23 cities come to malls, office buildings or any parking spot.

What's behind all this? "People do prefer to stay at home," says Cheryl Russell, editor in chief of *American Demographics* magazine. Baby boomers are often two-career couples shuffling kids from day care to piano lessons, and they'd often rather not have to run out for bread or to check a new drapery pattern. Companies find that such customers are willing to pay a premium — from 12.5% to 100% in some cases — for goods to come to them.

But delivery is still an emerging factor in business and experts aren't sure how big it will get. One key test will be the fast-food industry. The potential is huge: A study by Campbell Soup Co. and the Food Marketing Institute found we already spend $62.4 billion on take-home meals. So the wheels are turning at giant corporations to see if we'd rather have those meals delivered.

General Mills Inc. is experimenting with home delivery through The Order Inn, which makes complete meals that cus-

(cont.)

tomers re-heat. Lasagna costs $5.25 and prime rib goes for $10.95. After eight months of tests in Minneapolis, General Mills has decided to double — to 90,000 — the number of homes it serves.

On the other hand, Popeye's Famous Fried Chicken, a New Orleans-based chain of 701 fast-food stores — tested delivery and found that customers didn't use it.

Others are finding the same thing. Safeway Stores Inc. spokesman John Shepherd says one problem for grocers is that people are picky about produce. He says customers want "to go into the store and pick from among the apples, check for bruises, squeeze the oranges."

Some retailers say home delivery doesn't make sense for them. "As a store, our main object is to get people into the store to shop," says Sue Sorensen, a spokesperson for Dayton Hudson Corp. in Minneapolis. That way, while you're looking for one thing, you may buy a few other things, too.

A big hurdle: delivering is expensive. To keep costs down, today's deliverers use computerized inventory systems and they keep office or store space and staff to a minimum. They make appointments — saying they'll be there at 4 p.m. rather than just "next Tuesday" — so they don't make any unnecessary calls.

Some new firms cut costs by investing in nothing but the delivery system itself. Waiters on Wheels, for example, picks up meals from San Francisco's restaurants and takes them to homes for a fee of $3 to $5. After eight months in business, the company has picked up 5,000 regular customers. Such businesses show that consumers are becoming more willing to pay for delivery and that entrepreneurs will find ways to bring the goods to them.

In fact, one small Florida company — Palm Beach Milk Co. — is getting ready to deliver milk to homes in September.

And in San Jose, Calif., you can always call Poop Van Scoop. They'll clean up after your dog in your backyard for $5 a week.

61

Trains Double Up to Get Truck Business

New Car Setup Starts Rate War, Aiding Shippers

By Daniel Machalaba
Staff Reporter of The Wall Street Journal

The proliferation of double-stack container trains is igniting a rate war between truckers and railroads, benefiting shippers with lower freight rates.

More than 100 double-stack trains, which carry one container loaded above another, now ply the nation's long-haul east-west freight routes each week, compared with a handful five years ago. Double-stack rates between Chicago and Los Angeles dropped 15% in the past 12 months, as freight-hauling capacity continued to grow amid a slowdown in demand. Some analysts expect rates to fall further when additional trains are launched.

The transcontinental freight routes have become "extremely competitive," says John Koons, president of Country Wide Transport Services Inc., a truck company. Double-stack trains are "taking a lot of freight that used to be routed via trucks."

Efficiency Increased

More broadly, the double-stack trains are "increasing the efficiency of U.S. freight transportation and the competitiveness of U.S. manufacturers," says Gerard McCullough, deputy director of transportation studies at Massachusetts Institute of Technology.

The rate cutting affects long-distance east-west freight flows of more than $10 billion a year. Some analysts estimate that the industrywide rate drops spurred by double-stack competition are saving U.S. consumers between $500 million and $1 billion a year.

Among the biggest rate cuts are ones on the busy Chicago-Los Angeles corridor, where rates for some carriers plunged from about $1,500 for some of the bigger containers two years ago to $1,200 to $1,000 now.

Proctor & Gamble Co. recently shifted some of its business away from trucks to double-stack trains because of the rate cuts and improvements in double-stack service. The company now ships 20 container loads a week of potato chips, peanut butter and liquid detergent from its Midwest plants to the West Coast by rail.

In response to shipper defections, some truckers are slashing rates. Others are courting shippers further away from the major double-stack terminals. A few are fleeing transcontinental routes, focusing instead on shorter regional deliveries.

Country Wide is moving its headquarters from Pomona, Calif., where double-stack competition is keen, to Knoxville, Tenn. MNX Inc., a St. Joseph, Mo., trucker, is redeploying trucks to less competitive routes in the Southeast. Recently, MNX bought a shipping broker to gain access to the fast-growing double-stack market. Another trucker, CRST Inc., Cedar Rapids, Iowa, shelved plans to buy 50 more trucks, blaming rate declines.

"We're barely making money," says John Smith, president of CRST. "We're doing everything we can to keep costs down."

For decades the nation's railroads seemed helpless against trucking companies that siphoned off their most lucrative freight, leaving the rails with low-rated

bulk traffic. They fought back with piggyback—transporting highway trailers on flatcars—but managed to win freight mainly from their own boxcars.

Double-stacks represent the "first concrete example of a new rail intermodal technology taking traffic off the highway," says Lee Lane, intermodal executive director of the Association of American Railroads. By some estimates, double-stacks are capturing U.S. freight shipments of more than $100 million a year from trucks.

Bathtub-Shaped Wells

By stacking two containers on special rail cars, railroads nearly double train capacity and cut rail costs 25%. The double-stack trains carry containers in low-slung, bathtub-shaped wells that provide a smoother ride than piggyback trains.

American President Cos., an Oakland, Calif.-based ocean ship line, launched the first coast-to-coast double-stack train in 1984. It was originally designed to speed international cargo off the company's ships on the West Coast to inland destinations. But to balance the heavy flow of Asian imports on its eastbound trains, the company solicited domestic freight to fill containers that would have returned empty to the West Coast. Later, American President expanded its trains to carry domestic freight in both directions.

"Our international freight volumes gave us the base to create a domestic freight system," says Donald Orris, president of the company's domestic freight unit.

Other ship lines, and the rail units of CSX Corp., Burlington Northern Inc. and Santa Fe Pacific Corp., have launched their own double-stack trains. Now they are trying to lure U.S. domestic shippers to use the the trains by ordering thousands of large-capacity containers, expanding terminals, speeding up train schedules and reducing rates. Currently, domestic freight accounts for about 30% of the cargo on double-stack trains and the business is growing rapidly.

CSX and American President have begun to dispatch their own company trucks and drivers, rather than relying on independent drivers, to move containers between shippers' loading docks and their railheads. That will eliminate some shipment delays, they say. And American President is refunding freight charges when it fails to deliver on time.

Thinking Like a Trucker

Double-stack operators are also making organizational changes, hiring executives from the trucking industry, for example. "The rails have finally realized after trial and error that to be competitive with truckers you have to think and act like a trucker," says M. McNeil Porter, a former trucking company executive who is president of CSX's CSL Intermodal unit.

Some shippers aren't likely to shift freight to double-stack trains any time soon. "Motor carriers cover more routes, give better service and their transit time is less," says Peter Brock, transportation manager of J.C. Penney Co. The trains are restricted, particularly in the East, by bridge and tunnel clearances. And shipper surveys rate trucks higher than rail intermodal service in reliability, speed, door-to-door delivery and customer responsiveness.

But 3M Corp., Campbell Soup Co. and General Electric Co.'s appliance division

(cont.)

have recently switched some shipments to double-stack trains from trucks. One reason Procter & Gamble switched some of its freight to trains from trucks is that "they use less fuel and create less pollution and that's good for the country," says Fred Morris, the company's transportation director.

Nabisco Foods Co. also plans to divert certain shipments to double-stacks because the company is concerned about the growing shortage of long-haul truck drivers. "We're trying to protect ourselves by putting as much freight on rail as we can," says William Ditoro, transportation director of the RJR Nabisco Inc. unit. "We're trying to wean ourselves off trucks."

62

A SMART COOKIE AT PEPPERIDGE

After an epic battle of the baking titans, this company found itself a day late and a biscuit short. A new president has put leaven in its loaf and hot products on the shelves. ■ *by Bill Saporito*

THE COOKIE MACHINE is cooking full blast at Pepperidge Farm. Three years after slinking away from an epic marketing battle waged by giants like Procter & Gamble and Nabisco over crunchy-chewy cookies, and two years after a series of new-product fiascos, the Campbell Soup Co. subsidiary is back in the chips. Pepperidge has gone on the offensive with new "lumpy bumpy" cookies crammed with chocolate, raisins, nuts, and whatnot, hoping to dish out some lumps and bumps to the crunchy-chewy gang that started the Great Cookie War.

"Pepperidge Farm is a shining star," crows R. Gordon McGovern, Campbell's chief executive. Pepperidge, which represents 10.4% of Campbell's sales, increased operating earnings last year 33% to $51.1 million on sales of $455 million, even with heavy outlays for new products. Cookies, called biscuits in the industry, account for half of Pepperidge's revenue, and business has been absolutely boffo. For the year ended in August, the company increased its market share from 3.5% to 4.5%. In the $3-billion-a-year packaged ready-to-eat cookie business, a full point is a lot of dough.

Other Pepperidge lines include a mail-or-der house and Godiva Chocolatier. That division is also fattening up: Sales of its $20-a-pound chocolates rose 19% last year to about $40 million, and the company expects a similar increase in 1986. The frozen-food division forecasts doubled sales this year with the big success of a new frozen pizza. Pepperidge's only soft spot is bread, where it faces yeasty competition from supermarket bakeries. The company is whipping up new varieties of specialty breads it claims are difficult for the supermarkets to match.

Behind the fatter cookies is a thinner, quicker Pepperidge Farm, a model of how to cut costs while improving quality and service. In the early 1980s the company found itself spending a lot of money making the wrong products and delivering them—too slowly—to the wrong market. President Richard Shea, the fourth head of Pepperidge since McGovern left to run Campbell in 1979, took over in 1984 and methodically reestablished the company as a high-end, high-quality biscuit and bread baker. In his zeal for reform, he purged hundreds of products such as vegetable- and meat-filled frozen pastry and Star Wars cookies. He has lowered costs by selling plants and tightening production processes,

until recently as quaint as the homey New England image the company's advertising likes to project. Speed is what wins prizes in the baking game. By computerizing every operation from dough making to store inventory, Pepperidge is knocking hours, even days, off the time between baking and delivery.

Margaret Rudkin, a Connecticut entrepreneur, baked preservative-free whole wheat bread for her children and started Pepperidge Farm in 1937. Campbell bought the business in 1961. Under McGovern, who took over in 1968, Pepperidge grew on the strength of its quality. It went from a regional baker with $100 million in annual sales to a $400-million-a-year national packaged-goods maker.

McGovern's successors emphasized frozen foods, then undergoing tremendous expansion. The company produced all manner of pastry-wrapped fruits, vegetables, and meats but committed a tactical blunder, says McGovern: Because the products could not be zapped in microwave ovens, competitors' snacks were more convenient. And in the

REPORTER ASSOCIATE *Stephen Madden*

(cont.)

frenzy of activity to fill up the freezer case, the company put its biscuit and bread business on automatic pilot.

As frozen foods began to cool, the biscuits came under attack. Frito-Lay's Grandma's were the first cookies in the market with crunchy outsides and chewy insides, an attempt to mimic the homemade variety. Then, late in 1983, Procter & Gamble declared the Great Cookie War by introducing Duncan Hines cookies with a national advertising blitz. The market leader, Nabisco Brands, now RJR Nabisco, joined in; so did Keebler. Over two years the four companies together spent close to $100 million on advertising, an unprecedented—and unsustainable—amount.

IN THE MIDST of the shoot-out, Pepperidge made like Switzerland: It stayed neutral and produced chocolate. "There is no end to the debate around here about whether the cookie war affected us," says Shea. "I tend to believe not." Nonetheless, Shea admits that the war was a missed opportunity. The advertising hoopla sent waves of consumers looking for "new" cookies, and Pepperidge had none. Shea says, "We cut our marketing funds, folded our tent, and went home. If we had had the right offering, we could have had so many sales we couldn't have dealt with them." Instead, the company introduced a cookie licensed from the spectacularly successful *Star Wars* movies—just as the *Star Wars* craze was fading. The product was aimed at children, light-years away from Pepperidge's upper-crust, adult niche. Star Wars, the cookie, lost $2 million.

McGovern picked Shea to run Pepperidge because "we had to do something. He's got a very keen sense of good product, he values freshness, and these are the things that make Pepperidge go." If you met Shea at a party, you might not remember him the next day even if you had had only water to drink. A square, spectacled man, he appears every bit the food engineer who spent some of his first working years designing dehydrated potatoes and technology for angel food cake mixes. His does not look like the face that has launched more than 500 new products at Pillsbury, Green Giant, Borden's, and Campbell. Once you sit down with him, however,

Shea gives evidence of ample wit. He is one smart cookie.

Shea makes Pepperidge's three-step game plan sound simple: "You have to have a crystal-clear product strategy and a religious appreciation for quality. Once you get that right, you get on to production; and once you get that right, you get a big ad budget and blow the product out of there." He zoomed in on Pepperidge's products, telling managers that the company would sell only top-quality, top-priced goods. He junked more than 300 items with little economic analysis: He decided their fate with his taste buds, not marketing reports.

The company's new products are ultra everything. The American Collection—the lumpy bumpys—are so full of goodies that the manufacturing engineers had a difficult time getting the cookies to hold together. Another new line, called Distinctive Chocolatier, borrowed butter cookies with molded chocolate tops from Delacre, a Campbell affiliate in Belgium. According to the A.C. Nielsen market information service, crunchy-chewy cookie sales fell 50% in 1985 and are recovering modestly this year—while Pepperidge claims it cannot keep up with the demand for its lumpy bumpys.

WHILE PEPPERIDGE readied new products, the company's plants were in no shape to meet emerging competition. To compete with the supermarkets, the company had to be a low-cost manufacturer so it could offer retailers the prospect of high profits from brand-name bread. To compete with cookie stores and other cookie companies, Pepperidge had to get fresher. "We broke down all the reasons we couldn't do it, and reached new standards of freshness across all our lines," says Shea. The standards included people. He replaced 16 top executives and sold off four of his 11 plants.

The strategic problem, though, was information. Orders from drivers were assembled manually at regional sales offices and mailed to the bakeries. Now, with computers, the company has an almost instantaneous link among sales, inventory, and production. Hundreds of the company's 2,200 franchised drivers record the inventory at each stop along their routes with hand-held computers.

Periodically they phone the information directly to computers riding the hips of production managers on the bakery floor. Generally, national cookie makers deliver products to stores from inventory that is five to ten days old; nationally marketed breads may be five days out of the oven. Pepperidge has trimmed those times to less than five days on average for cookies and less than three for bread. "Our goal is to get the cookies from the ovens to the stores in 72 hours, and we're scaring the life out of that now," says Shea. A $78-million plant under construction in Lakeland, Florida, should lower the averages still further. The company went globe-hopping to bring in equipment from half a dozen countries that will allow it to make 100 varieties of products in a single shift—about ten times the number it can handle now.

SHEA ALMOST DUMPED the Richmond, Utah, frozen-food operation, which was operating at 14% of capacity (vs. a company average of 85%), when Campbell ordered him to shut it down. But after seeing the place and meeting the workers, he decided that the patient could be saved. "We just kept telling people to come to work until we found something for them to make," he says. Salvation finally appeared in the form of a frozen pizza made with croissant dough that Pepperidge introduced last year. Sales are running a third above projections.

With products and production taken care of, Pepperidge is working on Shea's third step, advertising, with an open checkbook. In the middle of the cookie war, the company spent less than $5 million on advertising for all products; in the last quarter of 1986 it spent $14 million, making it the fifth-largest advertiser among all food companies. With some factory capacity still on standby, Pepperidge has room for more new offerings. In the meantime, the company opened its second Pepperidge Tree restaurant last month in a mall not far from its Norwalk, Connecticut, headquarters. Neither Campbell nor Pepperidge has much experience in retail food service, but that shouldn't daunt Shea. He didn't know much about the cookie business either. **F**

HOW LEVI STRAUSS IS GETTING THE LEAD OUT OF ITS PIPELINE

Before Sandi K. Torres paid for two pairs of Levi's 501 jeans at the KG Men's Store in Englewood, Colo., the cashier "shot" the price tags with a laser gun and in seconds $15.99 flashed twice on the register. The secret to that speedy transaction ended up later in Torres' trash can.

A tag on each pair carries a universal product code, the black lines more familiar on dog food and magazines. Besides speeding Torres through the checkout line, the code informed Levi Strauss & Co. of her purchase, setting in motion a chain of events that will lead to more jeans being made to replace the pairs she bought.

SHORTER LINES. When Levi began slapping bar codes on jeans in 1985 it gave retailers a shove toward electronic methods of processing order, inventory, and sales information. Although well behind pioneers in the grocery and automotive-supply industries, Levi Strauss is one of dozens of apparel manufacturers communicating electronically with retailers. Systems like LeviLink affix bar-code labels on goods at the factory and provide elaborate software services to track the goods through the retail channel. In a few years, believes Craig Van Fossan, re-

PHOTOGRAPHS BY ROBERT HOLMGREN

LEVI'S 501s The product code is stitched on at the factory, easing distribution to stores—and speeding sales figures to Levi Strauss

tail consultant for Kurt Salmon Associates, "anybody who doesn't do it will be at a real competitive disadvantage."

Already, such national retailers as Sears, J. C. Penney, and Wal-Mart are spending millions installing bar-code scanners in their stores and getting ready for the data onslaught. The comprehensive systems provide what the industry calls a "quick response" to retail trends and regional preferences. That means the right merchandise is on the right shelves at the right time. Retail-

ers think it can give domestic goods an edge over imports.

The results are dramatic: LeviLink has reduced the time between the order and receipt of shipment from 40 to a dozen days in some places. At Designs Inc., a Levi-only retailer based in Chestnut Hill, Mass., information on items that have sold during the day is kept in each of the 44 stores' computers. Each night the company's mainframe computer collects that information, and on the weekend it sends Levi an electronic order. Levi typically will ship the goods within four days. Such "electronic purchase orders" currently represent 25% of the total orders for Levi's jeans.

In retailing, nimbleness equals profits. A Kurt Salmon study found that $100 billion of softgoods is sitting in the inventory pipeline, and one-quarter of potential sales from that batch may not materialize if the goods are not available in time. Retailers such as Wal-Mart Stores Inc. are quickly getting the message to suppliers: Use bar-code labeling, or find new outlets for your goods.

By Joan O'C. Hamilton in San Francisco, with Randy Welch in Denver

Reprinted from the December 21, 1987 issue of *Business Week* by special permission, copyright© 1987 by McGraw-Hill, Inc.

ADVERTISING / By Thomas R. King

Credibility Gap: More Consumers Find Celebrity Ads Unpersuasive

Want to buy a television set or a pair of sunglasses? How about a pizza, underwear or some baby shampoo?

Just stop by Orel Hershiser's place—they're all for sale. Mr. Hershiser, extraordinary baseball pitcher and pitchman extraordinaire, is on so many TV commercials these days that his agent struggles to remember them all.

As celebrities continue to cash in on their fame, consumers are having more trouble believing what stars say in TV ads. A study to appear in the next issue of Commercial Break, **Video Storyboard Tests Inc.**'s newsletter about TV ads, says the number of consumers who find celebrity  ads "less than credible" jumped to 52% in 1988 from 38% in 1987. The fastest loss of credibility was among younger viewers.

In addition, consumers don't think celebrities are very persuasive, Video Storyboards says. Consumers recently ranked celebrities as only the eighth-most convincing tool used in TV ads. Celebrities finished right behind "experts in the field" and slightly ahead of company presidents. In 1984, 22% of respondents rated celebrity commercials persuasive. Only 16% thought the same way in 1988.

"Consumers are more skeptical than ever of celebrities' motives for doing commercials," says Dave Vadehra, the news-letter's editor. The most recent data, he says, show the number of respondents who think celebrities are doing ads just for the money climbed to 64% in 1988 from 50% in 1987.

"I can't blame them," Patrick J. Cunningham, chief creative officer at ad agency **N W Ayer**, says of consumers. "Celebrities *are* doing it just for the money."

The survey showed a sharp increase—to 37% in 1988 from 26% only a year earlier—in the number of respondents who think celebrities don't even use the product they are pitching. Stars' credibility undoubtedly has been bruised by isolated incidents where Hollywood hucksters have tripped up. Madison Avenue is still haunted by publicly reported admissions that Cybill Shepherd doesn't eat the beef she endorsed and that Michael Jackson doesn't drink the Pepsi he plugged.

More recently, there has been some debate about the impact of Maxwell House coffee commercials showing TV weatherman Willard Scott and newswoman Linda Ellerbee in a format that imitates a news program.

Mr. Vadehra's findings seem to fall on deaf ears as Madison Avenue continues to parade out more and more stars. Recent entries include John Larroquette, star of TV's "Night Court," pitching Holiday Inn, and Tim Conway and Harvey Korman selling Fruit & Fibre cereal. Late last month, Lintas: New York, a unit of **Interpublic Group**, signed 10 National Football League stars including Boomer Esiason and Eric Dickerson for Diet Coke commercials. And another commercial with Mr. Hershiser, this one for Wheaties breakfast cereal, has just begun appearing.

A number of advertising executives admit stars have been overused and misused. "In most cases, celebrities are used as a crutch," says Sam Scali, president and creative director of **Ogilvy Group**'s Scali, McCabe, Sloves ad agency in New York. He adds: "Celebrities often are a waste of a client's money."

But even Mr. Scali's agency has a campaign running that features not one, not two, but three stars. The somewhat silly ads for Hertz Corp. show athletes O.J. Simpson and Arnold Palmer singing tunes such as "California, Here We Come" and "Moon Over Miami" as they whiz down a freeway in a rented car. Between the musical bits, actress Jamie Lee Curtis extols Hertz's prices.

Mr. Scali defends the campaign, saying Mr. Simpson embodies "speed," and speed of service is very important to car renters. Last week, Hertz put its account up for review, but it isn't clear the company is tired of celebrities. Hertz said the review was prompted by changing market conditions in its business.

Some industry executives say Madison Avenue is unlikely ever to kick the celebrity habit, no matter what surveys say. The U.S. public thrives on the comings and goings of celebrities, insists Penny Hawkey, president and executive creative director at **Bloom Cos.**' Bloom Agency, New York. "We are titillated by the lives of the rich and famous."

Promotion

65

High-Tech Hype Reaches New Heights

Companies Cite Dubious 'Firsts,' Exotic Numbers

By MICHAEL W. MILLER
Staff Reporter of THE WALL STREET JOURNAL

Recently the world bore witness to a revolution in man's conquest of information. A few days later, civilization embarked upon a new renaissance. Shortly after that, the pen, ink and paper became obsolete.

In case you missed these events, here's what happened. First, Sharp Electronics Corp. introduced a new hand-held computer—and that touched off "the next true revolution in man's conquest of information," a Sharp press release explained.

Then came Summagraphic Corp.'s new line of high-resolution digitizing tablets, which ushered in "the Second Renaissance," according to a company mailing.

Paper's demise came when Coda Music Software started selling a new music-transcription program. "The age of pen, ink and paper, the standard for 900 years, is over," Coda's press release stated.

Writing press releases for high-tech products is a feverish game without rules. The world's electronic industries bring out hundreds of new products daily, each attended by professional hyperbolists. On one recent Monday, a Wall Street Journal reporter on the high-tech beat received a record 60 pieces of mail weighing nearly eight pounds, including a chocolate "chip" from Advanced Micro Devices Inc., a maker of silicon microchips.

Getting attention for a new product is tough in any industry, but the challenge for high-tech publicists is, to use one of their favorite words, unique. The news usually turns on mind-numbing technical matters. And no other field has such a large number of start-ups all convinced that their product is the next Apple computer or Lotus 1-2-3 spreadsheet.

To examine the state of the art in high-tech press releases, this reporter scrutinized and cataloged every new-product release he received during a 30-day period—201 specimens in all. The results offer a look at the gambits publicists use in their struggle to stand out from the crowd.

FORCED FIRSTS

High-tech publicists consider it extremely important to find a category in which a new product represents a "first." And there is no verbal hoop through which they won't jump in order to make the claim.

"Cirrus Logic," one press release trumpets, "is the first semiconductor company to offer a co-processor specifically to enhance the speed and reduce the system cost of raster printers." The same release also calls Cirrus "the first semiconductor company to address the market for intelligent VLSI using proprietary, silicon compilation technology."

Sometimes it's better not to ask just how significant these firsts are. Consider the following from FoundationWare, a software company: "QuickVac is the first-of-its-kind software using FoundationWare Intelligent Sentence Translator (FIST) technology."

Is that a meaningful first? "Not really, to be totally honest," says Michael Riemer, a FoundationWare spokesman. "It's a nice little tutorial for people who aren't totally computer savvy."

MYSTERY MARKET RESEARCH

No new-product press release is truly complete without official research emanating from nowhere in particular and proving that the product's market is about to explode.

CTA Inc.—maker of "the first product for the Macintosh SE, Plus and II capable of reading even the most complex documents"—has this to say about the market for software that converts printed pages into computer text: "Analysts see a 14-fold increase in this sector of the industry over the next three years."

Where did CTA find these analysts? CTA publicist Margaret Mehling says her information came from a January 1988 article in PC Week, a computer magazine. As it turns out, the article attributes the prediction to CAP International, a market-research firm. That firm indeed predicted a fourteenfold increase, but over four years, not three.

Another example, from OROS Systems Inc., a biotechnology-products company: "The OROS kit would be used by companies developing injectable monoclonal-based therapeutics. This market is expected to grow from $5 million in 1988 to $600 million in 1991." Says who? "According to market-research data," is the press release's only attribution.

OROS President Michael Boss says the forecast comes from a report by Theta Corp., a firm specializing in medical market research. The Theta report, however, says the market for injectable monoclonal-based therapeutics is expected to grow from zero in 1988 to $475 million in 1991.

Asked about the discrepancy, Mr. Boss explains that OROS also added in Theta's forecast for monoclonal-based *diagnostic imaging* products. "I suppose we were a bit loose with the word therapeutics," Mr. Boss says. But, he notes, the OROS kit can indeed be used by both markets.

MEASUREMENT MANIA

When nothing else comes to mind, it's never hard for companies to find a number to brag about. Very exotic and precise numbers are considered especially slick.

A press release from Alcoa Fujikura Ltd. boasts that the company has developed new optical-fiber technology with "a through-put time per ferrule of one to three minutes." The press release from Coda Music Software [the people who put pen and paper out of business] promises that its music-transcription program can handle "nested tuplets up to 8 levels."

There are so many ways to measure a computer's speed that a company just isn't trying hard enough if it can't find one that favors its new machine. According to a release from Apollo Computer, for exam-

The Hype Hit Parade

High-tech PR's most overused words, based on number of occurrences in 201 new-product press releases:

#	Word	Count
1	Leading	88
2	Enhanced	47
3	Unique	35
4	Significant	30
5	Solution	23
6	Integrated	23
7	Powerful	20
8	Innovative	18
9	Advanced	17
10	High-performance	17
11	Sophisticated	17

(cont.)

ple, the company's new Series 10000 Personal Supercomputer is "34 times higher than a |Digital Equipment Corp.| VAX 11 780 in double precision Linpack ratings." The computer also is "four times faster than a Sun 4/260 in SPICE ratings."

GOBBLEDYGOOK

Again and again, our sample showed high-tech companies' curious reluctance to come right out and say just what it is they are announcing. The gobbledygook quotient was high even in releases written by outside public-relations firms, whose fortunes often depend on how many newspapers decide to run stories about the companies they represent.

Here's a particularly thick example from KVO Inc., a Beaverton, Ore., public-relations firm: "MicroCASE . . . today announced . . . a joint development effort between Cadre Technologies and MicroCASE that tightly links structured analysis and design CASE tools to software development and test tools in support of real-time embedded system design."

Manning Selvage & Lee, a New York public-relations firm, created this concoction: "NCR Corporation's SCSI Technology Group today announced a new dual-channel synchronous SCSI host adapter for Multibus which provides the Multibus user with two independent SCSI-to-Multibus channels on one standard Multibus card."

Interestingly, the people who wrote these releases say they are not entirely happy with them. KVO account manager Margie Yap says she tried to persuade MicroCASE to drop the techno-babble and instead emphasize the long-term economic impact of its new product, which is supposed to make software writers more productive. The company would have none of it. "They're all engineers," she sighs. "They say, 'This is a neat whizzy thing and engineers love it.' Talking about things like productivity, it's like 'Don't bother me with those details.' "

At Manning Selvage & Lee, publicist Suzanne Quigley says she actually drafted a much clearer version of the NCR release. It even defined the terms "dual-channel," "SCSI," and "Multibus." But, she says, NCR excised the explanations. "These companies are very snobby. They just figure, how could you not know that dual channel means you can hook up two peripherals on one board and free up a slot?"

Marketing officials inside MicroCASE and NCR argue that these press releases were aimed at technical publications and had to be written with them in mind. "There is a fear that editors who receive |a less technical release| would believe that they are being talked down to by the company," says Gary Stechmesser, NCR's director of public relations.

Caine O'Brien, a marketing manager for MicroCASE, agrees. He adds: "From my perspective, if we aroused your curiosity to the point where you were interested in talking to us, then we succeeded in the primary goal of getting some press attention."

66

Selling Software That's Hard to Describe

Lotus's Agenda Poses a Problem In Marketing

By WILLIAM M. BULKELEY

Staff Reporter of THE WALL STREET JOURNAL

CAMBRIDGE, Mass.—Lotus Development Corp. wants to sell you a $395 "personal information manager" for your computer.

What's a personal information manager? Well, it's a bit hard to explain. And that's Connall Ryan's problem. Mr. Ryan is product manager for Lotus's new program, Agenda, and for the past year and a half he has been wrestling with how to market the software.

Lotus, the No. 2 personal computer software maker, faces one of the most daunting of marketing problems—selling a brand new type of product. Marketers know how to push chewier candy bars, improved detergents and speedier word processors. But brand new things are something else. Says Elizabeth Suneby, Lotus's advertising manager: "We have to tell people what a personal information manager is and why Agenda is the best personal information manager."

Agenda is a product that helps users organize information. But a lot depends on the user's creativity in deciding what information to store and how it should be stored. Once that's done, Agenda sorts the information accordingly and makes the proper adjustments whenever changes are made. For example, a user might type "high priority—tell Susan about Tuesday's sales meeting." Agenda can then file the reminder in separate lists of things related to Susan—to the date, to the sales department and to priority items. Change the meeting date to Wednesday, and Agenda changes the other lists.

Early Strategy

To launch Agenda, which will be shipped to dealers starting today, Lotus is said to have budgeted $6 million—more than the annual sales of all but a few programs. The company has run cryptic teaser advertisements in computer magazines, given early copies of the program to influential "techies" and previewed it at trade shows. Among computer cognoscenti, it is probably the most eagerly awaited new software product of the year.

But there isn't any guarantee it will be a hit. Indeed, there isn't any guarantee that Lotus will succeed in explaining to buyers precisely what the new product is. Mitchell Kapor, former chairman of Lotus and co-author of the program, coined the term "mystery-ware" to describe Agenda, which he conceived because he was frustrated that the computer couldn't help him organize the dozens of notes and business cards he unloaded from his pockets every day. "I'm eagerly awaiting the results from the marketplace," he says, adding that Agenda could be "either a big success or just a market presence."

Software experts have equally mixed opinions. Stewart Alsop, editor of P.C. Letter, a Redwood City, Calif.-based newsletter, says that Agenda is likely to be "another very-talked-about program that falls flat on its face because you can't use both" Agenda and another program at the same time. Stock analysts say that Agenda won't help Lotus's bottom line for years. Says David Readerman, an analyst with Smith Barney & Co.: "My expectations are low. It's a real marketing challenge."

But some argue Agenda could be a big hit and create a new category of software. "This is fundamentally new and different. It's tremendously exciting," says Esther Dyson, editor of Release 1.0, a newsletter that covers computer software. "I think it's an extremely useful tool," says Mort Rosenthal, chairman of Corporate Software Inc., a Westwood, Mass.-based software distributor. He says he uses Agenda more than any other software.

Big software companies have proved inept at creating new software categories, mostly buying smaller innovative firms or developing products in existing categories. But creating a new category offers the potential for big sales and profits.

Having a new hit product is important to Lotus just now. Last year it got about two-thirds of its $395.6 million in revenue from sales of just one program: 1-2-3, a spreadsheet designed by Mr. Kapor that remains the industry's best-selling software. The 1-2-3 program is facing growing competition, and Lotus consistently has trailed competitors in entering other areas of the software market. Moreover, Lotus has suffered a string of setbacks in recent months, including a six-month delay in shipping an updated version of 1-2-3.

Mr. Ryan, the product manager, got his first look at Agenda in January 1987. Because the product was so different, he pushed to get outsiders involved far earlier than normally. "My job was to open up the doors and let the sunshine in," Mr. Ryan says. He started running focus groups asking participants to watch a demonstration and make lists of things it could do.

Rather than keeping the program inside Lotus through its gestation period, Mr. Ryan started testing it on 25 loyal Lotus users. He gave them the program, some skimpy directions and said, "Here's this thing that's very amorphous. I won't even tell you what it is. Try it and tell us what you're doing." One of the users, George Goodwin, an account manager at Royal Bank of Canada in Toronto, startled developers by using Agenda to sort electronic newswires.

Since last fall, Agenda has been given to some 200 testers, five times the norm for a new product. They persuaded Lotus to redesign the way the program appears on the screen to users, a process that delayed Agenda for several months.

Lotus also decided to show off Agenda early—something most software companies avoid for fear they'll be copied or that their product will seem old by the time it finally emerges. "We thought it was so new we had to get the conversational ball rolling," says Mr. Ryan. So Mr. Kapor demonstrated it publicly last November.

Whether the strategy will boost sales isn't clear. But it certainly boosted interest. Mr. Ryan says some 300 people contacted him proposing various products based on Agenda. Lotus says 12 books are being written about the program.

Symantec Inc., a Cupertino, Calif., software company was so impressed by the excitement generated by Agenda that it dubbed its new GrandView program, which organizes text in outlines, a personal information manager.

One problem is how to advertise Agenda. Recently, Lotus began running a series of ads in computer magazines with pictures of ducks in a row, a funnel, a safety net and other items meant to symbolize aspects of Agenda. With the shipping of the product, the company will run eight-page inserts that pull together all the symbols and relate them to Agenda.

Planting a Seed

Lotus is also trying to put Agenda in the hands of people who will use it and talk about it. The company will give away thou-

(cont.)

sands of copies to influential techies. "Compared to an ad, it's so cost effective to seed it," says Mr. Ryan. For the less influential, Lotus will sell $15 "crippled" versions that can't print or store information but will let users see Agenda's potential.

Mr. Ryan says that face-to-face demonstrations seem to be the best way to convince users. When he demonstrated it at the Capitol Users Group in Washington, D.C., 77 of the 107 members present said they would buy it. Lotus has brought its regional sales representatives to Cambridge twice for two-day sessions in how to demonstrate Agenda. They'll be giving more than 100 seminars in the next few weeks.

Mr. Ryan figures that if he finds enough people, the program will develop the sort of momentum that made Lotus 1-2-3 a corporate standard that large companies ordered by the gross. Already, a British company that gives time-management seminars has ordered thousands of copies to be distributed as part of its course.

But he says that unlike some past product launches, "we view it as the first leg of a long haul. I think we're beginning to realize that marketing is an incremental process."

ADVERTISING / By Joanne Lipman

Too Many Coupons in the Paper? Advertisers Rethink Promotion

Inundated by coupons? Tired of those coupon inserts spilling out of the Sunday papers and littering the house?

America's advertisers can help. After years of issuing more and more coupons, and of pouring money into coupons instead of into real advertising, advertisers are pulling back, convinced that coupon clutter has made the promotion less effective. The number of coupons is still growing, but at a slower pace, and advertisers are trying to put the brakes on even more, in a bid to concentrate instead on building a brand's image through traditional advertising.

Philip Morris units Kraft USA and General Foods USA both said last week that they are holding coupon levels steady or cutting back for many brands. Coupons are like "heroin," says David Hurwitt, a General Foods senior vice president. "It really is a narcotic. The more you do, the more you want. You get short-term highs from it. . . but coupons don't contribute much over the years to a brand's equity."

Kraft this year broke out of the coupon cycle for at least three of its brands. Joel D. Weiner, a senior vice president, says Kraft has poured "significant" double-digit ad budget increases into its Velveeta, Miracle Whip, and Macaroni & Cheese Dinner brands. At the same time, he says, all three brands are trying to lower slightly the number of coupons they distribute. "We have a definite strategic objective to decrease couponing, with the exception of when it is clearly valid for a new product or a line extension's introduction," Mr. Weiner says.

Big packaged goods companies have been trying for years to break out of the coupon rut. Now that some are starting to succeed, if only in a small way, ad agencies and media such as television and magazines are hopeful of picking up revenue once spent on promotions.

Coupon Trends, 1984-1988
(figures in billions)

YEAR	TOTAL COUPONS	% CHANGE	COUPONS REDEEMED	% CHANGE
1984	163.2		6.25	
1985	179.8	10%	6.49	4%
1986	202.6	13	7.12	10
1987	215.2	6	7.15	—
1988	221.7	3	7.05	-1

Source: Manufacturers Coupon Control Center, a unit of Dun & Bradstreet Corp.

McCann-Erickson based its recent, relatively optimistic ad spending forecast partly on evidence that companies are concentrating more on brand advertising. And network executives attribute the current strong "upfront" market of network ad sales in part to a renewed emphasis on brand advertising.

But advertising-hungry media may be disappointed. Although the growth in coupons has clearly slowed, some advertisers are simply pouring more money into other types of promotions—not into advertising. Mike Zisser, chairman of Beaumont-Bennett, a sales promotion firm, says he sees some budgets being diverted into trade promotion. In trade promotions, a company typically gives a retailer money to stock its product, advertise a sale on the product, or put up an in-store display.

And even though the number of coupons isn't growing much, the slowdown isn't necessarily freeing up dollars for media advertising, because the coupons are for larger amounts. So, while General Foods isn't issuing many more coupons than last year, it is spending more for them.

Coupons "haven't been coming down as a portion of the total budget," Mr. Hurwitt says. According to the Manufacturers Coupon Control Center, a Dun & Bradstreet unit, the average coupon redeemed in 1988 was 41.5 cents, up from 30.4 cents in 1983.

Advertisers are turning away from cou-

pons because they don't have much choice: Coupons simply don't work as well as they used to. Coupon clutter has taken its toll. In 1987, the number of coupons distributed grew by 6%, but the number of coupons redeemed stayed flat. In 1988, while the number of coupons again grew slightly, the number redeemed actually fell for the first time, bringing redemptions to the lowest level since 1985.

Mr. Zisser believes redemptions may fall again in 1989, and total coupons distributed could remain about flat. "Couponing is starting to lose its effectiveness," he says. "There's so much of it being thrown at the consumer at this point. I don't think the people investing in it are getting as much out of it." (Steven Martin, of the Coupon Control Center, says the total number of coupons is growing at 4% to 6% so far in 1989.)

As coupons lose their luster, advertisers certainly hope to spend more on traditional media advertising. But they may try to find other promotions that will build brands, as advertising does. Mr. Zisser says one of the fastest-growing areas, although certainly not new, is cooperative advertising, in which an advertiser gives money to a retailer to run a joint ad—a K mart ad featuring a Sony stereo system, for instance.

Mr. Hurwitt also proposes trying innovative promotions, like replacing coupons with a "frequent buyer program" based on airlines' frequent flyer programs. He says that advertisers should search for promotions that can help "build equity" in a brand, the way traditional advertising builds brands; he suggests cooperative advertising, or perhaps a promotion using several of a company's brands.

The prices paid for consumer goods companies are "vivid testimony to brand equity," Mr. Hurwitt says. "And that equity didn't get built by coupons."

But he adds that although General Foods has leveled off the number of coupons it distributes, he still isn't satisfied. "Healthy, aggressive discontent with the status quo is the only thing that will ever get that number down," he says.

Apparel Makers Play Bigger Part On Sales Floor

By ANN HAGEDORN
Staff Reporter of THE WALL STREET JOURNAL

If a shopper walks away empty-handed from the new Liz Claiborne boutique at Jordan Marsh in Boston, it's probably not for lack of service. In the 6,000-square-foot area, Liz Claiborne Inc. has posted 12 clerks—five at the cashier's counter and seven on the floor—double or more the number typically found in similar department-store sales areas.

Such participation on the part of apparel makers is becoming increasingly common. Under various financial arrangements, the manufacturers are designing their own departments to better show their wares, helping to train store employees and even dispatching their own salespeople to the floor, just as cosmetics and fragrance makers have done for years.

The motive, the clothing companies say, is better efficiency and quality of service. They argue that, to the shopper's eye, department-store merchandise is often unimaginatively displayed, and that many salesclerks don't know enough about the goods they sell.

For years, retailers and manufacturers have communicated poorly, with a resulting loss in sales and profits, says Kurt Barnard, publisher of Retail Marketing Report, a trade newsletter. "They have failed to understand each other's operating realities," he explains. Now, he adds, given the uncertain retail environment, "buyer and seller must work hand in hand in the interest of attracting customers."

Untrained Help

Part of the service problem has been the changing nature of the work force, says Alice Bird McCord, a senior vice president at the National Retail Merchants Association, a major trade group. As more part-timers are used, she notes, stores see less incentive to invest in training.

Some in the industry say the situation is also an outgrowth of the fact that retail executives have been preoccupied in recent years by expansion and by mergers and acquisitions in the industry. "They've diverted their attention from the sales floor to the financial office," says Mr. Barnard. "Meanwhile, the consumer has been taken for granted." Adds Alfred Fúoco, chairman of New York-based Evan Picone Inc.: "As store chains have grown larger, they've taken money out of their budgets for sales help. That has hurt us."

To address the situation, Evan Picone plans to double its eight-person staff of "rotators," or staffers who tour stores coaching salespeople and spiffing up displays. J.H. Collectibles, a women's sportswear maker based in Milwaukee, has begun sharing the cost of a salesperson with Bloomingdale's in New York. New York-based Tahari Ltd., a high-fashion women's apparel maker, has a similar arrangement with Bloomingdale's and Macy's in New York and with Macy's in San Francisco.

Liz Claiborne went so far as to hire its own architect to design the selling space at Jordan Marsh. It will open a similar shop in Marshall Field's in Chicago this spring. Besides providing in-store personnel, the company fields a staff of 15 consultants who travel the country teaching salespeople how best to sell Liz Claiborne clothes.

While none of the companies will detail the costs involved, they typically report sales increases of 20% to 40% in stores where they've launched such programs. They say that this additional volume has offset the added expense without the need to increase prices.

A Future Trade-Off?

However, skeptics say that, as more manufacturers get into the costly business of designing and staffing their own sales space, it's likely that either quality will fall or prices will rise. "It's not in the best interest of the American consumer," says Bernard Chaus, chairman of Bernard Chaus Inc., a New York apparel maker. "I resent very much the thought of us participating in any way in the infrastructures of stores, investing dollars where retailers should be spending."

Mr. Chaus and others think retailers may begin to pressure vendors into subsidizing the stores, awarding choice spaces to those who spend the most. "What you're seeing in this whole development is a form of discount to get better space," says Alan Millstein, publisher of the newsletter Fashion Network.

Some stores, too, dislike the trend. A spokesman for Strawbridge & Clothier in Philadelphia says: "If a wholesaler decides they want to spend their money to do our job, they are taking it out of the product, or they will jack up the price of their goods."

Nevertheless, most people in the industry say that apparel companies' presence on the sales floor will only increase, and that makers of other goods will join them. Ultimately, speculates Arthur Britten, a New York retail consultant, "it will all lead to vendors leasing their space. Like a mall owner, the department store will be a landlord of various stores."

Now if Ms. Wong Insults a Customer, She Gets an Award

* * *

A Store in China Announces Its '40 Worst' Salesclerks, As an Incentive to Reform

By Adi Ignatius
Staff Reporter of THE WALL STREET JOURNAL

XIAN, China—In this land of guaranteed employment, there is plenty of recognition for a job well done. You might be named a "model worker" and awarded a television set or a special bonus. Or, like proud employees at the Xian Instruments Factory near here, you might be handed a gold plaque declaring your firm a "civilized enterprise."

But, in a country that abhors the sordid capitalist practice of firing, what do you do when the workers of the world won't work? The Chinese are choosing a traditional medicine: When all else fails, try humiliation.

An Award for Me? No Thanks

Amid much fanfare recently, the Xian Department Store, which has about 800 employees, publicly named its "40 Worst Shop Assistants," a move meant to spur better performance from the tardy and the rude. The large retail operation in this medieval walled city even went a step further: It made the transgressor's workplace his pillory, hanging a plaque overhead, complete with picture, that proclaimed him a member of the "40 Worst."

"It's the only system we've found to pressure workers to do better," says Bai Shuzheng, the store's burly Communist Party secretary. He flashes a broad smile, showing off a solid row of silver teeth. "Those designated the 'worst' feel embarrassed," he reasons. "Otherwise, our efforts would have no effect."

Is it working? Listen to Chen Jie, a dimpled, 19-year-old salesclerk sanctioned for snapping at a customer: "I accept my punishment, since my error hurt the store's reputation," says Ms. Chen, who sells synthetic-fur coats. "Today, I view my little

three-foot shop counter as a window of socialist civilization." Amen.

The department store's campaign has vaulted it past the world of boots and winter coats and into the headier realm of labor-relations innovator. The official Xinhua news agency carried a report of the "40 Worst" list. Several other enterprises in the region, on the lookout for new motivators, have sent emissaries to study the store's technique.

Sorry, Not My Department

And no wonder. In many parts of China, poor service reigns. A salesclerk from New York could even learn a thing or two about rudeness here. Anna Chennault, a prominent Chinese-American businesswoman, was so angered by bad service at Beijing's largest Friendship Store that she fired off a letter to China's Communist Party newspaper.

"They don't know what friendship is," Mrs. Chennault complained of the salespeople. "They treat customers as though they were the enemy."

Xiao Xingcai, Xian Department Store's general manager, freely commiserates. "Service in China has been bad for a long time because the state has guaranteed everything to workers," he says. Hence, his store's new reverse incentive. "When a seller has a plaque at her counter identifying her as the worst assistant in the store," he says, "she'll improve quickly to get it taken away."

The big question was how to select the 40 lousiest workers from the store's huge staff. Managers decided to give the public a chance for catharsis. During October, they set up a ballot box at the customer-service desk and urged shoppers to vote for the worst salespeople. They found an all-too-willing electorate. Then, the managers culled their personnel reports and made selections of their own.

A staff meeting was convened, and the "40 Worst" had their day destroyed. The losers had to write self-criticisms analyzing their shortcomings and, worse, most had to forfeit their monthly bonus.

Offenses ranged from ignoring customers to throwing things at them. Hu Ping was one of the throwers. She was busy chatting with colleagues at her hardware counter when a woman approached and asked about buying an electric socket. The 18-year-old saleswoman ignored the

customer and then pointedly served others who arrived later. When the woman persisted, Ms. Hu reared back and launched a socket at her. "Here's your socket," she snapped. "Couldn't you see I was busy?" (Aside from wounded pride, there were no injuries.)

Wang Fuling, a slender 34-year-old shoe saleswoman, got singled out by her supervisor for repeatedly leaving her work station to chat with friends. Ms. Wang, dressed in a red parka she wears while serving customers in the unheated, cavernous store, complains she was cheated.

"It wasn't fair. I never left the shoe department to talk to friends," she protests, fingering her fake-diamond earrings. "I left to get soft drinks downstairs—and I wouldn't have had to do that if the store had provided us tea on the second floor."

And Chen Jie, the synthetic-fur coat salesclerk? In early October, a woman economics teacher stopped at her counter to buy a coat but rejected the first 11 Ms. Chen showed her because they were covered with dust.

"I told the woman, 'Of course they're dusty. They were transported all the way from Wuhan'" 400 miles away, recalls Ms. Chen. As the customer grew testy, Ms. Chen fired back: "Lady, I've never met a customer as rude as you."

That broadside cost the saleswoman dearly. Her customer marched over to the service desk and cast a vote for Ms. Chen as the store's worst assistant. Ms. Chen eventually won enough votes to make the designation official, and lost her November bonus—nearly a quarter of her monthly income. Just four months earlier, she had been selected one of the store's top salespeople.

The store's directors are now getting set to select a second batch of bad workers. In the name of fairness, they had also promised to designate one of the store's dozens of supervisors "The Worst Manager." But, oddly, that plan appears stalled. "It's a very complicated system," offers Mr. Xiao, the general manager, hoping the conversation will end there. He gulps nervously. "It's really too difficult to decide who's the worst manager," he concludes.

Nothing, no doubt, that a ballot box in the staff coatroom wouldn't solve.

TWO DAYS IN BOOT CAMP —LEARNING TO LOVE LEXUS

How Toyota grooms true believers to sell its new luxury line

I clench my hands nervously. I forget my customer's name. And I can't recall whether this car or its sister model has the special door seals. But despite my dubious talent, here I am playing saleswoman for Lexus, Toyota Motor Corp.'s new luxury car division. The exercise is part of a training course where some 90 sales and service people are learning how to build the classy image the Lexus division thinks it needs to succeed in this hotly competitive market.

The two-day seminar in Chicago is a marathon of lectures, quizzes, and role-playing. Constant reiteration of the division's highbrow philosophy sometimes gives it the feeling of a revival meeting. We are not mere car salespeople but a vanguard for change in an often despised industry, we are told. "The most important single factor in the Lexus division is what is in the hearts and minds of the people who make up this organization," intones General Manager J. Davis Illingworth Jr.

The emphasis is on personal attitudes, not product attributes. We do hear plenty about the cars: the $35,000 LS 400 and the sportier $21,000 ES 250. But after 450 prototypes, 2.7 million test miles, and $3 billion of investment, Toyota seems confident that its Japanese-made sedans will perform as planned. Instead, it frets that six years of effort could stall in the hands of an ill-mannered sales force. Toyota plans to sell 16,000 Lexus cars this year and 75,000 in 1990 through a separate dealer network.

Lexus appears to have a head start in its efforts to mold the best and the brightest. Of 560 trainees recruited for this and four other Lexus boot camps across the country, nearly 22% used to sell or service European luxury makes. Only 15% came from domestic lines, including Cadillac and Lincoln. The others worked for Japanese or multiline dealers. Nearly two-thirds of the Lexus trainees are under 40 years old, and 83% have at least some college education. There's not a plaid sportcoat in sight.

PROS AND CONS. While Lexus aims to be different, it's not ashamed to learn from the competition. The carmaker hired anthropologists to observe dealerships of Toyota and several rivals in three cities. The lessons for us: Know your product—and the competing models—thoroughly, as salespeople do at BMW. Shower customers with respect and courtesy, à la Mercedes. Avoid the cool, unemotional presentation common at Acura, Honda's upscale division. And shun the backslapping approach of Cadillac.

But how exactly should we do this? Some prescriptions are obvious: receptionists to greet customers, honest negotiations with buyers, and clean cars filled with gas after servicing. "I've been waiting for this style of selling for 10 years," confides Paul F. Wisowaty, a former Chevrolet and Toyota salesman who is now general sales manager at Lexus of Orland in Tinley Park, Ill. "I never did like beating on people."

We trainees are bombarded with inspirational speeches from the likes of Vince Lombardi Jr., son of the late Green Bay Packers' coach, and ex-convict-turned professional motivator Gordon Graham, who says: "When you say you can't, you immediately shut off all creativity." But too much dessert after dinner and too many football yarns begin to wither our can-do spirit. The speeches drone on until nearly 10 p.m.

BLUE THUNDER. To make sure the Lexus vision is taking hold, we're tested both days by a cheery host who seems to have escaped from a second-rate game show. On big screens at the front of the room appear multiple-choice questions and a countdown clock. We enter our responses on keypads at our tables. To fire the competitive spirit, we're assigned to teams—I'm with Blue Thunder. Each team's combined score is instantly charted on the center screen. I'm beginning to feel like one of Pavlov's dogs. What is the Lexus goal? Correct answer: "Complete customer satisfaction." The Lexus way is . . . "Not to compete but to excel."

The real moment of truth arrives on day two. After all the lectures, demonstrations, and test drives, we must finally try to sell the cars. We're told to tailor a presentation to the customer's specific interest—or "hot button." My customer's hot button: aerodynamics and styling. With a trainer posing as the buyer and an audience of four other salespeople, I launch into my spiel about the elegant ES 250. I repeat the word "aerodynamic" six times and I speak in a near monotone. But my group is kind. Their grades on my performance range from 73 to 96 out of 100. I rate highest on rapport and sincerity.

There's some comfort when my team wins the overall competition with a score of 93%. My teammates take home a piece of crystal engraved with the name Lexus in it. I leave with the knowledge that I haven't missed my true calling.

By Wendy Zellner in Chicago

NOW SALESPEOPLE REALLY MUST SELL FOR THEIR SUPPER

More department stores are changing to straight commission

John L. Palmerio, a 25-year veteran of the men's shoe salon at Bloomingdale's flagship store in Manhattan, thought working on commission would prove lucrative. He hasn't been disappointed. Since February, when his department switched from an hourly wage scale to a 10% commission on sales, Palmerio has been pulling in an extra $175, or 25%, in his average weekly paycheck. And overall sales in the nine-person department have increased 22%. "So far, everybody has done much better than we anticipated," he says.

But upstairs in women's sleepwear and lingerie, sales associate Andrea Collier isn't wild about the prospect of giving up the security of a base salary. "It makes me nervous," admits Collier, whose department will be converting to straight commission within the next few months. "You have to work a lot harder to earn the same money."

APATHY CURE. Palmerio and Collier are part of a quiet revolution sweeping department-store retailing. To boost sales and upgrade service, major retail chains are converting thousands of hourly sales employees to commission pay. Department stores have always had salespeople on straight commission. But in recent decades, the practice has been limited to high-ticket areas such as furniture, electronics, and men's suits, where extra salesmanship really pays off. Now, they're applying the idea throughout the store, forcing clerks who sell anything from bed linen to pots and pans to earn their keep. Says James E. Gray,

president of the 30-store Burdines chain in Florida: "In the olden days, there was room for apathy. Now, you've got to sell to stay employed."

The retailers hope to use commissions, and their promise of higher pay, to motivate staff and attract better salespeople. Many have been inspired by Nordstrom Inc., a Seattle-based department store that has moved east and captivated shoppers with its service-oriented merchandising. A key ingredient of Nordstrom's success has been its reliance on skilled salespeople paid by commission.

But the Nordstrom formula can't be easily duplicated. Years of understaffing, neglect, and poor merchandising have sliced department stores' market share for general merchandise, apparel, and furniture by three points since 1982, to 18% in 1988, according to trade journal *Chain Store Age Executive*. Simply switching to commissions won't solve such problems. "You do not create more customer-oriented salespeople by putting in an incentive," says Bernadette Duponchel, a consulting manager for the Management Horizons retail consulting unit of Price Waterhouse. "Customer service is part of a culture that has to be communicated throughout the organization."

HIGH TURNOVER. If handled poorly, commissions may even work against good service. "You are less harmed by someone who leaves you alone than someone who is attacking you," says Michael D. Sullivan, president of Merry-Go-Round Enterprises Inc., a chain of 610 apparel stores based in Joppa, Md. The company has used commissioned sales help since its founding in 1970.

Commissions haven't been a cure-all for Nordstrom's crosstown rival, Frederick & Nelson. The Seattle-based chain of 11 stores had about 90% of its departments on commission by 1987. "It's been slower than I had anticipated in terms of the benefits taking root," says Robert W. Presser, senior vice-president and director of stores. One problem: Sales staff turnover has increased from less than 5% a year to a disruptively high 18%. Part of that reflects the loss of longtime employees who could not meet more stringent performance standards. But even promising new hires have not made the grade. "It's not a question of age or tenure but whether people are really cut out to sell," Presser says.

While department stores see it as an investment that should boost sales, converting to commissions is expensive at first. The process costs $700,000 to $1 million per store, estimates James M. Zimmerman, president of Campeau's Federated and Allied chains. That includes training

MAKING COMMISSIONS PAY

Example covers earnings for a salesclerk in the women's ready-to-wear department of Bloomingdale's maintaining sales volume of $500,000 a year. Clerk is guaranteed a minimum about equal to prior year's salary, to be paid as a draw against commissions. Pension benefits will increase as compensation rises.

OLD PLAN		NEW PLAN	
$7 per hour for 1,950 hours	$13,650	5% commission on $500,000	$25,000
0.5% commission on $500,000	2,500		
TOTAL ANNUAL PAY	**$16,150**	**TOTAL ANNUAL PAY**	**$25,000**

DATA: BW

(cont.)

programs, computer changes, and pay, which often goes up immediately (table, page 50). Still, Campeau Corp. plans to have 90% of the sales associates in its nine department store chains on some form of commission by the end of 1990.

At Bloomingdale's, the crown jewel of Federated Department Stores Inc., 13 of the 17 stores now pay commissions across the board. In July, the company reached an agreement with Local 3 of the Retail, Wholesale & Department Store Union to put the 1,500 salespeople at its Manhattan store on commissions. Workers will earn 5% to 10% on sales, depending on the merchandise they sell. To prepare for the change, sales staffers will participate in a two-day symposium designed to explain the system and teach better sales techniques. "Intense training plays a critical role in the transition and relieves the apprehension employees may feel," says Margaret Hofbeck, senior vice-president for personnel and labor relations for Bloomingdale's.

EASING IN. At other retailers, the move to commissions has evolved more slowly. The Broadway, a department store chain owned by Los Angeles-based Carter Hawley Hale Stores Inc., began the changeover five years ago. "We started out with a group incentive first," says Cyndi J. Bohm, manager of the Montclair (Calif.) store. "If a department did better than the plan, everyone would share the extra pay. Then, beginning with apparel, The Broadway switched to individual commissions." All 113 department stores in Carter Hawley's five divisions are now fully on commission.

Is all this trouble and expense worthwhile for retailers? Store executives say that departments such as better apparel, handbags, and towels and linens often enjoy rapid improvements in sales after changing to commissions. But small-ticket areas such as food and stationery, where purchases often fall below $25, don't do so well. Still, commissions may ultimately help reduce expenses. Frederick & Nelson's selling costs as a percentage of sales fell by nearly 1% last year, even though the chain increased the number of sales staff hours by 10%. "We can add more people because they pay for themselves," Presser says.

It's harder to judge the impact of commissions on service. Any incentive to improve selling skills has to be a step in the right direction, though, and commissions do seem to help. But if department stores still give customers a hard time on refunds or exchanges, or don't hire enough sales help, or don't offer exciting merchandise, then pay incentives won't necessarily make them better places to shop.

By Amy Dunkin in New York, with Kathleen Kerwin in Los Angeles and bureau reports

72

Telemarketers Take Root in the Country

Computers Lead To Opportunity In Rural Areas

By BILL RICHARDS
Staff Reporter of THE WALL STREET JOURNAL

'**F**IVE YEARS ago this wouldn't have been possible,' says an economist. But with new technology, he adds, 'there's absolutely no reason why a lot of these companies can't operate in a rural area just as easily as they can in Los Angeles or New York City.'

BREDA, Iowa — Computers and cow towns are finding a perfect match.

Take Breda, for example. With the farming slump of the early 1980s, this tiny western Iowa community with a population of 502 was in trouble. It lost its high school, its car dealership and its rail connection, not to mention several farms.

Then an unlikely Samaritan appeared: Sitel Inc., an Omaha, Neb., concern that peddles insurance and credit cards by phone across the nation. Last year the telemarketer picked Breda for a new sales center, hiring 43 locals—mostly farm wives—to work its computers and phones at $4 an hour. Those jobs won't save the local farms if agriculture nose-dives again, but they are tiding over some struggling families.

"Times are tough," says Deb Kroeger, a farmer's wife and mother of four. "But they'd be a lot tougher if I didn't have this job." Adds co-worker Sharon Pudenz, whose husband farms in nearby Vail, Iowa: "You just don't find work like this in small towns like ours."

Saving Money, Saving Towns

Not until recently, anyway. But high technology and low wages are leading a growing number of companies such as Sitel to set up shop in rural communities like Breda. Development officials in Nebraska, North Dakota and Iowa—places often overlooked by manufacturers searching for plant sites—say they are getting a stream of inquiries from companies whose business is done mainly by telephone and computer. In Nebraska alone last year, small towns gained 350 new jobs from such firms. Sitel, one of the nation's largest telemarketers, has created 500 new jobs in the past 2½ years—mostly in Midwestern farm towns with populations under 2,000.

"For these companies," says Shirley Porterfield, a rural economist for the Agriculture Department, "location doesn't matter a whole lot anymore."

Last summer, Rosenbluth Travel Inc., one of the nation's largest travel agents, shifted its computer reservations system from its home base in Philadelphia to an empty storefront in Linton, N.D. The little town of 1,500, whose economy took a pounding with last year's drought, gained 40 new jobs from the move while Rosenbluth cut its overhead by 20%. Hal Rosenbluth, the agency's president, says he was so pleased that he is encouraging airlines and other companies with big computerized operations to consider similar shifts.

"Data entry," Mr. Rosenbluth says, "knows no boundaries."

Citicorp proved that fact when it transferred its credit-card operation to Sioux Falls, S.D., in 1981. Others such as Amoco Corp. and Deere & Co. have moved parts of their data-processing units to smaller cities, too. But only recently have advances such as fiber optics and electronic switch systems made truly rural areas practical for footloose employers.

The Time Is Right

"Five years ago this wouldn't have been possible," says Abner Womack, a rural economist at the University of Missouri. With new technology, Mr. Womack says, "there's absolutely no reason why a lot of these companies can't operate in a rural area just as easily as they can in Los Angeles or New York City."

Federal economists say the impact of the job switch to rural areas is still too new to show up on their charts. But here in Carroll County, where manufacturing and farm jobs have dropped, the spurt in computer-based jobs is apparent. Last spring, American Home Shield Corp., a Santa Rosa, Calif., concern that processes warranties for home-appliance systems, installed 50 new computers in a vacant lumber store in Carroll, Iowa, the county seat 12 miles from Breda. Behind a clutter of potted plants, dozens of women now handle calls from 38 states. Eventually, the company expects to put 400 people on its Carroll payroll, which would make it the county's biggest employer.

Michael Wahl, American Home Shield's regional service manager, says it costs his company 35% less to operate in Iowa than in California. Turnover—about 40% annually at the company's California service center—is barely noticeable here; just two people quit during the insurer's first year in Carroll. What's more, "the quality of the work force here is outstanding," he says. "And tardiness is a non-issue."

Telemarketing officials say they are especially attracted to small towns that have independent telephone companies with cash reserves and the desire to install high-tech equipment in return for new business.

Breda's telephone company fit that description. Two years ago it put up $90,000 to lay 13.5 miles of new fiber-optic cable, connecting the town with American Telephone & Telegraph Co.'s national fiber-optic network that runs just south of here. With fiber-optic cable, which greatly expands and improves an area's phone and computer-transmission ability, Breda suddenly had a sophisticated communications link to the outside world. And suddenly it had an appeal for Sitel.

The Midwest's central location also allows phone marketers to reach anywhere in the U.S. at the cheapest rate. And there's a plus: Midwesterners don't have strong accents, helping sales.

For the rural Midwest these new jobs have arrived just in time. Agriculture's roller-coaster economics has been clearing farmers off the land at the average rate of 37,000 a year during the 1980s. And traditionally, farm communities here have been too far from markets and too poor to expand their economic base.

Visible Effect

In Breda, the effect is visible. At five o'clock there is even a traffic jam—or what passes for one in a town with a two-

(cont.)

block downtown. Business is up at Zack's, the local cafe. And the town is even laying the groundwork for a new housing development with 34 lots, with hopes of seeing an influx of newcomers.

In all, Sitel and a second local business that uses computers to dispatch trucks throughout the U.S. will employ about 80 people in Breda by the end of the year, an unusually large employment base for a town of this size.

Many of those workers will come off the corn, hog and cattle farms that dot the rolling countryside here—people like Mary Ann Irlbeck. American Home Shield pays Mrs. Irlbeck $5.50 an hour to handle complaints about balky air conditioners and failing dishwashers. She calls her job "a godsend" that has allowed her husband, Michael, to devote himself full time to operating their grain and livestock operation.

"Mike was running himself ragged trying to hold down an outside job and farm too," Mrs. Irlbeck says. "The gates were broken and the hogs were running all over and he was turning into a bear."

When American Home Shield showed up, Mr. Wahl says more than 1,000 people applied for jobs, although the company didn't run a single "Help Wanted" ad.

Nonetheless, before then local development officials never considered such companies as potential employers. "They really opened our eyes," says Patrick R. Moehn, a Carroll County banker who heads the local development corporation. Now, he says, Carroll is sending a raiding party to California this month to try to talk another insurer into transferring jobs here.

"If I were a board member of a company somewhere else that was paying its people $12 an hour to sit in front of a computer," says Mr. Moehn, "I'd sure be asking my management why they weren't looking at moving here."

73

Direct Marketing for Packaged Goods

Firms Target Offers to Court The Individual

By Ronald Alsop

Staff Reporter of The Wall Street Journal

Printed with flowery lettering and embossed with a gold coat of arms, invitations to join the Dewar's Highlander Clan make the club appear quite elite.

"The Dewar's Highlander Clan is an exclusive family of individuals sharing a set of common values, including a respect for tradition, a devotion to authenticity and the conviction that quality never varies," the membership offer proclaims. It goes on to tell members of the "family" that they are entitled to discounts on Scottish kilts, crystal glassware and other merchandise and may even win free trips to England and Scotland.

Despite the flourishes, though, the Highlander Clan is really no great honor. People receiving the pitch from Schenley Industries Inc., the marketer of Dewar's scotch, just happen to be scotch drinkers whose names turned up on one of the company's mailing lists. Schenley expects to send nearly two million invitations.

Innovative If Not Exclusive

While the Highlander Clan may not be as exclusive as it sounds, it still is an unusual direct-marketing ploy for a packaged-goods company. Only recently have Schenley and other mass marketers begun courting consumers with catalogs, newsletters and other targeted promotions.

"Direct marketing is finally emerging at packaged-goods companies after a slow gestation period," says George Wiedemann, president of Grey Direct, the direct-marketing division of Grey Advertising. "It has taken a long time because there's this inertia to stick with traditional media advertising and coupons."

Direct marketing is often referred to as "relationship marketing" because it's a way for companies to get chummier with customers. Traditionally, the relationship between mass marketers and consumers has been anything but chummy. Although loyal consumers may watch a company's ads, clip its coupons and buy its brands for many years, they mostly remain nameless

and faceless to the marketer.

"But with direct mail, you're dealing one-on-one with people and creating a tighter bond with them," says Lynn Fantom, executive vice president at Kobs & Draft, the direct-marketing unit of the Backer Spielvogel Bates ad agency. "You can't talk to all your customers. Yet it may make sense to communicate by mail with heavy users of your brand or with influential people, such as athletic coaches for Gatorade and dog breeders for Kal Kan dog food." CPC International Inc., for instance, is pursuing dietitians and home economists through its Health Watch newsletter, which plugs Mazola corn oil.

Clubs are especially trendy these days. Consumers who aren't asked to join the Highlanders Clan might be inducted instead into General Foods Corp.'s Light-Style Club. To inspire more brand loyalty for its Crystal Light soft-drink mixes, the Philip Morris Cos. subsidiary is sending 320,000 people a LightStyle fitness newsletter and a brochure promoting T-shirts, beach towels and other products bearing the Crystal Light logo.

"The newsletter is expected to change people's attitudes about Crystal Light and their purchase patterns over a longer period of time," says John Kuendig, General Foods' director of direct marketing. "A coupon certainly affects purchasing, but the effect doesn't last very long."

More ambitious than its Crystal Light project is General Foods' quarterly children's magazine, "What's Hot," which has a circulation of about two million and plugs many of the company's brands through recipes and cents-off coupons. Produced for General Foods by Field Publications—which also publishes Weekly Reader—the magazine features articles about dinosaurs and the "ALF" TV show, for example. But it's mostly just a series of ads disguised as puzzles and games. A sample puzzle: "Help this cherry pie get to the yummy Cool Whip whipped topping and that hungry boy below."

The mass marketers often consider their direct-marketing forays top-secret. Clorox Co. has hired Wunderman Worldwide, a direct-marketing agency owned by Young & Rubicam, but won't say which brands Wunderman will handle. General Foods declines to discuss a direct-mail piece for Kool-Aid that will include a comic book and will be mailed in a few weeks. And RJR Nabisco Inc. refuses to talk about its direct marketing, though tobacco-

industry officials say it has amassed a data base of millions of smokers' names.

To target consumers directly, marketers often buy lists of names that match the demographic profile of their typical customers. Some also are building consumer data bases through toll-free telephone promotions. To receive a $1 coupon for Wella Corp.'s So Fine shampoo and conditioner, for instance, consumers must call a toll-free number that appears in cable-TV ads. So far, Wella has received about 400,000 calls and plugged the respondents' names into its computers.

Despite the recent burst of enthusiasm, however, the marriage between mass-marketed consumer products and direct-marketing promises to be bumpy. For one thing, their styles conflict. Packaged-goods brand managers live or die by monthly sales reports showing the impact of coupons and other short-term promotions. Direct marketers, on the other hand, take a much longer view. They think in terms of the "lifetime value" of a customer.

"Direct marketing also is very expensive for packaged goods, most of which have slim profit margins," says Jon Adams, president of the Integrated Communications Group of the FCB/Leber Katz Partners ad agency. "It costs much more to send a promotion by mail than to distribute coupons in a newspaper insert."

Excessive costs have forced a few companies to scale back their direct-marketing ventures or even scrap them altogether. Unilever PLC's Thomas J. Lipton Inc. subsidiary last year stopped selling exotic teas, shortbread and tea kettles through catalogs. Likewise, Brown-Forman Inc. discontinued its 88-page Lynchburg Hardware & General Store catalog of clocks, decanters, hats and other items stamped with the Jack Daniel's whiskey logo. This year, it plans to mail a much smaller promotional catalog for Jack Daniel's.

Because of costs, General Foods almost canceled plans for a toll-free 800-number promotion last year for a line of frozen entrees. An operator-assisted number would have cost up to $2.50 a call. But then the company realized that a computerized answering machine could do the job because callers were only being asked to leave their names and addresses. The reduced cost: about 75 cents a call.

Tobacco and liquor companies—mired in a sales slump—are especially aggressive these days in getting into direct marketing. With fewer people buying ciga-

(cont.)

rettes and hard liquor, it only makes sense to target a narrower audience and spend less on national advertising.

"The number of scotch drinkers is unfortunately declining each year, so it becomes more important for us to hold onto customers we already have with incentives like the Highlander Clan," says Chuck Levy of Venet Advertising, the agency for the Dewar's club.

Restrictions on Advertising

What's more, government restrictions may eventually force tobacco and liquor companies to market directly by mail to smokers and drinkers. "Tobacco companies want to start experimenting with direct marketing now because they don't know what their advertising options will be long term," says Ms. Fantom of Kobs & Draft. Her direct-marketing agency is working on a program for Philip Morris's Parliament Lights cigarettes.

Philip Morris also is resorting to direct-mail to promote its Benson & Hedges Quality Choices catalog of luxury goods. And last year, direct marketing helped the company persuade people to try its Merit brand. The company ran an anonymous ad betting smokers that they would prefer the mystery cigarette to their current brands. Smokers who took the blind challenge received two packs of unmarked Merits; a later mailing identified the brand.

According to Leo Burnett Co., Merit's ad agency, 1.8 million people participated, including 1.1 million smokers of other companies' brands. Of those, about 45% said the samples gave them a more favorable opinion of Merits.

"We're doing image-building promotions like the Benson & Hedges catalog to reinforce the quality theme of our advertising," says Ellen Merlo, a vice president at Philip Morris. "RJR, in contrast, uses direct-marketing mainly to distribute coupons for its cigarettes."

A spokeswoman for RJR Nabisco declines to elaborate on the company's direct marketing. "Our direct marketing is extremely proprietary," she says. "The competition would simply love to know more about what we're up to."

74

Marketers Resurrect Ads From the Past

Golden Oldies Offer Awareness That's Built-In

By Ronald Alsop

Staff Reporter of The Wall Street Journal

Ready to "take the Nestea Plunge" again? Nestle S.A., the maker of Nestea, certainly hopes so. After a six-year hiatus, the company is hauling out that musty but still memorable advertising slogan to try to make iced-tea lovers think Nestea instead of Lipton.

The original Nestea Plunge commercials—in which people fell backward into swimming pools—ran from 1973 to 1982. But one-third of the consumers Nestle recently surveyed thought the ads were still on the air. The ad campaigns that succeeded the Nestea Plunge were so forgettable that even Blair Gensamer, senior vice president for coffee and tea at Nestle, can't recall them.

"We tried to move onto bigger and better ideas, but nothing measured up," Mr. Gensamer says. "With the cost of media today, it would be a terrible waste not to take advantage of an asset like the Nestea Plunge."

Deja vu seems to have set in this summer on Madison Avenue. In addition to the Nestea Plunge, marketers are recycling ads from the past for such brands as Armour hot dogs, Raid bug killer and Ovaltine drink mix. Alex the beer-guzzling dog is once again starring in Stroh's commercials. (Actually, it's a new mutt because the Alex from the first campaign died.) And later this year, two other ad themes will make a comeback: Memorex audio tapes' "Is it live or is it Memorex?" and Timex watches' "It takes a lickin' and keeps on tickin'."

Easier and Cheaper

The creative juices haven't dried up at ad agencies. It's just that some people in advertising believe they may be able to breathe new life into faded but once-potent slogans, jingles and ad characters.

Marketers say resurrecting golden oldies is a lot easier and cheaper than trying to build awareness from scratch with totally new ads. Some advertisers also are capitalizing on baby boomers' longings for their childhood and teen-age years. Ovaltine ads, in particular, play on consumers' memories. They feature footage from the "Captain Midnight" television show, which the brand sponsored in the 1950s.

"Companies are coming back with old campaigns because baby boomers are feeling old and are afflicted with a great deal of nostalgia," says Leo Shapiro, who heads a consumer-research firm in Chicago. "They feel they left behind a simpler time and place that they'd like to return to."

John Miller, who became president of Armour Food Co. last year, received the inspiration for reviving the old jingle ("What kind of kids love Armour hot dogs?") when his co-workers at his former firm began singing it at a going-away party. "When I got here, I said we should be using that song because it's still so catchy," says Mr. Miller. "We simply updated it this year to have more of a Bruce Springsteen sound."

The Foote, Cone & Belding ad agency brought back Captain Raid, the animated Raid bug spray can, after consumers in focus groups spontaneously started talking about their memories of the character. "Captain Raid hasn't been in commercials for more than 10 years, but people described him as a hero, sort of the Clint Eastwood of insecticides," says Diane Peterson, account director at Foote Cone. "The people even put their hands on their heads to show how Captain Raid sprayed out his insecticide in the old ads."

But there is always the risk that reviving a classic slogan or spokesman will backfire and create an old-fashioned image for a brand. To guard against that, marketers tend to give their recycled ads a contemporary twist. The Captain Raid of 1988, for example, has rippling muscles and a futuristic look. And a woman in one of the new Nestea spots doesn't just tumble into a swimming pool; she falls onto an exercise mat that turns into a pool.

It's too soon to tell whether Captain Raid and the Nestea Plunge will work any marketing magic in their reincarnations. But advertisers acknowledge that those and many other campaigns probably suffered premature deaths. Too often, vintage ads are scrapped just for the sake of change. The not-invented-here syndrome is usually at work: A new agency or brand manager wants to make a big impression, and the fastest way is with new ads.

"Agencies and clients also will change campaigns because they get bored and assume everyone else is, too," says Ted Bell, director of creative services at the Leo Burnett ad agency. "But in fact, consumers may not be tired of our ads at all. The world isn't out there thinking about our campaigns every day the way we are."

Sometimes, nervous companies dump tried-and-true campaigns in response to new competition. That's what the marketer of Dial soap unfortunately did in the late 1970s. Feeling the heat from Procter & Gamble Co.'s Coast soap, Dial abandoned its ad theme, "Aren't you glad you use Dial? Don't you wish everybody did?" and came up with "A new Dial morning" instead. The new ads tried to match Coast's claims by promoting Dial as an invigorating soap with a refreshing scent.

"But our customers came back and said, 'That's not who Dial soap is,' and they stopped buying the product," says Richard Lies, general manager of Dial's personal-care division.

Mr. Lies blames "A new Dial morning" at least partly for the soap's market-share losses in the late 1970s and early 1980s. Its share of the bar-soap market slid to about 11% from 17%. It has rebounded a bit to 13.5%, however, since the company returned to the "Aren't you glad you use Dial?" line a few years ago.

Sara Lee Corp. walked away from the line "Nobody doesn't like Sara Lee" and experimented with other jingles that never quite caught on with consumers. Some of the flops: "It's so delicious it's Saralicious" and "When you Sara Lee love your family, they're going to Sara Lee love you back." Perhaps the only person in America who can still reel off those slogans is Bob Tarkington, group manager for consumer marketing at Kitchens of Sara Lee.

"It looked to us like the old slogan was wearing out, but after some other less successful campaigns, we decided to find a way to revitalize it," he says. The solution: Recruit Al Jarreau and Manhattan Transfer to perform jazzy new renditions of "Nobody doesn't like Sara Lee."

But advertising executives believe Dial, Sara Lee and other companies would have been better off if they hadn't killed their long-running themes in the first place. "After two or three lost years, 'Nobody doesn't like Sara Lee' will never have the same impact it once did," says Lou Centlivre, managing director of the creative department at Foote Cone in Chicago.

Varying the Formula

Sara Lee and other ad recyclers might have followed the example of Procter & Gamble and a few other companies that are prolonging successful, long-lived campaigns by varying the formula.

(cont.)

Rosie, the waitress in Procter's Bounty paper towel ads, was recently reunited with an old flame who's a Humphrey Bogart look-alike. "We don't want the viewer to turn his mind off because he already knows what's going to happen in the commercial," says Pat McGrath, president of Jordan, McGrath, Case & Taylor, Bounty's agency. "In this new commercial, people will see that Rosie has a personal life and doesn't spend her whole life behind a diner counter mopping up coffee spills."

Another old-timer, Madge the manicurist, ventures outside the beauty parlor in the latest Palmolive dish soap commercial. As she walks down the street to buy a newspaper, women shout, "I soaked in it" and hold out their hands for inspection.

Colgate-Palmolive Co. is so committed to Madge that it celebrated her 20th birthday last year with a bash in New York City and a free cake promotion for consumers who bought Palmolive. Says Ariel Allen, Colgate's vice president for creative services: "There have been brand managers and agency people who wanted to make their mark by replacing Madge, but we guarded against it. You're lucky when you get a campaign like this and should do everything you can to keep it alive."

75

Fighting Back

Chemical Firms Press Campaigns to Dispel Their 'Bad Guy' Image

Fears of Regulation, Lawsuits Lead Firms to Clean Up And Court Public Backing

Mishaps Undermine Efforts

By LAURIE HAYS
Staff Reporter of THE WALL STREET JOURNAL

The chemical industry is running scared.

Regulators are relentless. Citizens are angry. Disasters like Bhopal, Love Canal and Times Beach are still haunting memories. So after years of trying to tough it out, big chemical makers are trying a new tactic: An all-out effort to persuade the public that the industry is mending its ways. The goal is to calm apprehensions before even stricter laws and constraints are imposed.

Consider these recent examples:

—Du Pont Co. has vowed to stop making chlorofluorocarbons by the end of the 1990s. The chemicals, widely used in refrigerants and styrofoam, are suspected of eating away the Earth's protective ozone layer.

—Monsanto Co. has promised to reduce all its hazardous air emissions by 90% by 1992 though they currently meet federal guidelines.

—Dow Chemical Co. and the Sierra Club have endorsed jointly a proposed federal law that would sharply reduce hazardous-waste production. Dow itself has adopted an aggressive waste-reduction program.

—The Chemical Manufacturers Association has proposed for the first time to set operating and safety standards that its 170 members would have to meet to retain membership.

A Strong Backlash

Industry officials acknowledge that the campaign is born of desperation. Environmental activism is on the rise, carrying the threat of more government regulation, more lawsuits brought by citizens' groups against polluters, and heightened pressure to clean up contaminated sites, typically a very costly undertaking.

Chemical companies also fear a strong backlash as more and more information on pollution becomes known to the public. Under a recently enacted federal right-to-know law, for instance, chemical companies are required to notify the Environmental Protection Agency of all emissions of toxic chemicals.

Monsanto decided to reduce air emissions because officials are concerned about such reaction. "The demand for a cleaner environment hasn't peaked yet," says Harold J. Corbett, senior vice president. Cutting pollution voluntarily, he says, "is better than sitting back and waiting for more regulation to come along."

"Firms realize they have to deal with environmental issues on a self-interested basis," says Daniel Dudek, a senior economist for the Environmental Defense Fund, a not-for-profit advocacy group based in New York. "Otherwise, somebody else will make a decision for them that they will have to live with."

Media-Savvy Managers

Officials who fear such consequences include Robert D. Kennedy, chairman of Union Carbide Corp., which owns a majority of the Indian subsidiary that leaked poison gas and killed more than 2,000 near a plant in Bhopal in 1984. "An aroused public," he says, "can put us out of business, just like it put the nuclear industry out of business" after the incident at Three Mile Island. "The industry can and should improve its performance," he says.

Many companies are pressing a public-relations program designed to portray themselves as sensitive to the environment. To advertise its newfound awareness, Hercules Inc. hoists flags at its plants with symbols representing the Earth, air, water and fire. Its environmental-awareness program is dubbed "We Care." Hercules also rewards employees for adhering to federal, state and local anti-pollution guidelines.

The Chemical Manufacturers Association has gone so far as to publish a manual for plant managers with advice on how to win public support. It urges them, for example, not to "stonewall" when asked questions. They are also told to avoid such seemingly arrogant responses as "The risk of emissions from the plant is lower than the risk of driving to the meeting or smoking during breaks."

Public-Relations Fluff?

Across the country, managers are adopting friendlier, more open postures. In community advisory meetings, companies are trying harder to address concerns. Residents, environmental activists and local officials are invited to join the committees and set the agendas.

But the industry's efforts to portray itself as a sensitive corporate citizen still have a long way to go. Some skeptics dismiss the campaign as just so much public-relations fluff. "Coffee and doughnuts and a few sirens really don't take care of the problem," says Fred Millar, a director of the Environmental Policy Institute, a nonprofit environmental-advocacy group in Washington.

Others say the campaign doesn't begin to address problems caused by hazardous chemicals in the environment. Says Barry Commoner, a founder of the environmental movement and director of the Center for Biology of Natural Systems at Queens College in New York: "The cutting edge of the unsolved environmental crisis lies with the chemical industry. When [a chemical company] says they're doing their best, my first response is 'How come you didn't do this 30 years ago?'"

In addition, the industry's reassurances that safety is a top priority seem to ring hollow in light of frequent mishaps and accidents. Just last month, a chemical leak from a Monsanto plant in Sauget, Ill., sent 120 residents to the hospital with burning eyes, nausea and headaches. Four days later, in Nashua, N.H., 1,700 residents were evacuated from their homes after a leak from a W.R. Grace Co. plant that makes chemicals and pesticides created a vapor cloud.

Picketing the Plant

But many companies say they have learned the consequences of enraging the public. Ciba-Geigy Corp. is one of those. In 1984, hazardous waste from its chemical plant in Toms River, N.J., was found to have seeped into the groundwater of a neighboring residential area. A year later, in an unrelated incident, Ciba and four of its officials were indicted on charges of disposing of waste improperly at another site. (The case is pending; the company and the officials pleaded innocent.)

A public furor erupted, and it hasn't subsided yet. The incidents led residents to take a closer look at the plant's operations, and some didn't like what they saw. On several occasions, Toms River residents picketed the company's complex. Now, environmental groups are demanding that the company halt the discharge of treated waste into the ocean—a move that the company says would be very costly.

(cont.)

The mishaps have hurt in other respects, too. Several years ago, the company sought approval from local officials to build a $90 million pharmaceutical plant in Toms River. But its application to get zoning approval has become snarled in red tape, largely because of local resentment and increased scrutiny.

"Ciba's reputation is at an all-time low," says William Skowronski, a school official and a member of a local environmental group.

Making Amends

Now, Ciba is trying to make amends. It invited residents to join a committee to air their gripes against the company and discuss solutions. The company also donated $50,000 to a local environmental group to hire specialists to evaluate the company's plans to clean up contaminated sites. The consultants noticed an omission in the plans that neither the company nor federal regulators had spotted. Ciba agreed to remedy the oversight.

Ciba officials say they believe the efforts are helping mend relations with the community. And some local activists give the company credit for trying. "For the first time, citizens are being allowed to participate in the regulatory process," says Kathleen Terry, an attorney and president of the local environmental group.

The legacy of Bhopal also has been a powerful motivator for some chemical makers, among them Rohm & Haas Co.

The company operates a chemical plant in Philadelphia's Bridesburg section, an industrial zone that also is home to a coffee factory, a smelter and a city sewage-treatment plant. Foul odors often permeate the air here. Leaks and accidental chemical spills aren't unusual.

While many residents staunchly supported their industrial neighbors for the jobs they provide, Rohm & Haas has had its share of problems. The most infamous involved the deaths from lung cancer of 60 Rohm & Haas workers who had been exposed to a toxic chemical process between 1948 and 1971 in the plant's Building 6.

The company changed the process to make it safer, and two years ago, settled cases stemming from the workers' exposure for $25 million. But, alarmed by the incident at Bhopal, officials decided to take a harder look at all the plant's hazardous-chemical operations.

Today, Rohm & Haas has under way a program to upgrade safety procedures and reassure local residents that it intends to be a more responsible corporate citizen. To foster better relations with the residents of Bridesburg, plant officials meet with community leaders every month to discuss their concerns about plant operations.

The company also says it spent $5 million to analyze its handling of the most dangerous chemicals used at the plant. It has reduced inventories of those chemicals, and it monitors more closely the processes in which the chemicals are used.

For some companies, the battle with environmentalists has come down to bottom-line financial concerns. They hope, for example, to gain competitive advantages by anticipating future regulations. Du Pont is regarded as leading the phase-out of ozone-damaging chlorofluorocarbons. The EPA and an international group of producers had advocated only a reduction of the compounds, not their elimination. But now just about everyone supports the phase-out idea, and Du Pont appears closest to going commercial with alternatives.

'We Saw Opportunities'

But Du Pont says making chlorofluorocarbons was no longer very good business for the company anyway. Intense price competition squeezed profits, and overproduction forced it to write off some new manufacturing facilities before they were used. Elwood P. Blanchard, a Du Pont executive vice president, dubbed the business a "cash trap" for Du Pont.

In other cases, environmental liabilities have become so financially burdensome that companies have found they can save money by preventing pollution before it starts. Dow Chemical Co. saw in the mid-1970s that hazardous-waste landfills were increasingly costly burdens because of cleanups and lawsuits. Similarly, pollution-control devices are expensive. So the company began researching ways to produce less hazardous waste.

The result was a program started in 1986 that environmentalists now cite as a model for other companies. Its premise is production efficiency. Each financial quarter, Dow tracks an index that shows the process wastes as a percentage of production. So far, it says, air wastes have been reduced by 30%, water wastes by 20% and solid wastes by 15%—all before they even reach the pollution-control devices that filter them further. Dow's goal is to reduce waste an additional 10% to 15% next year.

Already, Dow is saving money. For example, by reprogramming a computer at a Louisiana plant where vinyl chloride is made, 10.5 million pounds of air wastes were eliminated. The value of the unreacted raw materials that would have become waste: $800,000 a year.

Says Ryan Delcambre, Dow's manager for waste reduction, "We saw opportunities."

ADVERTISING / By JEFFREY A. TRACHTENBERG

New Law Adds Risk to Comparative Ads

It's getting nasty out there. Makers of everything from jam to air fresheners to bug killers have launched ad campaigns that mimic or attack their competitors with a zeal that industry veterans say they have never seen before.

"Comparative advertising has become really pointed and mean," says Bob Wolf, vice chairman, Chiat/Day Advertising Inc. "One of the reasons is that manufacturers no longer compete for every consumer in a category. Now it's very precise, niche marketing."

It's also about to become more dangerous. In an article in the current issue of the Harvard Business Review, authors Bruce Buchanan and Doron Goldman write that the little-noticed Trademark Law Revision Act of 1988, which becomes effective this November, makes it easier for victims of attack advertising to sue.

Under the old Lanham Act, advertisers were prohibited from misrepresenting their own products. The new act prevents them from misrepresenting the qualities or characteristics of "another person's goods, sevices, or commercial activities."

This means companies that believe their brand names have been unfairly tarnished by attack advertising have protection under federal law, a significant change. Not only does the new act close a loophole often used by the defense, but it also covers all states.

"It's definitely pro-plaintiff," says Michael Epstein, a partner at Weil, Gotshal & Manges. "If you feel your company has been misrepresented, it will be easier to sue. I don't think there's going to be a tenfold increase in suits, but companies will have to be more careful about their advertising."

There are numerous examples of advertising that might be affected by the new act. Consider **Sorrell Ridge**, a maker of spreadable fruit jams and jellies. In Sorrell Ridge's TV campaign, created by **Follis & Verdi**, viewers are told that preserves made by **J.M. Smucker** Co. are mostly corn syrup, refined sugar, and just some fruit. Sorrell Ridge products, in comparison, are presented as consisting of all fruit and fruit juice.

Some viewers might take that to mean that Sorrell Ridge products are healthier than Smucker's. Although Sorrell Ridge's chief executive officer, Fred Ross, says the company doesn't see any problem with the commercials, he concedes the new law gives him pause. "We'll have to reconsider the direction we've taken," he says, even though he credits the campaign with boosting the company's sales by 50%.

Another recent example of tough comparative advertising is the fight between Lysol, made by Sterling Drug Inc., and Glade, which is made by **S.C. Johnson &** Son Inc. Last month Glade aired a commercial suggesting that the air doesn't smell good for Lysol users because Lysol is 75% alcohol. In turn, viewers recently saw a TV commercial for Lysol contending that Glade is more than 97% water and gas.

A Sterling Drug spokesman says the Lysol ad "was completely accurate." But under the new act, being accurate may not be total protection from a lawsuit.

"You can make a true statement but still give a false impression to a consumer," notes Daniel Ebenstein, a partner with the law firm of Amster, Rothstein & Ebenstein in New York. Without commenting on the merits of the Lysol ad, he says, "A product may contain mostly water, for example. But the remaining ingredients may be very significant. One issue is what you say, but a separate issue is the message you communicate."

Regarding the Sorrell Ridge ads, Richard Smucker, president of Smucker's, said, "We do make an all-fruit product, but their comparisons are against our traditional fruit line." Mr. Smucker said his company won't bring suit. S.C. Johnson officials declined comment.

Mr. Ebenstein doesn't think the new act will drastically change the body of law that has been written around the Lanham Act. But, he says, "This is a congressional acknowledgement that there ought to be a national remedy for false and misleading advertising, and that is likely to create more litigation."

Ford Decides To Fight Back In Truck Ads

By Joseph B. White
Staff Reporter of The Wall Street Journal

DETROIT—Ford Motor Co., tired of turning the other cheek in its truck advertising, is unveiling new TV commercials that slap back at archrival Chevrolet.

Ford's change of tactics and its decision to sharply increase truck advertising during the next three months will escalate one of Detroit's hottest marketing wars just in time for the spring selling season. The new strategy also suggests that when it comes to selling pickup trucks, it doesn't pay to be nice.

Ford had tried, since last fall, to avoid directly comparing its trucks with those of General Motors Corp.'s Chevrolet division. But Chevy hasn't been interested in a truce. Instead, it is bombarding consumers with flashy ads that belittle Ford trucks—by name—as underpowered and outmoded.

Now, sales of Ford's full-size and compact pickups are down 2.3% since Oct. 1, the beginning of the 1989 model year, while Chevy pickup sales have jumped 14%. Ford's original low-key 1989 campaign wasn't "articulating the reason for our leadership" in the pickup-truck market, says John Vanderzee, advertising manager. Ford is particularly worried that first-time pickup buyers are being lured into Chevrolet showrooms by the hard-hitting Chevy ads.

So Ford now will boast of "important features Chevy can't talk about" in the new ads for its full-size F-series trucks. The features include a standard engine with more pulling power, a "bigger, longer, wider, deeper" cargo bed, and lower price. Chevy officials declined to comment.

Ford's new commercials are still mild stuff compared with a Chevy ad that depicts a Ford truck being blown up by a keg of dynamite. That's because Ford officials believe truck buyers think Chevy's pyrotechnics are silly. "We believe this is the high road," Mr. Vanderzee says.

But not so high that consumers will miss the point. One new Ford commercial shows a Ford pickup hauling a helpless Chevy out of a ditch.

What's more, the new advertising for Ford's Ranger compact pickup will directly rebut a Chevy criticism that apparently was hitting home. The Ranger spot will highlight Ford's decision to offer four-wheel drive "at the touch of a button" as standard equipment. Until recently, this push-button four-wheel-drive system was an option on 1989 Rangers. Chevrolet, which has a standard feature allowing drivers to shift into four-wheel drive by throwing a lever, has been heckling Ford for lacking this feature in ads that show a Ford truck stuck in knee-deep mud.

Ford dealers say it's about time the company put some punch back in its truck ads. "You just can't sit there and let a guy beat up on you," says Dave Sinclair, a big St. Louis Ford dealer.

Dealers have reason to worry: While Ford boasts that nearly two-thirds of its customers are repeat buyers, the explosive growth in the truck market is coming from one-time car owners without any brand loyalty.

Besides creating the new commercials, which will hit the airwaves next Monday, Ford also plans to run more of them. The company will raise its truck-advertising spending during the next three months by 50% from a year earlier, Mr. Vanderzee says.

"If the consumer senses a momentum in this business," he says, "we want the momentum to swing back our way."

Quaker Oats Co. Is Sued by Texas Over Health Claims in Cereal Ads

By Jeff Bailey

Staff Reporter of The Wall Street Journal

The state of Texas sued **Quaker Oats** Co., charging that advertisements for its oatmeal and oat bran falsely claim that eating the cereal reduces cholesterol and the risk of heart attack.

The lawsuit, filed in Texas state court in Dallas County, is one of a number of actions being taken against food companies by a nine-state group of attorneys general known as the health-claims task force. Jim Mattox, Texas attorney general, said of Chicago-based Quaker: "We're in the middle of an oat-bran craze in this country that was primarily started by Quaker in order to sell its products. Consumers have been duped."

Mr. Mattox, who is widely expected to run for governor of Texas, isn't exaggerating by much when he calls it a craze. Quaker said that oatmeal sales, which had been flat for years, began skyrocketing in the fall of 1987—when studies showing that oatmeal can help reduce cholesterol were widely publicized. Quaker's oatmeal sales gained 25% in the 12 months following release of the studies, and rose an additional 9% the following year, when many new competitors entered the suddenly booming market, a Quaker spokesman said. The company expects oatmeal sales of about $500 million this year, he said.

In a statement, Quaker said its ads are "truthful and supported by valid, reliable scientific evidence." The company also said it is "extremely disheartening to see the attorney general obstructing . . . the goal of nutrition education."

At the heart of all this is a series of ads featuring actor Wilfred Brimley, a grandfatherly sort who played the baseball team manager in the Robert Redford film, "The Natural." In the ads, Mr. Brimley urges viewers to eat oatmeal, saying: "It's the right thing to do."

Quaker's ads say that the company's oatmeal and oat bran can help lower cholesterol levels—as part of a low-fat, low-cholesterol diet.

That qualification, however, appears in smaller letters on the cereal box, the lawsuit says. The lawsuit asks for a temporary restraining order against the ads. It asks that Quaker be forced to disclose in all ads the exact diet required—including how often and how much oatmeal to eat to achieve the desired results—and that the research cited was financed by the company.

Texas asserts in the suit that Quaker pitches oatmeal as a drug substitute, urging people to "self-medicate with Quaker oats" rather than seek the help of a doctor for high cholesterol or heart problems.

About a year ago, a health advocacy group questioned the health claims, and the Federal Trade Commission reviewed the ads, concluding last June that Quaker wasn't misleading consumers and that people realized that any benefit came within the context of a proper diet. During that period, the company has also been providing information to Texas, which is leading the nine-state task force in this matter.

A spokesman for Mr. Mattox said the task force's other states don't plan to file similar suits unless "they have to." The states hope the Texas action will force Quaker to change its ads nationally.

Quaker said it expects to successfully defend itself in the lawsuit and has no plans to alter its claims.

Double Standard For Kids' TV Ads

Non-Network Stations' Lax Rules Lure Toy Makers—and Rile Critics

By JOANNE LIPMAN

Staff Reporter of THE WALL STREET JOURNAL

In one Barbie doll commercial, America's favorite 30-year-old teen-ager looks just about the same as she always has. A bundle of plastic arms and legs, she's incapable of doing much of anything without the help of the little girls holding her.

But look at this second commercial. Set up on a strobe-lighted stage, Barbie and her buddies appear to move all by themselves, holding guitars and dancing up a storm amid flashing blue and pink lights. Clouds of smoke swirl about them, and a rock 'n' roll score is intercut with the shrieks of little girls. It takes a second viewing, and the pause button of a videocassette recorder, to notice the black-sleeved arms in the black background manipulating the dolls.

Why the difference? The first spot ran on network television, where standards for children's advertising are strict. The second ran on non-network TV, where there are often no such standards at all. And therein lie the seeds of a growing debate.

Critics say the disparity is an open invitation to abuse in children's advertising. And while no firm statistics exist, they contend that the problem is getting worse. A major reason: Proliferating independent and cable stations, they note, are drawing more advertisers—and child viewers—away from the networks. Indeed, with competition in the toy industry intense, many advertisers are feeling the lure of non-network TV's freer atmosphere.

Leaning on Technology

While the networks require such things as a realistic portrayal of a toy's abilities, Playmates Toys Inc. was able to use special effects in a non-network spot to make its talking Cricket doll dance, spin and gesture as well. The ad included the disclaimer "Doll does not walk" flashed on the screen—but that didn't stop Pilar Boehm, 5, from promptly asking her mother to buy her one. "I said, 'Can't you see it doesn't walk?'" Helen Boehm recalls. "But my daughter can't read."

Ms. Boehm is the director of the Children's Advertising Review Unit (CARU) of the Council of Better Business Bureaus. Of the more than 60 kid's TV commercials cited by the agency over the past five years, she says, all but two were non-network ads. The Cricket commercial, which CARU cited as being misleading, is typical of the group's targets.

In another case, a series of independent-TV ads for Sylvanian Families, a line of small animal figures made by Coleco Industries Inc./Tomy Corp., used stop-action animation to make the figures walk, jump and pick up furniture. CARU cited the spots as being confusing to kids. A spot for Voltron, a 26-inch-high, remote-controlled robot made by LJN Toys Ltd., showed the toy battling cartoon villains and zapping two of them with a laser, when the real thing basically just moved forward and backward. CARU questioned whether the ad exaggerated the toy's capabilities.

CARU, as a self-regulatory group, has its own suggested guidelines for kid's ads but wields no legal authority to change or pull them. Most advertisers abide by its suggestions, though. Coleco, for example, says it "agreed there was potential for confusion" and modified the spot in February by making a "clean break" between the fantasy and real-life segments. Playmates, which says it doesn't think its ad was misleading, and LJN, which didn't respond to calls for comment, have taken the commercials in question off the air.

"Children, especially young children, don't make the same kinds of distinctions we do of what is real and what is fantasy," says Dorothy G. Singer, a child psychologist and co-director of Yale University's Family TV Research Center.

In defending their commercials, many advertisers argue that such critics underestimate today's savvy children. "Kids aren't dummies," says Jerry Sachs, president of Sachs, Finley & Co., the Los Angeles ad agency that created the Cricket spot. As for that ad, he says, "children understand the difference between live action and animation. We sold I don't know how many hundreds of thousands of that thing, and I think we got two letters saying the child was disappointed. That's an incredi-

bly small amount."

Advertisers say, too, that a spot's failure to meet network standards doesn't necessarily make it a bad commercial. "People say you're trying to be misleading or deceptive, and that doesn't make good sense for us to do that," says Robert Moorman, a senior vice president of Tonka Inc.'s ad agency, Jordan, McGrath, Case & Taylor. Since most toys are part of large product lines, he explains, kids who are deceived "aren't going to want to buy any other part of the line."

Still, many toy makers concede that fierce competition is pushing them to test the limits of less-fettered TV outlets. After all, hundreds of toy makers are vying for a share of the $9 billion to $10 billion spent on toys annually. If toy stores carried just one of every kind of toy produced this year, their shelves would be crammed with some 40,000 items—and that doesn't include such electronic toys as video games.

At Mattel Toys Inc., "there was a period of time several years ago when we went to some non-network commercials hoping to be able to do better battle" with competitors, says Martin Miller, senior vice president of marketing research and planning for the company. "A lot of our competitors were going to non-network, and we thought, 'Oh, my goodness, we have to combat that.'"

A 1987 independent-TV spot for one of Mattel's Masters of the Universe dolls, for example, showed the toy appearing to pick up other figures automatically, while a voice-over intoned, "When Monstroid gets wound up, it grabs." In fact, figures had to be placed in its claws. A 1985 spot for Mattel's Rainbow Brite dolls was almost completely animated; it didn't even show the product until a brief shot at the end.

CARU questioned whether the first ad was misleading and whether the second gave kids unreasonable expectations. (Mattel's dancing-Barbie spot, which dates from the same period, wasn't challenged.)

While Mattel says it doesn't believe its commercials were misleading, it no longer creates different ads for non-network TV—and for a pragmatic reason. "When all is said and done, they didn't necessarily do a better job of selling the product," Mr. Miller explains. He says Mattel studied commercials for about 200 of its products over three years to determine whether network or non-network spots sold best. "We found absolutely no difference," he says.

As a result, Mr. Miller adds, Mattel "made a conscious decision in 1987" to stop making commercials that aren't network-legal. About half of the toy maker's annual $40 million to $60 million ad budget goes to network TV.

Other toy makers, however, are turning their attention *toward* non-network TV.

(cont.)

Among these are Tonka's Parker Brothers division, which currently advertises such games as Monopoly and Clue primarily on network. "We probably will have a concept this year that there's no way we could get through the three (major) networks," says John Hurlbut, senior vice president of HBM/Creamer Inc., Parker's ad agency. "We want a concept that is more exciting—more unusual—than the networks will allow."

While a third to a half of Parker's $15 million to $20 million ad budget usually goes into network TV, "that number is likely to go down," Mr. Hurlbut says. In explaining the move to non-network, he, too, cites growing competition for kids' dollars, which he says comes as well from other advertisers to children—such as cereal and candy makers—that aren't subject to the same restraints on network TV. Besides, he adds, non-network TV can be a less expensive way to reach kids.

More for Less

It costs about $7 for advertisers to reach 1,000 kids during Saturday morning network programs, but only about $4.50 to reach 1,000 kids watching syndicated programs on independent stations, according to Bohbot & Cohn Advertising Inc., a media buying firm specializing in the children's market. Cable is even cheaper, at about $2.25 per thousand kids.

For their part, non-network TV executives say they are responsible programmers and haven't heard complaints about kid's advertising. Cable-industry executives add that most large cable networks running kid's ads, such as Nickelodeon, have their own strict standards. "This is the first I've heard of anybody producing two different commercials," says Preston Padden, president of the Association of Independent Television Stations.

That silence may not last long. Action for Children's Television, an influential Boston activist group, is setting its sights on the issue. ACT has recently lobbied intensively for a bill, just passed by the House and expected to get Senate approval, that would limit the amount of commercial time in children's programs.

"ACT has been so busy focusing on macro problems that we haven't had time to focus on these differences" between network and non-network ads, says Peggy Charren, president of the group. "Now that we have our bill, we will be able to go back to looking at specific commercials. We did a lot of that in the 1970s, and we're going to do a lot of it in the late 1980s and 1990s."

A Sampling of Guidelines

Each of the major television networks has its own set of guidelines for children's advertising, although the basics are very similar. A few rules, such as the requirement of a static "island" shot at the end, are written in stone; others however, occasionally can be negotiated.

Many of the rules below apply specifically to toys. The networks also have special guidelines for kid's food commercials and for kid's commercials that offer premiums.

	ABC	CBS	NBC
Must not overglamorize product	✓	✓	✓
No exhortative language, such as "Ask Mom to buy…"	✓	✓	✓
No realistic war settings	✓		✓
Generally no celebrity endorsements	✓	Case-by-case	✓
Can't use "only" or "just" in regard to price	✓	✓	✓
Show only two toys per child or maximum of six per commercial	✓		✓
Five-second "island" showing product against plain background at end of spot	✓	✓	✓ (4 to 5)
Animation restricted to one-third of a commercial	✓		✓
Generally no comparative or superiority claims	Case-by-case	Handle w/care	✓
No costumes or props not available with the toy	✓		✓
No child or toy can appear in animated segments	✓		✓
Three-second establishing shot of toy in relation to child	✓	✓ (2.5 to 3)	
No shots under one second in length	✓		
Must show distance a toy can travel before stopping on its own	✓		

80

Haggling Grows Over Ad Agency Fees

Straight Commissions Come Under Attack by Clients Who Want to Pay Less

By JOANNE LIPMAN
Staff Reporter of THE WALL STREET JOURNAL

For years, **Hardee's Food Systems** Inc. dutifully paid its ad agencies a 15% commission, no questions asked, just like thousands of other ad agency clients.

Now, the questions begin.

The fast-food chain says it is considering a change in the way it pays its ad agencies, perhaps using a bonus system based on merit rather than a straight commission system based on how much it spends. "We generate about $9 million in (ad agency) commissions right now," says Gary Langstaff, an executive vice president, "and I don't know if we get $9 million worth of service."

Hardee's is joining a growing debate over how ad agencies should be paid. In recent years, the standard 15% commission, in which the ad agency takes 15% of the amount an advertiser spends on media time and space, has become the exception rather than the rule. Industry estimates vary, but many executives believe 65% or more of clients now use some other form of payment, such as a sliding commission or a fee. Much of the time, that works out to less than a straight 15% commission.

While the commission has been under attack for years, the debate over it is intensifying now because both agencies and their clients are under severe economic pressure. For the past few years, clients have been reining in their ad spending, and have tried to cut commissions after seeing how richly paid were the ad executives involved in the recent agency-merger wave. That in turn prompted ad agencies—once reluctant to discuss something as vulgar as money—to begin publicly lashing out at clients for not paying enough.

Ogilvy Group Inc., for example, pulled out of the finals of the Nissan competition last year, complaining that the compensation was far too low. Says Jack Bowen, chairman of ad agency **D'Arcy Masius Benton & Bowles**: "I'd say we dropped out of three or four competitions in 1987 because of the pay factor."

Most agencies, meanwhile, are looking

for ways to make up the slack. Keith Reinhard, chairman and chief executive officer of **Omnicom Group** Inc.'s DDB/Needham Worldwide unit, says DDB is exploring sharing licensing proceeds with clients if a character the agency creates becomes as popular, say, as Domino Pizza's "Noids." Currently, agencies don't profit if their creations become T-shirts or toys.

And negotiated compensation is more common. Today, says Alvin Achenbaum, whose **Canter Achenbaum Associates** negotiates agency fees for clients, "almost all

compensation agreements are negotiated."

Yet the growing emphasis on compensation threatens to make ad agencies more like commodities, which clients choose according to price rather than quality. Already, a small Philadelphia ad agency, **Harris-Edward** Inc., has published a price list touting such things as 30-second TV spots for $15,320 apiece and full-page color magazine ads for $5,760 each. No rivals are following that lead, but many acknowledge price proposals could become part of an agency's new-business pitch, right alongside creative ideas and credentials.

Last summer, taking a commodities approach, Godfather's Pizza Inc. dropped J. Walter Thompson Co. even though it was happy with its creative work. "We needed to bring (the price) more in line with what we could afford," says Charles E. Henderson, vice president of marketing.

The most common compensation arrangement now is a fee or reduced-commission arrangement, or a combination of both. But agencies are trying alternatives. Canter Achenbaum designed an "indemnification" clause for several clients, including **American Cyanamid** Co.'s Shulton unit, under which the ad agency must pay a seven-figure sum if it drops the client as a result of a merger. Small **Messner, Vetere, Berger, Carey** has discussed being paid based on a client's sales increases.

Bonus systems are also gaining popularity. R.J. Reynolds Tobacco, the **RJR Nabisco** Inc. unit, has been using one for about a year. Its agencies are happy with the plan, and some are considering similar ones for other clients.

Generally, however, most new compensation structures are vilified by ad agencies, which blame the compensation squeeze for many of their financial woes. Not that the 15% commission is the answer to everyone's problems, either. Clients still using it often demand extra services, like outside research the agency must pay for out of its own pocket.

Moreover, as clients create more brand extensions-new flavors, for example, "you've got four products there instead of one," says Mr. Bowen of DMB&B. "And guess what? They all come out of the same budget, and they aren't paying us any more."

Illustration by Stan Mack

Price

Grocery Chains Pressure Suppliers for Uniform Prices

By Alecia Swasy
And Gregory Stricharchuk
Staff Reporters of The Wall Street Journal

A fierce tug of war over pricing has erupted between grocery-store operators and consumer-product giants.

Two of the nation's biggest supermarket chains, **Winn-Dixie Stores** and **Kroger** Co., are trying to make manufacturers charge uniform prices for their goods across the country. The retailers say the change would let them streamline operations and save consumers money.

But several manufacturers, including **Procter & Gamble** Co. and **Pillsbury** Co., argue that regional pricing is a crucial part of their overall marketing strategy—and that abandoning it would, in fact, prove costly to consumers by curtailing special offers.

Uniform pricing would "restrict us from offering many of our normal promotional allowances and major sales events and would increase the average price of our products," Pillsbury says in a statement.

Decentralizing Chains

In recent years, consumer-product companies have sold a growing portion of their goods at prices set for specific regions. Steep discounts, for example, can be used to boost sales in an area where they are weak. Big grocery chains actually have fed this trend by decentralizing their own decision making.

But regional pricing has prompted energetic efforts to take advantage of the price differences. Supermarket chains and others often buy goods at low prices and warehouse them for future use or ship them to high-price areas.

Winn-Dixie and Kroger want to end these costly efforts, not by returning to centralized operations but by forcing manufacturers to standardize prices. In August, Winn-Dixie informed suppliers by letter that it would buy food and packaged goods for its 1,200 stores at the lowest price offered to any of its divisions. Last month

Kroger, with 1,300 stores, followed suit.

Joseph A. Pichler, president of Kroger, says the dispute is "highlighting the inefficiencies in buying" under the regional-pricing system. "There has to be a better way," he adds.

P&G says it won't yield on the matter. Winn-Dixie, in turn, has refused to reorder some P&G products.

Other chains, such as the **Great Atlantic & Pacific Tea** Co., which operates 1,170 stores, **Safeway Stores** Inc., with 1,161 stores, and **Albertson's** Inc., with 480 stores, say they are eagerly watching the clash. But they haven't indicated whether they will follow the lead of Kroger and Winn-Dixie.

Working against the grocery chains is the increasing consolidation in the food industry. And if **Philip Morris** Cos. succeeds in its current bid for **Kraft** Inc., some analysts say it will give the manufacturers more clout in this dispute. "The game we're dealing in now is one of economic power," says Richard Furash, a retailing analyst at Touche Ross & Co. in Boston. "The bigger you are, the better chance you have of prevailing."

But the retailers' insurgency suggests that they believe their own power has grown enormously in recent years. And they may be right.

The chains have gained critical leverage—including the ability to refuse shelf space to manufacturers' new products. That's a potent weapon because manufacturers have come to rely on prominent in-store promotions, where more and more shoppers make their buying decisions, to get new products off the ground.

Retailers also have an alternative to buying brand-name products directly from the manufacturers: If necessary, they can make purchases through middlemen called diverters, who buy goods when manufacturers are selling at special prices, then resell them to retailers. (Often, diverters are themselves retailers who buy excess goods on promotion.)

The insurgency also reflects changing

economic conditions. Consolidation among big food retailers has left many strapped with huge debt, forcing them to find ways to cut costs in an industry renowned for razor-thin profit margins. Retailers "have to push for every penny they can," says Richard J. Fox, associate professor of marketing at the University of Georgia.

Also, some bigger chains face growing competition from smaller counterparts that concentrate on generating high volume in basic goods rather than offering an array of services, such as in-store pharmacies, seafood counters and video rentals. For instance, Winn-Dixie has been under pressure from **Food Lion** Inc., a 540-store chain whose prices are standardized because the company makes purchasing decisions at a central location. "People have come to expect the same prices in all our locations," a Food Lion spokesman says.

Consumer Pressure?

For the near future, customers at both Kroger and Winn-Dixie—whose stores span the South and Midwest—may discover that they can't find some of their favorite brands. Shoppers also may find manufacturers flooding areas with coupons for brands that retailers have boycotted. Manufacturers could use such a tactic to try to force consumers to pressure retailers to restock discontinued brands.

Neither side will disclose which items are affected. Because big retailers often stockpile supplies, it may be too early to see big drops in store inventories.

Pillsbury, based in Minneapolis, also says Winn-Dixie is boycotting some of its products. But others, such as Pittsburgh-based **H.J. Heinz**, which produces everything from ketchup to baby food, and **Coca-Cola** Co.'s food subsidiary, maker of Minute-Maid orange juice and Hi-C beverages, say they are meeting with Winn-Dixie to try and work out a compromise.

Hugh Phillips, vice president of customer development at Coca-Cola Foods, says, "We're not interested in any confrontation with Winn-Dixie."

Space War

Supermarkets Demand Food Firms' Payments Just to Get on the Shelf

---

Some Overcrowded Grocers Get 'Slotting,' Other Fees; Even Kraft Plays the Game

---

Consumers Help Pay the Cost

By RICHARD GIBSON
Staff Reporter of THE WALL STREET JOURNAL

Jack Truzzolino thinks he has come up with a better pizza roll. If he has, customers of Safeway Stores Inc. will never know it.

He says Safeway, one of the nation's largest grocery chains, demanded $25,000 up front from his small Butte, Mont., specialty-foods company, just to make space for the product in freezer cases in its California stores.

Mr. Truzzolino won't pay. "It's highway robbery," he says. "We just can't afford it." (Safeway says it rejected the pizza rolls for other reasons, not the least of which was that it figured the product wouldn't sell.)

Thus, Mr. Truzzolino's pizza roll, and many products made by small companies, will never make it to shoppers in thousands of stores this year. New products—and in some cases, consumers' pocketbooks—are the casualties in a heightening power struggle between grocers and food manufacturers. Across the country, grocers are demanding growing amounts of cash, local-media advertising and promotion, and even changes in pricing policy in return for stocking new products.

Less Selection

As a result, supermarket shelves are rapidly becoming the world's most expensive real estate. Even a giant Philip Morris, which agreed over the weekend to acquire Kraft Inc. for $13.1 billion, isn't expected to dent the retailers' new strength. And if it does, using the powerful leverage of its General Foods and Kraft brands, that won't do anything to help medium-sized and small producers, who have accounted for much innovation in the industry.

In New York City, for example, Shoprite Stores asked for $86,000 to stock $172,-000 worth of Old Capital microwave popcorn, then tossed the brand out six weeks later when it didn't sell well. Curtice-Burns Inc. has to pay $1 million up front to chains across half the nation just to get shelf space for some of its $1.79-a-can pie fillings. And in New England, a supermarket chain asked Pillsbury Co. for more money to stock a new brownie than Pillsbury had budgeted for the product's introduction in the entire country.

At a minimum, the practice is narrowing the product selection available to consumers, though the size of store shelves also puts a natural limit on what can be offered shoppers. These days, small and entrepreneurial food concerns trying to field new products and brands are being blown off the battlefield.

"It's a sickness that pervades the industry," says Harold Greenberg, chief executive officer of Certified Grocers Midwest Inc., a grocery wholesaler.

New Big Guy on the Block

The trend reflects a fundamental shift in the balance of power between food retailers and manufacturers. In the past, big food companies bullied grocers, often telling them what products they had to take and at what price. But grocery chains have consolidated into regional giants with immense distribution clout. Armed with up-to-the-minute sales information from new computerized checkout-scanning systems, the retailers can quickly pinpoint what products are moving, and at what level of profit. Today, retailers are calling the shots.

As manufacturers get bigger, they are likely to pour more money into the battle for shelf space, raising the ante for new players. But even the consolidated food giants would still lack the clout to completely derail retailers' demands or to tip the balance of power back toward manufacturers. (In the case of Kraft, for example, the company pays fees only on its frozen food line. The practice is so ingrained that Kraft says it isn't certain whether even its combination with Philip Morris will make any difference.)

The business of delivering packaged foods to the consumer thus has become a high-stakes shoot-out. Most prevalent, and most open to abuse, manufacturers say, is a widening insistence by retailers on outright payments for shelf space. The fees, called "slotting allowances" in industry parlance, are payments for space, or slots, in grocers' warehouses.

It's Just Business

Supermarket operators say the fees re-

flect nothing more than a sensible business practice. Manufacturers spewed out more than 10,000 new food products last year, four times as many as a decade ago. There isn't enough space on store shelves to stock all the goods. And with profits in the grocery business razor thin—often just one or two percent of sales—it doesn't pay to build more stores with more shelf space.

What's more, manufacturers' market tests and advertising for the new products often are inadequate, so retailers aren't protected from costly failures. Instead, they are saddled with the cost of storing, labeling, shelving and then removing products that flop.

Enter the slotting allowance. The retailers see it as a form of insurance, a way of guaranteeing at least some profit, or reduced risk, in taking on a new product. A spokesman for Kroger Co. of Cincinnati, Ohio, says the fee helps make product introductions "a neutral event" for stores. And while the fee can be used to boost profits, some retailers contend it actually ends up in consumers' pockets, since the grocers may use the windfall to cut prices around the store. For example, Robert Wunderle, an executive with Supermarkets General Corp., says promotions and slotting paid by manufacturers "become a competitive factor in your pricing structure" in his company's stores.

The retailers claim they aren't twisting manufacturers' arms to get shelving fees. "There are four or five other people running up with cash saying, 'I'd rather have you take my product,'" says James L. Baska, a Kansas City grocery wholesaler and past chairman of the National Grocers Association. Adds Mr. Wunderle: "If a guy comes with a terrific new item and he's going to advertise it very strongly—meaning that customers are going to demand the product—and he offers no slotting allowance, we'll take the item in."

The practice has become just another cost of doing business. One manufacturer found that 69% of its major retail accounts wouldn't introduce new products without a fee. A big retail chain, insisting on anonymity, says the $15-per-store it charges to shelve a new item brings in $50 million a year.

To introduce a new frozen fruit juice bar, United Brands Co. doled out $375,000 in the New York City market alone, industry sources say. United Brands wouldn't comment. A spokeswoman for Shoprite's parent, Wakefern Foods Corp., confirmed that the chain accepted a slotting fee for Old Capital Popcorn and later removed the product from the shelf. "We just didn't sell

(cont.)

enough to reorder it," she said. "We had to go with the product that had the best sell-through for us."

Rent Check

Some supermarkets also ask "pay to stay" fees to keep products on their shelves more than a few weeks. Great Atlantic & Pacific Tea Co.'s New Orleans division recently asked Sargento Cheese Co. for a payment to keep its products in the dairy case. While Sargento refused, manufacturers worry that ongoing shelf rent charges will become commonplace.

In many cases the fees seem to bear little relationship to retailers' costs. Herbert H. Clarke Jr., sales manager for Jackson-Mitchell Pharmaceuticals Inc., says one Salt Lake City chain wants $2,000 to stock his brand of goat milk. He feels that's too much for a small market like Salt Lake City. Fee-setting, he complains, depends on "what kind of nerve these guys have got."

Slotting fees are particularly open to abuse, manufacturers say, because they are negotiated privately and sometimes paid in cash or in merchandise. One West Coast juice maker, who asked not to be identified, said a broker for one retailer once told him, "'I'll take whatever you've got, TVs, stereos, VCRs, whatever,'" presumably for use in store promotions.

Retailers typically charge what the market will bear. "If Ralph's [another large West Coast chain] is charging $100 per store and it has 130 stores in a market and we have 80, we'd be foolish not to try to get that as well," says Gary Michael, vice chairman of Albertson's Inc. of Boise, Idaho. "I'm not saying it's the best way to do business," he adds.

Tide's Draw

Partly because of slotting fees, says Gordon Crane, president of Apple & Eve Inc., a Great Neck, N.Y., juice company, "the cost of entry to launch a new product today is through the roof." Apple & Eve recently spent $150,000 to get a new fruit punch on grocers' shelves in some stores in the Northeast, the equivalent of about eight months' profit on the brand.

Retailers don't require slotting fees for all products, of course. Refusing to stock the handful of nationally branded products that command broad consumer loyalty would be counterproductive for retailers. So consumer-products giants such as Procter & Gamble Co. and Kraft get free access to grocers' shelves for such must-stock items as Tide detergent and Miracle Whip salad dressing.

Since rules governing slotting allowances are at best capricious, some manufacturers and lawyers contend that certain of the payments are illegal. The Robinson-Patman Act prohibits price discrimination between retailers within a given market, and thus would theoretically require manufacturers to pay all grocers the same slotting fees. But many in the industry doubt that's happening.

"I don't know for sure that every manufacturer who's offering [a payment] is offering it to every one of its competing" grocers in the same market, says Ronald A. Bloch, a Washington antitrust lawyer who once headed the Federal Trade Commission's oversight of the food-industry. Adds Willard F. Mueller, a former economist at the FTC and now a University of Wisconsin professor: "It's time the antitrust agencies take a hard look at this." The FTC, the agency that regulates product pricing, says it is just beginning to study the issue of slotting allowances.

The food companies, too, are worried about possible illegalities. Asked to discuss the matter, a General Mills Inc. spokesman says, "It's a sensitive issue. Nobody here wants to talk about it." A spokesman for a large Midwestern grocery chain alludes to industry "abuses," then refuses to say anything more. "If I talked about it specifically, the lawyers would have a field day on my body," he says.

Nevertheless, prosecution isn't likely. Discriminatory pricing would be hard to prove because slotting allowances are negotiated orally and in private. Proving that pricing practices have caused a specific injury, as courts have been requiring recently, would be difficult.

Manufacturers are loath to say how slotting allowances are affecting the suggested retail price they affix to their products. They don't want to say how much of the cost is passed on to consumers, though much of it likely is. Any additional cost "you put on a product will cost the consumer," says Patrick Smithwick, an industry consultant and former General Mills executive.

Frookie cookies is a case in point. One grocery chain's demand for $1,000 per store to introduce R.W. Frookie cookies in its 100 stores would have forced the cookies' retail price higher by 50 cents a package or more, says Richard S. Worth, the product's creator. A package of cookies that would have sold for $1.79 to $1.89, therefore, would have jumped to $2.29 to $2.39. Mr. Worth walked away from the chain.

Slotting allowances are just one of several examples of retailers' growing demands. Some supermarkets charge manufacturers for removing products from the shelves if they don't sell or are crowded out by the competition.

For You, a Special Deal

Other supermarkets insist that manufacturers buy unsold inventory back at full retail price, leaving manufacturers with little alternative but to write the goods off. If that happens, "I say 'No, you just keep it,'" says Phil Parsons, general manager of Perfect Pinch Inc., a small Chicago spicemaker.

More and more grocers are also requiring manufacturers to advertise heavily in local media—a step that benefits the grocer, but may not be part of a manufacturer's own marketing plan. Moreover, two of the nation's biggest supermarket chains, Winn-Dixie Stores and Kroger, are trying to make manufacturers charge uniform prices for their goods across the country, thus maximizing promotional allowances for retailers. Manufacturers are resisting, arguing that regional pricing is a crucial part of their overall marketing strategy.

Food buyers for one Texas supermarket chain, Furr's Inc., have even asked $500 just to make an appointment, according to one manufacturer. "I just laughed," said the sales manager of a Southern California candy company, who refused the demand. Furr's wouldn't confirm or deny the claim.

Some manufacturers have quietly begun campaigning to curb grocers' demands. Last May, George S. Davidson, chairman of Foster Canning Inc., sent a letter to his congressman, Rep. Delbert Latta of Ohio, saying: "This is nothing but a device to extort money from packers and squeeze all the independent and smaller processors off the shelves and out of business. We believe this is the most flagrant restraint of trade device yet conceived." He received a noncommittal reply.

Also, Quaker Oats Co. is trying to get retailers to accept a standardized introductory allowance for new products. The publisher of Food Distributors magazine, Brad McDowell, meanwhile, recently printed a series of editorials inveighing against what he calls "underhanded" practices and "payoffs" in the industry, including slotting fees.

But so far, such efforts haven't amounted to much. If anything, the practice of charging slotting allowances is growing in the retail business. Ken Partch,

(cont.)

editor of Supermarket Business, has been a
critic of the process for years, but acknowledges his criticism is largely futile.
"I feel like I'm screaming into the wind,"
he says.

Panasonic to Pay Rebates To Avoid Antitrust Charges

By Ann Hagedorn

Staff Reporter of The Wall Street Journal

NEW YORK—Panasonic Co. agreed to pay consumers $16 million to avert charges that it fixed retail prices on electronics products sold during six months last year.

About 665,000 people nationwide will be eligible for rebates of $17 to $45.

At a news conference yesterday, New York Attorney General Robert Abrams, whose office uncovered the alleged price fixing, said Panasonic, a Secaucus, N.J., subsidiary of Matsushita Electric Industrial Co. of Japan, attempted "the largest vertical price-fixing scheme in this nation's history. If the scheme had not been stopped, the cost [to consumers] would have been monumental."

In vertical price fixing, manufacturers typically demand that retailers adhere to minimum product prices. Such agreements violate antitrust laws. The Panasonic scheme was so elaborate and far-reaching, Mr. Abrams said, that his office will expand its investigation of price fixing in the electronics industry.

As part of the settlement, Panasonic agreed not to engage in the alleged activities for the next five years but did not admit to any wrongdoing. In a statement, the company flatly denied the allegations.

According to Mr. Abrams, Panasonic threatened to cut off the supply of its products if retailers refused to raise prices by an average of 5% to 10%. In several cases, Mr. Abrams said, Akiya Imura, the president of Panasonic, "personally and repeatedly pressured retailers to comply."

Because the settlement is intended to apply nationally, it is contingent on adoption by attorneys general in other states. Mr. Abrams said that if attorneys general representing at least 80% of the eligible consumers don't adopt the terms of the settlement within 60 days, the agreement will be terminated. In that case, he said, he would file a lawsuit against the company.

Though it was a retailer who triggered the attorney general's investigation by filing a complaint, some dealers were eager to cooperate with Panasonic, said one of the state attorneys in charge of the investigation. "There were retailers who were what we call rats," the attorney said at the news conference. "They would tip off Panasonic if they learned that another retailer was not complying."

The products, sold from March 1 through Aug. 31, 1988, include Panasonic and Technics brand videocassette recorders, camcorders, cordless telephones, answering machines and stereo equipment. Among the many retailers that complied with the scheme "in whole or in part," according to Mr. Abrams, were Circuit City Stores Inc., Dayton Hudson Corp. and K mart Corp. A spokeswoman for K mart said no executives could be reached for comment. Officials of Circuit City and Dayton Hudson couldn't be reached.

No charges have been brought against any of the retailers who allegedly were required to raise their prices.

Consumers who are eligible for reimbursement—and who had sent in a warranty form after making their purchase—will receive a letter and a claim form from Panasonic. The company also will advertise the terms of the settlement in national publications. And it will pay $2 million for the cost of administering the settlement, in addition to the $16 million in rebates.

Mr. Abrams said the scheme was first outlined during a corporate meeting last May, where a Panasonic vice president, whom he didn't name, directed other executives to closely monitor compliance. If dealers did not adhere to the new policy, there would be "chaos in the marketplace," the executive allegedly told the group, and Panasonic would "lose face with the entire industry."

In its statement, Panasonic denied all charges of unlawful conduct. Said Ralph Wolfe, senior vice president of sales: "Over the last few years, the serious erosion of profits in the consumer-electronics marketplace has been widely reported, and Panasonic sales policies are designed to address the need for dealer profitability." The purpose of the settlement, he said, is to avoid "costly litigation," though he added that the company is confident it "would have prevailed in any lawsuit brought by the state."

In trading yesterday on the New York Stock Exchange, Matsushita's American depositary receipts fell $2 each to $203.

Mr. Abrams, a Democrat, used the announcement of the settlement to take a shot at antitrust enforcement in the Reagan administration. "Major corporations, such as electronics makers, have gotten a message that practices which historically have been defined as clearly illegal will be winked at by federal regulators," Mr. Abrams said.

Charles Rule, assistant attorney general in charge of the Justice Department's antitrust division, countered Mr. Abrams's gloomy picture of the Reagan years. He said the government has been "very active" in its efforts to protect consumers from price fixing. For example, he said, there are now 160 grand jury investigations into alleged horizontal price-fixing schemes, compared with 50 in 1980. Horizontal price fixing typically involves agreements among competitors to set prices.

Court Says Indirect Buyers Can Sue Violators of State Antitrust Laws

By STEPHEN WERMIEL

Staff Reporter of THE WALL STREET JOURNAL

WASHINGTON—The Supreme Court, in an important victory for states and consumers, ruled that states may permit people who suffer indirect financial losses as a result of state antitrust-law violations to sue the violators.

The 7-0 ruling gives the states leeway to allow lawsuits by indirect purchasers under state antitrust laws, although such suits can't be filed under federal antitrust law. Indirect-purchaser lawsuits are an important tool for consumers to attack the practices of manufacturers, and also permits state attorneys general to file antitrust actions against manufacturers on behalf of consumers.

Fifteen states and the District of Columbia have laws allowing such lawsuits, including the four involved in the Supreme Court ruling—California, Minnesota, Alabama and Arizona.

Such suits are usually filed against manufacturers by people who purchase their goods from retailers or wholesalers, rather than directly. They typically are based on claims that a manufacturer engaged in a price-fixing conspiracy that inflated prices charged by middlemen, such as wholesalers or retailers, who weren't part of the scheme.

In 1977, the Supreme Court ruled that federal antitrust law permits lawsuits for damages only by direct purchasers. Since then, states have increasingly passed laws allowing such lawsuits under their own antitrust laws.

In May 1987, a federal appeals court in San Francisco relied on the Supreme Court's 1977 ruling to conclude that allowing indirect-purchaser lawsuits under state laws would interfere with enforcement of federal antitrust laws.

But the high court, in an opinion written by Justice Byron White, said that allowing such suits under state laws poses no threat to the use of the federal antitrust laws. The ruling is certain to spur similar legislation by other states.

The case arose when cement makers created a fund of more than $32 million to settle price-fixing lawsuits filed by numerous direct purchasers and by several states that were indirect purchasers themselves, or through local governments.

In 1984 and 1985, when a federal judge in Arizona began hearings on distributing the settlement fund, **ARC America** Corp. and other direct purchasers objected to any payments to indirect cement purchasers. The district judge and the San Francisco appeals court ruled that indirect purchasers couldn't receive any settlement funds, and the four states appealed to the high court.

Business groups such as the U.S. Chamber of Commerce argued in a friend-of-the-court brief against the validity of the state laws, saying they would interfere with the trials and payment of damages in federal antitrust cases. But the Justice Department backed the states in a brief.

Justices John Stevens and Sandra O'Connor didn't participate in the case and gave no explanation for their absence. *(California vs. ARC America Corp.)*

Employee Benefits Case

The justices, in a major victory for employees, ruled 9-0 that federal law doesn't prevent a state from prosecuting an employer who refuses to fulfill payment of promised wages or benefits to employees, such as reimbursement for unused vacation time.

The case involves a Massachusetts prosecution of the president of **Yankee Bank for Finance & Savings** for failure to pay two former bank vice presidents for unused vacation time, as promised by company policy.

The prosecution was based on a state law, similar to those in most states, requiring payment of all wages owed when a worker is fired. Because of legal questions about whether there could be a prosecution, the case was appealed to the state supreme court before a trial was held. The state supreme court ruled that the issue involved an employee benefit plan, that state law was pre-empted by federal law, and that the prosecution was prohibited.

In an opinion written by Justice Stevens, the Supreme Court reversed the 1988 ruling of the Massachusetts Supreme Judicial Court and said the promise to pay for unused vacation time wasn't an employee benefit plan covered by the federal pension and benefits law. The high court ruling sends the case back to Massachusetts for a trial.

Twenty states, the Justice Department and the AFL-CIO supported Massachusetts in the case. *(Massachusetts vs. Morash)*

Airline Liability

The high court ruled 9-0 that airline liability for accidents involving international travelers can't exceed limits set by international agreements simply because the airlines fail to properly warn passengers of the limits.

In an opinion written by Justice Antonin Scalia, the high court ruled against the families of the people killed when a **Korean Air Lines** jet crashed in September 1983 after it entered Soviet airspace and was fired upon by a Soviet military plane.

The 60-year-old Warsaw Convention limited airline liability on international flights. The Montreal Agreement, concluded in 1966 among a number of countries and airlines, set the liability limit at $75,000 a passenger in damages for injuries or death, and says passengers must be warned of the limit in writing on each ticket in 10-point type. Families of Korean Air victims argued that the airline used smaller, 8-point type and can't claim the $75,000 liability limit.

A federal appeals court in Washington in September 1987, rejected the argument and upheld use of the limit. But in cases involving other crashes, most other federal appeals courts have read the type-size requirement literally and have refused to limit airline liability.

Justice Scalia concluded that nothing in the language of the international agreements expressly says the airlines should lose the benefit of the liability limit for inadequate warnings. Had the ruling gone against the airlines, it might have exposed the industry to substantial damage awards in international air disasters. *(Chan vs. Korean Air Lines)*

FTC Accuses Six Large Book Publishers Of Price Bias Against Independent Stores

By Monica Langley
Staff Reporter of The Wall Street Journal

WASHINGTON — The Federal Trade Commission charged six of the nation's largest book publishers with illegally discriminating against independent bookstores.

In complaints issued yesterday, the FTC alleged that the publishers violated the Robinson-Patman Act by selling books at lower prices to major bookstore chains and at higher prices to independent stores.

The administrative complaints were issued against Harper & Row Publishers Inc., controlled by News Corp.; William Morrow & Co., a unit of Hearst Corp.; Macmillan Inc., a unit of Maxwell Communication Corp. of Britain; Putnam Berkley Group Inc.; Random House Inc., part of the Newhouse family's Advance Publications Inc.; and Gulf & Western Inc.'s Simon & Schuster Inc. The publishers are all based in New York. Those that provided comment yesterday on the commission's action said their pricing practices were fair.

The FTC alleged that the publishers used "discriminatory pricing practices" to sell or distribute books at lower prices to some retailers than other ones. The agency said the "favored purchasers" include the nation's three largest bookstore chains: Waldenbooks Inc., a unit of K mart Corp., Troy, Mich.; New York-based B.D.B. Inc.'s B. Dalton Bookseller; and Crown Books Corp., Landover, Md. The "disfavored purchasers," according to the FTC, are most, if not all, of the nation's independent bookstores.

The commission voted 3-1 to issue the complaints, with one commissioner not participating. FTC Chairman Daniel Oliver voted against issuing the complaints, saying he didn't think "there was reason to believe the publishers had violated the law."

The FTC said the publishers treat orders placed by bookstore chains as a single order, even if the books are separately packed, itemized and shipped to individual chain outlets. As a result, the chain stores are able to pay lower prices than independent bookstores "that receive shipments as large as or larger than the shipments to individual chain outlets," the FTC said.

The FTC also alleged that the publishers have provided services or facilities for promotion, display and inventory control to the chains without providing them to all purchasers on the same terms.

The FTC complaints said these practices have limited independent bookstores' ability to compete with the chains for "retail locations, expansion opportunities and sales to consumers."

In his dissent, the FTC chairman said the practices "probably have not injured competition," adding that the price differences are "probably justified by differences in the cost of selling to different purchasers." Mr. Oliver said the litigation isn't "in the public interest" because it "may force publishers to adopt less-efficient distribution methods and thereby lead to higher book prices for consumers."

William T. Loverd, vice president and director of corporate affairs at Random House, said the publisher is convinced the pricing of its books is "both lawful and fair." He added that the company is "surprised" the FTC would take such an action.

A Simon & Schuster spokeswoman said its pricing practices "have always been fair." The commission "is going to have a real fight on its hands," she said.

A Macmillan spokesman said the company hadn't seen the complaint and wouldn't comment until it had.

Barbara Husham, vice president and general counsel for Harper & Row, said, "We are convinced our trade practices are entirely proper and we are prepared to defend the action on its merits."

Officials of William Morrow and Putnam Berkley couldn't be reached.

The FTC allegations are to be reviewed in an administrative hearing to determine if the publishers have violated the law. If the FTC charges are upheld, the commission could forbid the publishers from price discrimination and require them to make special services available on equal terms to all book purchasers.

*—Cynthia Crossen in New York
contributed to this article*

IT'S NOT JUST A FILL-UP ANYMORE—IT'S AN EVENT

The current marketing frenzy has gas stations all pumped up

When Emanuel "Manny" Gianakakos took over a Shell service station in Lincolnwood, Ill., nearly four years ago, it was pumping red ink. Gianakakos spruced up the place, started giving away cold drinks, key chains, and coffee mugs, and began running specials on tune-ups and oil changes. Then, last December, Shell Oil Co. refurbished his station with $350,000 worth of flashy new canopies, signs, and high-speed pumps. The No. 1 U.S. gasoline marketer has also been pushing a series of new products in a national ad campaign. Today, Gianakakos can't pump fast enough: At 360,000 gallons a month, his sales are up sixfold from 1985. "People are coming back," he says.

So is gasoline marketing. Amoco, Exxon, Mobil, Chevron, and Shell are spending billions of dollars to jazz up their stations and push new grades of super-premium gas. And Gasoline Alley is starting to look like a shopping mall. At many of today's slick stations, you can pick up fresh doughnuts, pizza, and bread—and even rent a movie. You may be able to pay for your gas at a pumpside credit-card terminal. Or you may drive off with a free lottery ticket, a fistful of trading stamps, or a chit for a balloon ride, courtesy of your business-hungry local dealer. It's the sort of marketing frenzy that hasn't been seen since the industry's heyday in the 1960s, when oil companies launched fancy-sounding fuels—remember Shell's Platformate?—and dealers gave away everything from dishes to inflatable dinosaurs to draw in drivers.

But if it seems like the go-go years for gas again, the industry is also feeling a chillier blast from the past. After the Exxon Valdez tanker spill off the Alaskan coast on Mar. 24, Big Oil has been wriggling under intense scrutiny the likes of which it hasn't felt since the energy crises of the 1970s. The average price of all retail gas has risen 19% since early March, to $1.18 a gallon, according to Lundberg Survey Inc., an industry research firm. The industry blames the sharp rise in gas prices on OPEC, rising demand, and the cost of meeting new environmental rules. Still, suspicions of price gouging and worries about environmental damage have given the industry quite a black eye.

Oil companies would rather focus on a happier prospect: the start of the summer driving season. Increasingly, the industry is making its money at the pump rather than in the oil field. In 1988, refining and marketing profits for the top 23 oil companies doubled to $21.8 billion, while production profits fell, according to a survey by *Oil & Gas Journal*, a trade publication.

'A REVOLUTION.' Sales should be strong again this summer. But demand for gas is rising at less than 2% a year, and that heightens the battle for market share. To sharpen their retail operations, the majors have closed down thousands of money-losing stations in the past few years, abandoning entire regions. They're spending heavily to upgrade refineries and stations, enabling them to pump more gas through fewer outlets. "It's a revolution at the station," says Bryan Jacoboski, an analyst with PaineWebber Inc.

Amoco has been in the front ranks of that revolution. Starting in the early 1980s, it has pulled out of 16 states. It spent more than $100 million to modernize its remaining 3,700 stations while pressuring its 6,700 independent owners to follow suit. In 1987, it became the first major oil company to start phasing out leaded gasoline, replacing it with two high-octane grades, Amoco Silver and Ultimate, which it pushes with a $25 million-a-year ad campaign. "We give the customer what he wants," says Robert J. Rauscher, marketing vice-president. In the 29 states where it still sells gas, Amoco has increased its market share to 13.8% last year from 11.8% in 1983. In 1988, it had operating profits of $1.4 billion in refining and marketing on sales of $16 billion—almost as much as it earned from production.

Like Amoco, many oil companies are unveiling new products in their battle for the $85 billion retail U.S. gasoline market. Tapping Americans' renewed love for high-performance cars, they're hiking the octane ratings in their premium gasolines to as high as 94, tossing in additives to help engines run smoother, and topping it off with a fancy name. On May 22, Texaco announced a new line of System 3 fuels—leaded and unleaded—supported by a $20 million campaign.

Few cars actually need premium gas,

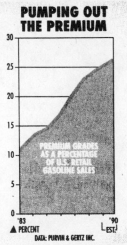

PUMPING OUT THE PREMIUM

PREMIUM GRADES AS A PERCENTAGE OF U.S. RETAIL GASOLINE SALES

▲ PERCENT

'83 — '90 EST.

DATA: PURVIN & GERTZ INC.

CHART BY RAY MELLEN

(cont.)

but ads often warn that lesser brands may cause engine damage. The tactic is working: Premium now accounts for 28% of the market, up from 12% in 1985 (chart, page 90), according to Lundberg Survey. For oil companies, the octane race makes sense: Premium grades cost only about 4¢ a gallon more to make than regular 87-octane gas, but they retail for as much as 15¢ a gallon more. And consumers will pay it. "Quality is the big motivation today," not price, says Gordon H. Thomson, vice-president of marketing at Exxon Co. USA.

In case the gas alone isn't enough of a draw, retailers have a host of other products for their customers. Ashland Oil Inc.'s Super-America stores sell fresh doughnuts and sandwiches, and they feature garden centers and cosmetics counters, as well as videotape rentals. In several cities, Amoco is testing joint ventures with fast-food outlets, including Dairy Queen, Dunkin' Donuts, and Burger King. In addition, repair services have been making a small comeback: About 2,700 of Exxon's 3,700 stations perform repair jobs.

WHITE HATS. Some dealers are even going back to full service—way back. Ron Cromwell, a Chevron dealer in Novato, Calif., replaced his staff's greasy blue uniforms with crisp white 1950s-style outfits, complete with matching white hats and black bow ties, and he graced the women's room with roses and a box of tissues. If an attendant fails to wash the windshield or check the tires, the driver gets a free fill-up. The result: Sales have jumped 29% since May, 1988, to 160,000 gallons a month. "You have to come up with new ideas to stay on top," says Cromwell.

Not every company is pulling into the full-service lane. In 1982, Atlantic Richfield Co. eliminated its credit card and began carving out a niche as the cheapest supplier in the West. It doesn't sell super-high octane gas and it doesn't do repair work, though most of its 800 stations include 24-hour convenience stores. Last year, Arco's stations averaged 200,000 gallons a month, up fourfold from 1982, helping it jump from No. 4 to No. 1 in California. "We skipped all the nonsense because we knew we couldn't be everything," says George Babikian, president of Arco Products Co.

Some critics say that the gimmicks are already wearing thin. If gas prices keep rising, motorists could be driven back to cheaper regular grades and to shopping for low-price brands. But don't tell that to Gianakakos or the other retailers. They're too busy pumping profits.

By Mark Ivey in Houston, with Lois Therrien in Chicago and Maria Shao in San Francisco

87

The 'Sale' Is Fading as a Retailing Tactic

In Pricing Shift, 'Everyday Lows' Replace Specials

By Francine Schwadel
Staff Reporter of The Wall Street Journal

Bargain hunters, beware. Retailers are starting to do away with something that gets your juices flowing: the sale.

In what is shaping up as a major shift in retail marketing, many big chains are scaling back regular prices and abandoning sales as their primary promotional weapon. Stirring in their usual dose of hype, the retailers call this new strategy "everyday low pricing."

The latest convert is none other than Sears, Roebuck & Co. Last year, the nation's largest merchandiser sold an astonishing 55% of its goods at "sale" prices. But as of today at noon, it is kicking the habit. After having closed its 824 stores for two days to remark its price tags, Sears will reopen with lower, more or less permanent prices, heralded by an advertising blitz. Sears says it still will run some sales, but for traditional reasons, like clearing out lawn mowers in the fall.

In adopting the strategy, Sears is joining a growing list. Last month, K mart Corp. expanded "everyday low prices" to cover 5,300 frequently purchased items, up from 3,000. Dayton Hudson Corp.'s Target discount chain, meanwhile, is running storewide tests of a similar pricing plan in Albuquerque, N.M., and Knoxville, Tenn. And Montgomery Ward & Co. recently broadened its low-price policy to most areas of its stores. The trend also extends to smaller retailers like some grocery chains and specialty outfits such as Eyelab Inc., a closely held eye-wear chain, and Workbench Inc., a home-furnishings retailer.

Sick and Tired Shoppers

Sales, of course, won't vanish, but the move toward everyday low pricing is "going to become very important," says Michael Wellman, K mart's vice president for marketing. A key reason, retail executives say, is that customers are fed up with constantly changing sale prices that make it hard to recognize a fair deal.

And rightly so. In recent years merchants have been so caught up in the craze

that they marked up goods just so they could put them on "sale" and still keep their average profit margins. Month-long specials and constant price promotions, even during Christmas and other peak shopping seasons, sapped the meaning from the word "sale."

"Customers no longer thought of regular prices as being real prices, because they weren't," says Morris Saffer, chairman of both Saffer Advertising Inc. and the Retail Advertising Conference, a trade group.

Two years ago, 55% of the 1,000 people surveyed by New York retailing consultant Walter K. Levy said they believed that the "sale" price of merchandise was the "real" price and that the "regular" price was artificially inflated. Although he hasn't repeated the survey, Mr. Levy says the proportion of people who believe they shouldn't pay "regular" prices probably has risen.

In backing away from sales, retailers do run the risk of alienating shoppers accustomed to buying marked-down items. But merchandisers adopting the new strategy believe that they can retrain shoppers—through advertising, such as Sears's initial blitz—to stop searching for sales.

Retailers say they are finding cost advantages in substituting lower regular prices for sales, enabling them to pass on more real savings to consumers. Among other things, they need fewer workers to ticket and re-ticket sale goods and to handle the big inventory bulges needed for specials. Advertising budgets can be trimmed. And merchandisers also hope to reduce the headaches that result from miscalculating the demand for sale goods.

Two years ago, for instance, Montgomery Ward employees spent 120 days filling 15,000 rain checks for a Smith-Corona electric typewriter the chain had marked down to $99 from $129. Ward officials anticipated selling 5,000, but demand was four times that. Running out of sale items also damages a retailer's image: "It just erodes your credibility," says Bernard Brennan, Ward's chairman.

Merchants expect consumers to appreciate the lower average prices, even if deep discounts aren't as plentiful. They also hope to lessen the chances for ill will, such as when a customer returns to a store only to find that a watch bought recently for 20% off is now selling at 40% off.

By lowering all prices, some merchants are even claiming a higher moral ground. Workbench, for instance, reduced its

prices about 15% last summer and decided to run only two annual sales instead of six, each of which had lasted a month or more. The New York furniture chain trumpeted the change by handing out "No Bull" buttons and fliers decrying "the phony pricing policies" of competitors that inflate "regular" prices so they can artificially reduce "sale" prices.

Warren Rubin, chairman, says the chain's move to what he calls "fair-value pricing" was prompted by "my unhappiness with the kind of merchant I had been." Workbench had stepped up its promotions over the past five years to keep pace with competitors, eventually selling as much as 85% of its merchandise at so-called sale prices.

"If they were real sales," Mr. Rubin says, "we'd be bankrupt."

The tide actually began to turn against the sale in the early 1980s as upstarts such as Wal-Mart Stores Inc., Toys "R" Us Inc. and Circuit City Stores Inc. started expanding. These stores keep prices low year-round, avoiding the yo-yo practice of marking them up and down, and consumers like it. Meanwhile, shoppers have learned from outlet stores that markups elsewhere are too high.

Mr. Brennan says Montgomery Ward started testing everyday low pricing because that was the strategy specialty-store competitors were using to grow rapidly.

Leo J. Shapiro, a Chicago market researcher whose firm bears his name, says consumers these days have a "love-hate relationship" with sales. In his surveys, as many as 85% of respondents say they don't pay full retail price for goods; but 60% to 70% of these shoppers feel they could have gotten an even better deal if they had shopped around more. "They love the idea that they bought for less," Mr. Shapiro says. "But they hate the idea that they could have gotten it for even less. They feel cheated all the time."

Just listen to Mary E. McKinley, a 63-year-old grandmother from Concord, Calif. Last Christmas she was so disgusted by retail pricing policies that she plans to give her five grandchildren checks this year.

Mrs. McKinley felt especially cheated when she bought two sweaters from J.C. Penney Co. early in the holiday season for $50 each, only to discover them advertised three days later for $29.99. She trudged back to the store and collected the $20 difference on one of the sweaters, but the other had already been mailed to Wales.

"I've always enjoyed shopping," she

(cont.)

says. "But when you see such a price change, it takes the fun out of it." Her advice to merchants: "Hey, set one price and keep it!"

Retailers acknowledge that some customers may defect, but sale-only buyers aren't the most prized patrons. "When we changed to low prices everyday [on food items in late 1987], we were forced to say goodbye to about 7% of our customers," says Norman Myhr, vice president of marketing and sales promotion for **Fred Meyer** Inc., a Portland, Ore., operator of grocery and general-merchandise stores. However, the deserters were primarily shoppers who had bought Meyer "loss leaders," and the chain actually attracted some new customers by making the switch. Overall, Meyer's market share slipped to 25% from around 27%. But, says Mr. Myhr, "the customer that's in the store [now] is a more profitable customer."

Will Department Stores Follow?

At the moment, most of the action in everyday pricing is occurring in discount and middle-market stores. While **Dillard Department Stores** Inc. is using the approach to price some items, most department stores—which typically serve a higher-income clientele—have sat on the sidelines, trying instead to cut down on sales by keeping tighter inventories.

Department stores could be next, though, and **Nordstrom** Inc. of Seattle may serve as a model. Its department stores are known for their good values on a wide assortment of quality merchandise. The chain, in the midst of a national expansion, hasn't felt compelled to copy the competition and run frequent sales. Instead, Nordstrom will hold only five sales this year.

Middle-market stores making the switch still run some specials, too. High-topped Converse All-Star sneakers, for instance, recently were on sale at Ward for $16.99—a 23% discount from the "everyday low price" of $21.99. A salesman says the sneakers regularly retail for $25.

"Consumers, in the research we've seen, tell us they still like to see a sale once in a while," says Ward's Mr. Brennan. But the spread between the everyday price and the sale price can't be too big, he says, or it hurts your believability.

88

A Price That's Too Good May Be Bad

Even in the bargain-minded world of private-label products, sometimes cheap can be too cheap.

Pathmark's Premium All Purpose Cleaner seemed to have all the elements of the perfect store brand. Its packaging plainly mimicked that of Fantastik, the top seller in the category. Its chemical composition precisely duplicated the national brand's, too. Best of all, Premium cost shoppers only 89 cents, compared with $1.79 for Fantastik.

But from its introduction in 1980, Premium gathered dust. In 1986, Pathmark decided consumers simply didn't understand the product. Store clerks stamped day-glo stickers on every bottle that read: "If you like Fantastik, try me."

Consumers declined the invitation, and Pathmark finally yanked Premium off the shelf earlier this year. "Clinically, it was an outsanding product in every respect," says Robert Wunderle, a spokesman for **Supermarkets General** Corp., Pathmark's parent. "We believe the price was so low that it discredited the intrinsic value of the product."

(Pathmark chose to withdraw the product rather than to experiment with raising prices, a lengthy and not always successful process, the chain says.)

Pathmark's experience isn't unique. The problem often crops up in the household-cleaner and health-and-beauty product areas, where hefty advertising budgets for national lines often make store brands look too cheap by comparison. For example, a 24-ounce container of **Stop & Shop** Cos. baby powder costs just $2.49. But the chain complains that most of its shoppers only crave Johnson & Johnson's time-honored classic, at $4.19 for the same size.

So just how cheap is too cheap? Conventional wisdom holds that in no-name, no-frills items—salt, sugar, flour and the like—the basement's the limit.

But the less apt a consumer is to believe that the private-label product is roughly equivalent to the national brand, the closer the private label should hew to the national brand's own price standard—to help consumers draw an implied quality comparison.

Rules of thumb vary, but Brian Bittke, president of Shurfine-Central Corp., says it's "unwise" to price food products more than 20% below, and nonfood products more than 25% below, national-brand counterparts.

"The further the distance from the national brand, the higher the credibility problem for consumers," says Peter Schwartz, president of Daymon Associates Inc., a private-label research and marketing firm. "Once you get outside the customer's comfort zone, the consumer pyschology becomes, 'Gee, they must have taken it out in quality.'"

—ALIX M. FREEDMAN

Marketing Strategies: Planning, Implementation and Control

89

Will U.S. Warm to Refrigerated Dishes?

Marketers Hope To Duplicate A U.K. Success

By Barbara Toman
Staff Reporter of The Wall Street Journal

U.S. food companies, struggling to jump on the gourmet-food wagon, are renewing their efforts to cook up fancy chilled fare.

Despite previous flops within this niche, **Campbell Soup** Co., Kraft General Foods and Nestle Enterprises Inc. all are test-marketing prepackaged, refrigerated fresh foods that need only be toted home and heated or lightly cooked. And **Nestle S.A.**'s Carnation Co. already sells a limited line of chilled fare nationwide and says it may expand.

Theirs is a risky bid to win over young, affluent tastebuds, inspired partly by the success of London-based **Marks & Spencer** PLC and the challenge that the company poses as it expands in the U.S.

Tight Lips on Strategies

Britain's second-largest retailer, Marks & Spencer sells food under its St. Michael private label. Last year, the company said it hoped to introduce American shoppers to its chilled fare through **Kings Supermarkets Inc.**, a small chain of upscale New Jersey grocers that it had just acquired. Except to say that a coming launch of new food lines would be "significant," a spokeswoman last week wouldn't elaborate on the company's plans. Marks & Spencer officials also declined to comment.

American competitors, meanwhile, are working on their own recipes for chilled food, not to be confused with frozen food. "Almost every major food processor is either in development or test market," says Richard Cristol, executive director of the Chilled Foods Association, an Atlanta-based industry lobby. And "everyone has been waiting with bated breath to see what [Marks & Spencer] is going to do. They certainly have the wherewithal and the expertise and the experience to do a fine job if they want to."

Perhaps. But anyone trying to sell chilled food in the U.S. faces a big batch of problems. Manufacturers haven't yet hit upon a formula for delivering a wide range

LINDA BLECK

of refrigerated fare to sprawling American markets. Even if the logistical problems are solved, U.S. shoppers, bombarded with an ever-expanding choice of deli sections and precooked carryout meals, might not go for chilled food, which has the disadvantage of being fairly pricey. Marks & Spencer, in particular, may find it needs to tailor its selections to suit jazzier American tastes and nutritional obsessions.

Marks & Spencer is a pioneer in prepackaged, refrigerated food. Its St. Michael fare has become a badge of British yuppiedom, with such fresh offerings as Salmon en Croute with cream sauce, Spaghetti Carbonara and Crepes Suzettes. Those dishes range in price from £3.39 ($5.34) for two servings of salmon, to £1.35 for the carbonara. The robust food business helped boost overall sales at Marks & Spencer, which also stocks clothes and housewares, to £5.12 billion in the year. ended March 31. Food accounted for £1.91

billion, or 37% of total sales.

In Britain, Marks & Spencer is renowned for its close relationship with farms and factories, and for its rigid demands for quality. The company even deploys its own specially designed trucks, called the Cold Chain, across Britain to its 264 stores daily.

Such a complex system is difficult to match in the U.S., where distribution chains are long. Indeed, James H. Moran, public-relations director for Campbell, cites distribution problems as one reason why the company withdrew its Fresh Chef line of refrigerated sauces, soups and salads two years ago.

Now, Campbell is trying again. In Philadelphia, it is test-marketing Fresh Kitchen, a new line of refrigerated sauces, entrees and desserts. "We think refrigerated [food] has a high potential," Mr. Moran says. "When we withdrew Fresh Chef, we said we would be back because this is a segment we are very much interested in." He declines to discuss Fresh Kitchen's test results or to say how Campbell might distribute the products nationally.

Culinova fresh entrees, launched in 1986 by **Philip Morris** Cos.'s General Foods Corp., hit similar distribution problems. Last December, shortly after Philip Morris bought Kraft Inc., the struggling line was scrapped.

But Kraft General Foods, the offspring of Philip Morris's acquisition, is pressing ahead with the Chillery line of entrees, salads, pasta and desserts originally developed by Kraft. It is test-marketing Chillery in Kansas City, with such offerings as beef teriyaki at $3.49, seafood salad at $2.89, and cheesecake for $1.39.

Like Campbell, Kraft General Foods declines to discuss specific future plans for its chilled food. But Mary Kay Haben, a Kraft General Foods vice president, confesses to getting "a real charge out of going into the [Marks & Spencer] store in London and seeing the cases and cases of chilled food. It's an energizer to see how the chilled-foods category has developed in the U.K. and to think about what it could be here."

Nestle, the Swiss giant, has jumped into the U.S. chilled-food market on two fronts. Its Nestle Enterprises subsidiary, based in Solon, Ohio, is test-marketing a line of upscale entrees and salads called FreshNes. Currently sold in Cleveland and Columbus, Ohio, FreshNes will move to more test markets this fall, says Milton C. Miles, president of Nestle's FreshNes unit, though he declines to name them.

Nestle's Carnation division already has nationwide distribution of chilled food. But so far, the Los Angeles-based unit sells only refrigerated pastas and sauces, packaged separately under the Contadina Fresh label. Food-industry experts say that those types of products are less temperature-sensitive than fancy entrees.

Carnation is looking at broadening its refrigerated-food line, says Richard Curd, a company spokesman, although he too declines to elaborate.

Mr. Cristol, the industry lobbyist, hopes that within a year technological breakthroughs will permit wider distribution of chilled food. He admits that the obstacles are formidable. "You've got to make the transporters aware of what they're carrying; food retailers have to understand how to rotate stock and watch shelf-life dates," he says. And supermarket refrigeration cases must be checked to ensure they maintain a constant temperature. Chilled food spoils quickly if mishandled.

To allay consumer fears about freshness, Campbell's Fresh Kitchen packages include a temperature-sensitive patch that turns blue if the food hasn't been refrigerated properly.

But the very concept of fresh refrigerated food still could prove tough to sell in the U.S. Like most Europeans, Britons are accustomed to shopping every day in stores where perishables dwindle by evening. Not so in the U.S. "Being in business in an American supermarket is defined as having all your shelves full," says Mona Doyle, president of the Consumer Network, a Philadelphia market-research and consulting firm.

As a British company, Marks & Spencer may face some handicaps in translating its recipes. Americans, for instance, follow food fads. A spicy St. Michael chicken dish might appeal initially, but "the American taste changes every day. What's hot today is gone tomorrow," says Philip Lempert, president of Lempert Co., a Washington, D.C., consulting firm for food marketing and advertising.

The dishes also have to be healthful, especially to lure the young, affluent crowd. Mr. Lempert says Americans will want to know if St. Michael food is low in fat and high in fiber or oat bran, a concept incomprehensible to most British shoppers.

"The question is whether Marks & Spencer can meet American needs," he says. "I'm not sure they understand the American palate."

Crowded Shelves

Chilled-food's biggest challenge, however, may prove to be the growing array of premium, easy-to-prepare food in big U.S. supermarket chains. **Safeway Stores** Inc., for example, is experimenting with carry-out Chinese food in 16 stores. Delis, salad bars and in-store bakeries have been staples at major supermarkets for years.

"There's a tremendous proliferation of take-home food," Ms. Doyle says. "That makes the competition for this kind of [refrigerated] product that much greater."

Price could also turn into a big consideration for a majority of shoppers. **Great Atlantic & Pacific Tea** Co., for one, believes most consumers want "gourmet quality but not at a gourmet price," says Richard de Santa, the company's communications director. So A&P sells refrigerated main courses at its 30 fancier Food Emporium stores in Manhattan and tony New York suburbs—not at its mainstream A&P supermarkets.

Mr. Lempert, the consultant, agrees that the market is limited. Americans "are willing to raise themselves one or two notches" up the scale of gourmet taste, Mr. Lempert says. But Marks & Spencer, in particular, "wants them to go from level one to level nine in one jump, and that might not work."

NOW ALPO WANTS TO DISH IT OUT TO KITTY

For pet-chow marketers, cat food is where the growth is

CEO KRUM WITH KLAUS THE CAT AND CHAUNCEY THE DOG

When Franklin W. Krum takes work home with him, he usually carries it in cans. Chauncey, his 15-year-old poodle mix, has eaten Alpo products all her life—as has Klaus, a two-year-old feline with a canine mind. "He licks your face and comes when he's called," says Krum of Klaus. "He's a very strange cat."

If Krum, who is chief executive of Alpo Petfoods Inc., has his way, though, Alpo-eating cats won't always be an oddity. Demographic trends are running against the walk-needing, attention-craving dog and in favor of the self-reliant, low-maintenance cat. With smaller homes, more one-person households, and more working women, the cat population is growing as the ranks of dogs shrink. Cats outnumber dogs in the U.S. by 58

million to 49 million, according to the Pet Food Institute.

As the only big pet-food marketer without a cat-food franchise, Alpo is already feeling the bite of those trends. The subsidiary of Britain's Grand Metropolitan PLC has seen its market share stagnate. Alpo, which is based in Allentown, Pa., must now sprout cat whiskers to remain competitive in the $5.7 billion pet-food industry.

Krum wants to build cat food into 40% of Alpo's business. But that poses something of a delicate marketing problem. The No. 1 seller of canned dog chow risks damaging its meaty, masculine image by moving into feline food. "The Alpo heritage in dog food may be as much of a liability as it is an asset," says Gary M. Stibel, a marketing consultant at New England Consulting Group. Alpo has been experimenting with its small Tabby brand of cat food, to learn the market. But Krum still isn't sure whether to take Tabby national or launch an Alpo cat food. "For us to get into the cat-food business, we'll have to do everything exquisitely well," he says.

BITS AND BITES. But Alpo hasn't always been that surefooted. The company has been slow to introduce new products, so despite its 24% share of the canned dog-food market, it has just 6.3% of the total pet-food market. Alpo's Stew Biscuits, for example, spent 4½ years in testing before a regional launch last October. In dog treats, where sales are up 59% since 1982, Alpo's Jerky Bits and Beef Bites, acquired with the purchase of Reward Co. in 1983, trail Ralston Purina Co.'s Bonz and Jerky Treats and Meaty Bones from H. J. Heinz Co.'s Star-Kist Foods

Inc. And a pet health-insurance tie-in with a veterinary group was scrapped after six months of testing in 1986. "Alpo has not been extraordinarily successful in new products," says Stibel.

Krum, who joined Alpo from Kellogg Co.'s Mrs. Smith's Frozen Foods unit in 1981, has had some hits. His Alpo Puppy Food, launched in 1985, has quickly reached $18 million in annual sales. Next on the plate is Alpo Lite, launched this spring with a $10 million ad push, Alpo's biggest new-product push since dry food in 1978. Capitalizing on the diet craze among humans, Lite boasts 25% fewer calories than regular Alpo and is aimed

PET FOOD'S TOP DOGS

Company	Market share
RALSTON PURINA	28.8%
CARNATION	11.8
QUAKER OATS	11.6
HEINZ	10.2
KAL KAN	9.4
ALPO	7.7

DATA: WHEAT, FIRST SECURITIES INC.

at the estimated 40% of dogs that could stand to shed a few pounds.

Between new products and acquisitions, Krum hopes that Alpo will grow from sales of $439 million last year to $600 million by 1993. But as Alpo noses its way onto new turf, a pack of formidable competitors is digging in. Quaker Oats Co., for example, acquired the Gaines dog-food line in 1986 and is spending heavily to relaunch its Cycle brand, which includes products aimed at puppies and at overweight dogs. Star-Kist will spend $25 million over the next two years to launch Reward, a premium dog food. And Alpo Puppy Food's success has bred imitators, from Quaker's Gravy Train Puppy to Kal Kan Foods Inc.'s Wel Pup. And Alpo's push into cat food will bring it up against industry leaders Ralston, Heinz, and Carnation, which has made strong gains with its Fancy Feast gourmet cat food.

Still, Alpo has shown a talent for landing on its feet. Anticipating the death of ad spokesman Lorne Greene last September, for example, Alpo readied an alternate campaign featuring ordinary people talking about their pets' longevity. As Krum notes, nimble marketing is the key to this business, in which the buyer usually doesn't evaluate the product himself. "If the dogs pushed the shopping carts, we wouldn't have to spend $35 million a year in ads," says Krum, who speaks from experience—having sampled a little Alpo in his day.

By Richard W. Anderson in Philadelphia

Reprinted from the September 19, 1988 issue of *Business Week* by special permission, copyright© 1988 by McGraw-Hill, Inc.

MENCHER/PICTURE GROUP

WILL $4 PERFUME DO THE TRICK FOR BIC?

Its fragrance line is clicking in Europe, and the U.S. is next

For Bruno Bich, being one of a dwindling number of smokers is a matter of more than social discomfort. Bich, the president and chief executive of Bic Corp., still flicks a Bic to light his big cheroot, but it's an increasingly lonely act. He admits that the prospects for disposable lighters, Bic's largest and most profitable line, aren't good.

People aren't likely to stop writing or shaving, so Bic's other core businesses, pens and disposable razors, aren't in imminent danger. But in these areas the Milford (Conn.) company, which is 61%-owned by French parent Société Bic, faces growing challenges from Gillette Co. and foreign rivals.

Now its search for a hot growth product has led Bic back to its French roots: Would you believe Bic perfume? Société Bic recently launched a mass-market fragrance line in Europe. The four scents are being sold beside Bic lighters, shavers, and

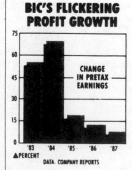

BIC'S FLICKERING PROFIT GROWTH

CHANGE IN PRETAX EARNINGS

75
60
45
30
15
0
'83 '84 '85 '86 '87
▲PERCENT
DATA: COMPANY REPORTS

pens at $4 for a quarter-ounce spray bottle. The line is doing well, and export to the U.S. is planned for next year.

Why perfume? "It's a $3 billion market at retail," says Bich, 41, son of company founder Marcel L. Bich. "There aren't that many consumer products today that offer the kind of growth we like to get." But critics say Bic is unsuited for the perfume business, where glitz and image are everything. The company's diversification record doesn't exactly exude the smell of success, either: Bic's six-year effort to build a business in sporting goods continues to lose money, and its brief leap into pantyhose hit a snag in the 1970s.

Still, Bic needs to try something new. Lighters accounted for 41% of its $290 million in sales and 55.6% of its $50.6 million in pretax profits last year, when Bic raised its share of the 500 million-unit market to 65% from 62%. And Executive Vice-

President Keith C. Koski expects additional sales jumps as Bic rolls out its Mini Bic to more outlets.

Nonetheless, the market is losing its spark. And Bic is bedeviled by product-liability lawsuits alleging that exploding butane lighters have caused deaths and injuries. One such suit was settled in 1986 for $3.2 million, and another was dismissed last March. But Bic has just been ordered to release hundreds of internal documents relating to safety tests and consumer complaints. The order, by a U.S. District Court judge, came in an $11 million suit filed by the estate of a woman who died in 1985, allegedly after a Bic lighter exploded in her hands. Bic says its lighters are safe and reliable.

LATE ROLLERS. In pens, Bic's strongest challenge comes from Boston-based Gillette, whose Paper Mate, Write Brothers, and Flair pens have close to 40% of the U.S. market, compared with Bic's 50%. Still, for all their savvy, both companies were late to introduce metal-point rollers, now the favorite in offices. Mitsubishi Pencil Co. brought rollers to the U.S. nine years ago, and currently has 10% of the total market.

Bic is trying to fight back with a new assault on the office, where it has only a 40% share, compared with its 60% of the retail pen business. In January the company set up a sales force aimed at the office market and launched print ads featuring endorsements of Bic's roller from novelists Robert Ludlum and Ken Follett. "Our huge opportunity is in the office," says Koski. Bic is increasing its total ad budget 15% this year, making up in part for a 26% cut in 1987.

In disposable shavers, Bic seems to be getting sliced to ribbons. Last year its dollar sales of shavers fell 5%. One reason: Gillette's 1986 introduction of its Microtrac razor as a low-priced alternative to Bic. Bic hopes to reverse the trend with a new, Greek-made shaver featuring a metal bar that stretches the skin to reduce nicking.

As for perfume, competitors have their doubts about how much cachet a $4 bottle of Bic will have. "If Bic commoditizes the thing too much, I don't think women will wear it," says Mark Laracy, president of Parfums de Coeur Ltd., which has built a $65 million business in knockoffs of luxury perfume labels.

Still, fragrance prices have soared, on average, more than 66% since 1981, so Bic's perfume could be "a promising concept," says analyst Diana K. Temple of Salomon Brothers. Bruno Bich is hoping that a little splash of *eau de Bic* will be just the bracer his company needs.

By Resa W. King in Milford, Conn., with Keith H. Hammonds in Boston and Ted Holden in Tokyo

Strategic Marketing

Enough about strategy! Let's see some clever executions

by Thomas V. Bonoma

Strategic brilliance can't compensate for dim tactical follow-through.

Researchers, teachers, and students must grapple with *marketing-as-practiced*, instead of focusing solely on strategic problems that can only define *marketing-as-conceived*. Otherwise, academic efforts to advance the discipline will be in great danger of prescribing symptomatic and inappropriate strategic cures for executional diseases.

The last 25 years have witnessed remarkable progress in management's strategic marketing sophistication. Marketing strategy models are available that allow the manager to create a veritable strategic barnyard of cash cows, dogs, and, for all I know, birds.

Other models capture no fewer than 27 of the key factors to the success of any firm's marketing moves, stir them up in a statistical stew, and fill management's plate full of clear prescriptions about marketing directions.

Trouble is, strategic brilliance isn't what's lacking in a world where customers who have paid $20,000 for an automobile can't get it serviced, where corporations nominated as "key accounts" by their vendors don't know who to call with a buying problem, and where airline travel, even "up front," is a dice throw of disappointments between the indigestible food and the surly service.

Those who do the marketing job— as opposed to those who conceive,

plan, and study it—are quick in their insistence that they know very well *what* they want to do for customers. But they have recurrent problems getting useful practice to occur in the intensely human thicket called the corporation.

If strategies often fail to work, it's usually not because the plans aren't clever enough (though, that's what you'd inevitably think if you read our journals). It's because of the near total academic, consulting, and research emphasis on strategic brilliance vs. tactical follow-through as the be-all and end-all of the marketing discipline.

This focus does far-reaching damage, not only to the poor devils who manage firms by targeting them so toward strategic modernity that their reason for being is sometimes forgotten, but also to the purveyors of this view who can deceive themselves and their students into believing that marketing lies more in the planning than the doing.

It's not even clear whether firms *can* be strategically differentiated any longer. For one thing, firms within the same industries tend to engage similar strategies because they are facing substantially the same set of environmental conditions.

Also, competitors in every industry have access to the same "strategy pool"—the MBAs from leading universities, the academics and consultants, and two decades of better living through strategic planning.

The consequence is that competitive differentiation from strategic leapfrogging will help fewer and fewer firms make the kinds of returns they need in these difficult times.

But, managing the quality with which the strategies are executed and seeking imaginative tactics for putting plans into practice can make all the difference. Unfortunately, most firms are far better at proposing effective action than at disposing it, as are most marketing academics.

With the help of 40 firms, almost 60 business units, and more than 500 middle and top managers, I've investigated the topic of quality marketing practices for the last six years.

I can report that there *is* a science, or at least an art, of good tactical marketing. Better yet, its methods can be researched, generalized across companies, and taught in the classroom to those who will run today's firms tomorrow.

An important finding from my work is that the management structures designed to help get the marketing job done well often become inimical to good practices, either because the routines degenerate into dysfunction over time or because of market changes.

This is especially evident when low-level marketing and sales systems are considered. One large tractor-trailer manufacturer, for instance, demands sales-call reports from its salespeople at the end of every month

(cont.)

before releasing expense checks.

Management doesn't *do* anything with these reports—at least nothing related to the key function of customer and competitive intelligence. Rather, it uses the reports as a way to check on and discipline the sales force.

As a result, the call reports often are a creative combination of fiction and memory, carefully crafted by reps to "cover themselves" from possible management retribution.

At more complex levels of marketing systems, the invidious effects of in-place systems are even more disabling to managers.

At industry-leading Frito-Lay, for example, all marketing systems are tuned to dominating the salty-snack business. The much vaunted store-door delivery system—which replaces warehouses with a very expensive sales-service system of over 10,000 drivers/salespeople—assures the grocer constantly fresh stocks of the bulky and very short shelf-life Fritos and Doritos.

It is this distribution system, more than any other of the company's innovations, which is responsible for Frito-Lay's dominance of the salty-snack

arena.

Yet, when Frito-Lay tried to duplicate this system just two aisles down, in the cookie aisle, the same elements that made it a success in salty snacks contributed to its troubles with cookies.

If a leading consumer marketer can't export its systems across two very similar snack categories, what does this say for marketing systems' flexibility in times of change and turbulence?

While structures—including systems, organizations, and budgeting and allocation rubrics—were inimical to good marketing actions in many corporations, the skills of the managers doing the job often were what produced good practices.

Often, managers acted to bridge the gap between poor corporate structures and marketplace requirements by exercising their own skills at managing inside and outside the company. As a result, the firm was, in a real sense, "subverted toward quality."

The best implementers found ways to get around control system inadequacies, often by constructing a set of informal "back of the envelope" monitoring methods which were simple,

but applied regularly to the state of the business.

At one company, for example, marketers routinely monitored the weather as a key leading indicator of future sales. When asked why they didn't analyze the multitude of data available from the electronic data processors, one marketer said, "We don't have 18 months to w   for those guys to convert the data we need into information."

But the key element in whether a firm was able or inept at executing marketing strategies was management's perception to and resolution of the structure-and-skills dynamic operating in the firm.

Those managers who understood that even successful structures become bureaucracies which lag behind current reality, permitted their marketers to be flexible in applying their skills to solving problems, even when these violated systemic rules.

Those who fell in love with the way things were, or ought to be, or had to be, insisted on a horrible kind of structural compliance from their subordinates that produced weak management, weak marketing, and weak practices. /MI

Thomas V. Bonoma, "Enough about Strategy! Let's See Some Clever Executions," reprinted from the February 13, 1988 issue of *Marketing News*, published by the American Marketing Association, Chicago, IL 60606.

93

How a Small Firm Survived Loss of Main Customer

By Barbara Marsh
Staff Reporter of The Wall Street Journal

CHICAGO—Losing a key customer is troublesome for any business. Losing a customer that accounts for 80% of a company's sales can be fatal.

Mellish & Murray Co., a 100-year-old bender of sheet metal, suffered just such a loss. Five years ago, the small metal-fabricating company was cut off by its main customer, W.W. Grainger Inc. of Skokie, Ill., which started making the products in-house. With the change, four-fifths of Mellish & Murray's sales vanished.

A loss of that magnitude "can cause a company to go under," says Norman Carlson, a Chicago-based partner in Arthur Andersen & Co.'s small-business practice.

"After we took the knife out of the heart," says H. James Murray, president, the company decided to stay in business. The road back to prosperity has proved long and painful, however, and has included a botched acquisition and some bad choices of new hires. Only gradually has the company worked out its problems. Although it has remained profitable through most of the trauma, sales are running at $4 million a year, well below the $7.5 million peak in 1985.

As such, the Mellish & Murray saga illustrates both the dos and don'ts of coping with the loss of a principal customer. And it's a good case study of just how easy it is for companies to fall into the one-customer trap.

Such companies are vulnerable because they "don't market, promote or hire good salespeople," says Rett Humke, a St. Charles, Ill., financial consultant to the Murray family, which owns Mellish & Murray. "You get very sluggish." He says it's dangerously easy for small companies to feel secure supplying companies such as McDonald's Corp. or Sears, Roebuck & Co., because the business comes in such large volume, with little effort, and payment is prompt.

When the giant drops the small supplier, consultants say, the supplier is faced with two alternatives: reducing the size of the business or replacing lost sales. And frequently there's little time to do either to save the company.

For the Murray clan, with four family members on the payroll, others working part time and still others counting on income from the company, shrinking the business wasn't an option. But replacing the lost sales entailed an about-face from the way they had operated.

Above all, the two brothers who run the company swore they would never repeat the mistake of relying so heavily on one customer. "Psychologically, we felt we'd been controlled by somebody above us," says Charles Murray, executive vice president. "We knew we had to diversify our customer base." And they set about acquiring proprietary products to do just that.

Mellish & Murray was solid enough financially to withstand the transition. As its sales to Grainger fell, the company slashed output and reduced inventories, freeing cash to finance acquisitions. And its bankers pitched in with additional financing.

Nonetheless, the Murrays stumbled many times in trying to teach themselves how to remake their company. A planned acquisition that didn't work out taught them a lesson in using advisers to advantage. The brothers, finding a company they wanted to buy, had their lawyer work with the seller's lawyer to hammer out terms, but the talks bogged down in legal nitpicking. "Thirty thousand dollars in attorneys' fees later, we still didn't have a deal," recalls Charles Murray.

As a result, when they attempted their next purchase—Reeve Electronics Inc.—the Murrays negotiated directly with the seller. They wrote the guts of the deal in a page and a half—and only then turned it over to the lawyers, who transformed it into 20 pages of legalese. The upshot: Legal fees ran just $15,000, and the deal went through.

However, Reeve itself turned into another lesson: know the product. Nobody at Mellish & Murray understood the research projects involving Reeve's line of high-frequency heating systems for industrial use. Though Reeve's former owner certainly did, his consulting contract with the Murrays ran out after a year. The company ended up relying on a salesman and a technical employee from Reeve, but even they didn't have the know-how for new-product development, the Murrays say.

With that in mind, the Murrays later acquired a maker of metal storage boxes—a business that fit comfortably with their traditional metal-bending business.

They also learned that their old accounting system couldn't handle their diversifying company. After buying Aeroflash Signal, a strobe-light manufacturer, Mellish & Murray erred by grossly underbidding the competition on a government contract for flash tubes, the bright lights that mark airport runways. At $16.50 a tube—about $8 below cost—the Murrays lost their shirts on the contract.

The problem was, their centralized accounting system didn't allow them to price the labor content as they should have, the Murrays say. So they installed separate accounting systems for their major product lines. Although their bid on a later flash-tube contract jumped to $27.80 a tube, they won again—and made a 15% profit.

Perhaps the best lesson for the Murrays in all of this was learning to rely once again on their greatest asset as a family business: themselves. At first, after being hands-on manufacturers for so many years, they were unsure of their sales and marketing instincts. So, for Aeroflash, they hired a costly sales director and sales team and relied on them to double volume.

But it didn't happen, says James Murray's daughter, Cari, 25 years old, armed with a finance degree and hoping to succeed her father as president someday. While office manager in 1987, she decided she might as well try contacting Aeroflash's neglected customers herself.

"Murrays have a way of doing things methodically," she says with pride, describing how she is flying to rural towns to see customers, calling on distributors and going to trade shows.

Her reward? She was promoted last year to treasurer and general manager of Aeroflash. And her division's sales for the first half of this year are right on track—up 10%.

Marketing Strategy Planning for International Markets

Nordson Is Poised to Compete in the '90s
Gear Has Appeal Abroad and Technological Edge

By Ralph E. Winter
Staff Reporter of The Wall Street Journal

WESTLAKE, Ohio—The 1990s, say the prognosticators, will be another tough decade for U.S. manufacturers as they face more intense international competition. But **Nordson** Corp. is the type of producer that is likely to prosper in that climate.

"The companies that succeed in the 1990s will be export-oriented, especially those specializing in equipment used to modernize industry," contends Lawrence Chimerine, chairman and chief executive officer of WEFA Group, a Bala Cynwyd, Pa., economic consulting concern. "They will have good foreign distribution and understand how to make their equipment attractive to foreign buyers."

Nordson, a medium-sized maker of specialized machinery, fits that bill. It makes sophisticated equipment, most of it electronically controlled, used to apply adhesives, sealants and coatings. More than half its 1988 sales of $240 million will come from overseas.

But that emphasis on foreign business can also cause problems, as it did when the dollar soared in the first half of the 1980s. A decade ago, the company's prospects looked extremely bright, with profits rising nearly four-fold between 1976 and 1980. But earnings then dropped and remained weak for five years.

Engineering Talent

Still, companies like Nordson, with its customized products, are better prepared to compete internationally than many other U.S. concerns. Engineering talent is a far bigger factor than hourly labor, which is a big plus when selling in countries like Taiwan, South Korea and Brazil. Moreover, huge research spending by the giant chemical producers that make adhesives and coatings helps Nordson stay in the forefront of manufacturing technology.

"Nordson represents the manufacturing company of the future," asserts Theodore H. Tung, senior vice president and economist with National City Bank, Cleveland. "The U.S. may produce less steel during the 1990s, but there will be more opportunity for companies that apply the latest technology to do some job better and more efficiently."

Nordson's profits support that contention. Analysts "won't be embarrassed" by estimates of $3 to $3.20 a share for the year ending Oct. 30, says William P. Madar, president and chief executive. Moreover, fiscal 1987 net of $24.7 million, or $2.35 a share, was up 79% from the previous year.

Mr. Madar also believes that the company is better positioned than a decade ago to maintain the favorable earnings trend. Mr. Madar was wooed in 1986 from Standard Oil Co. (Ohio) by Eric T. Nord, a Nordson founder and the current board chairman. The 48-year-old Mr. Madar took a gamble when he moved to a concern where the founding family still controls a stake exceeding 40%. Only six months earlier, Mr. Nord, now 71, had assumed the reins again after a professional manager failed to satisfy the family.

Pad to Pad

At Nordson, Mr. Madar has been using what he terms a "lily pad to lily pad" growth strategy, jumping from one new market to another nearby one "rather than leap across the pond or into an entirely different pond." With this conservative approach, Nordson "won't become dependent on the great Eureka or the great new business," he says.

The company tried both of those a decade ago, plunging into robotics and making a major acquisition in packaging machinery. Neither succeeded, contributing to the profit crunch early in the decade.

However, Nordson, with more than half its sales from abroad and all its production in the U.S., was hurt even more by the U.S. recession and the sharp rise in the dollar. Management, fortunately, grimly hung onto the company's market position in Europe and Japan.

In the past two years, the dollar's decline has helped fatten profits. Nordson is also benefiting from aggressive business spending here and abroad on new equipment that pares costs and improves product quality. For instance, heightened concern about product tampering and sanitation has made Nordson's adhesives equipment attractive because it helps assure leak-proof and insect-proof boxes.

Screws and Rivets

Moreover, manufacturers use Nordson's equipment to replace screws, rivets and welds with adhesives, cutting the cost of assembling items as diverse as electronic circuits and car doors. No single customer buys as much as 1% of Nordson's output, Mr. Madar says.

That's partly because Mr. Madar, an avid pheasant hunter, picks his targets carefully. Nordson plays down highly competitive, commodity-type products such as general-purpose glue guns and paint sprayers to concentrate on customized equipment for special market niches. In most Nordson sales, the materials to be applied are too expensive to waste, or precision is critical and the application complex.

Mr. Madar upset many veteran employees two years ago when, to sharpen Nordson's focus, he reduced the number of engineers working on standard painting equipment and reorganized the company along geographic lines instead of by major products. Those changes triggered the early retirement of 27 employees and the dismissal of 95 more, jolting this small-town company known as a paternalistic employer.

The regional organization could be a mistake, some insiders say, because managers may be spread too thin and make incorrect decisions on what products to develop and promote.

As business improves, Mr. Madar is cautiously rebuilding employment, which now stands at 2,050. However, he's primarily hiring those with electronics expertise who can devise and sell equipment that will ride the accelerating wave toward computer-aided manufacturing. "The electronic content of our equipment has increased dramatically," he says.

Despite that forward planning, Nordson would be tripped up again if the dollar soars. Mr. Madar is trying to hedge, but there isn't much he can do. He is increasing the overseas sales engineering staff so that more applications work can be done in the country where the sale is made. Also, the company is lining up local suppliers for the few standard parts of the systems.

Shelf Control

'Papa-Mama' Stores In Japan Wield Power To Hold Back Imports

With 56% of the Retail Sales, They Confront Big Chains That Carry New Products

Attacks on the Devil's Shops

By Damon Darlin
Staff Reporter of The Wall Street Journal

SHIZUOKA, Japan—Modern chain-store owners here don't worry about armed robbers. They worry about attacks by the small shopkeepers down the street.

Irate shopkeepers beat up a worker helping build one of this city's first convenience stores, a franchisee of Japan's Lawson chain. Later, gangs of outraged mom-and-pop shopkeepers wearing motorcycle helmets and kamikaze-style headbands repeatedly stormed the Lawson stores at night, screaming at employees and intimidating customers who patronized these "devil's businesses." Anonymous late-night callers, intent "on keeping the blood pure," harassed the store owners' families. Then, someone dumped excrement outside Takamasa Ohsumi's new Lawson store.

"I keep telling myself we have to keep going," says the battle-weary Mr. Ohsumi, sitting on an upturned milk crate in his stock room after several months of attacks. "We can't give up."

Captive Consumers

In Japan, a deep-rooted, even violent, resistance arises against the kind of modern distribution system that has long and efficiently provided Americans with cheap goods. The world's second-largest .consumer market—125 million people, affluent and eager to buy cheaper imports—is held captive by tiny stores.

And so, these "papa-mama" shops, as the Japanese call them, have a stranglehold on store shelves that could display American products. While providing excellent service, the shops also keep prices high, limit selection and, the U.S. government argues, obstruct imports. If American-style convenience stores, supermarkets and mass-market merchandisers had

free rein, imports—including American products—would stand a much better chance in Japan. But the papa-mamas would lose their cozy, but grossly inefficient, control of 56% of Japan's retail sales (vs. 3% for U.S. mom and pops and 5% in Europe).

Unfortunately for entrepreneurs such as Mr. Ohsumi, the bureaucrats back the bullies that terrorize his convenience store. The Shizuoka city government is trying to enforce "guidelines," which were created by small merchants and require a national retailer to get approval from all existing shopkeepers within a third-of-a-mile radius of a proposed store before opening it. That's why Shizuoka, a market the size of Atlanta, didn't have a single convenience store until Lawson, owned by retail giant Daiei Inc., began its battle to do business here. An estimated 60% of Japan's towns impose similar limits.

National Law's Restrictions

Moreover, the papa-mamas had the power to push through a national law decreeing that no retailer can open a store larger than 5,382 square feet—about a tenth the size of the tiniest K mart in the U.S.—without permission from a community's store owners. The powerful Ministry of International Trade and Industry administers the law in such a way that eight to 10 years pass before a store gets approval. Only about three dozen large stores open each year in all Japan—and usually at half the size requested.

Add other hurdles — the 71 licenses needed to operate a store and the existence of four times as many wholesalers compared with retailers as in the U.S.—and one concludes, as does U.S. Secretary of Commerce William C. Verity, that "there is something wrong here." Thus, although Japan has lowered most of its formal trade barriers—its tariffs are among the world's lowest and many product standards and discriminatory taxes are being eased—informal cultural barriers remain high.

In America, large stores such as Sears Roebuck and K mart led the import boom, sucking in products from many lands to lure shoppers with low prices. In Japan, foreign consumer products have difficulty getting in because only large stores, which are constricted, have the shelf space needed to experiment with new products from abroad. Of the $31.5 billion of Japanese imports from the U.S. last year, less than a quarter were consumer goods (as are most of Japan's exports).

Blocked Shelves

"Many American businesses can get their products on the dock, but they have trouble moving them onto the shelves where the Japanese consumers have a

choice," Mr. Verity says. Concerned with the way Japan's complex retail distribution system blocks imported goods, he has made changing it one of America's top trade grievances with Japan.

In some ways, the U.S. attack couldn't be better timed. Most Japanese, according to surveys, want a change. Innovative retailers, such as convenience-store operators and mass-market discounters, are eager to take advantage of the changing behavior of affluent Japanese. The distribution system is already beset by scrappy businesses bringing in lower-priced goods by bypassing official importers. And most papa-mamas are run by elderly Japanese, and death is thinning their ranks. The system "will loosen," says Hitomi Hashimoto, a retail analyst at Kleinworth Benson International. "But no one sees it happening any time soon."

That's a big problem. The system may change too slowly for Americans already frustrated with Japanese foot-dragging on other trade issues. The issue is so entwined with Japanese domestic politics that the government's reluctance to force changes ensures that Japan's retail system is one of the most contentious, frustrating issues the U.S. faces.

Take the main U.S. request, the abolition of the national large-scale retail-store law that lets small stores regulate expansion by big ones. Many Japanese bureaucrats sincerely want the law abolished because large stores would bolster the slowing Japanese economy.

But MITI officials say forthrightly that the best they can do is to loosen enforcement to enable new stores to open more quickly. The bureaucrats well know that the 1.6 million papa-mamas are a vociferous, politically powerful group. Shopkeepers are already irritated about the ruling party's plan to start a national sales tax, and a government move to abolish the retail law would further enrage papa-mamas and doom the tax plan. Japan's leaders who have staked their political careers on the new tax and are at odds with the farmers as well don't want to further rile an important voting bloc.

Like U.S. pressure on Japan's agricultural protectionism, an attack on Japan's retail labyrinth is an attack on its social-welfare system. Labor-intensive and inefficient, the retail system is almost the flip side of Japan's factories. The dusty, cramped stores and the attendant layers of distributors that deliver a half case of soy sauce or three boxes of disposable diapers at a time offer jobs to the marginally employable.

As a result, Japan's shopkeepers are

fiercely protective. And they keep Japan as the U.S. would be if frozen in time in the early 1960s—before the development of huge shopping centers, with the local TV shop still selling only Zeniths and RCAs, with Chevrolet and Ford dealers not even dreaming of handling a Japanese product.

But the U.S., with a far more open system, changed, and imports flooded in regardless of the cost to small retailers. The U.S. now has one shopping center for every 10,000 people, compared with Japan's ratio of one for every 100,000. Japan's system shuts out outsiders, Japanese or foreign.

The difference between the countries is illustrated by the fortunes of Korea-based Samsung Electronics. In the U.S., Samsung's products are starting to push aside Japanese competitors, grabbing almost 15% of the U.S. market for videocassette recorders and 20% of the microwave-oven market. But in Japan, Samsung doesn't sell a single full-fledged VCR, just a "play only" model, which doesn't record. It doesn't sell any microwave ovens, either—just fans, black-and-white TV sets, and a few other items totaling about $60 million annually. Its U.S. sales are 15 times that.

One reason for Samsung's difficulties in Japan: Half the consumer-electronics products sold in this country are handled by retail stores controlled by Japanese manufacturers, who have no intention of stocking competing Korean goods.

As a result, finessing the distribution system has been crucial to any foreign company claiming success in Japan. Mars Co.'s M&Ms became a major brand in Japan only after the company's sole agent, Mitsubishi Corp., helped get the candy into subway and train-station kiosks, right next to Japanese products. Bayerische Motoren

Werke AG has made the BMW a best-selling car in Japan by opening its own dealer system. Merck & Co. bought a minority position in Banyu Pharmaceutical Co., at least in part for Banyu's network of drug salesmen.

Ultimately, America's hope may lie less with the Japanese government and more with the major Japanese retailers, who are becoming adept at finding the cracks in the system and widening them. For instance, many papa-mama shops are seeing a decline in their sales and a lack of interest by the owners' children in the family store. Therefore, the convenience-store chains, the major ones backed by large retailers, send out recruiters who convince the owners that their children, who hate the dim, dusty store, would enjoy running a brightly lit outlet with employees, computers and 3,000 items. Ito-Yokado Co.'s 7-Eleven subsidiary says about 80% of its franchisees are former papa-mama stores. "If they have a feeling they want to stay in business, they have to come to that decision," a company spokesman says.

All that fits nicely with a demographic trend of more working women, who find it hard to get to a grocery store after work. Convenience stores, which now account for about 3.5% of retail sales in Japan, are growing at double-digit rates and should account for 6% of sales in 10 years.

This strong growth signals radical change in the complex wholesale system. An increase in convenience stores will reduce the layers of wholesalers as the chains modernize distribution, with many products being bought straight from the manufacturer and going directly to a central distribution center. For example, 7-Eleven has two rival milk companies shar-

ing the same delivery truck in one area of Japan. (Japan's 7-Elevens have an agreement with Southland Corp., operator and franchiser of 7-Eleven stores in the U.S., to use the store name.)

The retailers are also beginning to build large, American-style shopping centers. The trick, though, is finding distressed towns with local merchants worrying about declining sales. As Japanese become more mobile and roads improve, more shoppers think little of driving 10 to 20 miles to another area for a better selection.

Because that was happening to the city of Noda, 75 miles north of Tokyo, officials and even merchants actually cooperated with Jusco Co., one of Japan's biggest retailers, in building a shopping center.

"Our dream was to set up an American-style shopping center," a Jusco spokesman says. The three-story store will be 22,000 square meters, Jusco's biggest outlet. Surrounded by parking lots for 1,600 cars, the development will include restaurants, a swimming pool, a playground, a bowling alley and a drive-in theater. To mollify local merchants, 7,400 square meters were reserved for 92 specialty stores. Nonetheless, the negotiations took three years.

Whether such efforts will change Japan's retailing system to resemble America's is debatable. But experts agree that over the next 15 years, change will be inevitable, though slow. Even in Shizuoka, a hotbed of papa-mama reactionism and a city so typical that many manufacturers use it as a test market, change is afoot.

Matsuyo Hasegawa, whose family has run a small sake shop for 300 years, isn't concerned about the Lawson store down the street. She says the family plans to close the old shop and open a convenience store out in the suburbs.

PepsiCo Accepts Tough Conditions For the Right to Sell Cola in India

By Anthony Spaeth
And Amal Kumar Naj
Staff Reporters of THE WALL STREET JOURNAL

In a race to expand its world market share, **PepsiCo** Inc. accepted tough conditions from the Indian government to make and sell Pepsi-Cola in a country that booted out Coca-Cola in 1977.

The large Indian market for soft drinks has been supplied by local bottlers selling local products with such brand names as Thumbs Up and Campa Cola.

PepsiCo said the joint venture will make an initial investment of $17 million in an industrial facility to make soft-drink concentrate, along with fruit juice concentrates and snack foods from locally acquired produce, in the state of Punjab. The locally made soft drinks will be distributed through franchised bottlers.

In return for the entry into the country, PepsiCo agreed that the venture would export from the venture five times the value of its imported components. If that condition isn't met, PepsiCo won't be able to repatriate royalties and profits.

PepsiCo, based in Purchase, N.Y., also won't hold a majority stake; it will own 39.9% of the venture and a corporation owned by Punjab state and the Indian central government will have a 36.1% stake. The Tata Group, India's largest industrial corporation, will own 24%.

PepsiCo officials acknowledge the agreement's terms are harsh in comparison with similar accords PepsiCo signed to gain entry into the Soviet Union and China.

"We're willing to go so far with India because we wanted to make sure we get an early entry while the market is developing," said Robert H. Beeby, president and chief executive officer of the company's Pepsi-Cola International. "The Indian middle class is beginning to emerge, and we see that as a big growth market."

India has a population of 800 million people, and Indians drink about 2.4 billion bottles of name-brand soft drinks a year. Although that's a small number on a per-capita basis, industry analysts estimate the market is growing at 20% annually.

Pepsi's plant will make enough concentrate for 1.2 billion bottles of Pepsi a year. PepsiCo said it hasn't set a date when it would start selling the soft drink there.

Another reason for PepsiCo's move clearly was competition from its big rival, **Coca-Cola** Co., which is aggressively pursuing markets in China and the Soviet Union. "We found that it is better to [enter] a market with or ahead of Coca-Cola," said Mr. Beeby. He said Pepsi entered China a couple of years after Coke, and about 10 years ahead in the Soviet Union. "Viewing them [Coca-Cola] as our lead competitor, if we get into a big market ahead of them we are that much better," he said. "That was another reason for making such an attractive agreement with India."

Officials at Coca-Cola, based in Atlanta, had no comment on PepsiCo's move.

Coca-Cola left India after the government demanded that the company turn over its secret soft-drink formula to an Indian company and transfer other technical know-how to local management. The Indian government also announced that the soft-drink giant, along with other foreign companies, couldn't own more than 40% of their Indian subsidiaries, a ruling that was tantamount to diminishing the companies' control over their Indian operations.

PepsiCo also operated in India for about two years in the mid-1950s. A company spokesman said the company left the country because "we were unable to build a viable business there."

Mr. Beeby said the company doesn't see any problem meeting the condition that PepsiCo must generate exports five times the value of imports to the joint venture. PepsiCo will have to import some parts of the concentrate to preserve the secrecy of its soft-drink formula. But by agreeing to this ratio, PepsiCo has voluntarily agreed to a limit on its soft-drink sales in India, if it doesn't meet that condition.

To ensure that it meets the export-import condition, PepsiCo said the joint venture will build modern food processing plants that will use locally grown tomatoes, pears, apples, mangoes and other fruits to make fruit-juice concentrates, mainly for exports. The venture also will establish an agricultural research center to develop high-yield crops and disease-resistant seeds.

PepsiCo, whose soft-drink sales account for roughly a third of its business, is a leading processor of snack foods, and it also owns restaurant chains.

The joint venture will create 1,000 jobs and give work to about 15,000 farmers.

Western Ways

How a German Firm Joined With Soviets To Make Good Shoes

It Pushes Quality Control, Uses Imported Machines; Eager and Happy Workers

But Many Such Ventures Fail

By Thomas F. O'Boyle
Staff Reporter of The Wall Street Journal

LENINGRAD—It's 4:30 p.m., and outside a store, in the freezing cold and darkness, customers are waiting patiently for three, four, even five hours.

They are waiting for shoes. Perestroika has finally delivered the goods—and judging from the line, which stretches far down the street and is long even by Soviet standards, you'd think the shoes were being given away. But they are worth the wait, says one fur-capped man who, after two hours, still can't see the door. These are no ordinary shoes.

Although they look much like other Soviet-made footwear, the difference is the quality. "They won't leak, they'll keep your feet warm. They're much better than what you can buy elsewhere in Leningrad," the man explains, stomping his feet to shake off the cold. He hasn't seen the shoes, but his wife, tipped off by friends, told him they are out of this world.

From Another World

Actually, they come from a factory right around the block. In a way, however, they do come from another world. Since last April, the factory has been operated by Lenwest, a joint venture 40%-owned by West Germany's Salamander AG and 60%-owned by the Proletarian Victory shoe concern of Leningrad. Every day, the modern, well-lit, efficient plant churns out 4,200 pairs of basic, utilitarian shoes of a quality previously unknown in the Soviet Union.

The Soviets provide the labor and most of the raw materials. The Germans provide the know-how—plus the machines, the management techniques and the quality control. The Soviets mostly take orders—and watch, listen and perhaps learn. And although Lenwest's output is a mere one

million of some 800 million pairs of shoes produced in the Soviet Union last year, they are very important to the Soviets. Besides providing badly needed consumer goods, this joint venture and others like it, the Soviets hope, will help fire up their economy by increasing competition.

"There is no shoe manufacturer in the Soviet Union that compares with Lenwest," says the joint venture's chief bookkeeper, Fyodor Pavlov. Thrusting a Lenwest shoe into a visitor's hands, he asks, "How much would you pay for this?" Then he adds: "You saw how many people want to buy that for 80 rubles, that long line out there in the cold." Even though 80 rubles is slightly more than one week's pay for the average Soviet worker, "the market for this kind of shoe is limitless," Mr. Pavlov says, sounding more like an entrepreneur than a state-appointed bookkeeper.

Germany's Big Role

That Soviet citizens want better shoes and that the Soviet Union benefits from this kind of cooperation with Western firms are irrefutable. But what about the Western partners? When Moscow began opening up the Soviet economy by announcing, in January 1987, that it would allow such business ventures, Western companies eagerly lined up for what they saw as lucrative opportunities. The rush continues: Of the 200 or so joint ventures formed in the past two years, nearly half were registered in the past four months. Among Western nations, West Germany leads the pack, with 26 joint ventures already formed and dozens more being negotiated.

Now, many of the companies that got in are asking themselves whether joint ventures here really make sense. For Salamander, a major European manufacturer of good-quality, moderately priced shoes that has more than 1,600 retail outlets in West Germany alone, the answer is yes.

The Stuttgart-based company says that, based on Western accounting standards, Lenwest was profitable in its first year of operation, though Salamander won't disclose any figures. Both parties have agreed to reinvest the profits for at least three more years to double production capacity. Later this year, Lenwest will introduce 16 new models, including a few more stylish women's shoes decorated with bows. And Salamander has just opened a second shoemaking joint venture with another Soviet concern near Minsk.

Worth a Repeat

All things considered, says Werner Rost, Salamander's head of export sales in Stuttgart, "If we had to do it all over again, we'd make the same decision."

Salamander's success stems from vari-

ous factors, including its patience with the Soviet system, its willingness to reinvest profits during the start-up, its years of experience in the East Bloc and the Soviets' pent-up demand for quality footwear.

But for many companies, joint ventures may be more trouble than they are worth. Lenwest is one of only 20 or so ventures actually operating. Even savvy PepsiCo Inc. needed 15 months to find a suitable site for one of two planned Pizza Hut restaurants; it's still looking for the second.

Says Martin Kallen, the managing director of Monsanto Co.'s European operations: "You don't just walk in there and make a buck. The opportunities are limited, and you have to work hard to reap them." He predicts that the "failure rate of joint ventures is going to be high."

A major problem is the nonconvertibility of the ruble. Because the Soviet currency isn't freely changeable into other monies, Western companies' profits earned here must stay here—although some foreign companies get their profits in barter arrangements that give them Soviet goods that can be sold abroad.

Even more daunting are a raft of operational problems. Until December, when Moscow revised its laws, foreign companies couldn't own more than 49% of a joint venture; so, the Soviets always held the upper hand. In procurement and pricing, Western partners are at the mercy of what can be a capricious Soviet system, under which raw materials are doled out by the government according to the national economic plan and must be requisitioned more than a year in advance. And because prices for many basic goods are controlled, what a manufacturer may charge often doesn't reflect production costs.

"The value of a herbicide to a Western farmer is relatively well established. In the Soviet Union, it isn't," says Mr. Kallen, who tried for several years to negotiate a joint venture to make herbicides. Because food prices are strictly controlled, the price a Soviet farmer pays for a herbicide is also effectively controlled. That, plus the unavailability of raw materials, persuaded Monsanto to give up the project.

"Importing the raw materials would have meant that we had to export more of the final product than we were prepared to consider" to balance a probable deficit of hard currency, he says.

Some Major Advantages

Salamander also had to struggle. But because Lenwest took over a building previously occupied by the Soviet partner, the venture already had perhaps the most precious commodity in the Soviet Union: suitable work space. Luckily, telephones and

(cont.)

telex machines were also in place.

Salamander has three employees who live in a nearby hotel and supervise the production. They share one desk in a common office, a ramshackle room with peeling wallpaper and a conference table wedged up against piles of shoe boxes and cartons of files. They travel to Germany every month or so to visit their families, who chose to stay there. They don't speak Russian, and each has a translator during office hours. After work, they're on their own, but that doesn't really matter; they don't have much free time.

To Western businessmen, everything in the Soviet Union seems abnormal. Even routine tasks—from booking a hotel room to changing an airline reservation—can be formidable. "They have a completely different system," says Mr. Rost, Salamander's export chief, who, along with another Salamander executive and three Soviets, sits on Lenwest's supervisory board.

Signs of those differences abound. Just reaching a consensus on what is meant by "profit" isn't easy. Responding to that question, a bewildered Mr. Pavlov at first says: "We don't have that concept here." Then, after huddling with colleagues, he explains that although he thinks he understands the concept, he isn't comfortable with it. "This is a mutual learning process, and we've had to make adjustments to balance our two systems," he says.

Cautious Negotiators

Or consider the negotiations to form Lenwest, which were begun in April 1987 and concluded six months later. The Soviet delegation usually numbered about 20. "They tried to bring as many people as possible so they wouldn't make a mistake," recalls Mr. Rost, one of four who represented Salamander.

One principle on which Salamander insisted helps minimize conflicts. Because the Soviets outnumber Salamander on the board by 3 to 2, all board decisions must, under the venture's bylaws, be unanimous. But that provision hasn't headed off all problems. In filling the job for Lenwest's marketing chief, all five directors voted to hire a man recommended by the Soviets. He was sacked two months later.

"Most of the people who are employed there have no experience at all in the field of marketing," Mr. Rost says. "They've never sold anything. They have distributed goods." The new marketing chief comes from the Soviet foreign-export organization and has had sales experience.

Salamander has won a few battles on the marketing side. It obtained written guarantees from the Soviets allowing the joint venture to sell through its own outlets, such as the one at No. 36 Suvorovsky Prospect in Leningrad.

As many as five more stores may open this year in Leningrad and other cities, including Moscow and Kiev. "The demand is so great that with every new store we open up, there will be a line," Mr. Rost predicts confidently. The outlets give Lenwest a higher profit margin and more control over its shoe sales.

Raw-Material Problems

The biggest problem that it had to overcome was a shortage of first-class raw materials. "Our partners couldn't understand why, if we had the money, we couldn't buy the goods. We said, 'Because we haven't ordered them in advance,' and they said, 'That's nonsense,'" Mr. Pavlov recalls.

What wasn't available through the system had to be trucked 2,420 kilometers (1,450 miles) from Stuttgart—and purchased with precious Western currency. In the first few months, about 35% of the raw materials came from the West; now, all but 5% are Soviet-supplied.

Nevertheless, the Soviet system still frustrates the Germans. "You can't be as flexible here as in the West," says Wolfgang Meiser, a barrel-chested, gray-bearded plant manager. "In Germany, if you have a shoe collection that doesn't sell, you just change to another. You make new models with new material. It's no problem in Germany, but it would be a problem here" because raw materials must be ordered so far in advance.

Fortunately for Lenwest, the shoes have been selling, largely because of Salamander's near-fanatical attention to quality control. Quality is crucial to both partners. For the Soviets, it means goods that would be readily accepted in the West and hence more foreign trade. Although all of the Lenwest production is now sold in the Soviet Union, eventually the partners hope to export as much as 20% of it. Exports are important for Lenwest, too, because the hard-currency income can offset hard-currency spending on the three Germans' salaries (paid in marks), the raw materials purchased in the West, and sales promotions there. And because Salamander is required to buy either shoes or raw materials—soles, for instance—from Lenwest to balance the hard-currency ledger, it, too, wants top-quality production.

Comparable Quality

So far, Lenwest's quality is comparable to the best Western standards. All the machines—even the hand tools—are the same as those used in Salamander's German factories. In addition, each of the 735 Soviet workers got a month of training before starting to work. They also get on-the-job instruction from quality-control specialists from Stuttgart. As incentives, they earn a bonus for higher productivity but are penalized if the quality slips.

"We don't really mean to punish them," says Mr. Meiser, amid the clanking of machines stamping out leather parts. "But they have to learn that quality is absolutely the most important thing to us. We won't accept anything less."

On the whole, the German managers praise the Soviet workers. Although Lenwest has the right to dismiss workers, it hasn't had to. The Germans say that in productivity, entry-level skills, job enthusiasm and motivation, Lenwest workers match or exceed their West German counterparts. "We expected to encounter a lot more troubles in the employment area than we've experienced," says Alfred Hoeh, one of the plant managers.

That may be partly due to Salamander's strict controls. Although its system differs greatly from the typical Soviet factory, some workers here prefer it. One middle-aged woman who once worked at another shoe factory in Leningrad says she likes the more regulated environment.

"If there's a disturbance in the department," she says, "I go get Mr. Meiser, and he deals with the problem immediately. You don't have to tell him twice." She adds: "The workers from other factories envy the workers here."

Coke to Use 'Can't Beat the Feeling' As World-Wide Marketing Theme

By Michael J. McCarthy
Staff Reporter of The Wall Street Journal

ATLANTA—Using its first new international advertising pitch in six years, Coca-Cola Co. plans to roll out a campaign to nearly 100 countries.

The theme, "You Can't Beat the Feeling," already in use in the U.S. for the past 15 months, will replace "Coke is it!" overseas.

In addition to new radio and print ads, the international campaign has more than 12 television commercials—the most Coke has ever produced for the overseas market in one year. McCann Erickson Inc., part of Interpublic Group of Cos., will shepherd the project for Coke through its branches world-wide, with help from some affiliated agencies.

"We don't change campaigns easily or quickly," says Ira C. Herbert, Coke's executive vice president. The "Can't Beat the Feeling" ad campaign helped raise awareness of the company's U.S. flagship Coca-Cola Classic 50% this year over 1987, Coke said. And it thinks the campaign will do much of the same the world over.

The people who push archrival Pepsi aren't so sure. "It may be tough to export the current campaign internationally," says Bill Katz, senior vice president, management representative, for Omnicom Group Inc's BBDO, the ad agency that handles the PepsiCo Inc. account. Mr. Katz says his agency's data shows "Can't Beat the Feeling" has neither done exceptionally well nor exceptionally poorly in the U.S. compared with some recent Coke campaigns.

Although such things are tough to quantify, Coke's advertising strategies lately have been overshadowed by those of Pepsi, industry executives and marketers have said. Pepsi has pursued what it calls "big event" marketing, using highly visible events such as boxing championships or the America's Cup race, and attention-getting people such as Michael Jackson and Mike Tyson.

While conceding that Coke outmuscles Pepsi overseas, outselling it in some markets nine to one, Mr. Katz believes Coke's current U.S. campaign has its shortcomings. " 'Can't Beat the Feeling' is an ethereal thought," the competing ad executive says. "What is the feeling? Why can't you beat it? It just doesn't express anything."

The positive results of Coke's research in eight countries abroad, though, have made Mr. Herbert confident the theme will last the five to seven years typical of successful Coke campaigns. By the middle of next year, Coke said the initial TV spot, featuring a variety of young and old people dancing to the upbeat "Can't Beat the Feeling" song, will be seen by two billion people world-wide. The company will alter the commercial for certain markets. One version of the ad, called "Dance," will be shown in the Carribean, Africa and the South Pacific with the tune played in reggae style, and with more blacks appearing in the shot.

Not surprisingly, a pitch with a trendy phrase like "Can't Beat the Feeling" needs to be tailored here and there to work in foreign tongues. In Japan, for instance, the spots will say the equivalent of "I feel Coke." In Italy, "Unique sensation." In Chile, "The Feeling of Life."

West Germany proved a problem. No translation really worked, so the ad's lyrics will be in German, but because the the country has a relatively large bilingual audience, the last line will be in English.

Despite the wide cultural differences a global market presents, Coke believes its core target consumers—12- to 24-year-olds—are becoming increasingly homogenous. Because of the widening availability of commercial television world-wide, says Mr. Herbert, "a German teenager is interested in the same kinds of things as the guy from Peoria."

So, says Jack Morrison, Coke's vice president, creative services, as Coke executives kick around ad themes these days, the big question is: "Will the idea travel?"

United Front

Europe Will Become Economic Superpower As Barriers Crumble

But No Easy Pickings Await Foreign Firms Competing In World's Richest Market

A Giant Wave of Migration?

By PHILIP REVZIN
Staff Reporter of THE WALL STREET JOURNAL

PARIS—The vision of Europe as a single market and economic superpower is finally becoming a reality. In the process, Europe is becoming a battleground for the world's major corporations.

The region's striking revival results from the elimination of most trade barriers between the 12 once-squabbling nations of the European Community, a reform that will be nearly complete by the end of 1992. With 320 million prospering consumers, Europe by then will have become the world's single richest market. Its new economic muscle will permit it to compete more fiercely in the global business fray even as the market encourages America and Japan to compete more fiercely in Europe.

Nearly 300 separate barriers to inter-European trade are falling, freeing trucks to move from Denmark to Belgium, dentists to move from Belgium to Greece, and a cornucopia of goods and services to spill across the Continent and Britain. This, says the European Community Commission, could raise the region's rate of economic growth by 7%, cut consumer prices by 6% and create five million jobs.

The EC declares the trend "irreversible," and a kind of unity fever has suddenly seized European businessmen. Fewer than 30% of them were aware of the 1992 changes a year ago. Now, recent surveys show, nearly all of them are.

A majority of Europeans want to elect a president of Europe. Seminars and advertising campaigns promoting the new era abound. The once-obscure flag of Europe, a circle of 12 yellow stars on a blue background, waves from Copenhagen to Athens. True believers wear Eurowatches, the hours of which are marked by tiny flags of EC members.

Because of profound cultural and political differences, there may never be a United States of Europe. And with many of the economic rules still being written, it is impossible to predict exactly what post-1992 Europe will look like. Yet certain trends seem clear. Giant corporations will stalk the new Europe's landscape, more of them indigenous than they would have been five years ago. Europe 1992 is being designed by Europeans for Europeans, so that European companies will fatten on subsidies and protectionism.

Foreign fears of a Fortress Europe protected by one effective tariff wall, rather than 12 leaky ones, are real in some industries. Indeed, the U.S. is readying its retaliatory weapons in a current dispute. The U.S. threatens to increase by a prohibitive 100% the import duties on European meat products valued at $100 million a year if Europe insists on banning American beef from animals treated with growth hormones.

Acquisition Binge

Big European companies were among the first to join the 1992 bandwagon, seeking world-class size through acquisitions or alliances. The pace is now furious. France's nationalized metals group, Pechiney, last month snapped up Triangle Industries of the U.S. for $1.26 billion to become the world's biggest packaging company. Grand Metropolitan of Britain just won Pillsbury for $5.75 billion to become one of the world's biggest food and drink companies.

Siemens of West Germany and General Electric of Great Britain (which isn't related to the U.S. company of the same name) are bidding $3.1 billion for Britain's Plessey to form a European electronics powerhouse to rival the U.S. General Electric. Siemens is also taking control of IBM's Rolm division. British GE is forming a joint venture with Cie. Generale d'Electricite of France to create one of the world's biggest power-generating equipment makers.

For its part, CGE's Alcatel venture has become the world's second-biggest telephone company, incorporating ITT's European phone operations. Daimler-Benz of Germany is taking over state-owned Messerschmitt-Boelkow-Blohm, which would create a mammoth aerospace and defense group.

Europe Inc.

"European companies will be stronger competitors because they will view Europe as a single market," says Denis Lamb, U.S. ambassador to the Organization for Economic Cooperation and Development in Paris. "American multinationals have lost their monopoly on that strategic vision and are going to have to confront this new indigenous competition."

Europe is starting to muster its troops against the Americans, using, among other weapons, Japanese-like government subsidy programs. The EC's Eureka program is currently sponsoring 213 joint projects, at a cost that could exceed $4 billion, to produce electronics systems and goods ranging from high-definition television to robots to computer chips. IBM and other non-EC companies aren't formally barred from such programs, but they don't get a lot of the contracts.

Apple Computer, which three years ago was excluded from providing computers to French schools in favor of the French company Thomson SA, is trying to participate in a project called Delta, linking various European universities. Apple says that European academics want its Macintosh computers and that the forthcoming decision will be a test of EC openness. "There are hundreds of opportunities in government procurement that we never hear about," says Michael H. Spindler, president of Apple Computer International.

International Computers Ltd., a subsidiary of STC of Britain, has a "buy European" program aimed at reducing to 30% in 1992 from 70% now the amount of non-European-made components it uses. "We shall buy from European sources whenever we can," says Alan Roussel, head of ICL's new European Strategy Board. "We want to create a third force, like the U.S. and Japan, and, frankly, we're going to use the same methods they've used for years."

Those methods include protectionism. European officials stress that future access to Europe's market for outsiders will depend on "reciprocity," or how European companies are treated in foreign markets.

A stubborn defense by Europe of its costly farm policy, centered on reciprocity, torpedoed this month's GATT talks in Montreal. The sniping has begun in the hormone-treated beef battle. American banks fret that they could be denied pan-European banking rights because each Ameri-

(cont.)

can state has its own banking rules.

"Europe-1992 shouldn't be a fortress," says Francois Perigot, head of France's employers' federation, "Nor should it be a sieve." He is a big fan of reciprocity. But "another name for reciprocity," says MIT economist Lester Thurow, "is Fortress Europe."

The most formidable fortress is likely to be the automobile industry, already well protected. Over the years "national champions" have been nurtured, and often subsidized by governments, behind quota or tariff walls—Fiat in Italy, Renault and Peugeot in France, Volkswagen in West Germany—with market shares of up to 60% at home and between 10% and 15% of the total European market. They are prospering in a market expected to have grown to a record 12.6 million cars in 1988.

Japanese car makers could probably triple their current 11% market share if allowed to sell freely here. They would flood France and Italy, where restrictions currently limit them to less than 3% of the market. The debate in Brussels, the EC's headquarters, isn't whether to continue to limit the imports of Japanese cars after 1992, but how to do it and how severely.

Says Cesare Romiti, managing director of Fiat, which has a dominant 60% share of the Italian market and a leading 14.8% of the total European market: "We must be careful that 1992 is an opening for European companies, not only for U.S. and Japanese companies."

The stakes are high. "Over the next decade the European market should be the most promising market in the world in terms of sales value," says Mark Snowden, auto-industry analyst for Booz, Allen & Hamilton Inc. in Paris.

The French favor limiting Japanese autos to their current European market share for the four years following 1992 and counting as imported any car that doesn't have at least 80% "local European content," that is made in Europe with European parts. That would neatly exclude Nissan Motor's Bluebird, made in England but with only about 70% local content.

It wouldn't necessarily exclude American-made Japanese cars, although the terms of this provision are still being hammered out. Because the U.S. market is considered to be open to European cars, Europe would be open to U.S. cars made in America, though not necessarily to U.S. cars made in Japan.

The battle over the rules for car import quotas has highlighted major differences between the French and Italians, on one hand, and the British, who favor freer markets, on the other. Differences between EC members complicate the making of rules governing notary publics, beer labels and a variety of other things; 1992 won't end all of Europe's problems.

European unemployment remains 10% despite bouyant economies in West Germany, France, and Britain. Even those economies could sour fast in a world recession. The trickiest jobs—such as the leveling of sales-tax rates that range from zero to 38%, or establishing a single currency, a single political voice or a common language, won't be done by 1992, if ever.

The European Community Commission in Brussels has moved fastest on the easiest parts of the 1992 plan, such as establishing a single maroon passport that bears each member country's name *under* that of the European Community, and replacing with one form the 30 or more customs documents needed by a truck driver going from London to Naples.

EC officials talk of a giant migration, precipitated by the new freedom to travel, of perhaps 15% of Europe's population, nearly 50 million people, moving from one country to another over a period of decades.

The toughest problems, which would require each country to cede more of its sovereignty over political, social and economic policy to Brussels, have already spawned unseemly public arguments between politicians such as British Prime Minister Margaret Thatcher, who pleads for a "Europe of nations," and EC Commission President Jacques Delors, who says, only a little hyperbolically, that Brussels will make 80% of the political and economic decisions for its members within 10 years.

Mr. Delors's Socialist Party colleague, French Prime Minister Michel Rocard, opposes the EC's plan to harmonize sales-tax rates because the loss of revenue might force him to cut social programs.

Mrs. Thatcher has been the most biting. She fears that post-1992 Europe could have a central, stifling bureaucracy. "We have not successfully rolled back the frontiers of the state in Britain only to see them reimposed at a European level," she said in a speech in Bruges, Belgium, last September.

And she doesn't much like a French idea for a European Central Bank. "I neither want nor expect ever to see such a bank in my lifetime," she said in another speech. "Nor if I'm twanging a harp, for quite a long time afterwards."

Still, says another Briton, John Drew, who heads the EC's office in London: "European unity is the most powerful trend of the second half of this century. We had our civil war during the first half." He adds: "Now we're getting together, and it's irreversible."

100

Asia's Success-Story Nations Learning How to Consume
With Some Exceptions, Domestic Spending Soars as Living Standards Rise

Selling may have started the Asian economic miracle. Buying will continue it.

While an American shopping for a television set or videotape recorder probably wouldn't guess it, the Asian export boom of the past three years is cooling and is likely to slow further in 1989. But Asian consumers with full wallets are picking up the slack. With incomes and living standards rising over much of the region, consumer spending is soaring.

As a result, the Asian-Pacific region, despite potential problems in China, Indo-

This article was written by Steven Jones from reports by correspondents of The Asian Wall Street Journal.

nesia and the Philippines, once again is expected to continue to lead the world in economic growth. Bank of America predicts Asia will be the fastest-growing region during the next five years, averaging 4.3% annual increases in real gross domestic product. The bank estimates regional growth of 6% for 1988 (compared to a World Bank forecast of 3.5% for all industrial nations), slowing to 3.6% for 1989.

Japan and China are the most often-reported economic stories of the region, the former continuing its spectacular growth and spurring growth throughout the region by its domestic consumption and its foreign investment, the latter in danger of spinning out of control as double-digit inflation and rampant corruption have caused Beijing's leaders to slow the pace of economic liberalization.

The Fast Growing NICs

This article examines growth in the other nations of the region. That includes the four newly industrializing countries of South Korea, Taiwan, Hong Kong and Singapore as well as Thailand, where the cash registers are ringing.

"This is the story of people benefiting from the Asian economic miracle on a much greater scale than before," says William Overholt, director of economic research for BT Brokerage (Asia) Ltd., a unit of Bankers Trust of New York.

Retail sales in Hong Kong in May were 20% higher than in May 1987. Sales of cars and commercial vehicles are up 45% in Thailand. The surge in consumer spending in Taiwan is accompanied by an explosion in travel and spending abroad.

Even India's 100-million-strong middle class continues its buying binge. Consumer spending is up 10% to 20% from 1987 after rains broke a three–year drought.

"The growth is incredible," says Sanjiv Bhakat, vice president of Jagat Jit Industries Ltd., a major liquor and food-processing concern. "It's industry-wide." Mr. Bhakat says sales of his company's alcohol and malted-milk products are increasing 12% a year. A subsidiary's ice-cream sales are growing 40% a year. "We can't make enough," he says.

Cashing In

In Australia, Gordon Clarke is cashing in on the spending spree. The managing director of Mutual Pools & Staff Pty. anticipates "the best year in the last 15 years" and expects to build about 800 swimming pools and spas this year, 14% more than last year. But demand for fancier pools means sales are likely to jump 25% to $12 million.

Although the regional spending boom is accompanied by inflation, an expected slowing of export and economic growth next year should moderate price increases and nowhere save in China is inflation a major concern. The recession that many feared after the October 1987 global stock market crash hasn't materialized. With the major exception of petroleum, commodity prices are buoyant. This is good news, particularly for Malaysia and Australia.

Malaysia's economy is expected to grow 8% this year, up from 4.7% in 1987. "The recent growth figures mean we're back in line with the rest of Asia," says Kamal Salih, executive director of the Malaysian Institute of Economic Research. "The chore ahead for the government is to make sure that the export-led recovery moves toward an investment-led recovery."

Malaysia will benefit from strong overseas demand for palm oil. Rubber and tin prices also have raced beyond their depressed 1987 rates. Similarly, Australia predicts that strong prices for its mineral and agricultural exports will enable GDP to grow about 3.5% this fiscal year.

On the other side of the commodity coin is Indonesia, hurt by weak petroleum prices and lagging agricultural growth. Indonesia has boosted non-oil exports; this year, for the first time, oil and gas will account for less than half the nation's export earnings. The bright spot continues to be manufactured exports led by plywood and textiles.

Sluggish Demand

Indonesian consumer demand, in contrast to most of the region, remains sluggish, in part because of an austerity program under which the salary levels of four million civil servants have been frozen for three years, while inflation stayed at 9%. Indonesia's growth trails Southeast Asia's other market economies. Real GDP grew 3.6% in 1987 and this year will be "slightly better, but not that much better," says economy minister Radius Prawiro.

Economists say annual growth of at least 5% is needed to create enough jobs for the expanding labor force. They note that 5% growth can be reached in 1989 if oil prices reach $15 a barrel, or more than $1 higher than current prices.

While Indonesia must accelerate growth to keep pace with its burgeoning population, Hong Kong and Singapore are constrained by labor shortages. Singapore's real GDP is expected to expand by 9% to 10% in 1988, up from 8.8% in 1987, thanks in large part to an influx of foreign investment in export-oriented manufacturing. Japanese investors pumped in $190 million in this year's first half.

Asia's Economic Record
(Percent annual real GDP growth)

	1986	1987	1988	1989
Australia	4.6	2.7	3.6	2.9
China	7.8	9.4	9.8	7.8
Hong Kong	11.2	13.5	7.1	5.7
India	4.9	4.0	2.0	6.9
Indonesia	3.2	3.6	4.5	4.4
Japan	2.6	4.9	5.1	3.8
Malaysia	1.2	4.7	7.7	5.8
Philippines	1.5	5.1	6.5	5.8
Singapore	1.8	8.8	9.1	6.1
South Korea	12.0	12.2	10.3	7.4
Taiwan	10.6	12.3	7.4	6.5
Thailand	4.7	7.1	8.8	7.1

NOTE: GNP figures for China and Japan. Australia figures for years ending June 30; for India and Japan, March 31. 1988-89 figures are averages of private and offical estimates.

Consumer spending has jumped as Singapore nears full employment and wages rise. Economists say consumer demand is crucial to offsetting an expected cooling of exports next year. "Export growth will slow somewhat, but it won't drop dramatically," says a Singapore bank economist who predicts 7% GDP growth next year.

Singapore's main worries are outside its control. A recession in the U.S. would put the brakes on non-oil manufactured exports—a big portion of which go to America despite market diversification. Even if the U.S. avoids a recession, a chronic shortage of labor and a rise in job-hopping put a cap on production in some sectors and productivity in others. Half the country's industrial workers are non-Singaporeans and half of newly hired employees change jobs within a month.

Labor Shortages

Hong Kong's labor shortage prompts many businessmen to want immigration rules eased to admit more foreign workers, and construction begun on major projects like a new airport. Yet, Financial Secretary Piers Jacobs and others advise caution. He worries about slackening economic growth and signs of a further slowdown next year. "I don't get the feeling that 1989 is going to be a particularly easy year," says Mr. Jacobs.

GDP for 1988 is expected to grow 6%, down from the 13.5% pace for 1987. In the past decade, annual GDP growth averaged 8.4%. Hong Kong's export performance depends largely on its currency's link to the U.S. dollar. The edge this link once provided has slimmed now that the dollar is more stable.

The squeeze of high costs and the labor shortage is driving many local manufacturers across the border to China. The finished products of such manufacturers, if shipped overseas through Hong Kong, are called re-exports. In 1988, for the first time, Hong Kong's port and airport are expected to handle more re-exports than exports of locally made goods.

Wages also are rising sharply in South Korea, up an inflation-adjusted 18% this year. Many Koreans suddenly can afford to buy the consumer and luxury items, from cars to microwave ovens, they could only window-shop for a year ago. More than 60% of all households now have a color television, and the number of private cars has risen so rapidly that Seoul traffic managers have been unable to cope.

At the same time, the combined pressures of a rising won, tightened credit, higher wages and lower productivity are cooling the economy after two years of export-led runaway growth. The government expects GNP to increase about 10% this year, above earlier projections but below the 12% in 1987.

Digesting Growth

Some economic planners are delighted growth is slowing. "Our chief problem remains management of the surpluses," says a government economist. "We're still trying to digest the growth of the past few years. Unless we do, we may choke on our own success."

Taiwan, too, faces the problems of sudden prosperity. With per-capita GNP above $6,000, Taiwan's workers are becoming rich enough to dislike getting their hands dirty. The labor shortage is so acute that each unemployed person has almost three jobs to choose from and some companies pay employees a bonus if they bring in new workers.

Meanwhile, high-tech booms. Taiwan will export three million personal computers this year, up 50% from 1987. Long lines form outside discos that charge $20 a head, and $5 a beer, to dance to the beat of imported bands. "Labor and pollution are serious problems, but I don't think they will seriously hurt the economy," says Yu Tzong-shian of the government's Institution for Economic Research. "I think we can maintain 6% to 7% growth for the next decade."

Taiwan has become rich so quickly that it's still possible to rent a decent apartment for $300 a month and eat a meal at a noodle shop for $3. But $500,000 condos sell like hotcakes, while careful ordering is needed to keep a meal for two under $100 in many restaurants. And 7,000 new cars a month join Taipei's road congestion.

The newest Asian Tiger is Thailand, which has become the darling of foreign investors and where the economy is growing at the fastest pace in a decade.

Low wages and a large work force attract the investors, while suprisingly robust agricultural growth and booming tourism have also fired the economy. Real GDP growth is 8.3% to 9.3% this year and forecast to be between 7% and 8% in 1989. Incomes are rising and the cabinet recently approved the first pay hike for civil servants since 1981.

But producer prices were rising at a rate of 10% at midyear and consumer prices will rise as much as 5% this year. Interest rates have climbed to 9% from 6% a year earlier.

Even Southeast Asia's most-troubled market economy, the Philippines, has done reasonably well. Consumer-led recovery began in late 1986. "The economy is going great guns," says Solita Monsod, director of the National Economic and Development Authority, which predicts 6% GDP growth next year, slightly below this year.

Strong prices for coconuts and copper have helped as have low oil prices. But the recovery could stall without badly needed foreign investment and new stability in the financial system. Exports are rising, but not as fast as imports, leaving a worrisome trade gap for a nation burdened with a $29 billion foreign debt.

Marketing in a Consumer-Oriented Society: Appraisal and Challenges

CONSUMERS: A TOUGHER SELL

Older, busier, and harder to satisfy, Americans won't mind paying for convenience and service. But they can no longer be considered a mass market.

■ *by Christopher Knowlton*

NOT THAT ANYONE ever said it was easy, but consumer marketing is about to get harder. A trio of trends will create a new world in which marketers will have to learn new rules in order to prosper. The trends: the aging of the population, its evolving ethnic composition, and its insatiable demands for convenience and service. Managing the marketing task will become more complex as companies try to create attractive new images for older consumers and abandon the youth orientation that served so well for nearly two decades. As hundreds of new television channels and magazines spring up—as well as entirely new media, such as home videotext—marketers will also have to rethink their strategies for reaching purchasers.

For marketers the most profound and potentially profitable (or dangerous) trend of the Nineties will be the aging of America. In the year 2000, baby-boomers will be 36 to 54 years old, smack in the middle of their peak earning years. Though they will head 43.5% of all households, a slightly smaller percentage than today, those households will include more than half the U.S. population—145 million men, women, and children. Boomers will continue to make most of the buying decisions, accounting for 56% to 58% of the purchases in most consumer categories, according to the Futures Group, a management consulting and forecasting firm based in Glastonbury, Connecticut. But their tastes will change with age. They will buy fewer of Calvin's jeans and more of his couture; they will splurge for a Jaguar and junk the Toyota.

Middle-aged consumers will respond poorly to conventional youth-oriented advertising. Says Ken Dychtwald, a gerontologist and the founder of Age Wave, a communications firm: "Advertising based on fun, games, and sexual innuendo is not going to hit home with someone who has been purchasing for a lifetime." To sway an

older customer, advertising will be factual, emphasize quality, and appeal to the buyer's good judgment. A current magazine ad for Aiwa's new stereo recorders ($110 and up) does just that. It admits that Aiwa products are more expensive than Sony's, because "their tuners tune more accurately. Their tape players play more exquisitely. The largest weighs just eight ounces."

The boomers are entering the years that supposedly will convert them into savers. No one knows if they will suddenly start socking it away—so far they haven't—but they will surely give the financial services industry a boost as they prepare to pay for educating their kids and plan for their own retirements. Over two years ago John Hancock Mutual Life Insurance came up with its "Real Life, Real Answers" campaign. The ads, created by Boston's Hill Holliday Connors Cosmopulos agency, consist of such everyday scenes as a 40th birthday party or a young parent telling his daughter about his recent raise, with a brief financial profile of the person featured in the ad: "Age: 40, Salary (dual): $67,000, Home equity: $98,000." Says Peter Francese, founder of *American Demographics* magazine, "This campaign is perfect at reaching baby-boomers. It says, 'We, John Hancock, understand your financial future.'"

BABY-BOOMERS will settle down with age. They will face fewer opportunities to job hop and will put down roots in the communities where they plan to raise their families. Peter Francese expects that local foods, wines, and even magazines will become popular as this group grows more community oriented. But, having been raised with the jet age, boomers will continue to travel—and they can afford first class. Toronto-based Butterfield & Robinson, a travel agency that offers comfortable African safaris—17 days in Tanzania is $2,795 without airfare, European biking and walking tours are $1,795 for eight days of pedaling through Burgundy—has seen

bookings double in the last two years.

Although the boomers will continue to be America's biggest demographic group, the fastest growing will be those over 85. Now 1.2% of the population, the so-called old-old will account for 1.8%, or 4.9 million, by the turn of the century. Richard Hokenson, an economist at Donaldson Lufkin & Jenrette, notes that the Census Bureau began studying centenarians for the first time in 1980. That year 15,000 Ameri-

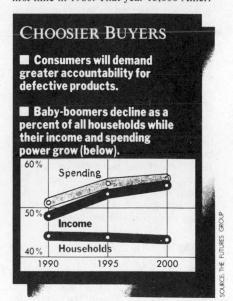

CHOOSIER BUYERS

■ **Consumers will demand greater accountability for defective products.**

■ **Baby-boomers decline as a percent of all households while their income and spending power grow (below).**

SOURCE: THE FUTURES GROUP

cans were 100 years old or more; today 45,000 are. Strongest demand among the old-old is for health care. One in five Americans over 85 resides in a nursing home or hospital. Francese sees the need for a new 100-bed nursing facility *every day* for the next 12 years.

EAGER TO MEET this demand, Marriott, the hotel and motel chain, will start building its third high-rise retirement commmunity aimed at the luxury market. Called the Jefferson and located just outside Washington, D.C., it will consist of 350 apartments and will offer such services as meals, transportation to and from the city, nursing care, and housekeeping. A two-bedroom unit will go for $240,000. Though the Jefferson won't open until the fall of 1990, some 1,900 retirees are already on the waiting list. Nonetheless, Marriott believes that greater growth potential is in the lower-income end of the market because well-fixed seniors can afford to hire nurses and stay in their own homes. The company has revised its strategy and now plans to build life-care facilities mainly for couples 70 and older with annual incomes as low as $25,000. To persuade seniors that these retirement homes will be attractive places to live, Marriott will customize the amenities, such as the number of prepared meals and visiting nurses, to the residents' needs.

Marketers have mistakenly stereotyped seniors as crotchety grandparents confined to rocking chairs. But consumer research shows that these buyers see themselves as ten to 15 years younger than their chronological years. Therefore, Allan Mottus, a marketing consultant, recommends that advertisers illustrate their copy with younger models but aim the text at older buyers. Age Wave's Dychtwald suggests that marketers can better reach seniors if they segment the group into those who still work and those who don't. He points out that retirees seldom use teller machines in banks because they are in less of a hurry than people who work and prefer the contact with tellers. The busiest bank branches in Fort Lauderdale and Sun City, Florida, he notes, have seating areas where retirees can socialize while they transact business.

THE TIDAL WAVE of boomers and seniors will not leave many youngsters in its wake. Population growth in the U.S. has slowed to about 0.9% a year, a trend that will continue through the Nineties. Immigrants—legal and illegal—from Asia, Mexico, and other Latin American countries will account for most of that growth because American women are bearing fewer children.

Hispanics, primarily Mexican and growing at five times the national rate, will increase 30% by the year 2000. Though culturally and economically Hispanics are a diverse lot—upscale Cubans have almost nothing in common with the largely downscale Mexicans, for instance—their broad spending patterns reflect some similarities.

For example, Hispanic households spend proportionately more per week on food than do members of other ethnic groups, and many of these households are headed by women, who are heavy buyers of cosmetics.

Avon could give lessons in how to reach these new consumers. The company recruits many of its Avon ladies from among the Hispanic immigrants who used its makeup in Latin America and translates much of its promotional material into Spanish for them. Last year seven of the company's top ten district sales managers were Hispanic women, and six were immigrants who scarcely spoke English when they arrived in the U.S. The Los Angeles region that includes the Barrio and the New York region that includes the Bronx reign as the company's two largest markets.

Along with their shifting demographics, consumers are undergoing broad changes in lifestyles mainly brought about by the increasing number of dual-career couples and households headed by women. Nothing sells to these time-pressed people like convenience, and they will gladly pay for services ranging from lawn care to day care. Anthony Adams, head of research for Campbell Soup, predicts that the $50 billion market for takeout food will double in the next decade. Two San Francisco entrepreneurs launched Waiters on Wheels last December, a home-delivery service ferrying hot meals from a growing number of the city's restaurants. Co-founder Constantine Stathotoulos says the company, which now has 16 employees, delivers 2,000 meals a week, primarily to working couples. In Minneapolis, General Mills is testing a similar concept called the Order Inn.

Trelleborg of Denmark builds the notion of convenience directly into the home. The company's environmentally efficient wooden houses are manufactured in Denmark in the form of precut Swedish pine and shipped to the U.S. where they are assembled in six to ten weeks. The houses come with 14-inch-thick walls and cement tile roofs that resist leaks and must be replaced only every hundred years or so. A typical 2,500-square-foot abode runs a steep $237,000, not counting the price of the land. But with virtually no marketing the company has sold 38 homes in New England in four years, primarily to trade-up buyers tired of leaky roofs and high energy bills.

CONSUMERS demand convenience in the form of accountability too. Ann Clurman of Yankelovich Clancy Shulman ad-

vises marketers to offer more warranties with their products to assure the customer that the manufacturer will be responsible in the event of a defect. American Express doubles the length of warranties and gives 90-day purchase protection on products bought with Amex cards. Faith Popcorn, chairman of BrainReserve, a marketing consulting firm, detects a growing aversion to sleaze kindled by the Washington and Wall Street scandals of the late 1980s. She warns marketers that the time has come to "talk straight" to buyers.

Not only will customers be busier, more experienced, and more demanding—they will also be more confused. The problem, as expressed by Laurel Cutler, the vice chairman of ad agency FCB/Leber Katz Partners: "Crowding, crowding, crowding." Already too many goods clutter too many store shelves, and too much advertising clamors for the attention of too few consumers. Of the 2,500 new products introduced each year, some 90% survive less than three years. Says Cutler: "You are dealing in a world where the leading shampoo—Head & Shoulders—has nine share points. Not 40 but *nine*." The Roper Organization forecasts an increasing "bifurcation" of consumer-goods markets into high-volume, low-priced lines and high-priced, individualized lines.

Success in this environment will require ability to scratch out market niches with annual sales of $50 million to $100 million rather than $1 billion, argues Richard Winger, a partner at Boston Consulting Group. Consider the food industry, once the champion mass marketer. Of the hundreds of food products introduced in the past five years, only eight have sustained $100 million in sales. Appropriately, all are convenience related; among them: Frito-Lay's Cool Ranch Flavor Tortilla Chips, Ragú Chunky Gardenstyle spaghetti sauce, and Swanson Homestyle Recipe TV dinners. Winger believes that opportunity for marketers lies in "creating new packages of things and emphasizing the service aspect of that bundle." The anytime-anywhere roadside assistance programs that Mercedes and Volvo offer car buyers is one example of a new package rather than a new product.

Nationwide marketers in the Nineties will have to spend more on local advertising or risk losing share to local brands. The mass-marketing strategy of the past 40 years is becoming inefficient as some mass-communication vehicles reach a smaller proportion of the population. Network TV

(cont.)

EIGHT SUPER-GROWTH MARKETS FOR THE NINETIES

Cellular telephones	The convenience of being able to use a phone anywhere will expand this million-phone market to at least ten million phones in use by the mid-Nineties.[1]
Facsimile machines	Fax machines will spread with the growing use of the home as an office, from 1.3 million machines today to 20 million to 25 million by the year 2000.[2]
High-definition TVs/VCRs	Better picture resolution should send aggregate sales of this new TV and VCR technology from zero to $13 billion by 2000 and $150 billion by 2008.[3]
Home satellite dishes	New satellites will make cheaper, smaller dishes more practical for areas cable can't reach. Dishes in use will jump from 2.4 million to 16.7 million by 1993.[4]
Generic drugs	As patents expire on expensive brand-name drugs, the cheaper generics will concoct sales of $25 billion by 1997, up from $200 million to $300 million today.[5]
Laptop computers	Their lightweight, portable computing ability will boost the number of laptops in use from 1.2 million units this year to nearly eight million by 1992.[6]
Storefront hospitals	Thanks to medical advances, fewer treatments require a hospital stay. That will help outpatient facilities become a $1 billion business by 1991.[7]
Sucrose polyester	Dieters will make Procter & Gamble's fat substitute—when approved by the FDA—a $1 billion product by the mid-1990s. Look for it in cooking oil, then in junk food.[8]

Sources: [1]Booz Allen & Hamilton; [2]Personal Technology Research; [3]National Telecommunications & Information Administration; [4]Frost & Sullivan; [5]International Resource Development [6]Dataquest; [7]Frost & Sullivan; [8]Drexel Burnham Lambert and Goldman Sachs.

has been losing viewers to cable for years and will continue to do so. Cable TV offers advertisers smaller, more homogeneous audiences. Mass market magazines do well conveying a complex message and building an attractive image for a product, but special interest magazines are becoming a popular way to reach a choosier customer.

Advances in direct marketing technology and the spread of databases made possible by the use of computer bar codes will also make it easier to reach the right customer. Last year American Express sold 7% of all the luggage bought in the U.S. by sending mailings to affluent cardholders whose charge records showed they spent heavily on other American Express travel-related merchandise.

MORE THAN A FEW shirts have been lost in home videotext services, but Prodigy, a system created jointly by IBM and Sears, seems to have the best shot at creating a shop-at-home market that works. Through a personal computer equipped with a modem a subscriber can shop at K mart or Neiman-Marcus, buy stocks, do his banking, book airline reservations, check movie listings, review *Consumer Reports*, and use dozens of other services. Prodigy is inexpensive: $9.95 per month gives subscribers unlimited use of the system. Walter Salmon, a Harvard business school marketing professor, thinks it holds particular promise for products the consumer is comfortable buying without touching, such as small appliances, books, and tapes.

Led by the baby-boomers—78 million strong, one-third of the population—U.S. consumers in the Nineties will be older, busier, richer, and harder for marketers to find. Such changes will make the decade a confusing time for consumer-goods companies and advertisers. But it will be a time also when marketing becomes more sensitive to the vagaries of the culture and more dynamic in its response to them. And that is sure to mean more sales. **F**

REPORTER ASSOCIATES *William Bellis and Darienne L. Dennis*

OOPS!

Marketers blunder their way through the 'Herb decade'

An ADVERTISING AGE roundup

The 1980s may be remembered as the "Herb decade" in consumer marketing.

Three years after Burger King Corp.'s celebrated promotion flopped, Herb the Nerd remains a popular example of what can go wrong in marketing: Rather than think Herb had *never been* to Burger King, consumers associated the negative character with the chain.

The 1980s were not without marketing successes, but Herb has become emblematic of a decade plagued by half-baked new products and misdirected advertising messages.

Taken together, they raise the question of the extent to which marketers have lost touch with the U.S. marketplace. Are marketers listening to consumers?

A rising chorus of voices indicates they haven't been, and that's a trend too dangerous to ride into the 1990s.

Consider these other examples of '80s marketing miscues:

● Fashion designers decided in mid-decade to reintroduce shorter skirt lengths. Women didn't buy the clothes or the decision, and retailers took a beating.

● Coca-Cola Co. in 1985 announced introduction of a new formula for its 100-year-old Coca-Cola. But it didn't understand the product's position as a piece of Americana, and "new" Coke was an immediate and continuing bust. The company had to bring back the original formula as a new brand.

● Adolph Coors Co. decided to change the name of its flagship premium brand to Coors Original Draft from Coors Banquet

(cont.)

beer to more accurately position its unpasteurized brew. Loyal Coors drinkers, however, thought the brewer had changed the formula, so Coors is dropping the draft label.

These are the most highly publicized examples of "Herb-marketing." What they have in common is a real, and often expensive, misunderstanding of consumers—what could be called a "Herb gap" between marketers and the consumer.

The origins of the problem are complex; marketers, agencies and researchers all point fingers at one another. But consumers themselves bear some responsibility.

"For the last decade we've been saying we're in an era of fragmentation," says Judy Langer, president of New York consultants Langer Associates. "We're not a mass society, as we were, so there aren't big waves of trends as there were in the past and that makes it harder to read the public.

"[Consumers] are more fickle and more demanding. I see consumers having relationships with brands, but it's more like they're dating than that they're married."

That has made serious consumer research more necessary, more difficult and more expensive. As such, it too often has become more easily ignored, some people say.

"Consumer research is tougher than before despite [improved technology] because now you need to know a lot about a lot of different segments," said Bill Robinson, chairman of William A. Robinson Inc., Ketchum Communications' Chicago-based sales promotion agency.

Potentially the most damaging source of the problem is shortsighted management: brand management run by MBAs more comfortable with numbers than with real people, and top management worried about quarterly results in an age of leveraged buyouts, corporate takeovers and corporate turnover.

"A lot of the money that used to go to research and development in American companies is now going to go to debt service," Mr. Robinson said.

Faith Popcorn, chairman of New York's BrainReserve marketing consultancy, said marketers have gotten lazy.

"I think marketers have, to a great degree, lost touch with the consumer because they don't have the time to get out and *personally* talk to people," she said. "They trust intermediaries, questionnaires, telephone interviews, but there's nothing like sitting down one on one and talking to people."

Observers say that loss of contact helps explain why, for example, the U.S. toy industry appears unable to create many products that capture children's imagination. Mattel's Barbie is 25 years old; the hot Nintendo videogame is an import.

Marketers respond that they could save millions of dollars if loss of contact were the problem. Rather than talk to 10 consumers on the corner, Frito-Lay talks to "150,000 to 200,000 consumers a year through one-on-one contacts," said VP-Marketing Dwight Riskey.

The toll-free number printed on each bag alone draws 100,000 calls yearly, he said, and that feedback is taken very seriously.

But that's after a product is on the shelves. In 1986, Frito-Lay was so sure it understood consumers' snack preferences that it rolled national—without market testing—a three-item cracker line called MaxSnax.

Even with network TV ad support, the line met with overwhelming consumer indifference.

Conceding that the national rollout had been premature, Frito-Lay pulled the line from store shelves, taking a $52 million tax write-off.

The debacle convinced Frito-Lay that true market testing is a necessity, even for a category leader.

"Consumers are changing rapidly. Our approach has changed. We need consumers to guide direction in terms of product improvement," Mr. Riskey said.

The problem isn't necessarily a lack of test marketing.

Coca-Cola Foods believed it had a great idea with Minute Maid Squeeze-Fresh, frozen orange juice concentrate in a squeeze bottle.

The idea was that consumers could make one glass of juice at a time rather than mix and store a half-gallon. The concentrate even stayed fresh in the refrigerator for five weeks.

But the product went into two test markets in 1987 and was soon labeled a bomb. According to insiders, consumers *loved* the idea and *hated* the product. It was messy to use, and no one knew how much concentrate to squeeze in the glass.

The company, it turned out, had

> *"I see all kinds of agencies going off in left field with their creative ideas and losing touch with the consumer. They're forgetting about the product itself, the redeeming benefits and values it has."*

spent more time considering package graphics than it did watching potential customers use the product.

Robert Kaden, president of researcher Goldring & Co., Chicago, ascribed the problem to lack of guts rather than lack of information.

"There's a problem here, but it's not a research problem; it's a management problem of believing what research says and overcoming momentum" to act on it, he said.

"We're beyond basics now, beyond consumer needs and into the realm of wishes and desires and emotional motivation," Mr. Kaden added. "That requires patience on the part of manufacturers, and it's not there.

"We used to talk about a three-year payout on new products; I haven't heard that in years. Now it's maybe a 12-month schedule. The attitude is, 'It had better work *now*.' "

That impatience also has changed the role of simulated test-marketing, computer models that project sales volume and market shares for new products based on estimated ad

(cont.)

spending, awareness, trial and repeat buying, and other variables.

These days, more real-world testing options are available, such as Information Resources Inc.'s BehaviorScan service. Some marketers say simulated test-marketing's role has changed from a way to quickly gauge acceptance to estimating the minimum in marketing support needed and the minimum in sales necessary to meet payout.

Gary Stibel, a principal in New England Consulting Group, Westport, Conn., traced the "Herb gap" problem to "advertising by the numbers.

"The biggest problem is with the new generation of brand managers who can't decide—and aren't allowed to decide—without numbers to back their opinions," he said. "Creative risks just aren't allowed."

Clay Timon, VP-worldwide advertising for Colgate-Palmolive Co., agreed that many consumer product marketers have been paying attention to everything *but* the consumer.

It's easy to become a slave to Wall Street's rabid desire for quarterly profits, he said. One result of that "is an overriding shift away from consumer ad spending to trade promotions that result in an immediate return to meet the financial objective."

The rise in trade promotion spending also traces to marketers' short-term thinking and willingness to have retailers do their research by finding out what sells. That's a poor substitute for true research.

"Retailers are asking for slotting allowances because there are so many new products flooding the marketplace and so many fail. They've been burned so often they're gun-shy," said Ron Paul, president of Chicago's Technomics consulting company.

"So many of those products aren't going to make it, but marketers are moving them out [to stores] because real research takes too long," he said. "They're saying, 'Let's do a couple of focus groups and let's get it out there.' "

Dick Bruno, corporate VP-marketing for Windmere Corp., which has developed several successful small appliances, said manufacturers *do* know consumers. But they've been persuaded to distrust their experience and knowledge.

"Clients know what sells better than anyone else, but too often they defer to ad agencies and marketing gurus to come up with strategic thinking, and what they get is way off target," he said. "The dynamics between clients and agencies are really falling apart, and you can see it in some of the misdirected ads on TV.

"I see all kinds of agencies going off in left field with their creative ideas and losing touch with the consumer. They're forgetting about the product itself, the redeeming benefits and values it has. They aren't using pragmatic, consumer-directed thinking based on research that ought to come directly from the client."

Automakers found they'd lost touch with consumers and have invested heavily and worked hard to regain that touch.

Darwin Clark, general marketing manager of General Motors Corp.'s Buick division, said the explosion of choices in cars made it harder for consumers to decide what they wanted and harder for automakers to discern their decisions.

"It's a very volatile market, and we're doing all kinds of market research to quantify what's going on," he said.

Focus group research certainly has its limits, said Ben Bidwell, president of product and marketing for Chrysler Motors.

"Consumers always put price way down [on a list] because they don't want to be labeled as 'Just looking for a deal.' But when they go to buy, price becomes all-important," he said.

To augment that kind of research, Chrysler now evaluates more lifestyle research.

"The real issue is trying to guess where [consumers] are going to be in 1992 or 1993," to account for automakers' long lead time, Mr. Bidwell said. The idea is to "find out what the avant-garde, Newport Beach, Calif., people are thinking today and try to project whether five years from now it's going to be big in Omaha."#

This story was written by Scott Hume in Chicago from reports by Pat Sloan and Lenore Skenazy in New York, Laurie Freeman in Washington, Raymond Serafin in Detroit, Jennifer Lawrence in Houston and Kate Fitzgerald in Chicago.

103

Courting Shoppers

Nordstrom's Push East Will Test Its Renown For the Best in Service

---

Retailer Banks on a Culture Of Equal Parts Hoopla, Incentive and Psychology

---

The Family's Balancing Act

By Francine Schwadel
Staff Reporter of The Wall Street Journal

SEATTLE—Nordstrom Inc. has always been paternal about its customers. The retailer serenades shoppers with live piano music, checks coats at the door and even provides baby-changing tables to speed a diaper switch.

So it wasn't surprising that, when the 88-year-old concern opened its first East Coast department store last year, it went to extraordinary lengths to preserve its reputation for service, a reputation renowned in the West. Rather than hire managers locally, Bruce, John and Jim Nordstrom, grandsons of the founder, transplanted 100 veterans to the new store in McLean, Va., outside Washington, D.C. Another 200 salespeople moved east at their own expense. When the store doors finally opened, fully half the staff was already steeped in the quirky Nordstrom culture—and customer coats were being properly checked at the door.

Expansion Ahead

But now Nordstrom is facing a much bigger test. Beginning in September, and extending over the next four years, the highly successful retailer plans to add 15 more stores to its 58-store chain. Many of them will be in the East and Midwest, including suburbs of New York, Chicago, Minneapolis and Baltimore. Stretching a company beyond its base is always risky, but it may be especially so for Nordstrom. The retailer, which advertises less than its competitors and relies more on word of mouth to draw shoppers, is entering new markets where it is generally unknown. It will be selling its wares at a time of slowing consumer spending. And its quick growth could well outpace its ability to train new missionaries to carry the company flag.

"I think they have a problem as they grow larger," cautions Stanley Marcus, the retired chairman of Neiman-Marcus, which struggled through an expansion of its own in the 1970s and early 1980s. He says it may not be as easy for Nordstrom to maintain standards as it was "when the stores were in one area and family members could check them daily."

But the Nordstroms are confident they can clone the company's unusual culture and keep service levels high. They point to their record so far: Over the past decade, Nordstrom has successfully expanded out of the Northwest into the hipper California market. As for the McLean, Va., store, it was profitable in its first year.

Corporate Harmony

The secretive Nordstroms—known inside the company as Mr. Bruce, Mr. John and Mr. Jim—usually refuse to explain to outsiders how their company works. Instead, they make self-effacing comments about their role in Nordstrom's remark-

Nordstrom Results
Sales
In billions of dollars, year ended Jan. 31

Net Income
In millions of dollars, year ended Jan. 31

able success. "It's just a lot of people doing a lot of things on their own," says Jim Nordstrom, a tall man with big hands who, at 49 years old, is the youngest of the founder's grandsons.

But don't be fooled by this aw-shucks attitude. The Nordstroms are shrewd busi-

nessmen, who typically open new stores in malls with track records of attracting affluent crowds. They are also masters at motivating their troops, at maintaining family harmony amid potentially explosive corporate decisions, and at decentralizing their business.

To understand the Nordstroms and their old-fashioned ways, you must climb two flights of stairs above the company's flagship department store in Seattle to its modest executive suite. Up here, the executives answer their own phones and the portraits of Grandpa Nordstrom and his two dead sons are done in charcoal instead of the usual corporate oils.

While it is clear who runs the show, the Nordstroms like to describe their organization chart as an upside-down pyramid, with them on the bottom. They eschew executive perks, such as having their own secretaries. Their small offices are identical in size. There is no czar.

Instead, the five top executives share power, insisting that titles mean nothing. Jim Nordstrom, his brother John and their cousin Bruce are all co-chairmen. Cousin Jack McMillan is president, and a family friend, Robert Bender, who grew up in Seattle with the Nordstroms and was their fraternity brother at the University of Washington, is senior vice president.

It is the family that's at the core of the Nordstrom mystique. The three Nordstroms and their cousin Jack each earned an identical $453,750 in salary and bonuses last year, while Mr. Bender earned somewhat less. And although the family members each control different amounts of Nordstrom stock—with values ranging from $74 million to $195 million—they all have an equal vote, along with Mr. Bender, on major policy questions, such as where to locate new stores. They don't move forward unless the decision is unanimous.

"Everybody has veto power," says Mr. McMillan. "It isn't used very often."

Balancing acts like this are rare in business, and rarer still among a founder's third-generation offspring. But the Nordstroms, who along with their extended family own 40% of the company's stock, say they are merely following in the footsteps of their fathers, who also shared power. "We were raised with an example," says a bespectacled Bruce Nordstrom, 55. "It really has a lot to do with turning the other cheek and saying, 'I want you to do what you want to do.'"

Take, for example, the family's decision a few years ago to sell the Seattle Seahawks football team, in which the Nordstroms had a majority stake. Jim Nordstrom considered the team a distraction from the retailing business. Bruce was uncomfortable with the publicity and the fact that young athletes earn so much. But John Nordstrom was the team's managing partner—and he loved it.

"He really didn't want to sell, he got so involved," says Mike McCormack, then the team's general manager. But Mr. Nordstrom ultimately went along with the family's desires. "He was reluctant to sell, but the decision was made," Mr. McCormack says.

A Family's Advantage

The family provides extraordinary management stability for the chain at a time when other stores are being rocked by takeovers and revolving-door owners. When B. Altman and Bonwit Teller were bought out in 1987, for example, their new parent, Hooker Corp. of Australia, redirected the chains into an ambitious, new expansion program. Now, Hooker is having cash-flow problems and has put the chains up for sale. Meantime, some apparel makers have held up shipments to the stores because of Hooker's problems.

Nordstrom, on the other hand, steams ahead. Each of the five top executives oversees a separate piece of the company, pushing most operating decisions down to the store level. They pore over daily sales reports but insist they don't give employees much direction.

Instead, they create an intensely competitive atmosphere by setting ever-higher sales goals and pitting employees against one another in contests. "People that respond to that kind of pressure are our kind of people," says Bruce Nordstrom.

Store managers, for instance, must publicly declare their sales goals at regional meetings. Then a top executive unveils what he calls the "secret committee's" sales target for each store. Unlucky managers who set goals below the committee's are booed. Those who exceed them are cheered. To egg on the crowd, the usually reserved John Nordstrom sometimes dons a letterman's sweater emblazoned with a big "N."

The executives also hand out monthly cash prizes to stores that provide the best service. The choice is made on the basis of scrapbooks bulging with letters from customers, copies of thank-you notes salespeople write to their customers and notes called "heroics" that salespeople write about each other.

Salespeople who do especially well are honored monthly as All-Stars. A Nordstrom shakes their hand and gives them $100, and the right to big discounts in the store. The most productive are inducted annually into the Pace Setters club, which also entitles them to big discounts. And the best managers get their names engraved on a plaque in the executive suite.

To promote service, employees are given the freedom to do almost anything to satisfy shoppers. Billie Burns, a former men's clothing department manager, once got a call from a regular customer who was racing to the airport and needed some clothes. Mr. Burns gathered up a bagful of blazers, slacks and underwear, charged them to the customer's account and met the man's car outside the store for the handoff. A saleswoman at the same store once soothed a frantic executive with a run in her stockings by delivering some nylons to the woman's office in time for her to change for a big meeting.

Do You Have That in a 12½-E?

This sort of attention to customers' needs started at the turn of the century with John W. Nordstrom. A Swedish immigrant who arrived in the U.S. with $5 in his pocket, he made his fortune mining gold in Alaska and the Klondike before opening a shoe store in Seattle with a partner in 1901. The two split philosophically, the story goes, the day Grandpa Nordstrom started ordering shoes in uncommon sizes.

Today, the Nordstroms, unlike other retailers, require virtually everyone to start on the sales floor, where they themselves started stocking shoes. They attract ca-

The Nordstrom Clan

Top, Brothers Jim and John, and right, cousin Bruce

reer-oriented college graduates partly because Nordstrom pays, in combination with an hourly wage, commissions ranging from 5% to 10% after employees meet certain sales quotas. The average Nordstrom salesperson earns around $25,000 a year, compared with less than $20,000 for clerks at other stores, where commissions nor-

mally aren't paid. A top performer at Nordstrom can make more than $80,000.

The company is also highly decentralized and growing rapidly. Even merchandise buying is decentralized, so company buyers in different areas can adapt to customers' tastes. The suburban Washington, D.C., store, for example, carries more formal attire than other Nordstrom stores.

All this leads to more opportunity for employees, especially since Nordstrom promotes only from within. Consider the case of Bob Love, a former Chicago Bulls basketball player. Mr. Love's stuttering landed him in what he calls "dead end" jobs after he retired from professional sports. Then he went to work busing tables at a cafe in a Seattle Nordstrom store. His hard work impressed John Nordstrom, who told him he would have to do something about his speech impediment to advance beyond menial work. So with Nordstrom picking up the tab, Mr. Love started seeing a speech therapist.

"They kept pushing me and were concerned about me," says Mr. Love, now corporate health and sanitation director for the chain's restaurants. "All I wanted was a chance. They gave it to me."

The Nordstrom culture does have its eccentric moments. Former employees in certain regions say that, in motivational seminars, they were encouraged to write and repeat upbeat statements called "affirmations." While still a salesperson, for instance, one former store manager told himself repeatedly, "I enjoy being a store manager at Nordstrom." Salespeople have also focused on such phrases as "I feel proud being a Pace Setter." Some employees consider it pop psychology, but others embrace the idea, writing chants aimed at changing their lives.

For suppliers, this corporate individualism—and splintered chain of command—can be vexing. When Michael Treiber, chief executive of Jones New York, a women's apparel maker, tried going to the top—as he does at other chains—he found Jim Nordstrom wouldn't talk business.

"We talked about the social amenities," recalls Mr. Treiber. "Other than a glad hand and a goodbye, that's all I got out of the conversation. He doesn't want to second-guess his people."

Nordstrom department managers, in fact, have so much freedom to hire and fire that some employees complain of favoritism. The company recently was sued in federal court in Seattle by the Equal Employment Opportunity Commission on age-discrimination charges.

Clearly, working at Nordstrom isn't for everyone. Consistently failing to meet sales quotas is considered a firing offense. "It's a very intimidating environment,"

(cont.)

says one Seattle-area saleswoman who requested anonymity. "They preach that as long as you're giving service, they'll take care of you. But that's not true. All they really care about is how much you sell."

Nordstrom employees today "have less job security than any other employees we have under contract," contends Joe Peterson, president of United Food and Commercial Workers Local 1001 in Seattle, which represents Seattle-area Nordstrom employees. Notably, however, the union hasn't been able to organize Nordstrom workers elsewhere because they typically earn more than clerks at other stores. But when the company recently suggested making union membership optional in its Seattle stores, a union poll showed employees overwhelmingly opposed to the idea. The union is threatening to wage a negative publicity campaign against the chain over the matter.

Just Repeat: 'I Know I Can Sell'

The three Nordstroms themselves might not have measured up to the standards they use today. "We weren't very good salespeople," says Jim Nordstrom. "I was the best, and I was lousy." Bruce Nordstrom says he once pushed so hard while fitting a young woman in a tight pair of flats that she tipped over in her chair.

The Nordstroms, all of whom are married, are as private in their personal lives as they are in their business affairs. John and Jim Nordstrom live along Lake Washington in a Seattle neighborhood where dense shrubbery shields their houses from public view. Their pursuits tend to be solitary ones. John, a varsity rower in college, runs 50 miles a week and skis. Two years ago, he climbed with crampons and ice axes to the top of Mount Rainier. Jim owns a 72-foot yacht, which he moors over summers at his fishing lodge in British Columbia. He flies himself back and forth in his own plane. His cousin Bruce also has a big boat, which he takes up to Jim Nordstrom's place in Canada in the summer.

All of the men want to retire by age 60, so it is likely that a new generation of Nordstroms will play a role in the company's coming expansion. Seven fourth-generation Nordstroms are already working their way up through the ranks. Three are store managers. Three are buyers. One runs a new management-training program in Southern California, which she calls the University of Nordstrom. There are also professional managers who will likely leaven the mix at the top.

For now, though, the company can bask in its success. Its sales per square foot rose last year to $380, nearly double the department-store industry average. And in 1988, when other big merchants were struggling, Nordstrom rang up a 21% sales gain to $2.3 billion.

What's more, the competition is starting to ape Nordstrom. Bloomingdale's, among others, is copying the company's practice of paying commissions to salespeople. And, though Nordstrom may still have the franchise on emergency deliveries of nylons, its rivals are taking note: Lord & Taylor has started special classes—to teach its clerks how to be friendlier.

104

Ethics Codes Spread Despite Skepticism

Critics Say They Look Good — But Help Little

By Amanda Bennett
Staff Reporter of The Wall Street Journal

In 1986, senior managers of Security Pacific Corp. proudly drafted the bank's first corporate ethics code. "We wanted to make our values manifest," recalls Irving Margol, an executive vice president.

But when they tried out the code on employees in focus groups, the managers got a rude shock. Point by point, the employees disputed the code's precepts. Security Pacific believes in open communication, the code said. Wrong, said employees: Management is reluctant to be honest. The company provides equal opportunity for everyone, was another point. Wrong again: Opportunities are manipulated and blocked by higher-ups, employees said. The company assesses the moral fitness of clients before we do business with them, management maintained. No, said employees: We take business where we can get it.

The managers considered abandoning the idea of a code, says Mr. Margol. Instead, they started a program to close "the myth and reality gap" by convincing employees that the code was serious and encouraging workers to abide by it.

Heightened Interest

Formal ethics codes are hot these days. Companies without them are scrambling to commit corporate values to paper. Companies that already have codes are rushing to update, disseminate and interpret them. Consultants are flocking to help with the task; conferences and seminars abound.

"The interest today is greater than it's ever been," says Alexander Horniman, a senior fellow at the Olsson Center for Applied Ethics at the Darden School of the University of Virginia.

But difficulties—and skeptics—abound. Some employees resist codes. They feel pressured to go along, and resent having their own values questioned. And ethics specialists say some codes are mere window dressing: They look good but aren't expected to interfere with the realities of the business world.

Ethics codes generally address such topics as conflict of interest, confidentiality of corporate information, misappropriation of corporate assets, bribes and kickbacks, and political contributions. Many begin with a statement of corporate mission. Some also contain sections on a corporation's responsibilities to its different constituencies, including customers, employees and shareholders.

Well-publicized cases of corporate malfeasance fuel interest in ethics codes. Many corporate codes date from the 1970s, when big foreign-bribery scandals were uncovered. Nowadays, corporate officers are looking at insider-trading convictions and government contracting scandals.

Some backers say ethics codes are particularly important these days to spell out corporate positions on difficult issues such as employee testing and privacy, insider trading and industrial espionage. At the same time, companies face growing scrutiny as the public and legislators become more concerned about business conduct.

"This generation of managers will be judged in large measure according to its ability to make sound ethical choices," and not just for its bottom-line results, Ronald Berenbein, senior Conference Board research associate, told a recent conference on ethics sponsored by the group.

Proponents of ethics codes also say they can help companies go through mergers, acquisitions and restructuring. "No unit we owned in 1977 is part of the company today," says Robert J. Bell, who helped Primerica Corp. develop a new ethics code before he recently retired as vice president and general auditor. The company's transformation from a packaging company to one engaged in financial services, specialty retailing and other fields stirred fears that employees in newly acquired units would unwittingly violate its policies on employee conduct.

So, from 1980 to 1985, Primerica put together an ethics code, expanding on existing elements, and began giving workshops to immerse new employees in the code and the corporate culture. For example, the company discussed with managers a hypothetical case study of a specialty retailing unit. Although paying retailers to buy goods is common in that field, Primerica made it clear that such practices would violate its ethics code's prohibition of payments and other inducements to make a sale, and wouldn't be tolerated.

When a company opts for a code, often the first difficulty is deciding how detailed to make it. Susan Spagnola, vice president and senior counsel of Chemical Banking Corp., says the company prefers a lengthy code because banking raises many legal and regulatory issues—which the bank feels are also ethical questions—that apply to all employees.

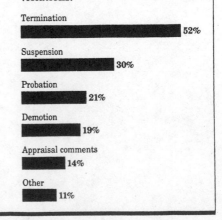

Setting the Standards–and Enforcing Them

In a survey of companies with ethics codes, these percentages said the following people participated in drafting the document:

Top management — 80%

Legal department — 44%

Directors — 24%

Founder or member of founder's family — 7.1%

Consultants — 2.2%

These percentages of surveyed companies said their ethics codes include the following penalties for violations:

Termination — 52%

Suspension — 30%

Probation — 21%

Demotion — 19%

Appraisal comments — 14%

Other — 11%

Note: Both charts include multiple responses

Source: The Conference Board

(cont.)

As in other companies with simpler plans, the bank also has separate policies on employee behavior in specific departments. But items in the ethics code "might be something all (employees) would encounter," Ms. Spagnola says. She cites a provision on gifts that is derived from the Federal Bank Bribery Act, which makes it illegal for bank employees to give or receive gifts with the intent of influencing or being influenced.

Minimalist Approach

Other companies take a minimalist approach. Levi Strauss & Co. moved from a 13-page booklet "filled with details and procedures" to a half-page statement of principles, says a spokeswoman. Among other items, the new code affirms the company's "respect for customers and employees," and it exhorts employees to avoid "real or perceived conflicts of interest."

Levi Strauss made the change to reflect its confidence in its employees' own sense of right and wrong, the spokeswoman says. And when employees can't figure out what to do, she adds, the company would prefer to have them turn to their manager or supervisor for guidance or support, rather than to a detailed document.

For similar reasons, some companies decide to do without a code altogether. After taking a close look at other companies' ethics codes, Mead Corp. decided that ethical conduct "can't be reduced to a code," says Thomas H. Schumann, human resources vice president at the company's fine-paper division. "You can't cover everything, and people think if it's not covered, it's OK."

Some companies, fearing legal repercussions, go out of their way to make sure the parties mentioned in ethics codes don't mistake them for legally binding documents. The Security Pacific code, for example, promises employees timely performance reviews—but also makes it clear that such a vow is a goal, not formal policy. Otherwise, "you could be open to legal suits," says Mr. Margol. A fired employee, for instance, could sue on the ground that he or she hadn't had a performance review in a long time.

Still, whether detailed or general, ethics codes often come under attack for the same reason: Much of what is contained in the codes, ethics specialists say, doesn't really address ethics in general, but rather is intended to protect the corporation. A Washington State University study of ethics codes at 202 Fortune 500 companies found that while 75% fail to address the company's role in civic and community affairs, consumer relations, environmental safety and product safety, more than 75% deal with conflicts of interest—which can affect the bottom line.

Kirk O. Hanson, a lecturer at Stanford University's business school and a consultant in business ethics, says most ethics codes "are compliance documents reflecting legal standards the company wishes employees to observe" on "negative and punitive" topics, including conflict of interest and insider trading.

Another criticism is that codes often put too much of the burden to be ethical on employees, while not addressing ways in which companies can create an atmosphere that facilitates ethical behavior by employees. For instance, a code could instruct managers not to put undue pressure on subordinates to accomplish goals. Without such provisions, "the message is, 'You people should behave ethically regardless of what else is going on in the company,'" says Barbara Ley Toffler, a partner in Resources for Responsible Management, a Boston-based consulting group that deals with corporate ethics. "It's focusing on people and not on the environment."

Indeed, codes sometimes run directly counter to actions that employees are all but forced to take. This can create strain—and resentment—in the workers.

Making Payments

For example, U.S. companies are banned by law from paying bribes overseas. But doing business abroad without such payments is often difficult, so many companies make such payments—on the books and thus legally—under different names, such as "facilitating payments." Employees often feel the payments, though legal, violate the spirit of corporate ethics codes.

At one big telecommunications company, Ms. Toffler found the issue of such payments caused "tremendous pain" among the affected managers. "This was a company with a reputation for responsible and ethical behavior. They felt the company was doing a number on them, and they were doing the company's dirty work."

A study of Champion International Corp.'s ethics code by the Business Roundtable, a group of senior business leaders, found that the lower the level of employees, the greater was their cynicism and hostility toward ethics codes. The phrase "the Champion way" is meant to indicate high business standards and fair treatment of employees. But researchers found that at a mill in Maine, " 'That's the Champion way' was often applied derisively to management actions with which employees disagree."

A Champion spokeswoman acknowledges that such skepticism exists there. But she notes that employees at the mill have been influenced by their turbulent recent past, which included a hostile takeover battle with another company before the mill was acquired by Champion in a friendly merger.

105

CFC Curb to Save Ozone Will Be Costly
Task Will Require World-Wide Cooperation

By Laurie Hays
Staff Reporter of The Wall Street Journal

Saving the Earth's protective ozone layer isn't going to be an easy job.

Du Pont Co.'s acknowledgment last week that the ozone is at risk has focused attention on the severity and urgency of the problem. Du Pont's solution is simple: stop making the chemicals that are believed to be the culprit. But the world has become so heavily dependent on those chemicals, known as chlorofluorocarbons, or CFCs, that accomplishing the goal will be risky and costly.

The task will require world-wide cooperation and good substitutes. It will cost hundreds of millions of dollars in research and plant construction. Moreover, weaning the world too quickly from CFCs could eliminate tens of thousands of jobs, trigger bankruptcies and even cause new health risks.

"Du Pont has certainly sent a strong signal to those who thought they'd wait it out and not do anything," acknowledges Kevin Fay, executive director of the Alliance for Responsible CFC Policy, which represents producers and users of CFCs. "But how fast can we do it?"

Adds Karl Loos, vice president of chemicals and plastics at Arthur D. Little, a Boston consulting firm, "We're in turmoil. We're all looking for the answers and they aren't clear right now."

First Concerns

Invented in the 1930s, CFCs make refrigerators and air conditioners produce cool air. They're used in plastic foam and cleaning agents. They were once used as propellants in aerosol containers until the practice was banned in the U.S. in the late 1970s. Without CFCs, food would spoil, office workers would wilt and cars would be less comfortable. In the U.S. alone, CFCs represent a $28 billion industry that employs about 715,000 people in 5,000 companies.

It wasn't until 1974 that scientists raised the possibility that CFCs might be eating away at the ozone, the layer of stratosphere that screens out the sun's harmful ultraviolet rays. The rays can cause skin cancer, eye ailments and other health problems as well as environmental damage to crops and fish populations.

CFC producers—Du Pont is the largest of the five major U.S. suppliers—began back then looking for substitutes. The research effort today involves hundreds of scientists. Du Pont estimates it has invested about $30 million so far, including $10 million last year. It expects to spend even more this year. Though other companies are spending somewhat less, the problem has been given top priority in the industry, officials say.

The stakes are high. Companies may invest hundreds of millions of dollars in new plant construction to make substitute products, so they want to be sure the substitutes aren't toxic and don't fail to serve the purpose. Early on, for example, Du Pont thought it had come up with a good substitute for cleaning electronic equipment and then discovered the compound caused sterility in male rats.

Risky Shortcuts

Products may be obsolete by the time they are ready to market. Such was the case in the late 1970s when **Pennwalt** Corp. developed a replacement for CFCs in aerosol cans. By the time the company had finished testing the product for toxicity, aerosol users had moved on and decided to use a hydrogen compound instead.

"We were left with an approved product and no market," says Peter Miller, manager of Pennwalt's Isotron division.

There also may be production problems. At **Allied-Signal** Inc., the second-largest CFC producer in the U.S., Bernard Sukornick, director of fluorocarbon research, cites the risks of investing in commercial plant production for a new product before it is known from pilot studies whether the final manufacturing process is indeed adequate.

"We're taking considerable risks and shortcuts," says Mr. Sukornick, "We're risking much more from a financial point of view than this type of industry usually takes."

In the rush to find substitutes, it is difficult to assess whether a product is the best possible outcome. "As a scientist I can't stand here and tell you that I have gone through every combination," says Mr. Sukornick. "I know I haven't looked at the problem in enough ways to be satisfied intellectually, but I have no time. I have to take what I've got and go with it."

For manufacturers that use CFCs in their products, the risks aren't as easy to define. They are potentially devastating if the process moves too quickly. Under the worst circumstances, producers would stop making CFCs before substitutes are available. Shortages would develop, prices would skyrocket and manufacturers of appliances such as refrigerators would go bankrupt.

Users' Dilemma

Du Pont's plan to cease CFC production has heightened anxieties. Although the

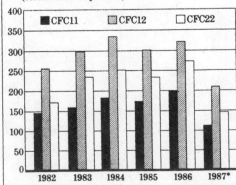

U.S. Chlorofluorocarbons Industry

Refrigerants production
(In millions of pounds)

Legend: ■ CFC11 ▨ CFC12 □ CFC22

(Bar chart, years 1982, 1983, 1984, 1985, 1986, 1987*, vertical axis 0 to 400)

CFC-dependent industries

INDUSTRY	ANNUAL REVENUE (In billions)	NUMBER OF JOBS
Air Conditioning	$12.9	150,000
Refrigeration	6.0	52,000
Service/maintenance	5.5	472,000
Plastic foams, food freezants and sterilants	2.5	41,000
Cleaning agents	3.0	10,000

Sources: Alliance for Responsible CFC Policy; International Trade Commission

*First six months

company promises "an orderly transition to the total phase-out," it could stop making CFCs at any time. If others followed and substitutes weren't available, shortages could develop that would put some customers out of business.

In addition, the Du Pont announcement runs the risk of encouraging Congress to legislate restrictions that the industry would find unpalatable, according to industry officials.

"If Du Pont says we choose to get out of this, Du Pont goes on," says Mr. Fay of the CFC Alliance. "But GE can't just say we won't make refrigerators. It's a much tougher position for user industries." Adds Arnold Braswell, president of the Air Conditioning and Refrigeration Institute, which represents manufacturers, "We're very nervous."

Yet another challenge is cooperation. While Du Pont has boldly stated its intentions to eventually cease production of CFCs—it hasn't said when it will do so—no other producer has yet jumped on the bandwagon. Du Pont estimates that it makes 25% of the world's CFCs, but recognizes that it can't solve the world's problem alone.

Indeed, Du Pont's plan goes significantly beyond the Montreal treaty signed by 31 countries last fall. The treaty calls for a 50% reduction in 1986 levels of CFC production by 1998, but not a total phase-out.

For CFC users, the dilemma is different. Richard Barnett, chairman of the CFC Alliance, says equipment manufacturers won't retool their plants until they can know with certainty which CFC substitutes the producers will stick with. When these customers retool, he says, "it has got to be right. They can't afford to change two or three times."

106

THE CASE FOR LOW TECH

Electronic gadgetry isn't worth much to people who need a good charcoal stove

YOU'VE BEEN READING in these pages about floating trains, high-definition television, supercomputing and many other hi-tech wonders. But of the five billion people on the planet, how many could draw any real benefit from such things?

Not that many. The real beneficiaries are a few hundred million people in the developed countries. This technology is of little use to most of the world's people, who can't afford the technology and who haven't the skills to apply it. And yet, all too often, this is what gets transferred to the struggling nations of the underdeveloped world.

The aid programs of the past few decades have brought billions of dollars of technology to the Third World, but they are an embarrassing legacy. Whatever the perceived benefits to donors and recipients—diplomatic gains and exports for the aid givers, symbols of modernization for the recipients—the practical benefits are illusory.

Moreover, the problem is worsened by the growing gap between North and South. As the U.S. and Japan pull away from the rest of the world technologically—and even from Europe to some extent—less and less American and Japanese technology is of any value to people in developing countries. Instead of getting what they could really use, the poor cousins in the family of nations wind up with technology that is inappropriate and wasteful.

Like the $40 million French-financed airport at the Tanzanian capital of Dar es Salaam. It has all the modern airport trappings—air conditioning, video monitors and a loudspeaker system among them—and when it was completed in 1984, it was hailed as a monument to progress in Africa. Some monument.

An unknown but doubtlessly huge percentage of the Tanzanian population can't afford to fly anywhere, for one thing. The nation is so poor that few people have electricity, much less air conditioning. And even those who can buy a ticket have trouble getting off the ground; many flights in Tanzania are routinely canceled because of a chronic shortage of fuel. That's only one shortage. Tanzania is having trouble producing even such essentials as bricks and cooking oil.

Which leads to this: Isn't there technology from the U.S., Europe or Japan that would be of more value to the average Tanzanian than a video-display monitor telling him about canceled plane flights that he couldn't afford to take anyway?

Of course, and it is the most basic kind of technology: better backhoes, stoves that use 50% less charcoal, hydraulic palm-oil presses, simple wheelchairs, a substitute for cement, a pedal-operated cassava grinder or a way to store milk for five days in a village with no electricity. It is these things, not supercomputers and

jetports, that spell progress to the poor of the world.

But much of the time they have gotten instead failed megaprojects, white elephants that in many cases have proven to be obscene wastes of time, money and manpower—bridges that nobody crosses, idle sugar-processing plants rusting in the jungles, grain silos where there is no grain.

These massive miscalculations have been compounded by numerous smaller ones. Not long ago, for example, an agency of the Dominican Republic charged with giving money and technical assistance to small business gratefully accepted the gift of a mainframe computer. Mainframe computers are wonderful things, no doubt, but in a country where electricity outages occur almost daily, their biggest impact on small-business development has been to paralyze it while everyone waits for the juice to go on again.

Looking back over a bleak landscape of failures large and small, experts in aid to underdeveloped countries sometimes seem close to despair. We tried big projects, they say, and many of them sank of their own weight. We tried smaller ones and a lot of them flopped, too. We watched Dutch scientists design a wood-burning stove, only to find it was less efficient

than an open fire. We sent medical inoculants, but the local water was so impure they couldn't be used.

And as these individual projects—large or small—have failed, some economists and policy makers have figured that broad economic changes would help the struggling poorer nations. Get world prices right and things will turn around, they say. But these macroeconomists, too, have turned largely pessimistic; commodities prices have mostly headed down, instead of up. Let the world's money slosh around among the developed nations of the northern hemisphere, the pessimists seem to be saying. Lend the world's excess cash to good credit risks like the U.S.—the biggest debtor of all. Forget about the poorest nations; their futures are bleak.

A better idea would be to concentrate our energy, ingenuity and will on providing practical solutions to the most basic problems in poor countries—a reliable supply of food, sturdy housing, clean water. We can still afford this kind of aid, and the technology either exists or is in promising stages of development.

In Woods Hole, Mass., for example, a small company called Ecological Engineering recently installed a sewage-treatment plant at a Vermont ski resort that uses gravity, sunlight, animals and plants to process wastes through a series of tanks. Building a plant like this to serve a city of 100,000 might cost about $3 million, a fraction of the usual cost. Among the interested parties are Ghana, Ivory Coast and Sierra Leone, all African coastal states whose fishing industries are threatened by fouled ocean waters.

In Guatemala, a non-profit U.S. outfit called Appropriate Technology International is creating a vertically integrated wool industry by developing new cross-breeding, shearing and spinning techniques, and by organizing artisans' cooperatives to sell the final products—blankets, scarves, rugs. In India, borrowed agricultural technology has led to better seeds and a "green revolution" thought impossible to achieve a decade ago.

In extending help, the developed nations might do well to remember that the simplest ideas often have the greatest impact, and that local people often know best how to apply them. People like Kamwanna Wambugu of Tigoni, Kenya, a school principal turned entrepreneur.

A couple of years ago, Mr. Wambugu had an idea. He imported a little basic technology, adapted it to village needs and came up with something of vital importance to his countrymen, something others had tried and failed to develop: a better, charcoal-burning stove.

High technology counts, but what much of the world needs are things like better stoves. And a lot more men like Mr. Wambugu. ▦